MW01093842

New Perspectives on South-East Europe Series

Series Editors: **Spyros Economides**, Senior Lecturer in International Relations and European Politics, London School of Economics and Political Science, UK.

Kevin Featherstone, Professor of Contemporary Greek Studies, London School of Economics and Political Science, UK.

Sevket Pamuk, Professor of Contemporary Turkish Studies, London School of Economics and Political Science, UK.

Series Advisory Board:

Richard Crampton, Emeritus Professor of Eastern European History at St Edmund Hall, University of Oxford.

Vladimir Gligorov, Staff Economist specialising in Balkan countries, The Vienna Institute for International Economic Studies, Austria.

Jacques Rupnik, Senior Research Fellow at the Centre d'études et de recherches internationales, Sciences Po, France.

Susan Woodward, Professor, The Graduate Programme in Political Science at The City University of New York, USA.

South-East Europe presents a compelling agenda: a region that has challenged European identities, values and interests like no other at formative periods of modern history, and is now undergoing a set of complex transitions. It is a region made up of new and old EU member states, as well as aspiring ones; early 'democratising' states and new post-communist regimes; states undergoing liberalising economic reforms, partially inspired by external forces, whilst coping with their own embedded nationalisms; and states obliged to respond to new and recurring issues of security, identity, well-being, social integration, faith and secularisation.

This series examines issues of inheritance and adaptation. The disciplinary reach incorporates politics and international relations, modern history, economics and political economy and sociology. It links the study of South-East Europe across a number of social sciences to European issues of democratisation and economic reform in the post-transition age. It addresses ideas as well as institutions; policies as well as processes. It will include studies of the domestic and foreign policies of single states, relations between states and peoples in the region, and between the region and beyond. The EU is an obvious reference point for current research on South-East Europe, but this series also highlights the importance of South-East Europe in its eastern context; the Caucasus; the Black Sea and the Middle East.

Titles in the series include:

Ayhan Aktar, Niyazi Kizilyürek and Umut Özkirimli (*editors*)
NATIONALISM IN THE TROUBLED TRIANGLE
Cyprus, Greece and Turkey

Kevin Featherstone, Dimitris Papadimitriou, Argyris Mamarelis and
Georgios Niarchos
THE LAST OTTOMANS
The Muslim Minority of Greece, 1940–1949

Alexis Heraclides
THE GREEK-TURKISH CONFLICT IN THE AEGEAN
Imagined Enemies

New Perspectives on South-East Europe
Series Standing Order ISBN 978–0–230–23052–1 (hardback) and
ISBN 978–0–230–23053–8 (paperback)

You can receive future titles in this series as they are published by placing a standing order. Please contact your bookseller or, in case of difficulty, write to us at the address below with your name and address, the title of the series and one of the ISBNs quoted above.

Customer Services Department, Macmillan Distribution Ltd, Houndmills, Basingstoke, Hampshire RG21 6XS, England

The Last Ottomans

The Muslim Minority of Greece, 1940–1949

Kevin Featherstone
Professor of Contemporary Greek Studies, London School of Economics and Political Science, UK

Dimitris Papadimitriou
Reader in European Politics, Department of Politics, University of Manchester, UK

Argyris Mamarelis
Research Fellow, European Institute, London School of Economics and Political Science, UK

and

Georgios Niarchos
Research Fellow, European Institute, London School of Economics and Political Science, UK

First published 2011 by
PALGRAVE MACMILLAN

Palgrave Macmillan in the UK is an imprint of Macmillan Publishers Limited, registered in England, company number 785998, of Houndmills, Basingstoke, Hampshire RG21 6XS.

Palgrave Macmillan in the US is a division of St Martin's Press LLC, 175 Fifth Avenue, New York, NY 10010.

Palgrave Macmillan is the global academic imprint of the above companies and has companies and representatives throughout the world.

Palgrave® and Macmillan® are registered trademarks in the United States, the United Kingdom, Europe and other countries.

ISBN: 978–0–230–23251–8 hardback

This book is printed on paper suitable for recycling and made from fully managed and sustained forest sources. Logging, pulping and manufacturing processes are expected to conform to the environmental regulations of the country of origin.

A catalogue record for this book is available from the British Library.

A catalog record for this book is available from the Library of Congress.

Printed and bound in Great Britain by
CPI Antony Rowe, Chippenham and Eastbourne

'του Τσίφτη,
για τις μεσημεριανές ιστορίες'

Contents

Boxes

Tables

Maps and Plates

Maps

Plates

Abbreviations

AFZ	Anti-Fascist Women's Front (*Antifasiste Front Zhena*)
AGS	American Geographical Society
ALP	Agrarian and Labour Party (Παράταξις Εργατών Εργαζομένων)
AMAG	American Mission for Aid to Greece
ASKI	Contemporary Social History Archives (*Αρχεία Σύγχρονης Κοινωνικής Ιστορίας*)
AYE	Diplomatic and Historical Archive of the Greek Foreign Ministry (*Υπηρεσία Διπλωματικού και Ιστορικού Αρχείου του Ελληνικού Υπουργείου Εξωτερικών*)
BCA	Turkish Republic Prime Ministry Republican Archives (*Başbakanlık Cumhuriyet Arşivleri*)
BCF	Balkan Communist Federation
BCP	Communist Party of Bulgaria
BOA	Prime Ministry Ottoman Archives (*Başbakanlık Osmanlı Arşivleri*)
CAB	Records of the Cabinet Office
CSA	Bulgarian Central State Archives (*ЦЕНТРАЛЕН ДЪРЖАВЕН АРХИВ*)
DIS	Directorate of Army History (*ΔΙΣ – Διεύθυνση Ιστορίας Στρατού*)
DSE	Democratic Army of Greece (*ΔΣΕ – Δημοκρατικός Στρατός Ελλάδας*)
DU	Democratic Union (*Δημοκρατική Ένωση*)
EAM	National Liberation Front (*Εθνικό Απελευθερωτικό Μέτωπο*)
EAO	National Guerrilla Bands (*ΕΑΟ – Εθνικές Αντάρτικες Ομάδες*)
ECA	Economic Cooperation Administration
EDES	National Republican Greek League (*ΕΔΕΣ-Εθνικός Δημοκρατικός Ελληνικός Σύνδεσμος*)
EES	Greek National Army (*Ελληνικός Εθνικός Στρατός*)
EKKA	National and Social Liberation (*Εθνική και Κοινωνική Απελευθέρωση*)
ELAS	National Peoples' Liberation Army (*ΕΛΑΣ – Εθνικός Λαϊκός Απελευθερωτικός Στρατός*)
ELIA	The Hellenic Literary and Historical Archive (*ΕΛΙΑ – Ελληνικό Λογοτεχνικό και Ιστορικό Αρχείο*)
FEK	Greek Government Gazette (*ΦΕΚ – Εφημερίδα της Κυβερνήσεως*)
FO	Records created and inherited by the Foreign Office
GAK	General State Archives (*ΓΑΚ – Γενικά Αρχεία του Κράτους*)
GES	(Greek) Army Headquarters-General (*ΓΕΣ – Γενικό Επιτελείο Στρατού*)
GWRA	Greek War Relief Association
HoC	House of Commons Parliamentary Papers on line

HS	Records of Special Operations Executive (SOE)
HQ EMT	DSE Headquarters of Eastern Macedonia and Thrace
HW	Records created and inherited by Government Communications Headquarters
IMRO	Internal Macedonian Revolutionary Organization (*VMRO – Vnatrešna Makedonska Revolucionerna Organizacija*)
KKE	Communist Party of Greece (*Κομμουνιστικό Κόμμα Ελλάδος*)
LP	Liberal Party (*Κόμμα Φιλελευθέρων*)
MAD	Units of Raiding Squads (*ΜΑΔ – Μονάδες Αποσπασμάτων Διώξεως*)
MAY	Units for Rural Security (*MAY – Μονάδες Ασφάλειας Υπαίθρου*)
MFQ	Maps and plans extracted to flat storage from records of various departments held at the Public Record Office
NARA	National Archives and Records Administration
NC	National Coalition (*Εθνικός Συνασπισμός*)
NOF	National Liberation Front (*Narodno Osloboditelen Front*)
NPU	National Political Union (*ΕΠΕ – Εθνική Πολιτική Ένωσις*)
OSS	US Office of Strategic Studies
PAO	Pan-Hellenic Liberation Organisation (*ΠΑΟ-Πανελλήνιος Απελευθερωτική Οργάνωση*)
PNL	Party of National Liberals (*Κόμμα Εθνικών Φιλελευθέρων*)
PP	People's Party (*Λαϊκό Κόμμα*)
PRO	Public Record Office
RP	Reformist Party (*Μεταρρυθμιστικό Κόμμα*)
SEKE	Greek Socialist Labour Party (*ΣΕΚΕ – Σοσιαλιστικό Εργατικό Κόμμα Ελλάδος*)
SNOF	Slav-Macedonian National Liberation Front (*Slavjano Makedonski Narodno Osloboditelen Front*)
SOE	Special Operations Executive
UNRRA	United Nations Relief and Rehabilitation Administration
UNSCOB	United Nations Special Committee in the Balkans
UPN	United Party of the Nationally-Minded (*ΗΠΕ – Ηνωμένη Παράταξις Εθνικοφρόνων*)
WO	Records created or inherited by the War Office Armed Forces Judge Advocate General and related bodies
WW	World War
YVE	Defenders of Northern Greece (*ΥΒΕ – Υπερασπιστές Βορείου Ελλάδος*)

Place Names

*The following list contains the names of villages and towns mentioned in the book. It is not an exhaustive list of all settlements in the area. In the first column, settlements appear in the Latin alphabet based on their official name today. In the second column names appear in the official language of the state they currently belong to. The third column contains alternative names used locally and/or in neighbouring countries.

**Throughout the text all place names appear in the Latin alphabet based on their official name today. When primary sources are quoted, place names appear in their original form followed by their current official name in brackets (for example, 'Salonika' [Thessaloniki]). In some translated primary sources, the authors have exercised their discretion in identifying the correct place names.

Western Thrace

Agras	Άγρας	Küçük, Sirkeli
Aigeiros	Αίγειρος	Kavaklı
Alexandroupolis	Αλεξανδρούπολη	Dedeağaç, Dedeagach, Дедеагач
Alkyoni	Αλκυόνη	Altıcılar
Amaranta	Αμάραντα	Yahyabeyli
Amaxades	Αμαξάδες	Arabacıköy
Ambvrosia	Αμβροσία	Ortacı
Ano Drosını	Άνω Δροσινή	Üntiren
Ano Mytikas	Άνω Μύτικας	Yukarı, Aralıkburun
Ano Vyrsini	Άνω Βύρσινη	Hacıören
Aratos	Άρατος	Karacaoğlan
Archontika	Αρχοντικά	Celebiköy
Arisvi	Αρίσβη	Ircan
Arriana	Αρριανά	Kozlubekir
Asomatoi	Ασώματοι	Bulatköy
Avaton	Άβατον	Beyköy
Bakses	Μπαξές	Bahçe
Chloe	Χλόη	Hebilköy
Didimoteichon	Διδυμότειχο	Dimetoka, Dimotika, Димотика
Dimario	Δημάριο	Demircik
Drania	Δρανιά	Kozdere
Drosero	Δροσερό	Yeni Mahalle
Echinos	Εχίνος	Şahin
Eranos	Έρανος	Otmanören

Erasmion	Εράσμιον	Taraşmanlı
Esochi	Εσοχή	Üşekdere
Evlalon	Εύλαλον	İnhanlı
Evmoiro	Εύμοιρο	Emirler
Evros	Έβρος	Meriç, Maritsa, Марица
Feres	Φέρες	Ferecik
Folea	Φωλέα	Yuvacılı
Genisea	Γενισέα	Yenice
Gizela	Γκιζέλα	Karagözlü
Glafki	Γλαύκη	Gökçepınar
Gratini	Γρατινή	Ircanhisar
Iasmos	Ίασμος	Yassıköy
Ifaistos	Ήφαιστος	Kalkanca
İliopetra	Ηλιόπετρα	Göynüklü
Isalos	Ίσαλος	Uysallı
Kalhas	Κάλχας	Kalfa
Kallithea	Καλλιθέα	Neşeliköy
Kallyntirio	Καλλυντήριο	Kalendereköy
Kardamos	Κάρδαμος	Gerdeme
Kato Drosini	Κάτω Δροσινή	Küçüren
Kato Mytikas	Κάτω Μύτικας	Aşağı, Aralıkburun
Kato Virsini	Κάτω Βύρσινη	Kuzören
Kechros	Κέχρος	Mehrikoz
Kentiti	Κεντητή	Gencerli
Kerasia	Κερασιά	Kirazlı
Kimi	Κύμη	Kezüren
Komara	Κόμαρα	Kumarlı
Komotini	Κομοτηνή	Gümülcine, Gumuldjina, Гюмюрджина
Koptero	Κοπτερό	Yalımlı
Kosmion	Κόσμιον	Küçükköy
Kotani	Κοτάνη	Koşnalar
Kotinon	Κότινον	Kocina, Mahallesi
Kotyli	Κοτύλη	Kozluca
Kremasti	Κρεμαστή	Kurthasanlı
Kyrnos	Κύρνος	Kırköy
Lambron	Λαμπρόν	Satıköy
Leyki	Λεύκη	Bedili
Lykeio	Λύκειο	Kurcalı
Livas	Λίβας	Ayvacık
Lofarion	Λοφάριον	Lefeciler
Maggana	Μάγγανα	Büyük, Otmanlı
Medousa	Μέδουσα	Memkova
Mega Dereio	Μέγα Δέρειο	Büyük, Dervent, Bölgesi
Mega Pisto	Μέγα Πιστό	Büyük, Müsellim

Melitena	Μελίταινα	Ballıca
Melivia	Μελίβοια	Elmalı
Mesohori	Μεσοχώρι	Kurtbeyli
Metaxades	Μεταξάδες	Tokmakköy
Miki	Μύκη	Mustafçova
Mikro Dereio	Μικρό Δέρειο	Küçük, Dervent
Milia	Μηλιά	Bektaşlı
Mirtiski	Μυρτίσκι	Musacık
Mischos	Μίσχος	Çepelli
Mosaikon	Μωσαϊκόν	Karamusa
Mytikas	Μύτικας	Aralıkburun
Nea Vyssa	Νέα Βύσσα	Bosnaköy
Nestos	Νέστος	Karasu, Mesta, Места
Nymfaia	Νυμφαία	Yanıköy
Oraion	Ωραίον	Yassıören
Orestiada	Ορεστιάδα	Altunkaraağaç
Orfanon	Ορφανόν	Öksüzlü
Organi	Οργάνη	Hemetli
Pachni	Πάχνη	Paşevik
Pagouria	Παγούρια	Bayatlı
Palaia Morsini	Παλαιά Μορσίνη	Büyük Mursallı
Palladion	Παλλάδιον	Palazlı
Pandrosos	Πάνδροσος	Dereköy
Paterma	Πάτερμα	Payamdere
Pelagia	Πελαγία	Denizler
Polyantho	Πολύανθο	Narlıköy
Polyarno	Πολύαρνο	Kuzoba
Polysito	Πολύσιτο	Hızlıca
Porto-Lago	Πόρτο-Λάγο	Karaağaç
Potamia	Ποταμιά	Çepel
Ragada	Ραγάδα	Kızılağaç
Samothrace	Σαμοθράκη	Semadirek
Sappes	Σάππες	Şapçı, Sapchi, Шапчи
Sarakini	Σαρακηνή	Sarancına
Satres	Σάτρες	Sinikova
Selero	Σέλερο	Gökçeler
Sidiro	Σιδηρώ	Demirören
Sidirohori	Σιδηροχώρι	Alren Pınar
Smigada	Σμιγάδα	Çalabı
Sminthi	Σμίνθη	Dolaphan
Sostis	Σώστης	Susurköy
Soufli	Σουφλί	Sofulu
Strymonas	Στρυμόνας	Struma
Stylari	Στυλάρι	Baraklı

Sydini	Συδινή	Elmalı
Sykorrachi	Συκορράχη	Çobanköy
Symvola	Σύμβολα	Semetli
Thermes	Θέρμες	Ilıca
Vaniano	Βανιάνο	Balabanlı
Velkion	Βέλκιον	Bekirköy
Vourla	Βούρλα	Fırlaç
Vrysika	Βρυσικά	Subaşköy
Xanthi	Ξάνθη	İskeçe, Ksanti, Ксанти
Xylagani	Ξυλαγανή	Kuşlanlı
Ziloti	Ζηλωτή	Zeynelli

Bulgaria

Batak	Батак	
Beden	Беден	
Brachigovo	Брацигово	
Dospat	Доспат	
Gabrovo	Габрово	
Harmanli	Харманли	Harmanlı
Haskovo	Хасково	Hasköy, Kardzhali, Кърджали, Kırcaali
Kresna	Кресна	
Kumanovo	Куманово	Kumanova
Mugla	Мугла	Muğla
Pazardjik	Пазарджик	Tatar, Pazarcık
Perushtitsa	Перущица	Peruştiçe
Peshtera	Пещера	Peştere, Peristera, Περιστέρα
Petrich	Петрич	Petra, Petritsa, Petritsi, Πέτρα, Πετρίτσα, Πετρίτσι
Plovdiv	Пловдив	Filibe, Filippoupolis, Φιλιππούπολη
Smolyan	Смолян	Paşmaklı
Stara Zagora	Стара Загора	Eski Zağra, Palaio Zagori, Παλαιό Ζαγόρι
Svilengrad	Свиленград	Mustafa Paşa
Tamrash	Тъмръш	
Trigrad	Триград	

Turkey***

Akhisar	Asprokastro, Ασπρόκαστρο
Bandırma	Panormos, Πάνορμος
Bozcaada	Tenedos, Τένεδος
Çanakkale	Dardanelles, Δαρδανέλια
Edirne	Adrianople, Αδριανούπολη, Odrin, Одрин
Enez	Ainos, Αίνος

Erdek	Artaki, Αρτάκη
Gökçeada	Imvros, Ίμβρος
İpsala	Ypsala, Ύψαλα
İstanbul	Istanbul, Constantinople, Κωνσταντινούπολη
İzmir	Smyrna, Σμύρνη
İzmit	Nicomedia, Νικομήδεια
Keşan	Kessani, Κεσσάνη, Keshan, Кешан
Kirklareli	Saranta Ekklisies, Σαράντα Εκκλησιές, Lozengrad, Лозенград, Kırkkilise
Malkara	Malgara, Μάλγαρα
Samsun	Amisos, Αμισός
Tekirdağ	Raidestos, Ραιδεστός, Rodosto, Родосто
Uzunköprü	Makra Gefyra, Μακρά Γέφυρα, Uzunkyopryu, Узункьопрю

***Pronunciation of Turkish letters

C – sounds like *j* in 'jam'
Ç – sounds like *ch* in 'church'
Ğ – lengthens preceding vowel
I – sounds like *a* in 'cereal'
İ – sounds like *i* in 'pin'
Ö – sounds like French *eu* as in 'leur'
Ş – like *sh* in 'sharia'
Ü – sounds like French *u* as in 'tu'
V – lighter than *v*, sounds almost like *f*

Preface

It takes little imagination on the part of the foreign reader to recognise the sensitivity attached to the fate of a Muslim minority in Greece, especially as the bulk of its members proclaim their 'Turkishness'. There are few case studies that might be written relevant to Greco-Turkish relations that are more politically sensitive. The minority has constituted the 'enemy within' for many Greeks and a 'repressed' minority to most observers from Turkey. Since the 1980s, their plight has been highlighted by a number of international organisations concerned to protect human rights. In the following decades, successive Greek governments have sought to address their condition. They became 'a cause' to fight over.

Yet, the history of this minority has been barely studied in a serious, academic manner. This is curious, given that the history surrounding their position has frequently proved contentious. Of particular interest here, are the actions and experiences of the minority during perhaps the most momentous decade of recent Greek history: the 1940s. This was a decade that witnessed the events of the Second World War – invasion followed by brutal occupation – and the Greek Civil War – with brother against brother. What did the minority (or its component communities) do during the 1940s? How did they react to invasion, occupation, and civil turmoil? What explains their response?

The present study seeks to address these questions and to attempt to fill an important gap in the historiography of the minority and of Greece and Turkey. The focus is not a general history of the period. The narrative of the book follows a chronological sequence, but it is structured around a set of key dimensions to contextualise the response of the minority.

The starting point for this project had been an apparent puzzle. Despite many reasons to expect the contrary, the minority had in fact remained passive and disengaged from the tumultuous events of the 1940s. The initial question to address, therefore, was a deceptively simple one: *why*? The instinct was to locate the minority in a wider geo-strategic setting of Greco-Turkish relations, affected by the discourse of the minority as a strategic resource. With the progression of the fieldwork, however, it became more and more evident that the position of the minority had to be placed in its local context. Rather than being clouded by the grand politics of geo-strategic relations, this was a puzzle that had to be answered locally. As such, other themes arose that could be better approached through the lens of political sociology, studies of nationalism, of war and occupation, etc. These led us to delve into issues of identity, of the cohesiveness or otherwise of the 'minority', of social structure and geography, of the local conditions that might sustain a more assertive reaction, and of Communist politics. As such, the 'puzzle' became enlarged and it cut across disciplines and literatures. Telling a 'dog that didn't bark story' is complex in itself. Though some might, inevitably, have questioned the veracity of the puzzle fewer would have easily predicted the path needed to explain the non-response.

The book stems from research conducted over several years by the authors and funded by the Arts and Humanities Research Council, the main public funding body in the UK in this academic area. The grant awarded by the AHRC (AH/D502616/1) allowed for extensive travel to obtain archival materials and personal interviews. The authors wish to express their appreciation of the award: the present study would have been impossible without it.

The research has taken the authors into new and challenging academic areas. Mamarelis and Niarchos brought to this research a specialist background in the local history of the Civil War and in minorities and Greco-Turkish relations (respectively), drawing on their doctoral theses. The core of the present project stemmed from a natural confluence of their interests. For Featherstone and Papadimitriou, by contrast, much of this terrain was uncharted. Their background is in political science. Moreover, to some extent, the authors were entering established areas of modern Greek studies, dominated by figures rightly regarded as iconic. The task of crafting a case study that would contribute to the hinterland of historical and social studies on Greece and the region that had thrown up such luminaries was daunting. Friends said we were courageous, though they might have been more direct and said foolhardy.

To some, on both sides, there may be wariness that three Greeks (and a Brit) endeavoured to write a history of the Muslim minority. Rather than accepting such suspicions as legitimate, however, the authors invite the reader to examine not only their findings, but also the rigour with which they have endeavoured to obtain evidence to support their arguments. The empirical sources are extensive and diverse: they encompass previously unseen archival material from Greece, Bulgaria, Turkey, the UK and the US as well as a vast range of local publications and personal interviews. At the core of our research endeavour has been our commitment to activate and cross-check all available sources.

Moreover, some may question the usage here of the term 'Muslim minority', rather than that of 'Turkish minority'. No position is taken on the identity of the minority today. But the evidence of the 1940s strongly suggests that there were several, conflicting identities held within the minority. Moreover, the tension between a modernist 'Kemalism' and more traditional Ottoman norms and values on the eve of the outbreak of the Second World War indicates that identification with 'Turkishness' was somewhat problematic. The designation in the book's title of 'The Last Ottomans' is intended to convey not only the historical derivation of the minority, but also the cultural transition underway within the minority at this time. This is a bygone age and it should not be confused with present day assumptions.

Over the course of the research, some of the findings have been reported in various settings and valuable feedback obtained. Presentations have been made in Birmingham, Cambridge, Columbia, King's College London, the LSE and Yale universities. The research has also been reported to several conferences. Of particular interest was a public seminar organised in Komotini, Western Thrace, in June 2008. This enabled the authors to outline their research to the local community and to obtain valuable feedback from it. This connection with the locality (and all its inhabitants) had been an important priority from the outset.

In a study of this scale, we have incurred many debts. A number of people and institutions have provided much-needed help and support. First and foremost are those who allowed us to interview them about their personal recollections of life in Western Thrace in the 1940s. Sometimes these interviews were on a one-to-one basis, whilst others took place in groups. Often their own family members and friends were interested to hear of this neglected history. We are very grateful to Vasilis Bornovas, Abdülhalim Dede, Ali Hüseynoğlu, Agapi Kandilaki-Yfanti, Charalambos Kontogiannis, Antigoni Papanikolaou and Konstantinos Tsitselikis who, from their own different perspectives, helped us to understand this complex community. In addition we would like to acknowledge the support of the 'Western Thrace Turks Solidarity Association' of Turkey which facilitated our contacts with émigrés. Our special thanks go to its Chairman, Erol Kaşifoğlu, and its Secretary-General, Recep Üstün.

Our archival research in Bulgaria and Turkey benefited tremendously from the support of Dr. Stefanos Katsikas and Burcu Çulhaoğlu respectively. Without them, important evidence relating to this story would have escaped our attention. We have also benefited from the comments and advice of many friends and scholars. Philip Carabott (KCL); Thalia Dragona (University of Athens); Renée Hirschon (Oxford); Abby Innes (LSE); Stathis Kalyvas (Yale); Şevket Pamuk (LSE); Stefanos Pezmazoglou (Panteion); and, Sotiris Rizas (Academy of Athens) each read earlier drafts of at least some of the chapters. In addition, John Breuilly (LSE); John Hiden (Bradford); Martyn Housden (Bradford); and Jennifer Jackson Preece (LSE), offered invaluable guidance. Special thanks are due to Umut Özkırımlı (Bilgi University) for his advice and support. Most of all we would like to extend our gratitude to Vemund Aarbakke (Aristotle University, Greece) and George Kazamias (University of Cyprus) for their patient review of our drafts. The input of each of these colleagues greatly improved the quality of the study. Any errors that remain are the sole responsibility of the authors. Eleni Xiarchogiannopoulou (LSE) provided expert research support for the project.

Our respective universities provided welcome support for this project. Mamarelis and Niarchos were employed as Research Fellows by the LSE.

Featherstone benefited from sabbatical leave from the LSE and from the support of its Hellenic Observatory. Papadimitriou worked on this book during two spells of sabbatical leave from the University of Manchester spent at Princeton and Yale respectively.

The tolerance and professional support of the team at Palgrave in the production of this manuscript is much appreciated.

It is impossible to name all those who have helped us. On a personal level, to conduct the research as a team – with its members each contributing their different strengths – has been an unqualified pleasure. At the same time, the project has imposed on those around us. As we finish this endeavour, we wish to record our appreciation of the love and support offered by our families and friends. The book is rightly dedicated to them.

KEVIN FEATHERSTONE
DIMITRIS PAPADIMITRIOU
ARGYRIS MAMARELIS
GEORGIOS NIARCHOS

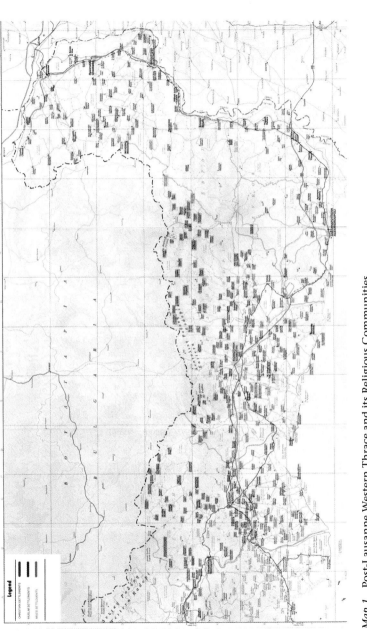

Map 1 Post-Lausanne Western Thrace and its Religious Communities

Source: Adapted on the basis of information provided by Aarbakke (personal notes); *Leykoma Thrakis kai Makedonias 1932*; De Jong 1980; Lithoxoou 2006.

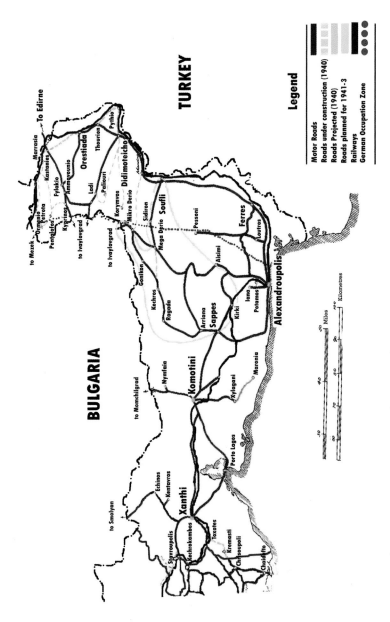

Map 2   The Transportation Network of Western Thrace in 1940

Source: Adapted from MFQ/1/458.

1
Introduction

1.1 An historical puzzle: the Muslims of Western Thrace during two wars

In the aftermath of the First World War (WWI) and a compulsory exchange of population, a sizeable and specific minority of Muslims were left within Greece, as a legacy of the old Ottoman Empire. Located near the north-east corner of Greece (Western Thrace), they found themselves in a rapidly changing society – 'foreigners' in a re-defined homeland. The region as a whole, however, had experienced repeated changes of authority and borders as a result of the decline of the Ottoman Empire and the rise of Bulgarian and Greek nationalisms. As such, it had been the land in-between conflicting irredentist aspirations. The Treaty of Lausanne of 1923, alongside the Greco-Turkish population exchange, provided (through the principle of reciprocity)[1] guarantees for the 'Muslims' of Western Thrace, recognising that they had a distinct identity and may be vulnerable to new threats. In the inter-war period, they represented about a third of the population of their region. With the onset of the Second World War (WWII), the Balkans were once again plunged into instability, which continued after the 'peace' with the arrival of Tito in Yugoslavia and the eruption of the Greek civil war. These separate events sustained not only an instability of authority, but also generally re-awakened ambiguities of identity, the assertion of rights, and new disputes about states and borders.

Not withstanding these conditions, the Muslims of Western Thrace remained overwhelmingly passive and detached from the conflicts of WWII, the Greek civil war and the struggles over borders. Looking back at

---

[1] The section of the Lausanne Treaty on the 'Protection of Minorities' refers to the minority obligations of Turkey for its 'non-Moslem' minorities. Article 45 of the same section provided that: 'The rights conferred by the provisions of the present Section on the non-Moslem minorities of Turkey will be similarly conferred by Greece on the Moslem minority in her territory'.

this formative period of twentieth-century history, the 'non-response' of the minority appears as an historical puzzle. Like Orthodox Greeks of the same age, Muslim men had been conscripted into the Greek Army to stop Mussolini's invasion and many appear to have fought bravely. But, after the defeat of Greece, this vulnerable minority passively accepted its own marginalisation. It suffered badly under a brutal Bulgarian occupation, but it showed little resistance. It did not form a resistance or insurgency organisation of its own and very few of its members willingly joined either the Communist or nationalist forces. Some took the exit option and fled as refugees to Turkey, though this was not without its own problems. Moreover, Ankara – for its own strategic reasons – opted not to publicly raise issues as to the fate of the Muslim community of Western Thrace for most of the 1930s and 1940s.

The case contrasts with that of others. In Epirus (north-west Greece), for example, a substantial number of Chams – an Albanian ethnic minority – were seen as supporting Mussolini's invasion and many later collaborated with the Axis.[2] None of these responses were very evident for the Muslims of Western Thrace. Further, in Macedonia at the end of the occupation a Slav minority pursued a separatist agenda supported by Yugoslavia. By contrast, in Western Thrace, the Muslim minority did not (nor was it prompted to do so by its 'kin-state' Turkey). Moreover, for their part, the Greek Communists had earlier sought 'independence' for both Macedonia and Western Thrace, later modified to a call for 'full autonomy' for their minorities. Yet, the Communists prioritised Macedonia, rather than Western Thrace and this circumscribed their engagement there.

A number of questions thus arise for the case study of the Muslims in Western Thrace. Why did the minority remain passive and disengaged from the conflicts? Why did Turkey, as the kin-country, not take up its cause more strongly? Why did the resistance movement – and the Greek Communists, in particular – fail to develop a stronger relationship with this 'oppressed' minority? More generally, what were the effects of occupation and civil war on the minority's orientation and existence?

A number of factors that help to explain the outcome in Western Thrace could reasonably have been expected to have led to a different historical course. Several can be highlighted here. The region had undergone successive changes of regime – all those continuously resident in the area over the age of 30 had lived through four different sets of rulers – and Bulgaria's occupation in 1941 was but the latest manifestation of competing irredentism. Rule over the region was thus hardly settled. Moreover, for its part, Turkey, as the Muslim minority's 'kin-country', under its new leader Mustafa Kemal (soon to be 'Kemal Atatürk') had, in its 'National Pact' (*Misak-ı Milli*) of 1920,

---

[2] A moderate number of Chams joined the ranks of EAM-ELAS but that happened in 1944 and in the context of the conflict between EAM-ELAS and EDES. Manta 2004: 188–190.

called for a plebiscite in Western Thrace to determine its fate (Aarbakke 2000: 25; Clark 2006: 98–99; Yıldırım 2006: 25, 33).[3] Though Turkey and Greece had later signed a 'Friendship Pact' in 1930 and embarked on a new era of rapprochement, when the Axis attacked the region, Ankara did not feel bound by any of these understandings and, instead, acted as an independent (and unpredictable) agent. Then, and later, Turkish nationalists saw the Muslims of Western Thrace as 'outside Turks' (*Diş Türkler*).[4] Gains might have been identified for Turkey – a state built on nationalism – had it accommodated itself more with the Axis Powers and sought territorial rewards for doing so.

In 1922, the Muslim population had been in the majority in Western Thrace and had held 84 per cent of the land (Oran 1994). They had formed the social base of the hegemonic power – they were the *millet-i hakime* (sovereign nationality) in the Ottoman system while Orthodox Greeks were the *millet-i muhakkime* (dominated nationality) (Oran, 1994). Now, many of those remaining in Western Thrace in 1941 suffered glaring economic and social inequality from the new local majority of the Greek Orthodox, though not necessarily of all the in-coming Greek refugees. This reversal of fortune made the minority a potential resource for conflict and insurgency.[5] For their part, the Greek Communists – pressed on the matter by their Bulgarian counterparts – clearly shared something of this assessment in their earlier declarations on the region. However, their later ambivalence and inconsistency in this respect introduced further complications into the local strategic puzzle.

---

[3] The 'National Pact' was approved by the Ottoman Parliament on 28 January 1920. It was based on the declarations of the Congresses of Erzurum and Sivas, organised by the Turkish Nationalist Movement in which Mustafa Kemal was the key figure. The Pact communicated Turkish nationalist claims towards the Great Powers in response to the Moudros Armistice (1918). Its six articles recognised the freedom of the Arabs; called for plebiscites to determine the fate of Ottoman territories occupied by the Allies (such as Western Thrace); asserted Turkish claims over Istanbul, guaranteed the rights of all minorities and demanded the withdrawal of Ottoman capitulations (Smith 1959: 17–27 and 153–155; Sonyel 1975: 13–21). For the original text of the Pact in French see Toynbee 1922. According to Aarbakke (2000: 25), Kemal subsequently moderated his position with regards to Western Thrace and withdrew his support for a plebiscite there. His u-turn on this issue is revealed in his speech at İzmit (16 and 17 January 1923), the full text of which was censored and only became available in the early 1990s.

[4] The term *Esir Türkler* ('Enslaved Turks') is also popular amongst Turkish nationalists. Other commonly used terms for kin Turkish diasporas are *Soydaş* and *İrkdaş*.

[5] Moreover, there appears to have been some 'parallel' history of assertiveness to build upon. Yıldırım (2006: 186–187) notes that the Turkish refugees leaving Greece promoted a degree of unionisation amongst local tobacco workers after settling in Turkey. A particular case in Samsun (Northern Turkey) involved refugees from Kavalla on the Macedonia-Thrace border.

Moreover, the geography of the region – and the population distribution of the Muslim minority – may be thought conducive to resistance and guerrilla activity. The Rhodopes were certainly inaccessible, though they lacked sufficient depth to allow a guerrilla force to attack and hide. On the other hand, the insular and closely-knit Muslim communities would have offered the potential for local insurgents to melt-away, lost in anonymity, if there had been a local will to do so. The failure of a Communist-led guerrilla force in the civil war to attract local support would later prove the importance of this point.

The passivity, disengagement and marginalisation of the Muslim minority in the 1940s is essentially a two-part puzzle, covering the factors relevant to the occupation during WWII and the struggles of the subsequent civil war. The primary task of this book is to address this puzzle and the explanation offered covers a range of factors – both those signalled already, as well as others.

In order to set the case study in perspective, Chapter 2 considers a number of background aspects. These centre on the relevance of geography and demography; of nationalism and the spread of Communist ideology; of the consequences of the Treaty of Lausanne; and of the legacies of inter-war politics and social norms. As such, the chapter begins to examine what kind of minority the Muslims of Western Thrace can be said to be. The present study is not conceived as primarily a case of nationalism (lapsed or otherwise) or of national identity. However, much of the subsequent discussion will be better understood if the underlying conception of a 'nation' and of its 'identity formation' is clarified. For these purposes, we accept Walker Connor's formulation of a nation being composed of a group who believe they are ancestrally related (1994: 212). In this context, a national minority is one that shares a sense of nationhood (a common past and future) with, in this case, an external kin-state. Importantly, Walker Connor warns that 'national consciousness is a mass, not an elite phenomenon' and this study seeks to delve into the 1940s as experienced at the grass-roots level (1994: 223).

Smith, with his ethno-symbolist approach, goes further. National identity, he argues, is 'the maintenance and continuous reproduction of the pattern of values, symbols, memories, myths and traditions that compose the distinctive heritage of nations and the identification of individuals with that heritage and those values, symbols, memories, myths and traditions' (2000: 796). The extent to which these conditions apply in the case of the Muslims of Western Thrace will be explored in subsequent chapters.

Following Chapter 2 as a scene-setter, the subsequent narrative develops in a broadly chronological fashion, to allow the story to unfold, whilst structuring the analysis around key themes. Chapters 3 to 5 present the case study of the Muslim minority during the WWII, from Mussolini's attack and the Bulgarian occupation of 1941 through to the withdrawal of Bulgarian forces in October 1944. Chapter 6 covers the interim period between the end of the WWII and the 1946 elections, a period shaped by significant ambiguity of authority and low intensity conflict. Chapters 7 and 8 then extend the study to the escalating violence of the Greek civil war.

The study inevitably touches on a number of social science dimensions relevant to the historical explanation. These range over political sociology, international relations, and studies of nationalism. The Muslim minority of Western Thrace was located within traditional, agrarian settings divided between isolated mountainous villages and lowland communities in villages and towns, with either a homogeneous or heterogeneous character. How did this setting impact on the minority's response? Previous studies of war and of civil war have highlighted factors that favour (and discourage) resistance and insurgency. How far is this case consistent with them? From an international relations perspective, the minority was identified with a 'kindred' state: Turkey both projected and accepted a role as guardian of those left behind by the retreat of the Ottoman Empire. What strategic conditions affect how states take up the cause of their kin communities abroad? Finally, the vulnerabilities and suffering of war confront issues of identity and of inter-communal relations. How did the Axis occupation and the Greek civil war affect the self-identity of local Muslims, their sense of common cause or 'groupness' and their relations with other ethnic groups? What were the foundations of national identity and of nationalism underpinning these orientations? These questions provide a frame within which the unfolding case study is structured and the findings on each of them are considered in the Conclusion.

1.2 Positioning the case study

Before turning to the case study, some readers will welcome a discussion of how it fits into the existing literature on the subject and also, later, of how the present study was conducted. One of the main preoccupations of this book was to build upon, but greatly extend, the scope of the existing literature on the region and the minority. No other published work, in any language, has confronted the 'puzzle' that has been identified here and the historiography of the Muslim minority, in general, is very limited.

There are, however, diverse literatures that relate to the present case study, albeit from different perspectives and foci. There is a sizeable general literature on the Axis occupation and on the civil war, with recent attention being given to the sociology of civil conflict, the strategies of the main protagonists, and the impact of the British and US intervention in Greece.[6]

---

[6] Iatrides 1981; Wittner (1982); Richter 1985; Fleischer 1988; Vlavianos 1992; Hondros 1993; Sfikas 1994; Barker 1996, 2002; Close 1998; Koliopoulos 1999; Clogg 2000; Mazower 2000, 2001; Margaritis 2001; Kalyvas 2003a, 2006; Carabott and Sfikas 2004 and Marantzidis 2006a.

Scholarly focus on the regions of Eastern Macedonia and Western Thrace is more limited by comparison, although a number of significant contributions have been published over the past decade.[7] Yet, in this literature the coverage of the particular case of the Muslim minority has been very limited and fragmented. More general studies on the position of the Muslim minority have lacked adequate detail for the 1940s and have been predominantly placed within the wider context of Greco-Turkish relations.[8] In recent years a number of scholarly works have focused on the violation of human rights in Western Thrace[9] and on the social anthropology of the Muslim minority,[10] but their scope has not been extended back to the period of the 1940s. Even the most significant study of the minority by Aarbakke (2000) mainly focuses on post-1974 developments and contains only limited coverage of the 1940s. More recently, the publication of the memoirs of Mihri Belli (Captain Kemal) (2009) and the book by Ali and Hüseyinoğlu (2009) have provided some important insights into the local history of that period, supplementing the incomplete and highly partisan account offered by Batıbey (1976).

Despite recent additions, however, significant gaps still remain in our understanding of the historical, social and political context that shaped the position of the Thracian Muslims in the middle of the twentieth century. Indeed, this period was a key phase: it came just before the Greco-Turkish conflict over Cyprus erupted in the mid-1950s. This was a conflict that would place the Muslim minority within a new discourse of contending nationalisms and strategic interests and a new equivalence with the Orthodox minority of Istanbul. As such, it is important to determine the experiences and orientations of the Muslim community of West Thracian minority *before* the new conflicts took over. Addressing such gaps can also serve to challenge popular Greek discourses of the minority based on the suspicion of it being 'the enemy within' or too-ready Turkish assumptions of its unequivocal identification.

---

[7] See, for example, Marantzidis 2001, 2006a; Kotzageorgi-Zymari 2002 and Chatzianastasiou 2003.

[8] Oran 1986, 1988; Popovic 1986; Vaner 1988; Bahcheli 1990; Alexandris et al. 1991; Alexandris 1992; Volkan and Itzkowitz 1994; Dalègre 1995, 1997; Tsioumis (1997; 2006); Akgönül 1999; Herakleides 2001; Papadimitriou 2003; Ker-Lindsay 2007; Özkırımlı and Sofos 2008 and Akgönül 2008.

[9] Bayülken 1963; Helsinki Watch 1990, 1999; Tsitselikis and Christopoulos 1997; Trubeta 2001; Meinardus 2002; Christopoulos and Tsitselikis 2003; Yağcıoğlu 2004 and Dragona and Frangoudaki 2006.

[10] Zenginis 1994; Brunnbauer 1998; Todorova 1998; Küçükcan 1999; Neuburger 2000; Tsibiridou 2000; Demetriou 2002; Michail 2003; Mavrommatis 2004; Papanikolaou 2007 and Eminov 2007.

1.3   A note on sources and methodology

Any historical case study poses questions of access to relevant and reliable material. These problems are exacerbated when: many of those directly involved have died; the community under study has become subject to a highly-charged discourse as the 'enemy within'; the memories of those who survive from the period may be tainted by subsequent events and experiences; and, archive material is not easily accessed and the information it provides is often partial, missing events or conditions at the local level.

The present study set out to overcome these challenges by seeking to cross-check accounts from whatever sources were available. Fortunately, in the course of the research, a substantial amount of empirical material in varied forms was collated. The types of source-material used in the study are, in the main: information from national archives in Greece; Turkey; Bulgaria; the UK and the US, to capture all three regional players and the international powers relevant to the local situation and security in the area; local archives; local newspapers (in both Greek and Turkish language); and personal interviews, across ethnic or political divides, with some of those directly involved in the events of the 1940s in Western Thrace. Separately, each source carries inherent problems of validity and reliability; in combination, however, the risks are significantly reduced.

With respect to the archive material utilised in this study, it was perhaps inevitable that the main bulk of the information would come from the Ministry of Foreign Affairs in Athens and its Diplomatic and Historical Archive (AYE). The records of the Ministry's Directorate of Political Affairs were the most relevant as it was, and remains, the main agent of the Greek government in managing 'minority affairs'. The vast majority of this material has never been utilised before. The material is, of course, limited for the 1941–44 period, but it is vast for that of the civil war. Altogether, the information facilitated a chronology of events in the region, as well as the evolution of Greco-Turkish relations before and after WWII. In the context of the civil war, it also displays the suspicion of the authorities towards the Muslims of Western Thrace.

A number of other Greek archives were accessed for the study. The General State Archives (GAK) in Athens, Kavalla and Thessaloniki (and, to a lesser extent, those in Alexandroupolis, Komotini and Xanthi) offered fragmented, but sometimes in-depth, information on Western Thrace in the 1930s and 1940s. Notable collections are the Archive of Foreign and Minority Schools in Kavalla, which provides invaluable insights with respect to the education of the minority and the Xanthi Prefecture Archive (the file on the 1940s is located in Thessaloniki), which contains useful material on the civil administration of the Muslim community. A substantial part of the archive of the Directorate of Army History (DIS) has already been published in edited collections. The material here allowed the tracing of the operations of the Greek National Army (EES) both during the 1940–1941 war against Italy and the course of the civil war. Further reference was made to the archives of the Hellenic Literary and Historical Archive (ELIA) in Athens (particularly the archive of General Vrettos) and Thessaloniki (particularly the 'Archive of Bulgarian Occupation in Macedonia and Thrace' and the archive of Harisios Vamvakas); the archives of Eleftherios Venizelos (at the Benaki Museum, Athens); the National Statistical Service (Athens), the Vovolinis Archive and the Contemporary Social History Archives (ASKI) in Athens and the Institute for Balkan Studies (IMXA) in Thessaloniki. Though more fragmented in their coverage, these sources proved important for both the pre-war era and the 1940s.

It was important to the study that it was also based on information obtained from archives in Turkey. Unfortunately, access to such state archives is frequently tightly restricted, particularly for foreign scholars. Crucially, the archives of the Ministry of Foreign Affairs were denied to outside investigators. Whatever the motive for this, the consequence is that serious, balanced research is made highly problematic. Such hurdles are antithetical to the desire that Turkey's place in Europe be properly understood. With access to the Republican Archives in Ankara (BCA) restricted, the only alternative was to use local partners. Via this route, the material obtained for this study was extensive, though it is not possible to completely verify the extent to which it provided full coverage of government policies and actions. The material covers the 'high politics' of the period only limitedly, but it was invaluable for its account of the educational and immigration issues affecting the minority in Western Thrace. Access was obtained to the Ottoman Archives in Istanbul (BOA) and these proved relevant to the coverage of the Balkan Wars, WWI and the Greco-Turkish War of 1919–23. Interesting insights into the position of the Western Thracian Muslims amidst a collapsing empire and the advance of Balkan nationalisms were revealed.

A broader picture was also provided by the access obtained to the Bulgarian Central State Archives (CSA) in Sofia. This material provided a very different account of events from the one presented by the Greek authorities. In addition to the invaluable information on the policies of the Bulgarian government in the area during the first half of the 1940s, the contents revealed a fascinating insight into the mindset of Bulgarian officials in Western Thrace. Hence, the apparently widespread discontent of non-Bulgarians in the area against the policies of the occupying forces rarely registered on the radar of the Bulgarian administration. The tone of the reports from the newly conquered territories in both Eastern Macedonia and Western Thrace is largely one of routinised administration, of 'business as usual'.

To counteract the pitfalls of relying on a history written at the governmental level, the case study presented here also utilises a wide range of local material. This allowed a deeper understanding of how the various communities at the grass-roots level viewed the events of the 1940s. The material included a number of Greek language newspapers: such as *Proia* (Morning News), *Eleftheri Thraki* (Free Thrace), *Proodeutiki* (Progressive) and *Ergatikos Agon Thrakis* (Labour Struggle of Thrace). Alongside these, the local Turkish-language newspaper, *Trakya* (Thrace), was extensively used. A particular insight into the attitudes and activities of local Muslims loyal to the Greek Communist forces during the civil war was provided by the newspaper *Savaş* (War – Struggle) which is frequently quoted in Chapters 7 and 8.

Beyond the regional and local perspectives, the case study frequently draws on the reports housed in the archives of the British and US governments, as two international powers with a crucial role in the fate of the area. As is often the case with historical research on Greece, the Public Records Office (PRO) in London has been a major source of information for this study. In particular, the archives of the Foreign Office, the War Office, the Cabinet Office, the Government Communications Headquarters and the Special Operations Executive (SOE) shed light on the position of the Muslim minority within the context of Greco-Turkish relations and the British response to its evolution. An unlikely, but very illuminating, source with regards to the nationalist movements in the wider region of Thrace during the nineteenth century have been the Parliamentary Papers of the House of Commons.

On the other hand, the archival material uncovered in the National Archives and Records Administration, Maryland (NARA), USA was rather limited with regard to the local Muslim community in Western Thrace. More significant was the evidence on the activity of the US security operations in Evros (during WWII) which, nevertheless, was rather peripheral to the core focus of this study. This early form of US engagement in wartime Europe is, indeed, a fascinating topic requiring further investigation.

Alongside the national, local, and international archives, the study has relied on the testimony of individuals (on both sides of the religious divide) who experienced the events of the 1940s in Western Thrace. In total, nearly 60 separate interviews (with more than 90 interviewees) were conducted in Western Thrace, as well as with émigrés in Istanbul, Uzunköprü, and İzmir. Overall, the interviews obtained covered different sides of the ethnic and political divides. Yet, it is not possible to estimate how well such interviews reflected the attitudes and experiences of the local population of the 1940s. Indeed, one lacuna that remains here is a full account of the experiences of the Bulgarian population who settled in (and were later evicted from) Western Thrace during WWII. That said, the present study has benefited enormously from the interviews that were obtained. The interviews were semi-structured in their format, balancing the checking of information obtained from other sources with the personal recollections of the interviewee. The majority of the interviews were conducted on a one-to-one basis, although a number of them involved larger groups. Given local sensitivities these interviews were not recorded and the identity of those who contributed is protected. For more details on the background of the interviewees, the reader is referred to the Appendix at the end of this book. The direct quotes included in the narrative that follows were reproduced from the notes of the interviewers, who remain fully responsible for any inaccuracies. The accounts offered by the interviewees allow the 'grand' historical narrative to be connected to the experiences of those who lived through the events. Of course, oral history contains its own research viruses as a result of the lapse of time and subsequent events clouding the memory. Again, evidence from such sources has been cross-checked with that obtained from archive material written in the relevant period.

The study that follows has thus confronted many conventional research challenges, as well as some particular to the case and the problems of access and sensitivity. Inevitably, the documentary material will be incomplete. Interviewees may offer a partial account. History is written in the present, shaped by the personalities of the authors and of contemporary conditions. Set aside these constraints, however, is the fact that the case study is based on extensive evidence from multiple sources, many of which can be re-examined by a sceptical reader. Hopefully, these features have reduced the risks and may increase the confidence in the portrayal that is offered.

2
The Muslim Community of Western Thrace in Context

2.1 Introduction

In 1923, the American Geographical Society (AGS), seeking to convey the context of recent events to its readers, declared that 'The debatable ground of Thrace has long been a political storm belt' (AGS 1923: 127). Indeed it had and for a variety of reasons. Before examining the events of the 1940s, it is therefore necessary to examine the longer-term setting and inheritance of the region. The demography of Western Thrace had been subject to major changes and this was to prove a significant factor structuring the 1940s experience of its various ethnic groups. Further, the historical inheritance of such groups had shaped their distinct identities. Indeed, as this chapter will outline, previous events had shown not a sense of shared nationhood, but rather the juxtaposition of competing historical narratives (and irredent-isms) within Western Thrace. More particularly, the Lausanne Treaty (1923) had intentionally 'minoritised' the Muslim population and this affected its identity and the discourse surrounding it. Thereafter, the establishment of the Republic of Turkey had challenged the minority socially and politically by counter-posing a new nationalism, based on a secular modernity, with traditional Islam. This created local political rifts amongst the Thracian Muslims that remained unresolved by the 1940s and these undermined its own political cohesion. At the same time, the minority was marginalised, but not excluded, from the politics of its host state, Greece. The over-arching international context had also changed: from one of political and military conflict between Greece and Turkey, to one of rapprochement between these contending powers. Ankara had become less publicly concerned with its brethren in Western Thrace. Each of these developments – of location, identity, leadership, and the counter-veiling interests of Turkey – was to form the crucial backdrop to how the Muslim minority would later respond to occupation and Civil War.

The Chapter addresses each of these legacies, to provide an overview of the condition and inheritance of the minority prior to the 1940s. It begins with geography and demographics, proceeds with failed local nationalisms and the 'minoritisation' of the Muslims, and concludes with the political disposition of the minority.

2.2 The physical and human geography of Western Thrace

Location, location, location

The events unfolding in this book are centred in Western Thrace, the north east border region of post-Lausanne Greece covering a total area of 8580 sq. km. In 1940 the region was home to some 360,000 people with a diverse ethnic, religious and linguistic background (Table 2.1). Geographically, Western Thrace is contained within the area bounded by the Rhodope Mountains to the north, the River Nestos to the west, the Aegean sea to the south and the River Evros to the east. The Rhodope Mountains (*Rhodopes*) form a dominant feature in the geography of the region. They are a striking 100–120 kilometres wide, forming a formidable physical barrier between the Upper Thracian plain on the north, the fertile Aegean plains to the south and the large plains of River Evros on the east. The range contains ten peaks over 2000 meters (6561 feet) that are separated by a succession of deep gorges and narrow valleys, providing for a naturally inaccessible and inhospitable terrain.

Despite its close geographical proximity to the metropolitan centres of Istanbul and Thessaloniki, the outlook of Western Thrace in the early twentieth century came to be shaped by its isolation and backwardness, caused by nationalist turmoil and chronic under-investment during the prolonged decline of the Ottoman Empire. The construction of a railway link between Istanbul and the port of Alexandroupolis in 1874 and the eventual extension of the line to Thessaloniki in 1896 opened up new opportunities for the economic development of the area, but much of this potential was damaged by the outbreak of the Balkan Wars and the local antagonisms in the run up to WWI. The road network in the area was also extremely poor, particularly with regards to the communication between the Rhodope Mountains and the Aegean coastline, where most of the fertile plains of the region are located. A British traveller in 1916 recorded only one such road suitable for 'wheeled traffic', making it possible to link Komotini to Haskovo (in Bulgaria) 'within a day' (Woods 1916: 287).

By the late 1930s, the preoccupation of the Greek military dictatorship of Ioannis Metaxas with Bulgarian revisionism, had led to the construction of a series of defensive forts along the Greco-Bulgarian border (known as the 'Metaxas line'), resulting in a significant improvement of the local transport network, such as the modernisation of the road between Komotini and Nymfaia and the construction of a new road linking Xanthi with Echinos. Yet, despite this investment, the vast majority of Muslim villages scattered in the Rhodope Mountains remained out of easy reach from the main low-land towns and villages and only limited contact was established between them for commercial exchange in local markets.

As elsewhere in the Balkans, the remote and inaccessible terrain of the Rhodope Mountains encouraged a significant degree of banditry, most prominently illustrated by the legendary Bulgarian *Hayduk* (*Klephtis*) Petko Voyvoda, but also by the notorious 'Miss Stone Affair' in 1901.[1] However, following the incorporation of Western Thrace into the Greek state in the 1920s, there are no reported incidents of banditry in the area. This stands in sharp contrast to the experience of other mountainous areas in the Greek mainland (particularly in Central Greece), where banditry remained a challenge to the authority of the Greek state well into the 1940s. (Jenkins 1961; Koliopoulos 1987; Jelavich 1997: 61–62, 73–76, Vol. I; Brewer 2001: 80–81, 126–127; Koliopoulos and Veremis 2002: 221–225). Indeed, many such bandits became closely involved in the resistance against the Axis, offering precious knowledge of the local terrain and significant know-how on guerrilla warfare. In Western Thrace there was not the same resource to call upon.

Contextualising the narrative of this book within the physical setting of Western Thrace is essential for the understanding of its main protagonists during the 1940s and the options available to them. Indeed a number of strong geographical cleavages are directly relevant here: both between town and village, as well as within the rural population itself. A major point of distinction was between those living in the larger, ethnically mixed, towns (such as Xanthi, Komotini)[2] and those residing in smaller rural settlements (see Map 1). In addition, within the rural population itself, a significant degree of ethnic, linguistic and cultural diversity prevailed, particularly between the villagers of plains or the *yaka* (the foot) of the Rhodope Mountains and those in the highlands (*balkan*) (Demetriou 2004). The degree of multi-ethnicity also varied across the different provinces of Western Thrace, with Rhodope and Xanthi sustaining a much greater percentage of minority populations than Evros (see below and Table 2.3).

---

[1] The affair centred on an American missionary who was kidnapped for ransom (near today's border between Bulgaria and Greece) by Bulgarian operatives of the Internal Macedonian Revolutionary Organisation (IMRO-VMRO) (Carpenter 2003; Sonnichen 2004: 259–288). On Petko Voyvoda see Karamandjukov (1934) and Trifonov (1988).

[2] According to the Greek census of 1928 there were only three local towns with a population of over 10,000 inhabitants: Xanthi (35,912), Komotini (31,551) and Alexandroupolis (14,019). Other significant population centres included: Didimoteicho (8690), Orestiada (8656), Soufli (7744) and Sappes (5 352). The total population of Western Thrace for that period was 303,171.

By the late 1930s the pattern of Western Thrace's ethnic mosaic had been largely consolidated, ending decades of demographic upheaval resulting in the uprooting, settling and re-settling of hundreds of thousands of people. The history of these population movements has attracted vast attention from Balkan historiography.[3] However, to the present day, their extent and impact remain an area of significant controversy in the academic literature (and the public discourse more widely) where both statistical data and scholarly interpretation are the subject of much contestation.[4] Table 2.1 presents a summary of the various demographic estimates relevant to the population mix of Western Thrace during the period 1893–1951.

Whilst a detailed discussion of these estimates falls outside the scope of this study, it is relevant to note that three periods of major migratory flows had shaped the human geography of Western Thrace by the early 1940s:

- The displacement of nearly 370,000 Muslims from Bulgarian lands between the Treaty of Berlin (1878) and the outbreak of the Balkan Wars (1912) (Karpat 1985: 75).[5] Of those displaced, significant numbers settled in the plains of Western Thrace, which was already home to a substantial body of Muslims. During the same period a number of Bulgarian-speaking Muslims (Pomaks) fled southwards from the northern Rhodope Mountains in fear of Bulgarian reprisals in the aftermath of the 1876 Batak massacre (see below). The impact of this movement on the Ottoman provinces (*Kazas*) of Gümülcine and Dedeağaç (covering a substantial part of today's Western Thrace) was tremendous with the local population rising from under 59,000 in 1878 to 281,709 in 1893 and 381,153 in 1907 (Karpat 1985: 118, 124, 167).[6]

- A further major population movement resulted in the demise of the Bulgarian population in Western Thrace, following the end of the WWI. As Table 2.1 indicates, in 1893 the Ottoman census registered 31,876 Bulgarians in the *Kazas* of Gümülcine and Dedeağaç (Karpat 1985: 124). Yet, in the aftermath of the Second Balkan War (1913) – with much of Western Thrace under Bulgarian control – the Bulgarian population in the area grew rapidly as significant numbers of Greeks were evicted from the area (Geragas 2005: 73–76; Kyriakidis 1919: 161–166; Pallis 1925: 6). However, the decision of the Allies to cede the administration of Western

---

[3] See Indicatively Macartney 1930 and 1934; Morgenthau 1930; Eddy 1931; Ladas 1932; Pentzopoulos 1962; Oran 2003; Clark 2006; Yıldırım 2006.

[4] See, indicatively, Carnegie Endowment 1914; Hirschon 2003; Keyder 2003; Kalionski and Kolev 2004; Kontogiorgi 2006; Aktar 2006; Tsitselikis 2006.

[5] Turan (2005: 83) puts that number to 350,000.

[6] Between 1878 and 1907 the population of the Ottoman *Sancak* of Edirne grew from 652,676 to 1,133,796 (Karpat, 1985: 119, 124, 167).

Table 2.1 Estimates on Western Thrace's Population Mix, 1893–1951

Census	Total	Turkish-speaking Muslims (Turks)	Greeks	Bulgarians[a]	Bulgarian-speaking Muslims (Pomaks)	Jews	Armenians	Roma[b]
Ottoman Census 1881/2–93[c]	281,709	210,594[d] (74.8%)	37,681 (13.4%)	31,876 (11.3%)	n/a	639 (0.2%)	609 (0.2%)	n/a
Ottoman Census 1906/7[e]	391,153	283,605[f] (72.5%)	49,142[g] (12.6%)	45,537 (11.6%)	n/a	1616 (0.4%)	949 (0.2%)	201 (0.05%)
Bulgarian Census Nov. 1919[h]	220,480	77,726 (35.3%)	32,553 (14.8%)	81,457 (37.0%)	20,309 (9.2%)	n/a	n/a	n/a
Allied Census Mar. 1920[i]	206,690	74,730 (36.2%)	56,114 (27.2%)	54,092 (26.2%)	11,848 (5.7%)	2985 (1.4%)	1880 (0.9%)	n/a[j]
Greek Census Dec. 1920[k]	191,000	84,000 (44.0%)	68,000 (35.6%)	35,000 (18.3%)	n/a	n/a	n/a	n/a
Greek Census May 1928[l]	303,171	84,669 (27.9%)	192,372[m] (63.4%)	7 (0.002%)	16,740[n] (5.5%)	2974 (1%)	3244 (1.1%)	1435[o] (0.5%)
Greek Census Oct. 1940[p]	360,219	97,535 (27.1%)	242,879 (67.4%)	0	15,000 (4.2%)	2537 (0.7%)	2268 (0.6%)	0
Bulgarian Census Mar. 1942[q]	216,920	71,301 (32.9%)	96,092 (44.3%)	43,526 (20.1%)	n/a	n/a	n/a	n/a

Continued

Table 2.1 Continued

Census	Total	Turkish-speaking Muslims (Turks)	Greeks	Bulgarians[a]	Bulgarian-speaking Muslims (Pomaks)	Jews	Armenians	Roma[b]
Greek Census Apr. 1951[r]	336,954	85,945 (25.5%)	225,792[s] (67.9%)	9[t] (0.002%)	18,664 (5.5%)	34 (0.01%)	549 (0.2%)	1143[u] (0.3%)

[a] Includes all Bulgarian-speaking Orthodox Christians.
[b] Includes both Muslims and Orthodox Christians.
[c] Figures adopted from Karpat (1985: 119, 124, 167). Includes the Kazas of Gümülcine (Komotini) and Dedeağaç (Alexandroupolis) only.
[d] Includes all Muslims.
[e] Figures adopted from Karpat (1985: 119, 124, 167). Includes the Kazas of Gümülcine and Dedeağaç only.
[f] Includes all Muslims.
[g] Includes Greek Catholics.
[h] Figures adopted from Aarbakke (2000: 28). In these statistics there is also reference to 8,435 'others' (presumably Roma, Armenians, Jews and Levantines).
[i] Figures adopted from Dalègre 1995 (vol. 2).
[j] Altinoff (1921: 177) makes reference to 1834 'Bohemians etc'.
[k] Figures adopted from Pallis (1925: 17). Pallis' statistics also referred to 4000 'others' (presumably Roma, Armenians, Jews, Levantines). The official publication of the census makes reference to a total population of 199,470. The 1920 census, however, contains no detailed breakdown of figures for Northern Greece. See Ministry of National Economy (1928).
[l] Ministry of National Economy (1935).
[m] 183,248 Greek-speaking Orthodox Christians plus 9124 Turkish-speaking Orthodox Christians.
[n] The census made reference to 16,747 Bulgarian-speaking people, stating that 16,740 of them were Pomaks.
[o] Of which 590 were Christians.
[p] Figures adopted from (Papaevgeniou 1946: 23). The official publication of the census makes reference to a total population of 359,923. The 1940 census, however, contains no detailed breakdown of figures. See Ministry of National Economy (1950).
[q] Figures adapted from Kotzageorgi (2002: 190). The statistics also makes reference to 6001 'others' (presumably Roma, Armenians and Jews).
[r] General Statistical Service of Greece (1958: 208–209, 244–247).
[s] 217,881 Greek-speaking Orthodox Christians plus 7911 Turkish-speaking Orthodox Christians.
[t] Appear as speaking the 'Slavic' language.
[u] Of which 840 were Christians.

Thrace to Greece in 1920,[7] (coupled with the Greco-Bulgarian population exchange of 1919), sealed the fate of the local Bulgarian population (Michailidis 2003). The Greek census of 1928 made reference to just seven Bulgarians living in Western Thrace. Within less than a decade, one of the three main ethnic groups in the area had been uprooted in its entirety.

• The aftershocks of the Greco-Turkish war in 1922–23 produced yet another demographic upheaval for Western Thrace, with profound implications for the size and outlook of the Greek community in the area. According to the Allied census of 1920, nearly 56,114 Greeks lived in Western Thrace. The collapse of the Greek campaign in Asia Minor in 1922, however, produced a mass exodus of Greeks from Turkey.[8] Within the context of the Treaty of Lausanne (1923) that ended the war (see below), the two governments agreed the compulsory exchange of nearly 1,200,000 Orthodox Greeks from Turkey (excluding those residing in Istanbul, Gökçeada and Bozcaada) with 350,000 Muslims from Greece (excluding those residing in Western Thrace).[9] The substantial number of refugees that eventually settled in Western Thrace is reflected in the Greek census of 1928 which registered nearly 140,000 more Greeks than the Allied census of 1920. Out of the ashes of the Greek nationalist project (*Megali Idea*), the ethnic mix of Western Thrace had changed forever. Former majorities were now in the minority, and the Greeks emerged a dominant ethnic group in the area.

The territorial changes envisaged by the Treaties of Neuilly (1919) and Lausanne (1923) resulted in the wider region of Thrace[10] been split into three, with Bulgaria gaining Thrace north of the Rhodope Mountains, Turkey controlling Thracian territory east of the River Evros, and Greece acquiring Western Thrace. Yet, for the hundreds of thousands of those displaced along the way, their memory of 'Thrace' must have included much wider frames of reference than the somehow artificial territorial demarcations agreed on the diplomatic table. The majority of the newly-arrived Greek settlers in Western Thrace, for example, had originated from Northern and Eastern Thrace which were now under 'foreign' and 'hostile' hands (see Table 2.2).

---

[7] Western Thrace was formally ceded to Greece by the Treaty of Lausanne in 1923.

[8] The harassment of the Greek population by the Young Turks had started since 1915 with large scale deportations of Greeks from areas such as Thrace, The Black Sea coast and western Anatolia (Alexandris 1992: 43).

[9] Estimate provided by Eddy 1931: 201; Hirschon 1998: 36–39; Ladas 1932: 438–442; Yıldırım 2006: 2006: 91,127.

[10] Following the 1864 administrative reform of the Ottoman Empire (*Tanzimat*), the whole of Thrace had been placed under a single administrative unit within the *Vilayet* of Edirne.

Table 2.2   Settlement of Greek Refugees in Western Thrace, 1924

	Xanthi Province	Komotini Province	Alexandroupolis Province	Orestiada/ Didimoteicho Province	Total
Thracians	6241	10,674	12,522	20,480	49,917
From Asia Minor	2938	1626	2924	82	7570
Pontians	1683	888	2160	7	4738
Caucasians	137	841	923	–	1,901
From Bulgaria	268	3044	1829	2544	7685
Total	11,278	17,082	21,950	23,113	73,423

Source: Leukoma Thrakis-Macedonias 1932.

Equally for the tens of thousands of Bulgarians and Muslims (both Turks and Pomaks) uprooted from across Thrace, the trauma of their lost liveli-hoods would have been a recent and raw memory. For those (on all sides) craving the stability of an imperfect status quo, the war clouds over Europe during the late 1930s instilled little confidence in the permanence and security of their new lives. For others with a point to make, the unfolding European crisis opened up new possibilities to settle old scores.

Distant neighbours

Western Thrace in the 1930s and 1940s contained many mixed communities, with different *ratses* (races) – a term used locally (Herzfeld 1980; Danforth 1989). Greeks, Turks, Pomaks, Roma, Jews, and Armenians lived in parallel, but distinct communities. The largest ethnic group in the region, the Greeks, predominated across the Prefecture (Νομός) of Evros and in the Province (Επαρχία) of Xanthi (see Table 2.3). In the aftermath of the 1923 popula-tion exchange, the booming towns of Alexandroupolis and Xanthi also sus-tained a large majority of Greek population (by four-fifths and two-thirds respectively), in contrast to Komotini where the population was more evenly distributed (Ministry of National Economy 1935 and Table 2.4). The influx of Greek refuges in the 1920s also altered the population mix in rural areas, with 243 new 'Greek' settlements established in the lowlands of Western Thrace (Leykoma Thrakis-Makedonias 1932: 168). By contrast, in 1922 the Muslim population had been in the majority in Western Thrace and had held 84 per cent of the land (Bayülken 1963: 150–153; Oran 2003: 102).[11]

---

[11] For a much different estimation of land ownership in Western Thrace see Aarbakke (2000: 57–61).

Table 2.3 Distribution of Population in Western Thrace According to Language, Greek Census 1928

Prefecture (Νομός)/ Province (Επαρχία)	Greek	Turkish	Bulgarian	Roma	Other	Total
Evros						
Alexandroupolis	22,256	1,881	0	12	1,483	25,632
Didimoteicho	30,332	6,343	0	110	933	37,718
Orestiada	27,086	6,637	0	298	256	34,277
Samothrace	3863	1	0	0	2	3,866
Soufli	19,151	1,765	2	28	289	21,235
Sub-Total	*102,688*	*16,627*	*2*	*488*	*2,925*	*122,730*
Rhodope						
Komotini	29,467	36,800	755	402	2,273	69,697
Xanthi	44,343	27,565	14,260	547	2,551	89,266
Sappes	6750	12,801	1,730	38	159	21,478
Sub-Total	*80,560*	*77,166*	*16,745*	*987*	*4,983*	*180,441*
Total	**183,248**	**93,793**	**16,747**	**1,475**	**7,908**	**303,171**

Source: Ministry of National Economy (1935: Table 7.9).

Table 2.4 Evolution of Population in the Main Towns of Western Thrace, 1920–1951

	1920	1928	1940	1951
Komotini	21,294	30,136	31,217	29,734
Xanthi	16,584	33,712	28,961	25,700
Alexandroupoli	6963	12,009	15,472	18,580
Didimoteicho	n/a	8204	7791	8136
Soufli	n/a	7307	7482	7435
Orestiada	n/a	3246	6652	12,832
Sappes	n/a	1808	2351	n/a

Source: Ministry of National Economy 1928; 1935; 1950; 1958.

By the late 1930s the Greek community had established itself as the economic elite in the area and provided the overwhelming majority of local civil servants and administrators. The significant presence of the Greek army in Western Thrace also boosted the profile of the Greek community in the area. By contrast to the elites in the main towns, however, large sections of Greek population (particularly the newly arrived refugees) faced a harsh existence as small plot farmers or as workers in the tobacco industry which remained a hugely important employer in the area (particularly in Xanthi). Although the Greek community maintained some degree of interaction with other ethnic groups in the area, its social life overwhelmingly revolved around extended family networks and the Greek Orthodox Church as well as membership of a flourishing number of cultural institutions which played a key role in shaping the content of 'Greekness' in the 'newly liberated' areas of Macedonia and Western Thrace.

Within the Muslim *ratsa*, the Turkish-speaking community formed the largest group numbering over 84,000 people according to the Greek census of 1928 (see Table 2.1). The largest concentration of Turkish communities was in the Prefecture of Rhodope, particularly in the Provinces of Komotini and Sappes where they formed clear majorities (Table 2.3; Dalègre 1997: 22). A significant presence of Turkish communities was also visible in the Western Thracian plains and across the *yaka* of the Rhodope Mountains as well as in some of the highland villages north of Komotini. Vibrant Turkish *Mahalle* (neighbourhoods) existed in both the towns of Xanthi and Alexandroupolis, whereas the Turks of Komotini formed the largest urban community of Muslims in Western Thrace. The Turkish population in Evros was, by comparison, much smaller and concentrated mainly on the north-western areas of the Prefecture (neighbouring Rhodope).

In the urban areas and the few ethnically-mixed villages in the low-lands, the Turkish communities lived peacefully alongside the Greek major-ity, but social integration was rather limited to commercial transactions or occasional inter-community gatherings in local festivals. In this sense, the situation in Western Thrace paralleled the inter-mingling of Orthodox Christians and Muslims in Anatolia (Hirschon 2009: 29).[12] Yet, the limits of such 'multi-ethnicity' were evident. Marriages, for example, were over-whelmingly arranged within the context of small localities, with very few brides 'given' outside the village, let alone to members of different ethnic or religious groups.

Overall, the outlook of the Turkish community was deeply entrenched in the Islamic tradition and the social order of the Ottoman Empire with which many local Turks felt a strong affinity. The predominance of patriarchal structures and a strong reliance on family networks and religious institu-tions provided for a conservative and rather insular form of social organisa-tion, particularly in the small rural communities where the vast majority of the Turkish population lived and worked as subsistence farmers. In more urban settings, a greater degree of cosmopolitanism was evident amongst the local Turkish elites of merchants, professionals and large land owners. The activism of the Turkish Consulate in Komotini in promoting 'Kemalist progress' (for example, in sponsoring local associations or influencing local education provision) was also significant in this respect. In subsequent years, the cleavage between 'Ottoman traditionalists' and 'Kemalist progressives'

---

[12] Hirschon (2006) and Örs (2006) in their respective studies of Asia Minor refu-gees in Greece and the Christians in Istanbul note the friendly contact and good memories of Christian-Muslim interactions.

would become a major feature of intra-minority politics to shape the local landscape in the run up to the turmoil of the 1940s (see below).

Alongside the 'Turks' were the Pomaks, a fellow Muslim minority with a more complex and disputed history than most, even in the Balkans. The historiography of the Pomaks questions who they are (an autochthonous or immigrant group); whether their conversion to Islam was voluntary or forced; and whether they should be considered as ethnically Bulgarian, Turkish, Greek or something else (Konstantinov 1997: 33; Todorova 1998; Brunnbauer 1998; Küçükcan 1999; Neuburger 2000; Tsibiridou 2000; Michail 2003; Anagnostou, 2007; Broun, 2007). In any event, with no Ottoman *'referentiel'* the Pomak community in the mid-twentieth century appeared to have had a greater sense of their own separateness, shaped by their Muslim religion and Bulgarian language. Their geographical isolation would have been relevant in this regard. The 1928 Greek Census identified 16,740 Pomaks, of which the vast majority resided in the highland villages of the Xanthi Province (see Table 2.3). Some 2000 Pomaks were also reported to be living in remote areas of the Provinces of Komotini and Sappes, along the Greco-Bulgarian border (in the Eastern Rhodope Mountains).

In economic terms, the Pomak community was far poorer than the lowland Turks. Their main economic activity revolved around forestry, small-scale animal breeding and subsistence agriculture. Given their geographical isolation, contacts between the Pomaks and other local communities were infrequent, particularly since most commercial transactions between the highlands and the lowlands were conducted by the Vlachs and Saracatchans (Dalègre 1997: 25). In this context, the cultural specificities of their community had persisted for centuries and remained largely unaffected by the demographic turmoil of the 1920s. A central feature of this culture was a strong attachment to the land and the Islamic tradition, with the Pomak community supplying a significant body of religious personnel across the region. The cultural distinctiveness of the Pomak community would have also been supported by overwhelming levels of village endogamy. In subsequent decades, internal migration towards Xanthi and Komotini and increased numbers of mixed marriages with lowland Turks radically altered the meaning of 'Pomakness' (Poulton 1997; Demetriou 2004). In the 1930s, however, there is little evidence to suggest that the first point of Pomak self-identification was of being 'Turkish'. The Pomak community became 'Turkified' later, especially after WWII.

In addition to those identifying as 'Turks' and as 'Pomaks' were the Roma (also referred to as 'Gypsies'), a vibrant feature of the local human landscape, albeit marginalised by both Christians and Muslims alike. As long ago as the 17th century, the Ottoman traveller, Evliya Çelebi, noted:

> The original home of the Gypsies of Rumelia has been this town of Gümülcine [Komotini] ... The Rumelian Gypsies celebrated Easter with the Christians, the Festival of the Sacrifice with the Muslims, and Passover

with the Jews. They did not accept any religion, and therefore our imams refused to conduct funeral services for them. It is because they are such renegades that they were ordered to pay an additional haraç [tax for non-Muslims]...There are numerous Gypsies in the vicinity of the town, whether singers, musicians, or counterfeiters and thieves... (Friedman and Dankoff 1991: 155–156)

Estimating the numbers of Roma in Western Thrace during the inter-war period is very difficult. The 1928 census identified nearly 1500 members of the Roma community, two-thirds of whom were Muslims (see Table 2.1). However, Aarbakke (2000: 35) casts doubt over the accuracy of population statistics on the Roma, whereas Nikolakopoulos (1990–1991: 171) and Andreades (1980: 11) estimated their number during the early 1950s to over 5000. Unlike their kin elsewhere in Greece, the Roma of Western Thrace were granted full Greek citizenship by virtue of their inclusion in the non-exchangeable Muslim population after Lausanne. Such 'official recognition' brought upon them certain obligations vis-à-vis the Greek state (i.e. conscription), but did not mitigate their extreme marginalisation (Zenginis 1994: 20–21).

Locally, the non-nomadic Roma were to be found on makeshift settlements in Xanthi, Komotini, Alexandroupolis and Didimoteichon where they remained excluded from the main areas of economic activity (agriculture or services), and coerced into forming a pool of occasional labourers or small-scale semi-legal marketers (Poulton 1997: 91). Harassed by the Greek authorities, the Roma community was also isolated by their fellow Muslims in the lowlands who were contemptuous of their non-adherence to the Islamic duties of frequent prayers and fasting. There were no instances of inter-marriage between the two groups and many local Turks regarded the Roma as being 'not one of us' (*onlar bizden değil*) (Zenginis 1994: 50). By contrast, some interviewees suggested that relations between the Pomaks and the Roma were marginally better.[13]

The Jews of Western Thrace, whose presence in the area dated back to the fifteen century, formed another piece of the local ethnic mosaic. According to the 1928 census the community numbered nearly 3000 people and was exclusively concentrated in the larger towns of the region (see Table 2.1). According to Enepekides (1969: 170) in 1940 there were some 819 Jews in Komotini, 900 in Didimoteicho, 550 in Xanthi, 140 in Alexandroupoli and 197 in Orestiada. The community maintained Synagogues and primary schools in all major towns (the school of Komotini had 200 pupils) and a number of vibrant community centres such as *Achadout* in Xanthi and *Macabi* in Xanthi (*Leykoma Trakis-Macedonias* 1932: 258, 268). Many members of the Jewish community featured prominently in local economic

---

[13] Interview 21.

life either as traders or skilled silversmiths. As elsewhere in Greece, the Jews of Western Thrace maintained high levels of educational attainment and a rather cosmopolitan outlook, although marriages were very much kept within their own community. During the Balkan Wars a significant number of Western Thracian Jews emigrated to Thessaloniki and Istanbul (Altinoff 1921: 11).[14] Those who remained in the area had to tread carefully so as to maintain a neutral position in the local power struggles between the Greeks and the Bulgarians. Although careful 'local diplomacy' did not extinguish low-level anti-Semitism in the area, it did avert major incidents of anti-Semitic persecution similar to those witnessed in other parts of eastern and central Europe during the 1930s.

Of similar size to the Jewish community of Western Thrace were the Orthodox Christian Armenians.[15] According the 1928 census, there were 3244 Armenians in the region (see Table 2.1), concentrated in separate neighbourhoods in the towns of Komotini, Xanthi and Alexandroupolis (Papaevgeniou 1946: 23). Despite their religious affinity to the Greeks, the Armenians spoke their own language (although many also spoke Greek and/or Turkish) and maintained a distinct cultural profile. This was supported by a network of churches, social clubs and schools, the largest of which (with 70 pupils) was located in Komotini (Leykoma Trakis-Macedonias 1932: 259). The size of the Armenian community in Western Thrace had increased substantially since the turn of the century with the influx of many Armenian refugees fleeing persecution in the Ottoman Empire. Indeed, during the Greco-Turkish population exchange of 1923 more than 45,000 Armenians from Anatolia arrived in Greece, whilst a substantial number sought refuge in Bulgaria. Writing in the early 1920s, Altinoff described the Armenian community of Western Thrace as insular and apathetic towards local politics, living on a very modest income generated by commercial activities (1921: 11). During the inter-war period relations between the Armenian and the Muslim communities remained tense, but isolated incidents of violence never escalated into community-wide confrontation.[16]

---

[14] Also see Central Board of Jewish Communities in Greece, www.kis.gr

[15] As noted in Table 2, nearly 5,000 (mostly Turkish-speaking) Orthodox Christian Pontians settled in Western Thrace in the aftermath of the Greco-Turkish population exchange of 1923. However, there is little evidence as to the extent to which this community became integrated or remained distinct from the Greek majority in the area. For details on the Pontians in Macedonia see Marantzidis 2001.

[16] For incidents of intercommunity violence in the area see AYE/1927/93.3, 'The present condition of the Turkish minority of Thrace and the grievances of the Turkish Embassy', Athens, 25 June 1927. AYE/1930/25, 9th Sub-Committee for the Population Exchange to the Greek Delegation at the Mixed Commission, Komotini 24 February 1925. BCA/43323/301000/25370623, Commission for the Population Exchange and Refugee Settlement, to the Prime Ministry, 28 February 1924; BCA/6176/301000/63214, The President of the Turkish Grand National

The Armenians enjoyed comparatively better relations with the Greeks, although during WWII their collaboration with the Bulgarian authorities would provoke much hostility (see Chapter 4).

*   *   *

It is evident from the above that the physical and human geography of the region had a number of important consequences for the cohesiveness and self-identity both of the Muslim minority as a whole and its constituent parts. The local diversity (structured by both geography and history) formed an important feature of the landscape with significant implications for the way in which the minority would experience the events of the 1940s. These will be explored in more detail in subsequent chapters.

2.3   Stillborn attempts for Thracian statehood

The protracted decline of the Ottoman Empire brought the wider region of Thrace (encompassing Eastern/Western Thrace and Eastern Rumelia) to the forefront of competing nationalist narratives and, at a later stage, exposed it to the agenda of socialist internationalism. This was indeed a process mirroring developments in many other parts of the Balkan Peninsula, although Thrace offered its own unique set of ethnic, linguistic and religious peculiarities. Greek claims over the area were already well-articulated within the context of the *Megali Idea* (Skopetea 1988; Clogg 1992: 47–97; Llewellyn Smith 1998: 1–20; Koliopoulos and Veremis 2002: 227–262). For Bulgaria too the aborted Treaty of San Stefano (1878) had offered a glimpse of the glories of national unification and expansion towards the Aegean Sea (Crampton 1997: 66–86; Jelavich 1997: 335–361, Vol. I). Turkish nationalism, by comparison, had arrived late, but its vigour could not be underestimated (Ahmad 1969; Kazancıgil and Özbudun 1997; Poulton 1999: 72–133; Landau 2004: 21–57; Gökalp 2005). Neither could its potential to galvanise support by virtue of its linguistic and/or religious affinity to the local non-Christian population. The spread of the Communist ideology in the Balkans offered a similar galvanising effect, with the potential of creating an audience that cut across the existing ethnic/cultural/linguistic/religious cleavages.

Such an invasion of nationalist and Communist modernity, however, must have felt rather overwhelming for Western Thracian Muslims who seemed in no hurry to abandon the traditional Islamic ways that had underpinned their existence for centuries. Western Thrace, in that sense, was different

---

Assembly, to the Prime Ministry, 7 November 1926; BCA/10253/301000/12387412, Foreign Ministry, to Prime Ministry, 16 October 1923.

from Macedonia. There, scattered pieces of a distinct Macedonian identity had survived the furious onslaught of Balkan nationalisms and were, later on, expertly manipulated by the Greek Communists and Tito's Yugoslavia. Although the ethnic properties of this identity were (and remain) contested, its Orthodox Christian heritage was never in doubt, particularly after the purging of the Muslim populations from Macedonia in the 1920s.

In Western Thrace the Muslim community stayed, whereas the local Bulgarian population lacked the nationalist vigour of their kin in Macedonia. The diverse cultural, linguistic and ethnic identities, both within and across the main religious divide, provided infertile ground for the development of a distinct brand of 'Thracian' nationalism that could be manipulated for the benefit of any one sub-group or kin country. The spread of the Communist ideology faced similar difficulties on the ground, particularly with regards to its appeal to local Muslims. The stillborn attempts for an independent Thracian statehood, either under nationalist or Communist guises, since the 1870s reinforces the metaphor of a mosaic of identities not conducive to a shared sense of 'nationhood'.

The Tamrash (Тъмръш) Rebellion (1878–1886)

The first attempt for the creation of an independent statelet in the Rhodope Mountains came in the aftermath of the Treaty of San Stefano (1878) by the Pomak population in the Tamrash region (today's Dospat in Bulgaria) who opposed the prospect of a Bulgarian administration in the area. Two years earlier, in 1876, local Pomaks under the leadership of Ahmed Ağa of Tamrash (*Tamrashliya*)[17] and Ahmed Ağa Barutanlijata were instrumental in perpetrating the massacre of the Christian inhabitants of Perushtitsa, Peshtera, Brachigovo and Batak when the latter were suspected of organising a Bulgarian rebellion against the Sultan (Lory 1989: 184–186; Simon 2000: 62–63). The Batak massacre, described by the British diplomat, Sir Evelyn Baring, as 'perhaps the most heinous crime that has stained the history of the present century' (Miller 1913: 365), caused widespread indignation across Europe (Gladstone 1876). The massacre also provided the spark for the outbreak of the Turco-Russian War the outcome of which had tremendous implications (through the Treaties of San Stefano and Berlin) for the entire Balkan Peninsula.

According to Dalègre (1995: 130–131), the insurgency was initially confined to the area south of Plovdiv, but was later extended towards the Rhodopes and the Arda valley. As early as July 1878 the British Ambassador to Constantinople maintained that the insurgents had declared themselves 'an autonomous Pomak nation' under the leadership of British-born Stanislas

---

[17] For the life and deeds of Ahmed Ağa of Tamrash see Lory 1989.

Graham Bower St. Clair, also known under the name Hidayet Paşa.[18] By the summer of 1879 a total of 17 Pomak villages had agreed to submit to the leadership of Ahmed Ağa from Tamrash and organised a separate 'government' with a number of portfolios distributed to local Pomak notables such as Hacı Hasan Ağa from Trigrad, Hacı Mehmet from Beden and Molla Eyüb from Mugla (Papadimitriou 2003: 82).[19] In 1881 four more villages from Tatar Pazardjik (Pazarcık) joined the insurgency which now extended its authority over 19,000 inhabitants and commanded an army of 8000 (Miller 1913: 414; Papadimitriou 2003: 77). The authorities of the new statelet collected their own taxes and dispatched an Ambassador to Plovdiv who was also instructed to issue visas to those wishing to visit its mountainous territories (Simon 2000: 55).[20] However, the underlying anti-Bulgarian sentiments that fuelled the rebellion soon became irrelevant following the recognition by the Ottoman Empire of the annexation of Eastern Rumelia by the Bulgarian principality in 1885.[21] The final demarcation of the border between the two countries that followed in 1886 brought most Pomak villages of Tamrash and Kardzhali under the Ottoman Empire, thus putting an end to the very reason that had let to the outbreak of the rebellion in 1878. Following their return to the Ottoman Empire, the Pomaks of Tamrash continued to enjoy

---

[18] The precise role of St. Clair in this rebellion remains a topic of considerable uncertainty in the literature. Papathannasi-Mousiopoulou (1984) and Mehmet (2007: 45) maintain that St. Clair was supported by the British government as a countervailing influence to the advance of the Russian Empire towards the Aegean. However, speaking in the House of Commons in 1878, the British Ambassador to Constantinople Sir A. Layard expressed little sympathy towards the activities of 'Mr St. Clair and his friends' (HoC, 1878–79 [C.2204] [C.2205] Turkey. No. 53 (1878). 'Further correspondence respecting the affairs of Turkey', No. 9, Sir A.H. Layard to the Marquis of Salisbury, Therapia 27 July 1878). According to Lory (1982: 194) the insurgency led by St. Clair did not spread across the entire area that later became known as 'insubordinate'. Lory also maintains that St. Clair had served in the British army but later settled in an estate by the Black Sea. He disliked both the Russians and the Bulgarians and he served in the Ottoman army in Bulgaria in 1877–1878. Several British, Spanish and Polish adventurers participated in his insurgency. St. Clair was eventually removed from the Rhodope Mountains in December 1878.

[19] The statelet of Tamrash is referred to with different names in Balkan historiography. Amongst the most common are *Temporary Turkish State of Rhodope* (*Rodop Türk Devlet-i Muvakkatesi*), *Tâmrâshka republika* (*Тъмръшка република*), or the 'insubordinate villages' (*nepokorna sela*). Turkish bibliography gives particular emphasis to names implying the existence of an actual 'Republic'.

[20] See for example Malkidis and Kokkas 2006: 22–27; See also Papathanasi-Mousiopoulou 1984: 119–124; Tsioumis 1997: 27–29; Marushiakova and Popov 2002: 4–5; Soilentakis 2004: 332–333, Vol. I.

[21] Following the Treaty of Berlin of July 1878 (that revised the Treaty of San Stefano), Eastern Rumelia had been recognised an autonomous principality (under a Christian Prince) within the Ottoman Empire.

widespread autonomy whilst some of their leaders were decorated by the Ottoman authorities (Miller 1913: 415; Dalègre 1995: 138).

The Republic of Gümülcine (1913)[22]

If the events of 1876–86 were fuelled by Pomak fears about what *might* have been the implications of Bulgarian rule for their communities, the second attempt for the creation of independent Thracian statehood was the result of the *actual* Bulgarian control of Western Thrace in the aftermath of the Balkan wars in 1912–13. The Muslim minority – particularly the Pomaks in the Rhodope Mountains – suffered bitterly at the hands of the Bulgarians who initiated an aggressive policy of 'Bulgarisation' and 'Christianization' against a community whom – due to their linguistic proximity – they regarded as 'lapsed brothers'. The villages around the tobacco-rich area of Xanthi were particularly hard hit.

A report produced by International Commission for the Inquiry into the Causes and Conduct of the Balkan War (funded by the Carnegie Endowment for International Peace) provided details on the forced conversion of the Pomaks:

> The Moslems were ranged in groups. Each group was given some baptismal name, generally a name honored in the Bulgarian church or in Bulgarian history. An exarchist pope then passed from group to group and took aside each of his catechumens *sui generis;* and while sprinkling his forehead with holy water with one hand, with the other he compelled him to bite a sausage. The holy water represented baptism, the piece of sausage renunciation of the Moslem faith, since the Koran forbids the eating of pork. The conversion was completed by the issue of a certificate adorned with a picture of the baptism of Jesus, the price of which varied between one and three francs…The converted were obliged to give up their fez, and the converted women to walk in the streets with their faces uncovered. (Carnegie Endowment 1914: 155–156)

An eyewitness account submitted by a local Bulgarian intellectual to the same Commission recalled:

> Those who stand for the thought and the honor of our country ought to know that our authorities have, in the countries on the frontier inhabited by the pomaks and recently liberated, acted in a way which is a disgrace to their country and to humanity. One aim alone was kept in sight – that of personal enrichment. Conversion was only a pretext. It did not save

---

[22] The name of the city in Bulgarian was *Gumuldjina*. Often Greek documents at the time referred to Komotini by that name.

the poor pomaks from atrocious treatment except where the priests with whom they had to deal were conscientious men. Such cases, however, were rare. The ecclesiastical mission was beneath criticism. High rewards were paid, but the priests sent to carry out this task in the pomak villages were drunkards and criminals who could not be kept in Bulgaria. The behavior of the police was monstrous. In Bulgaria no one has and no one can have any idea of the atrocities committed by prefects, heads of police, and priests. (Carnegie Endowment, 1914: 157–158)

The Bulgarian supremacy in Thrace (both Western and Eastern) in the aftermath of the First Balkan War (1912) was partially reversed in the summer of 1913 with the outbreak of the Second Balkan War which led to the capture of Alexandroupolis, Xanthi and Komotini by Greek forces and the recovery of Edirne by the Ottoman Army. A few months later, however, the Treaty of Bucharest (August 1913) ceded Western Thrace to Bulgaria (Carnegie Endowment 1914; Schurman 1914; Melas 1958; Hall 2000). The prospect of the area returning under Bulgarian administration galvanised all the non-Bulgarian local population into action. Joint committees of Muslims, Christians and Jews were set up to protest to the Great Powers and pressurise Greece and Turkey to intervene (Papathanasi-Mousiopoulou 1982). The Committee for Union and Progress under by the Young Turks were the first to oblige. A Turkish Committee for Thrace (*Türk Garbi Trakya Komitesi*) was created aimed at undermining the Bulgarian administration in Western Thrace and promoting the idea of autonomy. The Greek government was more cautious. Despite pressure from local church leaders, the Greek Premier, Eleftherios Venizelos, was reluctant to openly default from what had been agreed at Bucharest. Nevertheless the Greek government was anxious to retain a strong Greek presence in the area (many Greeks had fled since the arrival of the Bulgarian administration) and encouraged local Greeks to cooperate with the Muslims in making joint representations to the Great Powers (Georgantzis 1993: 119–127).

The Ottoman government, which did not participate in the negotiations leading up to the Treaty of Bucharest, also endorsed the demand for Thracian autonomy. Soon after the departure of the Greek army from the area, it began to support the formation of local guerrilla groups (many of which were close to the Young Turks) in their fight against Bulgarian soldiers and irregulars. On 31 August 1913, weeks after the signing of the Treaty of Bucharest, Ottoman-supported rebels entered Komotini and Xanthi unopposed and proclaimed the creation of a Provisional Government of Western Thrace (*Garbı Trakya Gecici Hükümeti*).

The 'Provisional Government' enjoyed considerable cross-community support and included representatives from the Turkish, Greek, Pomak, Armenian and Jewish communities. It was headed by Hafız Salih Mehmetoğlu and commanded a 30,000-strong army, drafted by volunteers from all the ethnic groups of the region (under the orders of Süleyman

Askeri). The provisional administration also provided for the establishment of a Parliament of 25 members, an Executive Committee of 16 members, three directorates (ministries) of military, justice and economy, the creation of courts, the collection of taxes, the payment of salaries to the civil servants, the introduction of a state flag, the provision of passports (bilingual, in Turkish and Greek) and the publication, by the prominent local Jew, Samuel Karaso, of the newspaper *L' Independent* in French and Turkish (Dalègre 1997: 56; Soilentakis 2004: 71–74, Vol. II; Vakalopoulos 2000: 280–281).

Strong international pressure for the full implementation of the Treaty of Bucharest, however, soon placed a heavy burden on the Ottoman authorities' initial support for the 'Provisional Government'. In view of the important Istanbul conference for the delineation of the Bulgarian-Ottoman border (in which the Empire was on the defensive), Ottoman Foreign Minister Talaat Bey recalled Muslim and Christian leaders from Western Thrace and pressured them to dissolve their government and accept the provisions of the Treaty of Bucharest. The 'Provisional Government' reacted angrily to this suggestion and, on 25 September 1913, Eşref Kuşçubaşı and Süleyman Askeri proclaimed the establishment of the Independent Government of Western Thrace *(Garbı Trakya Bağimsiz Hükümeti)*, also known as the *'Republic of Gümülcine'*.

The Republic was doomed from the start. The Treaty of Istanbul signed between the Ottoman Empire and Bulgaria a few days later settled the border issue and officially ceded Western Thrace to the latter. Without vital Ottoman backing, the Republic turned to its secondary patron, Greece, for support. The Greek government responded by offering the port of Alexandroupolis, which was still under its control, to the Republic and promised to dispatch armed bands to support their Anti-Bulgarian struggle. This was too little too late. Keen not to jeopardise relations with Bulgaria, the Ottomans despatched another delegation to Western Thrace in order to reassure the insurgents that the Treaty of Istanbul provided clear guarantees for the protection of the Muslim community. However, no such guarantees existed for the non-Bulgarian Christian population (Papathanasi-Mousiopoulou 1982: 61–62). In the end, the resolve of the Western Thracian leadership was broken. On 20 October 1913 the Republic of Gümülcine ceased to exist. More than 2000 Turkish officers and volunteers returned to the Ottoman Empire, while the Muslim leadership of the 'Republic' left for Eastern Thrace.[23]

---

[23] The practices of the Bulgarian administration forced many Muslims to flee from Western Thrace. Ottoman documents depict the hardship faced by those who left as well as the preoccupation of the government in Istanbul to halt this wave of immigration by forbidding Western Thracian Muslims to migrate *en famille*. BOA/ HR.SYS/2426/37, Sublime Porte, Interior Ministry, Directorate-General of Tribes and Immigrants, to Foreign Ministry, 28 September 1916. BOA/HR.SYS/2424/54, The Sublime Porte, The Office of the Şehbender [Consul] of Dedeağaç [Alexandroupolis], to the Foreign Minister, 16 August 1916.

The Turkish Republic of Western Thrace (1920)

The return of the Bulgarian administration in Western Thrace brought with it the resumption of the Bulgarisation campaign, particularly against the Pomaks and the Greeks (Popovic 1986: 144; Papathanasi-Mousiopoulou 1991: 84–87; Geragas 2005: 48–49). Yet the successful implementation of the Bulgarian national project in Western Thrace was soon to be fatally undermined by Bulgaria's decision to enter the WWI on the side of the Central Powers. On 17 September 1918 the victorious Entente signed an armistice with Bulgaria and a few weeks later Allied forces entered Sofia to enforce the armistice terms. For the Greeks who, after much internal recriminations, had eventually entered the war on the side of the Entente, this was a moment of opportunity.

The terms of the armistice included, amongst others, the gradual withdrawal of Bulgarian troops from Western Thrace and the despatch of a small Anglo-French force under Colonel Allier to the area in order to protect the Xanthi-Constantinople railway line. Meanwhile, the Greek army, under the command of the French Commander-in-Chief of the Allied Armies of the Orient, D' Esperey, remained in reserve in Eastern Macedonia. The prospect of the Greek army returning to Western Thrace alarmed the Bulgarian government[24] that was now ready to accept Western Thrace as a French protectorate – a proposal that was eventually rejected by France (Georgantzis 1993:163–166, 229–231).

In the meantime, Greek Colonel Mazarakis[25] continued his plotting against the Bulgarians. In December 1918 he encouraged his personal friend Ismail Hakki, a leading Turkish figure in the Bulgarian parliament (*Sobranje*), to submit a memorandum on behalf of eight Turkish and Pomak members of the *Sobranje* to D' Esperey and the Allied Conference in Paris asking for the removal of the Bulgarian administration and the deployment of Greek troops in Western Thrace.[26] A similar letter was sent to Eleftherios Venizelos himself,

---

[24] BOA/HR.SYS/2461/77, Ottoman Consul of Dedeağaç [Alexandroupolis], to Foreign Ministry, Directorate-General of Political Affairs, 15 January 1919.

[25] Colonel Mazarakis headed a 55-strong Greek delegation alongside Entente officials during the armistice negotiations with Bulgaria.

[26] According to reports from the Ottoman government, the treatment of Western Thracian Muslims in the hands of the Bulgarian administration grew increasingly harsh towards the later stages of the war. The Ottoman Consul in Dedeağaç [Alexandroupolis] wrote:

'The Bulgarians are engaging in acts that are more violent than those which took place during the Balkan War. They recently entered the neighbourhoods of Komotini committing atrocities beyond imagination. They transgressed the honour of Muslim women and seized all food, condemning Muslim people to starvation'.

BOA/HR.SYS/2454/37, Sublime Porte, Interior Ministry, Directorate-General of Public Security, to the Foreign Ministry', 9 June 1918. For similar comments see also

in order to promote their demands to the Allied Council.[27] The memorandum was a welcome gift to Venizelos during the Paris Conference, but outraged both Bulgaria and the Ottomans who grew increasingly suspicious of the rising Greek influence in the area (Petsalis-Diomidis 1978: 90–91). Eventually, under instructions from the Allied Council in Paris, D' Esperey appointed General Charpy as Governor of Western Thrace with the task of supervising the withdrawal of the Bulgarian Army and establishing the *Thrace Interalliée* administration until the resolution of the area's final status.[28]

In the ensuing power battle for control of the *Interalliée*'s civilian authorities, the Greeks were more resourceful than their opponents. Owing to the support of some Muslim representatives (such as Hafız Salih Mehmetoğlu), Greek-born Emmanuel Doulas was elected President of the Consultative Council.[29] The Greeks also gained the upper hand in the districts of Xanthi, Dedeağaç and Didimoteichon (Altinoff 1921: 17–19; Geragas 2005: 59–63).[30] These developments alarmed the Muslim community (and the Ottoman Empire) who saw their numerical strength on the ground not reflected in the power structures of the Allied administration. Venizelos' assurances that all Muslim populations in Thrace and Eastern Macedonia would enjoy widespread autonomy (including a local parliament, representatives to the Greek parliament and one Muslim minister in the Greek government) were not enough to allay the suspicions of the Turkish Committee for Thrace and the Young Turks (Petsalis-Diomidis 1978: 161–172).

Yet the leadership of the Muslim population in the area was confused and, at times, divided over the best course of action.[31] Those close to the

---

BOA/HR.SYS/2457/19, Sublime Porte, Interior Ministry, Directorate-General of Public Security, to the Foreign Ministry, 1 August 1918.

[27] AYE/1945/41.3, 'Letter of Muslim (Pomak) MPs of the Bulgarian *Sobranje* to Eleftherios Venizelos', 31 December 1918.

[28] In the meantime, Greek troops under Allied command occupied Xanthi in October 1919.

[29] The Interalliée system of administration provided for the creation of a 15-member Consultative Council to assist General Charpy in the exercise of his executive powers. The membership of the Council reflected the ethnic mosaic on the ground: five seats were allocated to Muslims (Hafız Salih Mehmetoğlu, Osman Ağa, Bedim Bey, Hassan Bey and Tevfik Bey), four to Greeks (Formozis, Papathanassis, Lamnides, Stalios), two to Bulgarians (Georgieff, Dotchkoff), one to Jews (Karasso), one to Armenians (Roupen) and two to Levantines with French nationality (Doulas and Badetti). In administrative terms the region was divided into two 'circles' and six provinces: Xanthi, Gümülcine, Dedeağaç (circle of Gümülcine) and Soufli, Didimoteicho, Karaağaç (circle of Karaağaç). The administration of the circles was placed under an Allied military commander assisted, in each district, by a civilian administrator drawn from the largest ethnic group in the area.

[30] The other three districts were placed under Turkish administrators.

[31] For an insight into the machinations within the minority during this period see Batıbey 1970.

Young Turks favoured self determination based on the numerical superiority of the Muslim community in the area. Others looked to Italian patronage for counter-balancing the advancing Greek hegemony (Geragas 2005: 86–87), whereas the Pomaks in the Rhodope Mountains were more amenable to negotiations with the Greeks.[32] The lowest common denominator of local Muslim preferences at the time seemed to have been a desire to end Bulgarian rule. A common view as to the future administration of the area proved much harder to accomplish.

In May 1920 the Allies handed over military control of the area to the Greek army, which days later began its advance towards Eastern Thrace. The latter was eventually ceded to Greece by the Sevres Treaty (10 August 1920). The Greeks were in a triumphant mood. Reporting from the newly conquered territories to the Greek Ministry of Foreign Affairs, the Representative of the Greek Government to the Head of the *Thrace Interalliée* (General Charpy), Harisios Vamvakas noted:

> Our understanding with the Muslims (and I mean the people, not the leadership, which is mainly attached to [the Turkish Thracian] Committee) has been accomplished … Turks keep coming to me expressing their devotion to us. The French General has been convinced by now that the majority of non-Greeks are positively disposed towards us.[33]

The Turkish Thracian Committee and the Young Turks, however, had different plans. Alarmed by the prospect of permanent Greek control over Eastern and Western Thrace), the Committee opened channels of communication with Bulgaria with a view to supporting the creation of an independent Thracian state. A first step towards this direction was taken, on 25 May 1920, with the proclamation of a Turkish Republic of Western Thrace (*Garbı Trakya Devleti Muvakkatesi*) in the village of Hemetli (Organi) in the Rhodope Mountains. The 'Republic' was headed by Peştereli Tevfik Bey and its military forces were placed under the command of influential Kemalist officer Ali Fuat Cebesoy (or Fuat Balkan).[34] Although a number of ministerial portfolios were allocated by

---

[32] ELIA/37/02, 9th Brigade, Xanthi to the Headquarters-General, Smyrna, 11 February 1920.

[33] ELIA/37/02, Greek Delegation in Western Thrace, Vamvakas, to Politis, Foreign Minister, Athens, 26 March 1920. For similar comments see ELIA/37/02, Greek Delegation in Western Thrace, Vamvakas, to Politis, Foreign Minister, Athens, 13 May 1920; ELIA/37/02, Ahmet, Mufti of Gumuldjina district to Vamvakas, 29 April 1920.

[34] In July 1915 Ali Fuat had created a revolutionary movement in Drama (Eastern Macedonia), aiming at protecting the local Muslim population from Bulgarian and Greek oppression. Shortly afterwards he established a 'Committee for the Liberation of Western Thrace' (*Batı Trakya Kurtuluş Komitesi*) and occupied several Muslim

the new 'President of the Government',[35] the 'Republic' never really developed state-like institutions and soon descended into a guerrilla movement against the Greek army in a period when the latter was preoccupied with its campaign in Asia Minor campaign. Following the conclusion of the Lausanne Treaty (which demarcated the Greek-Turkish border and ceded Eastern Thrace to Turkey) the 'Republic' was starved of its vital channels of support from Turkey. Not long afterwards, its leadership was arrested and sentenced to death, but was subsequently allowed to return to Turkey (Minaidis 1984: 120–121; Popovic 1986: 144–145; Georgantzis 1993: 339–340).[36] In Eastern Thrace, the provisions of Lausanne also put a natural end to the operations of the guerrilla force led by Kemal's ally Cafer Tayyar (who was also supported by Bulgaria) that resisted the presence of the Greek army in the area during the Greco-Turkish war (Papathanasi-Mousiopoulou 1975: 154–163; Kalionski and Kolev 2004: 308–309; Atatürk 2009: 185–186, Vol. I, 650–655, Vol. II).

The question of Thrace within the context of socialist internationalism

The spread of the Communist ideology in the Balkans following the Bolshevik revolution in Russia produced new challenges to the tri-partite division of Thrace envisaged by Neuilly and Lausanne. Already since 1920, the Balkan Communist Federation (BCF), set up within the context of Comintern, had made significant progress in coordinating the activities of Communist parties in the Balkans in pursing '...the unity of the Balkan countries into a Balkan Republican Federation' (Nefeloudis 1974: 22). The Communist Party of Bulgaria (BCP) played a dominant role in the context of the BCF, since it was the oldest, best organised and most popular communist party in the Balkans. Within its ranks there were some of the best known international communist leaders such as Georgi Dimitrov, who headed the BCF from 1923 to 1933 and acted as Secretary-General of the Comintern between 1935 and 1943.[37]

Given the Bulgarian misgivings over Macedonia and Thrace, both issues made an early appearance on the agenda of the Comintern and BCF. In 1922, for example, the Comintern had denounced the settlement of the Greek refugees from Asia Minor in Macedonia and Thrace, claiming that their establishment in these areas served imperialist aspirations for the reshuffling of the local population mix and played to the hands of Greek

---

villages in the area. However, in September 1917, Fuat was forced to flee to Turkey. See Popovic 1986: 144.

[35] Vice President and Minister of Justice: Gümülcine Mufti Bekir Sıtkı Bey, Minister of Foreign Affairs: Mahmut Nedim Bey, Minister of Internal Affairs: Hasan Tahsin Bey, Minister of Finance: Sabri Bey and Minister of Infrastructure: Mustafa Doğrul Bey.

[36] The leadership of the Republic was exchanged for a group of Istanbul Greeks who were tried for treason by the Kemalist regime because of their active support of the Allied occupation of Istanbul in 1918–1923.

[37] In 1945 Dimitrov became Secretary-General of the Bulgarian Communist Party and served as Bulgarian Prime Minister between 1946 and 1949.

capitalists. Shortly afterwards, in November 1923, the 6th Plenary Session of the BCF issued a lengthy resolution on Macedonia and Thrace. For Macedonia, the resolution recognised its strategic importance for the entire Balkan Peninsula and acknowledged that it would not be possible for any one Balkan country to assume its sovereignty without oppressing large sections of the local population. (Dagkas and Leontiadis 1997: 105).

Similar imperatives were identified by the BCF with regards to Thrace (see Box 2.1).

Indeed the granting of autonomy to Macedonia and Thrace was seen by communist planners as the first step towards the emancipation of their respective peoples. Eventually the two regions were to become autonomous Republics within the framework of a Balkan Federation of Socialist Republics. Six months after the resolution of the BCF, the 5th Plenary Session of the Comintern made explicit its commitment towards the creation of a 'United and Independent Macedonia' and a 'United and Independent Thrace' (Dangas and Leontiadis, 1997: 136).

These ideas on the status of both Macedonia and Thrace gained further impetus when the Communist Party of Greece (KKE – *Κομμουνιστικό Κόμμα Ελλάδος*) – previously SEKE (*Σοσιαλιστικό Εργατικό Κόμμα Ελλάδος* – Greek Socialist Labour Party) – acceded to the Comintern in November 1924. The earlier accession of the Greek Communists to the BCF (in 1920) had already exposed them to the influence of the Bulgarian Communist Party (Woodhouse 2002: 10). Now, full membership of the Comintern, further strengthened the internationalist profile of KKE and its dependence on foreign guidance. According to Grigoris Farakos, who became a senior member of KKE, '... the worst consequence of this dependence was the sub-jugation of the KKE to the slogans of the Bulgarian Communist Party for a "united and independent Macedonia and Thrace" – also endorsed by the

---

Box 2.1   Resolution of the 6th Conference of the Balkan Communist Federation on the National Question, 8–26 November 1923

The population of Thrace is also ethnically mixed and has become an apple of discord between Turkey, Bulgaria and Greece during the imperialist world war and the recent Greco-Turkish war. Thrace, was successively under the domination of the Turks, the Bulgarians and the Greeks, and today is divided among them, remaining an apple of discord, capable of fuelling another military conflict. Like the population of Macedonia, the Thracian population has struggled through the years for its political and national independence and has been an object of manipulation in the hands of smaller and bigger countries for the realisation of their expansive policies. The protracted war has turned this flourishing place into rubble and imposed a new yoke of political and national slavery on its population. A significant part of its ethnicities was compelled to abandon their properties and immigrate to other countries. Therefore, there can be no other way, but the creation of an autonomous Thrace.

Source: Dangas and Leontiadis, 1997: 107–108.

Comintern – and its involvement in the controversies of the Balkan countries over the Macedonian issue' (Farakos 2004: 25).

Despite its strong commitment to the principle of self-determination, however, the KKE made no organised attempt to infiltrate the Muslim community in Western Thrace. This contrasted sharply with its official rhetoric which, in 1925, maintained that 'the issue of the independence of Thrace (Eastern and Western), must be discussed in a clearer way and become more popularised among the refugee populations of Western Thrace and the Turkish minorities of that region' (KKE 1974: 79). By the mid-1930s, under pressure from its political opponents and sections of its own membership, the KKE's line on 'independence' for Macedonia and Thrace was dropped in favour of a more general commitment to 'full equality for minorities' (KKE 1975: 296; Lymberiou 2005: 63). However, the greater penetration of all minority groups (Macedonians, Turks, Albanians, Jews, etc.) in Greece was re-iterated as a party priority during the 5th Conference in December 1935 (KKE 1975: 306).

Yet, despite the significant inroads made by KKE among Macedonian Slavs, its influence over the Western Thracian Muslims remained minimal. This discrepancy would, later on, have major implications both for the development of resistance activity in the area during WWII and the ability of the KKE to build bridges with the local Muslim population during the course of the Greek Civil War (see Chapters 4–8).

* * *

The struggle for control of the wider region of Thrace since the Bulgarian uprising of 1876 bore all the hallmarks of fluidity in the face of nationalist resurgence that accompanied the dying days of the Ottoman Empire. Under conditions of rapidly declining Ottoman sovereignty and intense international involvement in the area, pre-existing local identities were de-constructed, re-invented and (re)-adjusted in order to respond to an overwhelming pace of change and a constantly shifting balance of power. Western Thrace was no exception to this pattern. At one level, the rise and rapid fall of the three attempts for independent statehood during that period revealed the difficulty of articulating a regional ('West-Thracian' or more generally 'Thracian') nationalist narrative that was independent from the existing (or the emerging, in the case of Turkey) national paradigms that encircled it. Neither could this gap be filled by the Communist ideology, particularly since the Muslim community remained almost totally isolated from it. Hence the stillborn attempts for independent Thracian statehood can be best understood as instinctive responses driven by short-term strategic imperatives, rather than the culmination of longer term processes of national or ideological emancipation shared by all local communities.

For Western Thracian Muslims, in particular, the fate of the three republics was both a reflection of their own community's internal diversity and the diluted purpose of their patron (the Ottoman Empire). The strong

Islamic outlook of the local Muslim community made it less receptive to the nationalist ideals or the Communist ideology that swept the Balkans in the late nineteenth and early twentieth century. In this sense, the Muslims of Western Thrace lacked both the 'ideological conviction' and the 'national patronage' enjoyed by their Greek and Bulgarian counterparts. The Ottoman Empire, as the community's 'natural' protector during that period, offered ambiguous signs of support and was certainly unable to deliver. Later on, the consolidation of Kemalism in the new Turkish Republic was to have major implications both for the self-identification of Western Thracian Muslims and their expectations from their kin country. These will be discussed in more detail in subsequent sections of this chapter.

2.4   The 'minoritisation' of the Muslims of Western Thrace

The Muslim community of Western Thrace emerged onto the geo-political landscape largely because of the Treaty of Lausanne that ended the Greco-Turkish war of 1919–1923. This originated its legal identity and its status as the only national minority recognised by the Greek government. The Muslims had become 'minoritised' (Cowan 2001), beyond the ideological construction of 'Hellenism', identified by international treaty but subject to a domestic legal framework that set them apart and left them enduring much inequality (Christopoulos and Tsitselikis 2003). Greek identity was non-inclusive; the prevailing culture could not countenance non-Orthodox being 'Greek'. If it were needed, the local actions of the Greek state sustained an identity of separation (Dragona and Frangoudaki 2006; Haslinger 2003; Trubeta 2003), wary of its identification with the new Turkey. The Lausanne Treaty shaped the way in which much of the subsequent local, bilateral and international discourse on Western Thracian Muslims was constructed.

The official signing of the Lausanne Treaty (23 July 1923) was preceded by the conclusion, on 30 January 1923, of a bilateral Convention Concerning the Exchange of Greek and Turkish Populations which provided (Article 1) for the compulsory exchange of all 'Turkish nationals of the Greek Orthodox religion established in Turkish territory, and of Greek nationals of the Moslem religion established in Greek territory'.[38] As already noted, the Convention exempted from its provisions the 'Moslem inhabitants of Western Thrace' and the 'Greek inhabitants of Constantinople' [Istanbul].[39] These groups

---

[38] The exchange was made retroactive to include those who had migrated since 18 October 1912.

[39] The Greek Orthodox inhabitants as Gökçeada and Bozcaada were also exempted. The Convention made no reference to the Chams (Albanian-speaking Muslims) of Greek Epirus who were largely excluded for the compulsory exchange. It is estimated that only 2993 out of a total of 20,160 Chams in area were transferred to Turkey (Divani 1999: 218–246; Manta 2004: 25–43).

were subjected to special protective measures that were outlined in the provisions of the Treaty of Lausanne (see Box 2.2).

As instruments of securing peace, the Convention and the Treaty of Lausanne were controversial acts. Both documents equated religion with national identity in a local context that was far too complex to sustain such simplistic dichotomies (Alexandris 2003; Oran 2003; Seferiades 1928). In addition the labels used to define the Muslim population in Western Thrace were inconsistent, containing, interchangeably, references to both 'Muslims' and 'Turks' (Oran 1994). In subsequent decades this discrepancy gave rise to an enduring bilateral feud with significant legal and ideational

---

Box 2.2 The Treaty of Lausanne (1923): Main Provisions on the Protection of Minorities

Article 37

Turkey undertakes that the stipulations contained in Articles 38 to 44 shall be recognised as fundamental laws, and that no law, no regulation, nor official action shall conflict or interfere with these stipulations, nor shall any law, regulation, nor official action prevail over them.

Article 38 [Basic Rights]

The Turkish Government undertakes to assure full and complete protection of life and liberty to all inhabitants of Turkey without distinction of birth, nationality, language, race or religion.

All inhabitants of Turkey shall be entitled to free exercise, whether in public or private, of any creed, religion or belief [...]

Article 39 [Civil and Political Rights]

Turkish nationals belonging to non-Moslem minorities will enjoy the same civil and political rights as Moslems.

All the inhabitants of Turkey, without distinction of religion, shall be equal before the law. [...]

No restrictions shall be imposed on the free use by any Turkish national of any language in private intercourse, in commerce, religion, in the press, or in publications of any kind or at public meetings. [...]

Article 40 [Communal Property]

Turkish nationals belonging to non-Moslem minorities...shall have an equal right to establish, manage and control at their own expense, any charitable, religious and social institutions, any schools and other establishments for instruction and education, with the right to use their own language and to exercise their own religion freely therein.

Article 41 [Education]

As regards public instruction, the Turkish Government will grant in those towns and districts, where a considerable proportion of non-Moslem nationals are resident, adequate facilities for ensuring that in the primary schools the instruction shall be given to the children of such Turkish nationals through the medium of their own language. This provision will not prevent the Turkish Government from making the teaching of the Turkish language obligatory in the said schools.

Article 42 [Religion]

The Turkish Government undertakes to take, as regards non-Moslem minorities, in so far as concerns their family law or personal status, measures permitting the settlement of these questions in accordance with the customs of those minorities. [...]

Article 43 [Religion]

Turkish nationals belonging to non-Moslem minorities shall not be compelled to perform any act which constitutes a violation of their faith or religious observances [...]

Article 44 [International guarantees]

Turkey agrees that, in so far as the preceding Articles of this Section affect non-Moslem nationals of Turkey, these provisions constitute obligations of international concern and shall be placed under the guarantee of the League of Nations. [...]

Turkey further agrees that any difference of opinion as to questions of law or of fact arising out of these Articles...shall, if the other party thereto demands, be referred to the Permanent Court of International Justice. [...]

Article 45 [Reciprocity]

The rights conferred by the provisions of the present Section on the non-Moslem minorities of Turkey will be similarly conferred by Greece on the Moslem minority in her territory.

Source: Carnegie Endowment 1924.

implications. The emphasis placed by Lausanne on religious identity and freedom had already been provided for in previous international treaties involving Greece such as in 1830 (with respect to Catholics) and 1881 (with respect to the Muslim populations of Thessaly and Epirus).[40] What was new with the agreements such as that of Lausanne was the concern for collective rights and their protection under an international body, the League of Nations (Mazower 1998: 54).

Indeed, the Treaty of Lausanne was one of a series of international agreements under the auspices of the League which sought to provide minority protection in the Baltic and central European states. The Polish Minorities Treaty, signed between Poland and the League on 28 June 1919 provided a model for other states, with a similar treaty signed by Czechoslovakia

[40] Similar international examples can be found in the cases of Belgium (1830) and Romania (1878).

(10 September 1919) and declarations subscribing to similar principles by Finland, Lithuania, Latvia and Estonia.[41] The Polish Minorities Treaty had 'assumed a model character for similar agreements across Central and Eastern Europe and for a variety of ethnic minorities in other countries' (Wolff 2003: 32; also Mair 1928: 36). Moreover, such a treaty was itself motivated by a desire on the part of the Great Powers to avoid the problems posed for minority rights by the earlier experience of the Balkan Wars of 1912–1913 (Mazower 1998: 52).

Yet, the new Poland had posed difficult questions of whether a homogeneous, 'ethnically-pure' state should be created or one of a more heterogeneous character. The latter conception prevailed: only two-thirds of the population would be ethnically Polish (Mazower 1998: 53). The Polish Minorities Treaty thus endeavoured to guarantee full minority rights as well as the free use of minority languages in the private sector, to provide 'adequate facilities' for their use in the judicial system, and to protect the rights of minorities in the educational system (Woolsey 1920; Coakley 1990). 'The object of the minority treaties', the British Foreign Minister Austen Chamberlain argued in 1925, 'was to secure for the minorities that measure of protection and justice which would gradually prepare them to be *merged* in the national community to which they belonged.' (quoted in Hiden and Smith 2006: 388). The provisions of the Lausanne Treaty clearly reflected these wider European developments, though how far the 'nationalist' sentiment of the Muslims of Western Thrace was comparable to some of those of German minorities in central Europe remains a moot point. In any event, the Greco-Turkish population exchange had taken the League of Nations into un-chartered territory: this was the first 'compulsory' population exchange to be sponsored by an international organisation in the history of international law. The notion was later taken up by the British in Palestine in 1937 and, then, by Hitler and Mussolini (Schechtman 1946: 22).[42] The exchange was to traumatise both Greek and Turkish societies for decades thereafter.[43]

In bilateral terms, the principle of reciprocity enshrined in Lausanne (Article 45), placed the Muslims of Western Thrace and the Orthodox Christians of Istanbul within the strategic frame of Greco-Turkish relations (Niarchos 2005; Tsitselikis 2008). Disputes arose immediately. Both the Greek

---

[41] The relevant treaties were agreed as follows: Finland (27 June 1921), Lithuania (12 May 1922), Latvia (7 July 1923) and Estonia (17 September 1923).

[42] The idea of a voluntary population exchange between Greece and her Balkan neighbours was later floated by the United Nations (UN) in 1947 (Claude 1955: 194).

[43] See the accounts of Hirschon (2006) and Örs (2006). Iğsiz (2008: 451) writes of the '65-year Turkish silence surrounding the 1923' exchange, broken only by the documentary novel of Kemal Yalçin in 1998 'The Entrusted Trousseau: Peoples of the Exchange'.

and the Turkish governments complained to the 'Mixed Commission' set up to administer the exchange. The Bulgarian government also complained to the League about the plight of their kin in Macedonia and Thrace (Cowan 2003). Members of the Muslim minority in Western Thrace do not appear to have themselves petitioned the League or the Commission: representation went via the respective governments, usurping the role of the grassroots. This is in stark contrast to the petitions from multifarious sources submitted to the League concerning the plight of 'Macedonia', for example (Cowan 2007, Cowan 2003). On occasions, unresolved disputes prompted direct appeals to the League. Greece complained about the interpretation by Turkey of who was entitled to remain in Istanbul (Mair 1928: 198). The Turkish authorities reciprocated (in 1923) with a complaint about Western Thracian Muslims whose property had been confiscated by the Greeks or who had suffered financial loss in the aftermath of the Greek land reform (Aarbakke 2000: 54–55; Ladas 1932: 478–480).[44]

However, in December 1925, the two governments performed a remarkable u-turn and informed the League that they sought the termination of its investigations into their respective appeals (Divani 1999: 177–182). They had instead agreed on a process of bilateral negotiation. Eventually, outstanding exchange issues and territorial claims were resolved when Venizelos visited Ankara and signed, in October 1930, the Friendship Pact (Treaty of Ankara) between Greece and Turkey (Anastasiadou 1982; Alexandris 1992: 171–190; Sarris 1992: 59–66, 250–272; Hupchick 2002: 345). The Pact initiated a period of rapprochement between the two countries that lasted for most of the following decade.

As a result, the fate of the Muslim minority disappeared from the international agenda and Ankara made no significant attempt to promote the rights of its kin in Western Thrace. This stood in sharp contrast with many of the minorities of central and eastern Europe who pursued an energetic campaign for greater cultural autonomy via the creation of the European Nationalities Congress in Geneva in 1925 (Hiden 2004; Smith and Cordell 2008). Leaders such as the Baltic German Paul Schiemann presented avant-garde notions of non-territorial cultural autonomy, seeking to revise understandings of the role of the nation-state (Hiden 2004). Diplomatic expediencies in the aftermath of the Greco-Turkish rapprochement, however, meant that similar debates never made inroads into Western Thrace (Bamberger-Stemmann, 2000). The implications of the Pact for regional security in the run-up to WWII are analysed in Chapter 3.

---

[44] Further disputes over land entitlement between the majority Greeks and the minority Turks were to occur after 1953 when the Ministry of Agriculture in Athens decided to expropriate property for landless farmers. Most of the expropriation was of land that the Turkish minority felt belonged to them (Oran 1984: 362).

The more general point, though, is that Turkey – granted a *droit de regard* over Greece's Muslims since the Treaty of Constantinople in 1881 (Tsitselikis 2008: 72), a role reinforced by the Lausanne Treaty – placed its interests as a 'kinship state' below those of its geo-strategic interests in the region. This contrasted with the expansionist strategies being pursued in central Europe in this period. Although the context changed fundamentally over the course of the 1940s, later chapters will show that Ankara's local engagement in Western Thrace (via its Consulate in Komotini) was rarely matched by its rhetoric and actions on the international stage. Much of the focus of the case study, therefore, is set at the local level. Developments within Turkey, however, had a great deal of local impact, both ideationally and as a strategic resource for the minority's competing factions.

2.5   The political orientation of the minority during the 1930s

Turkey is relevant to the West Thracian case not only as an external foreign policy actor, but also as a domestic *referentiel* for identity amongst the Muslim community. This feature is crucial to the understanding of the changing orientation of the community in the pre-war period.

Between Ottoman 'traditionalism' and Kemalist 'progress'

The consolidation of the Kemalist regime in Turkey in the aftermath of Lausanne, unleashed a cultural whirlwind that disturbed the balance of power within the traditional Muslim community of Western Thrace (Dalègre 1997; Aarbakke 2000; Özkırımlı and Sofos 2008). Having first forced the last Sultan of the Ottoman Empire to flee in November 1922, Kemal went on to abolish the institution of the Caliphate. The Caliph was seen both as a successor to the Prophet Mohammed and as the political leader of a united Muslim world – the Caliphate. The institution had been revered across the Muslim nations for some 1350 years and with the Ottoman Sultans latterly acquiring the Caliph title, it gave Istanbul an international prestige.[45] The Kemalist government soon closed shrines, *sharia* colleges (*Medrese*), uniting public education, and replaced *sharia* law with civil law (Toynbee and Kirkwood 1926: 149–181; Lewis B. 1965: 256–263; Lewis G. 1965: 72–83; Kinross 1995: 340–353, 384–387; Mango 1999: 361–414). The revolutionary

---

[45] Kemal had started by allowing the last Sultan's cousin (Abdulmecid) to remain as Caliph, but in April 1924 he suddenly went the full distance and did away with the Caliphate notion altogether, when it seemed possible that the latter might serve as a figurehead for moves at political restoration (Armstrong 1932: 220–229, 243–250; Kayali 2008: 144).

impact was tremendous, 'the scale and speed of this assault on religious tradition and household custom, embracing faith, time, dress, family, language, remain unique in the *Umma* (the Muslim world) to this day' (Anderson 2008).

Kemal's radical new ideology might have been a mix of diverse and, often, contradictory principles, but underlining them all were themes of modernisation and of emulating 'Europeanness'. The basic principles – known as the 'six arrows' – rested on republicanism; nationalism; populism; etatism; revolutionism/reformism; and laicism/secularism (Shaw and Shaw 1977; Pesmazoglou 1993: 268–285; Karal 1997: 16–23; Ahmad 2003: 87–90; Akşin 2007: 228–232; Kasaba 2008). Unlike Metaxas in Greece later, his regime was certainly not socially conservative. Alongside the secular initiatives, there were changes in the written language (the adoption of the Latin alphabet and universally-used numerals), the Gregorian calendar and Western working week, the banning of the fez and restrictions on women wearing the headscarf (*hijab*), alongside the enfranchisement of women (Armstrong 1932: 291-,293; Lewis B. 1965: 254–273; Lewis G. 1965: 90–113; Kinross 1995: 411–424, 465–472; Mango 2008: 164).

A new Turkish nationalism had to be created and overcome divisions of identity. Kemalism originated an historical identity for the Turks as a people emanating from Central Asia and spreading their civilisation westwards (Akçura 1991). This 'land of origin could only be imagined' (Keyder 2005: 9). In its extreme form, the historical myth claimed an *ur* status for the Turkish language: that is, that the root of the latter had bequeathed all other languages according to the notorious 'Sun Language Theory' (Keyder 2005: 7; Özkırımlı and Sofos 2008: 66). A 'concept of Turkishness was constructed which glossed over real diversity in an attempt to present the remaining population as homogeneous', an invention that served to rival the competing nationalisms of the Greeks, Armenians and Arabs' (Keyder 2005: 7). A more ethnocentric Turkish consciousness evolved (Ahmad 1969: 154), in which the 'Anatolian villager' was transformed from the symbol of Ottoman backwardness, to the 'guardian' of the Turkish nation's enduring virtues (Karpat 1982: 165; Poulton 1999: 81–89; Smith 1999: 143). The rural idyll would resonate with the bulk of the minority in Western Thrace, though the geographical reference for the new identity – Anatolia – was distinct and distant. Indeed, the move of its capital to Ankara was consistent with the myth – to a place 'without significations, to a city where there is no *there*' (Keyder 2005: 9; italics in original). Kemalism was not the first to invent a national or a contested history, but it was perhaps one of the most audacious.[46]

---

[46] In a similar vein, identity in the Balkans had undergone a dramatically changed context with the rise of the new states, creating their 'new' nationalisms (Kitromilides 1990: 25).

In Western Thrace, the ascendance of Kemalism met a rather sceptical audience as the local Muslim community exhibited an overwhelmingly Islamic outlook. The cleavage between Kemalists (or Young Turks) and traditionalists (Old Muslims) became more apparent with the arrival, in 1923, of a number of prominent Ottomans, who fled Turkey following the establishment of the new Republic.[47] The new arrivals formed part of a larger group of dissidents, who became known as the '150' (*Yüzellilikler*), based on a list of names declared as *personae non gratae* by the new Turkish government. Amongst those who settled in Western Thrace was the last Şeyhülislam (highest ranking Islamic scholar) of the Ottoman Empire, Mustafa Sabri, who went on to become a major rallying-point for opponents of Kemalism in the area. Sabri's immediate family, for example, took control of key minority schools and published the influential Islamic newspapers *Yarin* (Tomorrow) and *Peyam-y-Islam* (News of Islam).[48] Following Sabri's expulsion from Western Thrace in 1931 (see below), the voice of the traditionalist camp was articulated through the establishment of the *Association of Muslims of Greece* in 1932 (under the chairmanship of Hafız Salih Mehmetoğlu; a key local ally of the Liberal Party in the area – see below) and the *Committee of Islamic Unity* (1933) as well as the writings of Hafız Ali Reşat (of Circassian descent) and Hüsnü Yusuf.

On the other side, the Kemalist camp drew heavily on the support of the newly-established Turkish Consulate in Komotini and sought to propagate its ideology through the creation of Youth Associations such as the *Xanthi Youth Association* and the *Turkish Youth Union* founded by the influential local teacher Mehmet Hilmi in 1927 and 1928 respectively. Hilmi, who was briefly imprisoned and exiled by the Greek security services, was also instrumental in the publication of a number of pro-Kemalist newspapers, such as *Yeni Ziya* ('New Light'), *Yeni Yol* ('New Road') and *Yeni Adım* (New Step) (Tsioumis 1995: 122). Later on, the publication of *Ülkü* (Ideal) by Ismail Sadık Şahap and *Milliyet* (The Nation) by Hamdi Hüseyin Fehmi and Osman Nuri further strengthened the Kemalist voice on the ground. Hamdi Hüseyin Fehmi was later to become an MP (see below) and a prime suspect for the Greek secret services who regarded him as the main agent of Turkish nationalism in the

---

[47] Amongst those who fled Turkey (not all of whom settled in Western Thrace) were members of the Sultan's family, high-ranking political and military officials as well as a number of Circassians who had collaborated with the Greek Army in Asia Minor and Thrace. For more details on the Circassians who settled in Western Thrace see AYE/1927/91.1, Police Command-General of Thessaloniki, to Gendarmerie Headquarters-General, Department of Public Security, 'Activities of the Circassian and Turkish anti-Kemalists in Greece', 16 December 1927.

[48] For estimates of the Greek authorities on how many from the '150' had settled in Western Thrace see AYE/1927/93.3, Administration-General of Thrace, to the Ministry of Interior, 'The current condition of the Turkish minority of Thrace and the complaints of the Turkish Embassy of Athens', 25 June 1927.

Pomak areas of Xanthi.[49] Osman Nuri also acquired significant prominence as the editor of *Trakya* newspaper and, after the war, as a minority MP in the Greek Parliament (see subsequent chapters). In the field of education, the clash between the two camps within the minority became particularly intense as Kemalist teachers promoted aggressively secular reforms and the Latin alphabet. The traditionalists reacted by sacking Kemalist teachers in the schools they controlled and by refusing to provide religious services to those with known modernist sympathies (Aarbakke 2000: 77–80; Malkidis 2004).[50]

The minority's internal feuds were watched keenly by the Greek security services in the area.[51] The rise of Kemalist activists in the 1920s had caused considerable concern to the local authorities. In 1927 the Rhodope Gendarmerie drafted a list of 42 individuals who, it argued, should not be issued with an *etablis* certificate and hence be transferred to Turkey under the terms of the population exchange Convention. The list included, among others, Mehmet Hilmi and his associates in *Yeni Adım* (Sabri Ali and Mustafa Nakâm), the director of the Turkish Gymnasium in Komotini (Hacıyusufoğlu Hafız Halim), as well as a number of local Muslim tobacco workers who were suspected of communist sympathies.[52]

Yet, at the diplomatic level, the Greek government came under strong pressure from Ankara to expel the nucleus of anti-Kemalist opposition from Greece.[53] During the course of the negotiations for the 1930 Greco-Turkish

---

[49] AYE/1930/B/28/I, 4th Army Corps, Intelligence Bulletin, December 1929 'Foreign Propagandas – Turkey', undated.

[50] See also AYE/1929/37, Administration-General of Thrace, Department of Education, Komotini, to the Interior Ministry, Department of Education, Athens, 9 April 1928.

[51] See, for example, AYE/1930/B.28.I, 4th Army Corps, Information Issue of December 1929, No.2, Part 3, 'Foreign Propagandas, Part I, Turkish'; AYE/1926/61.2, Administration-General of Thrace to the Foreign Ministry, 13 May 1926; AYE/1927/93.3, Administration-General of Thrace to the Interior Ministry, 'The present condition of the Turkish minority of Thrace and the complaints of the Turkish Embassy', 25 June 1927; AYE/1926/5.1, Higher Gendarmerie Command of Thrace, Komotini, to Gendarmerie Headquarters-General, Athens, 'Activities of Turkish Propaganda in Thrace', 4 October 1926.

[52] AYE/1929/B/61, Rhodope Gendarmerie, Komotini, 14 July 1927. For Greek perceptions of Turkish propaganda in the area see also AYE/1926/5.1, Consulate-General, Constantinople, to Foreign Ministry, 18 November 1926 and AYE/1926/61.2, Administration-General of Thessaloniki to Foreign Ministry, 13 May 1926.

[53] For more details on the Turkish claims, the response by the Greek Government and the surveillance of Circassians around Greece, see AYE/1927/91.1, Army Headquarters-General, to the Gendarmerie Headquarters, 2 October 1927. AYE/1927/91.1, Department of Public Security, Athens, to Foreign Ministry, 31 August 1927. AYE/1927/92.2, Administration-General of Thrace, Komotini, to Foreign Ministry, 19 October 1927. AYE/1926/5.1, Department of General State Security, Fessopoulos, to the Higher Refugees Directorate, Department of Political Refugees,

Friendship Pact, Venizelos eventually agreed to expel a number of individuals from the group of '150' to the Middle East, including Mustafa Sabri who settled in Egypt. The purges against prominent members of the '150' marked a turning point in the policy of the Liberal Party which, throughout the 1920s, had offered its covert support to the traditionalist camp. The rise of Kemalism in Western Thrace was further supported by the electoral machinations of the *anti-Venizelist* camp in the mid-1930s (see below). Whilst these developments challenged the supremacy of local traditionalists on the ground, the internal power struggle over 'the soul' of the Muslim community continued well into the 1960s. The manifestation of this conflict during the 1940s will be examined in subsequent chapters of this book.

The electoral behaviour of the Muslim minority in the 1930s

The electoral representation of the Muslim community during the inter-war years became enveloped within the wider polarisation and instability of the Greek political scene. The dominant feature of this period is the bitter confrontation between *Venizelists* (led by Eleftherios Venizelos' Liberal Party) and *Anti-Venizelists* (led by the People's Party of Panagis Tsaldaris). The all-consuming power struggle between the two camps had its roots in the run-up to WWI, but in the aftermath of the Asia Minor disaster it acquired renewed venom which drew sharp divisions across most issues of domestic and foreign policy, including the very future of the Greek Monarchy which was eventually abolished between 1924 and 1935.[54] From the *pro-Venizelist* revolution of 1922 to the Mataxas dictatorship in 1936, a total of seven Parliamentary elections took place, leading to a turnover of 24 governments, under 13 different Prime Ministers.[55]

The electoral representation of ethnic minorities was also heavily implicated in polarisation of the period. For the *Venizelist* camp the trauma of the 1920 election defeat (in the aftermath of Venizelos' moment of glory at Sevres), was blamed on the *anti-Venizelist* vote of the minority population in the *New Lands* (i.e. the areas conquered by the Greece during the Balkan Wars and WWI) which, under the majoritarian electoral system of the time, cost the Liberal Party a small, but crucial for the overall majority in Parliament, number of seats. The Muslim community in Macedonia and, particularly, the Jews of Thessaloniki bore the main brunt of Liberal

---

Athens, 4 August 1926. AYE/1927/91.1, Directorate of Public Security, Athens, to Gendarmerie Headquarters-General, Department of Public Security, 23 October 1927. AYE/1927/91.1, Thessaloniki Police Department, to Gendarmerie Headquarters-General, Department of Public Security, 'On the movements of the Circassians and anti-Kemalists in Greece', 16 December 1927.

[54] For an authoritative account of the history of the inter-war period in Greece, see Mavrogordatos (1983).

[55] During the same period Senate elections took place in 1929 and 1932 (for one third of Senators).

Party's anger (Mavrogordatos 1983: 236–42). Hence, upon its return to power following the Asia Minor disaster, the *Venizelist* camp changed the electoral law and implemented a policy of separate electoral colleges for the Muslims of Western Thrace and the Jews of Thessaloniki which entitled each minority group to a fixed number of MPs in Parliament.[56] Although this change was portrayed as an attempt to improve minority representation in the national scene, the real agenda behind this move aimed at the exact opposite: putting an end to the position of minorities as 'arbiters' of Greek elections (Mavrogordados 1983: 239). Under the new arrangements, a total of four Muslim MPs were to be elected in the Greek Parliament on the basis of Muslim-only lists filled in Western Thrace.

The implementation of a separate electoral college for the Muslim minority in four out of seven Parliamentary elections between 1923 and 1936 determined the main characteristics of the minority's electoral representation during that period (see Tables 2.5 and 2.6). The most important feature in this respect was the very loose association between local Muslim lists and the national party-political scene. Although Muslim lists often used names that indicated some affiliation to national parties (such as 'Liberal', 'People's', 'Agrarian', etc.), the reality was that contact between local candidates and the leadership of national political parties remained, by mutual choice, minimal (Nikolakopoulos 1990–1991). Indicative of this apparent disconnection is Mavrogordatos' claim that, unlike the Jews of Thessaloniki, the Muslims of Western Thrace not only did not oppose the idea of separate electoral colleges, but indeed complained when they were abolished in 1934, following a decision of the Council of State which found them to be unconstitutional (1983: 246).

The question of the Muslim electorate's ideological orientation is also related to their disconnection from the national party-political scene. Aarbakke is, indeed, right in pointing to the paradox of the overwhelmingly *Venizelist* Muslim vote in Western Thrace in all post-Lausanne elections until 1934, even though the Liberal Party was the main proponent of assimilation policies in the *New Lands* (2000: 73). The most plausible explanation of this paradox might have laid with the minority's own sense of vulnerability and the imperative to be on good terms with the party in power (i.e. the Liberals between 1922 and 1933). This may also explain why minority support for the People's Party grew substantially in the aftermath of the 1933 election which brought defeat for the *Venizelist* camp. The lack of strong ideological conviction amongst the Muslim electorate is further reflected in the low levels of support for the Greek Communist Party (KKE) which, despite its electoral strength amongst the Christian population in Western Thrace, never really managed to make significant inroads in the minority during the inter-war period (see Table 2.5).

---

[56] In the meantime, the Turkish population of Macedonia had disappeared following the compulsory population exchange between Greece and Turkey in 1923.

Table 2.5 Parliamentary Elections in Western Thrace, 1926–1936

Year	Anti-Venizelists		Venizelists		Agrarians		KKE		Others	
	Muslim vote	Christian vote	Muslim vote	Christian Vote	Muslim vote	Christian vote	Muslim vote	Christian vote	Muslim vote	Christian vote
1926	7.0	9.7	86.6	65.9	0.5	6.1	5.5	18.2	0.4	–
1928	–	4.6	71.2	86	–	–	–	6.8	28.8	1
1932	–	10	86.3	73.3	6.6	4.7	3.6	12.0	3.4	–
1933	–	20.5	96.6	62.6	–	–	2.9	16.6	–	–
1936	44.7	25	43.3	57.9	5.5	8.6	6.5	8.4	–	–

Source: Nikolakopoulos (1990–1991): 178–179).

Given their considerable isolation from the national party-political scene, the pattern of electoral behaviour of Western Thracian Muslims was overwhelmingly shaped by local conditions. The power-struggle between Kemalists and Traditionalists was central in that respect. For most of the 1920s, the traditionalist camp within the minority dominated electoral politics, assisted, in part, by the muted support of the governing Liberals. Although the attribution of ideological labels (along the Kemalist-traditionalist axis) to Muslim MPs of that period is by no means an easy undertaking, it appears that the electoral fortunes of Kemalist candidates improved significantly in the early 1930s (see Table 2.6). This was the result of both the expulsion of the '150' (see above) and the more concerted effort of the People's Party to penetrate the minority vote for its own electoral benefit. A major turning point in this process was the electoral victory, in the 1934 Senate by-election, of Hatip Yusuf Salioğlu, a committed Kemalist who defected from the Liberals and joined the PP (Nikolakopoulos 1990–1991: 177). Yet, the electoral cleavage between Kemalists and traditionalists did not map evenly onto the division between *Venizelism* and *anti-Venizelism*. Indeed, as Nikolakopoulos argues, the collaboration between the Kemalist Hamdi Hüseyin Fehmi and the traditionalist Niyazi Mumcu was crucial in delivering the district of Xanthi to the PP during the 1936 election (1990–1991: 180).

Important cleavages in the electoral behaviour of the minority also emerged along ethnic and/or geographical lines. In the district of Xathni, for example, the Pomaks in the Rhodope Mountains and the Turks in the lowlands (and the town of Xanthi) voted overwhelmingly for 'their' respective candidates (Nikolakopoulos 1990–1991: 184). Similarly, Aarbakke argues that 'family dynasties' were far more powerful in Komotini (rather than Xanthi) where some of the 'big beasts' of minority politics, such as the long-serving MP Hafız Ali Galip, had established their power bases (2000: 75–76). Underlying these local specificities was an overall system of electoral representation based on deeply entrenched networks of patronage. In this context local MPs (along with other community notables) became extremely influential 'mediators' between the local Muslim population and the official Greek state (or, through the Komotini Consulate, the Turkish Republic). Widespread levels of illiteracy and very limited knowledge of the Greek language in the minority heartlands made this function all the more important. The purpose of such clientelistic networks was often based on economic imperatives, most importantly the need of local agricultural small-holders to maintain good relations with influential 'middlemen' to the national or international markets (Aarbakke 2000: 74). The example of the Xanthi MP and wealthy tobacco merchant, Hamdi Hüseyin Fehmi, is indicative in this respect.

Highly personalised channels of electoral representation were, of course, a systemic feature of Greek political culture that was visible well beyond Western Thrace. However, the international, national and local conjunctures affecting minority politics during the interwar years made the operation of such clientelistic networks all the more profound and significant. It is

Table 2.6 Minority MPs during the Inter-war Period, 1923–1936

Elections	Elected MP	District	Party[a]	Affiliation[b]
1920[c, d]	Hafız Salih Mehmetoğlu	Komotini	LP	Traditionalist
	Hafız Ali Galip	Komotini	LP	Moderate Traditionalist
	Arıf Arifzade	Komotini	LP	Kemalist
	Hasan Abdürrahimoğlu	Xanthi	LP	Kemalist
1923[e]	Mustafa Ağa Deveci	Komotini	LP	Moderate Traditionalist
	Hoca Mestan Efendi Ahmetoğlu	Xanthi	LP	Kemalist
	Emin Beyzade Hasan Dimetokalı	Evros	LP	Kemalist
1926[c]	Hafız Ali Galip	Komotini	DUP	Moderate Traditionalist
	Mustafa Ağa Deveci	Komotini	LP	Moderate Traditionalist
	Şükrü Mahmutoğlu	Xanthi	DU	Moderate
	Fehmi Bey Haşimzade	Xanthi	LP	Kemalist
1928[e]	Hafız Ali Galip	Komotini	LP	Moderate Traditionalist
	Cezayirli Muhtar Ali Rıza	Komotini	LP	Traditionalist
	Niyazi Mumcu	Xanthi	LP later PP	Traditionalist
	Halil Hüseyin Karaçanlı	Xanthi	LP	Kemalist
1929 (Senate)	Hafız Salih Mehmetoğlu	n/a	LP	Traditionalist
1932[e]	Hafız Ali Galip	Komotini	ALP	Moderate Traditionalist
	Mustafa Ağa Deveci	Komotini	LP	Moderate Traditionalist
	Hatip Yusuf Salioğlu	Komotini	LP, later PP	Kemalist
	Hasan Abdürrahimoğlu	Xanthi	LP	Kemalist
1933[e]	Hafız Ali Galip	Komotini	ALP	Moderate Traditionalist
	Mustafa Ağa Deveci	Komotini	LP	Moderate Traditionalist
	İbrahim Demir Serdar Zade	Xanthi	LP, later PP	Kemalist
	Hasan Abdürrahimoğlu	Xanthi	LP	Kemalist

Continued

Table 2.6   Continued

Elections	Elected MP	District	Party[a]	Affiliation[b]
1934 (Senate by-election)	Hatip Yusuf Salioğlu	n/a	PP	Kemalist
1935[c, f]	Hatip Yusuf Salioğlu	Komotini	PP	Kemalist
	Mehmet Mustafaoğlu (also known as Baytar Mehmet)	Komotini	PP	Kemalist
	Niyazi Mumcu	Xanthi	PP	Traditionalist
	Hamdi Hüseyin Fehmi	Xanthi	PP	Kemalist
1936[c]	Hafız Ali Galip	Komotini	NC	Moderate Traditionalist
	Hamdi Hüseyin Fehmi	Xanthi	PP	Kemalist

[a]Indicates loose association with 'national' parties, as local Muslim lists often run as 'independents'.
[b]As ascribed to them by secondary sources. A significant element of contestation and uncertainty remains over these affiliations.
[c]Election conducted through mixed electoral colleges.
[d]Elections not contested by Anti-Venizelists (in Thrace).
[e]Election conducted through separate Muslim colleges.
[f]Elections not contested by Venizelists (nationally).
LP: Liberal Party (Venizelist); PP: People's Party (Anti-Venizelist); DU: Democratic Union (Venizelist); ALP: Agrarian and Labour Party (Venizelist); NC: National Coalition (Venizelist).
Sources: Aarbakke 2000: 71–77, 681; *Azınlıkça*, Issue 38, June 2008; Nikolakopoulos 1990–1991: 171–185; Öksüz *2002:143*–145; Tsioumis 1995; PEKEM/BAKEŞ, Ministry of National Economy 1928a, 1931a, 1931 1933, 1935a, 1938.

within this context, that the shifting loyalties of many of the local Muslim MPs of that period should be understood and interpreted. No other personal journey is ridden more with the moral consequences of 'choosing sides' than that of the Xanthi MP Hamdi Hüseyin Fehmi: the son of a leading figure from the 'Republic' of Tamrash who fled to Western Thrace and was later elected a Greek MP (under a Kemalist ticket), before becoming a Bulgarian collaborator during WWII, only to pledge his loyalty to the post-war Greek government and support its territorial claims to the Pomak regions of Bulgaria (Tsioumis 1995: 123–124). The role of Hamdi Hüseyin Fehmi and other minority notables during the 1940s will be discussed in more detail in subsequent chapters.

*   *   *

The study of the minority's political orientation during the 1930s sets an important explanatory framework in which its behaviour during the

1940s is to be understood and contextualised. The ascent of Kemalism in Turkey and its reverberations across Western Thrace shook the very foundations upon which the local Muslim community operated for centuries. Hence, the rift between Kemalists and traditionalists introduced an additional electoral (and, more widely, social) cleavage over and above the ones already visible along ethnic and/or geographical lines. The power struggle within the Muslim community also intersected with the highly polarised nature of Greek politics at the time, centred on the schism between *Venizelism* and *anti-Venizelism*, in which the position of minorities (both as electoral commodities and potential threats to the security of the country) became increasingly central. The net result of these complex and often contradictory dynamics was a predisposition towards 'non-action'. This reflected the inability of the Muslim community to rally around a single leadership (or a charismatic 'leader') as local loyalties remained divided between competing power-centres and highly personalised channels of electoral representation. The premise of such competition varied over time and circumstance. It often acquired ideological (Kemalist/traditionalist), ethnic (Pomak/Turkish), party political (LP/PP), geographical (Komotini/Xanthi; highlands/plains) characteristics or a combination thereof.

The introduction of a separate Muslim electoral college entrenched further the highly localised nature of minority politics during the interwar period and reflected wider Venizelist mistrust against minorities as 'arbiters' of Greek elections. The fact that the minority itself was supportive of this measure is illustrative of its own sense of marginalisation and disconnection from the national political scene. On the one hand, the existence of a separate Muslim college undermined any prospect of structuring local politics along non-ethnic lines. Yet, on a different level, the college allowed the local Muslim population, to elect 'their' representatives and, through them, to exercise some leverage on the Greek authorities. Minority politics might not have been pretty, but at least they purchased a minimum degree of loyalty to the Greek state and provided an important 'safety valve' for venting local frustrations. In this sense, the example of the Western Thracian Muslims stood in some contrast to the Macedonian Slavs. The latter were not recognised as a minority by the Greek government and, consequently, were never allowed to develop their own representative structures. In the decade that followed, the different trajectories followed by the two groups underlined the relevance of this divergence.

2.6   Conclusion

On the eve of WWII, the Muslim minority of Western Thrace displayed certain core traits that would prove crucial to its later behaviour. Two of these have been amply portrayed in this Chapter.

Firstly, the minority was internally fragmented and it lacked the potential for action that derives from a sense of unity. The mix of ethnic, social and cultural identities within the region represented a 'glorious *olla podrida*' (Macartney 1934: 135). With a reversal of fortune, the previous majority was now the 'minority', protected by the Lausanne Treaty. Alongside the Greek Orthodox majority and the relatively small numbers of Armenians and Jews, the Muslim minority was neither socially cohesive nor geographically concentrated. It comprised the Turkish-speakers, concentrated largely in the lowlands in both homogenous and mixed communities; the Pomaks located mainly in isolated mountainous villages; and the Roma, both itinerant and non-itinerant, with the latter established in makeshift settlements on the peripheries of the main towns. Apart from any social barriers, local geography itself made travel and communication between these locations often difficult. In terms of the minority's identity, they were 'Muslim' (a third of the Roma were not), but they were differentiated by language, culture, economic circumstance and distance. Neither the Pomaks nor the Roma tended to self-identify as 'Turks'. Neither was there a sense of a shared Thracian identity or 'nationhood': the three attempts at establishing a separate state had failed, in the context of conflicting irredentisms. Even amongst themselves, the 'Turks' were socially and politically divided.

The secularist, modernist ideology of Kemalism seemed alien to traditionalist 'Ottomans'. 'Modernity' was a cleavage fostered by Ankara in a community that had been partially denuded of its historic social elite (following the collapse of the Empire) and one that was numerically skewed towards agriculture – often at a subsistence level – and the tobacco industry. The minority experienced modernity largely as an import – or as a social manifestation within the majority Greek community – confronting the relative 'backwardness' of its poorer strata (Janos 1982). The Greek state intervened into the minority's religious affairs – usually, though not consistently, to favour traditionalists, rather than Kemalists. Yet, new local civil associations emerged to allow Kemalism to advance its cause within the minority. But the general context remained one in which the ability of the disparate Muslim minority to produce a common leadership was severely hampered. It lacked the means by which it could enunciate a common interest or voice, radical or otherwise.

Yet, a second feature of the Muslim minority was that, though it suffered much discrimination and marginalisation from the Greek state, it was not actually excluded from its political processes. The creation of a separate electoral college was clearly motivated by a desire to avoid them affecting the construction of majorities in Athens, rather than for reasons of fostering their own cultural expression. Participation promised an outlet for frustration and also offered scope for local clientelism, status and patronage networks within the community. Whilst a strong and shared leadership was absent, more particularistic political representation of the Muslim minority was not.

The most basic condition that Lausanne's minority lacked was 'groupness'. This parallels the findings of Brubaker et al. in their much more contemporary study of the Hungarian minority in the Romanian city of Cluj (2006). They warn of the dangers of too easily attributing 'identity, agency, interests, and will to groups' – the processes and internal relations cannot be assumed (2006: 11). In Cluj conditions existed for 'an explosive and potentially violent ethno-nationalist conflict', but locals responded on the whole with equanimity and detachment (2006: 4–5). A predisposition to nationalist conflict could not be assumed and the minority failed to act as a 'group'. There are parallels here in the will and capability of the Muslims in Western Thrace to exert leadership in the inter-war period, even when confronted with much discrimination (and, later, in how it was to react to the external shock of Axis invasion).

A further feature of the Western Thrace case is the role of Turkey as the 'kinship' state. Again, there is a parallel with the Brubaker et al. study. Having also started with an interest in national minorities and their kin-states, they similarly found that this dimension was less consequential than was that of local socio-political conditions. In the case of Turkey, foreign policy calculations overcame kinship politics leading Ankara to avoid provocative statements about the Muslim minority in this period. This retreat was only qualified by its local actions via its Consulate in Komotini to encourage the shift of the minority towards Kemalist modernity. But the geo-strategic imperative that had led to the Friendship Pact with Greece in 1930 prevented Ankara from rousing the Muslims of Western Thrace with an antagonistic nationalist rhetoric.

By examining the long-term conditions of the Muslim minority, this Chapter has developed significant parts of the frame for the subsequent case study of the 1940s – the fragmentation and lack of groupness, the marginalisation but not exclusion. The role of Turkey has already been signalled as being one of relative absence, but its impact on the events leading to the invasion of Greece will be more fully explored at the start of the next Chapter.

3
On the Path to War

3.1 Introduction

The previous chapter outlined how Western Thrace in the 1930s had come to enjoy a certain level of stability. This chapter adds to that account how Greco-Turkish rapprochement provided a conducive context for the local stability. With the threat of war, both Greece and Turkey set about constructing common security alliances.

Yet, with developments elsewhere in Europe, this stability and rapprochement was to be blown asunder. The bulk of the chapter considers how war came to Western Thrace and the initial response to it. Events unfolded quickly and unpredictably. The dictatorial government of Ioannis Metaxas in Athens had judged that the main threat would come from Bulgaria. It therefore set about building its defences and imposing a security clampdown in Western Thrace, focusing in particular on the 'unreliable' Pomaks. However, the initial attack came elsewhere: Mussolini's troops invaded in the north-west. With Greece thwarting the Italian advance, Nazi forces marched through Bulgaria in the north-east. Greece now consciously decided to commit its resources to maintaining its defences against the Italians, leaving its north-east border exposed. Greece had a further surprise: despite their earlier alliance, Turkey was now seen as reneging on its commitments to Athens, fearing it itself might be invaded by the Axis. Western Thrace was soon overrun by the Germans and then by their Bulgarian vassals. Viewed locally, the world had been turned upside down.

The present chapter outlines the geo-strategic moves that led to war and examines the strategy pursued by Ankara. With Turkey's position compromised – and with both the Axis and the Allies seeking its favour – it could not act openly on the international stage in support of its kin-community in Western Thrace. Thus, the chapter leaves the international stage and examines the immediate local conditions, before returning to how Turkey sustained its neutrality throughout the war.

3.2 Shifting balances in the Balkans: the international context prior to WWII

The stability that came to Western Thrace in the inter-war period was due, in no small measure, to a détente between Greece and Turkey, the like of which had not been seen before or since. With the Liberal leader, Eleftherios Venizelos, returning to power in 1928, Athens pursued conciliation with Turkey. This would allow it to absorb its refugees and modernise its economy and infrastructure. In Ankara, Kemal Atatürk had similar preoccupations, having embarked on a massive domestic reform programme and for this he needed peaceful borders. This synergy of interests sustained a rapprochement with declarations of friendship that would today seem like political suicide in both domestic systems. Thus, Venizelos declared in 1933 that soon the two countries would form an 'Eastern Federation' together. Turkish Foreign Minister, Rüştü Aras, followed up with a statement that Greece and Turkey 'have almost become one country' (Alexandris 1982: 160–161). The amity was well-meant (compounded by a shared threat from Bulgaria), though a cynic might have observed that it would last as long as neither was tested too far.

The rapprochement had begun with the Ankara Convention (June 1930), which sought to address some of the thorny issues inherited by the population exchange of 1923. A few months later (October 1930) a wide ranging Friendship Pact was signed that included a number of individual agreements ranging from naval armaments to commercial cooperation (Pallis 1930; Miller 1931; Ladas 1932: 567–583; Anastasiadou 1982).[1] The following year, the Turkish Prime Minister, İsmet İnönü, visited Athens in an atmosphere of conciliation and friendship. The rapprochement was further developed by the Greco-Turkish Entente Cordiale of 14 September 1933 (see Box 3.1).

These diplomatic moves had local effects. The most important of these was the creation, with the consent of Venizelos, of the Turkish Consulate of Komotini, which since 1923 operated as a simple consular office, under the jurisdiction of the Turkish Consulate of Thessaloniki. In addition, a series of military, political, educational and cultural exchanges took place following the Friendship Pact. Sports meetings between Greek and Turkish teams became a frequent feature. In one such exchange in 1932, Mihri Belli, who later emerged as a key figure in Western Thrace during the Greek civil war, had his first contact with Greece as a young student (Belli 2009: 19–20).[2] Similar exchanges were also organised locally in Western Thrace. For

---

[1] In the same period Greece supported the proposal at the League of Nations to include Turkey in the discussions on the Briand Plan of 1929, submitted by France and aimed at the creation of a 'European Union'. Then, as much more recently, France blocked Turkey's inclusion. See Barlas and Guvenç 2009.

[2] Interview 1.

Box 3.1   Key Provisions of the Greco-Turkish Entente Cordiale, 14 September 1933

Article 1

Greece and Turkey mutually guarantee the inviolability of their common frontiers.*

Article 2

The high contracting parties agree that in all international questions in which they are interested, a preliminary consultation conforms to the general direction of their policy of understanding and collaboration and to their respective and common interests.

Article 3

In all international conferences of limited representation, Greece and Turkey are disposed to consider that the delegate of one of them will have the mission of defending the common and special interests of the two parties and they agree to unite their efforts to assure this common representation [...].

Article 4

The present pact is concluded for a period of ten years. If it is not denounced by one of the high contracting parties one year prior to the date of its expiration, it will remain in force for a new period of ten years' [...].

Note: *This guarantee referred to the Greco-Bulgarian and the Turco-Bulgarian frontiers, not to the Aegean, so as not to 'provoke' Italy, which controlled the Dodecanese Islands (Alexandris 1982: 161; Pikros 1996: 30).

Source: Kerner and Howard 1936: 231.

---

example, in September 1938 a friendly match took place in Xanthi between the local football club *Aspis* and the Turkish *Edirne Spor*. The event attracted much local attention leading to an official reception for the members of the Turkish team by the Mayor of Xanthi. The decision of the Turkish hosts to wear badges with the Greek flag after the match (which the Greek team won 8–0) must have certainly helped the festive spirit (Exarchou 2000: 265).

The bilateral ties were further strengthened as instability across Europe spread. Both Greece and Turkey became signatories of the Balkan Entente (also known as the Balkan Pact) which in addition included Romania and Yugoslavia. The Balkan Entente was signed in Athens in 1934, following four years of intensive political, diplomatic and cultural exchanges initiated by four Balkan Conferences (Kerner and Howard 1936; Svolopoulos 1973; Türkeş 1994).[3] The Pact (which was concluded within the framework of the League of Nations) sought to 'guarantee' the inviolability of Balkan borders

---

[3] In Athens (1930), Istanbul (1931), Bucharest (1932) and Thessaloniki (1933).

Box 3.2 Pact of Balkan Entente between Greece, Romania, Turkey and Yugoslavia, 9 February 1934

Article 1

Yugoslavia, Greece, Romania and Turkey shall mutually guarantee the security of their Balkan borders.

Article 2

The High Contracting Parties undertake to reach agreement on measures which must be taken if cases should arise that could affect their interests as defined by the present Agreement. They assume the obligation not to take any political action towards any other Balkan country which is not a signatory to this Agreement, without a prior mutual notification and not to assume any political obligation towards any other Balkan country without the consent of the other Contracting Parties.

Article 3

The present Agreement shall come into force upon its signing by all the Contracting Powers and shall be ratified within the shortest possible time. The Agreement shall be open to any Balkan country for accession which shall be taken into favourable consideration by the Contracting Parties and shall come into effect as soon as the other signatory countries notify their consent.

Source: League of Nations 1934a: 154–159.

(see Box 3.2); an objective that was severely compromised by the refusal of Bulgaria to join it.[4]

An additional Protocol to the Pact confirmed that all previous defence agreements (such as the 1933 Greco-Turkish Entente) between its signatories remained in force (article 5), but urged all contracting parties to start the negotiation of new bilateral defence conventions within six months of the conclusion of the Pact (article 4). The Protocol also provided that if a non-Balkan power, assisted by a Balkan ally, attacked one of the members of the Balkan Entente, all signatories would unite to fight against the aggressor (article 3) (League of Nations 1934: 158–9). This clause (particularly with regards to 'defining' the non-Balkan aggressor), however, met with reservations from Greece and Turkey, both of which wanted to avoid a confrontation with Italy and the USSR and preferred to confine the 'mutual assistance' clause within a purely Balkan framework (Kerner and Howard 1936; Svolopoulos 1973: 247–294, 1974; Türkeş 1994: 132–139; Papagos 1995: 40–63, 1997: 457–502).

Shortly after the signing of the Balkan Pact, Greece and Turkey initiated a new round of negotiations in order to extend their 1933 Greco-Turkish

---

[4] Albania was not invited as it was already in the sphere of influence of Italy, which encouraged revisionism.

Entente to a full-fledged defence convention. The draft agreement was scheduled to be signed in Geneva in January 1935 but was eventually cancelled because the chief Greek negotiator, the Minister of War, Georgios Kondylis, was opposed to a formal defence alliance with Turkey (Alexandris 1982: 162). However, the spirit of rapprochement resumed in the aftermath of the abortive pro-Venizelist coup of 1935 and became evident during the negotiations for the revision of the status of the Straits of Istanbul (Bosphorus) in 1936. During the Athens coup attempt, Turkey deployed its troops along its borders with Bulgaria in order to deter the government in Sofia from taking advantage of the situation by launching an attack against Greece (Alexandris 1982: 162–163; Svolopoulos 1997: 250–251). On the other hand, the sensitive issue of the status of the Straits, was resolved with a *quid pro quo*: the Montreux Convention (1936) annulled the respective clauses of the Lausanne Treaty and ended the demilitarisation of the Straits, handing over their control to Turkey. Ankara, for its part, did not object to the *de facto* re-militarisation of the Greek islands of Lemnos and Samothrace, which were initially placed under a demilitarised zone by the Treaty of Lausanne (Economides 1989: 191–192; Pazarci 1989: 121; Pikros 1996: 52–53).

Greece now sought to revive the negotiations to strengthen its entente with Turkey. In 1936, the Commander-in-Chief of the Greek Army, General Alexandros Papagos, asked for clarification on the understanding of the term 'common frontier' which was referred to in the 1933 Greco-Turkish Entente (see Box 3.1), which, he feared, would not provide Greece with protection in case of an attack from Bulgaria in Western Thrace. According to Papagos' recollections, the Turkish Foreign Minister, Rüştü Aras, in informal correspondence, explained that he understood the term 'common frontier' to include both the Turco-Bulgarian and the Greco-Bulgarian frontiers. Papagos sought to formalise this understanding by sending a draft defence convention to his Turkish counterpart in November 1939. This time, however, it was the turn of the Turkish government to drag its feet, claming that no bilateral defence treaty was necessary as these issues were adequately covered by the respective provisions of the Balkan Pact (Papagos 1995: 55–63).

In any event, the friendly spirit continued. When, during his visit to Ankara in 1937, Ioannis Metaxas (Greece's dictator since 1936) was confronted with Turkish concerns over Greek irredentism, he was keen to remind his hosts that 'Greece, honestly, does not have and cannot have in the future any aspirations outside its borders'.[5] The Greek Premier reassured his Turkish counterpart, İsmet İnönü, that:

> We will live in peace until our borders acquire a simple symbolic character. Besides, the firm and persistent aspirations our northern neighbours

---

[5] AYE/1940/8.A/3/2, Greek Embassy, Ankara, Raphael, to the Foreign Ministry, B' Directorate of Political Affairs, 29 October 1937.

[have] for access to the Aegean is in itself enough of a reason to support each other. (Kalantzis 1969: 38)

Similarly, Kemal Atatürk wrote to Metaxas in 1937:

The borders of the Balkan countries constitute a single frontier. Those who may have plans for [the change of] this frontier will expose themselves to the burning rays of the sun and I advise them to beware … Our frontiers are the same and the forces which defend them are one and inseparable. (Metaxas 1964: 275, Vol. DI)

Greece's strategy increasingly focussed on a possible threat emanating from Bulgaria. Indeed, Metaxas prepared the country to face an eventual assault from the north (Papagos 1997: 209). His fears were openly expressed in a letter to the Greek Ambassador in London in April 1939:

Bulgaria's change of the attitude in the aftermath of Italy's occupation of Albania is of great concern and we are worried that this is due to encouragement [given to Bulgaria] by the Axis. The statements of the Bulgarian Prime Minister in the Committee of Foreign Affairs of the *Sobranje* [the Bulgarian Parliament] clearly reveal the Bulgarian intentions and claims: the [return to the] 1913 frontiers, as the minimum prerequisite for the accession of Bulgaria to the Balkan Pact. (Metaxas 1964: 370, Vol. DI)

When Bulgaria and Yugoslavia drew closer together, the challenges to Greco-Turkish relations soon became apparent and the Balkan Pact appeared to lose its coherence. Yugoslavia reached a bilateral agreement with Bulgaria (Friendship Pact) on 24 January 1937 without consulting the other member of the Balkan Entente, followed by a Friendship Pact with Italy in March of the same year. With relations between Yugoslavia and Bulgaria significantly improved, both Greece and Turkey feared that a south Slavic rapprochement could potentially dominate the Balkans. For Metaxas, cooperation with Turkey was of paramount importance in order to deter Bulgarian aggression. Eventually, new Greco-Turkish negotiations led to an Additional (to the 1930 Greco-Turkish Friendship Pact and the 1933 Greco-Turkish Entente) Treaty, signed in Athens on 27 April 1938 (see Box 3.3)

Despite its friendly undertone, however, the Additional Treaty was ridden with contradictions. Article 4, for example, implicitly confirmed the commitment to the mutual guarantee of the 'common frontier' enshrined in the 1933 Greco-Turkish Entente (which remained in force until 1943). At the same time, article 1 of the Treaty made reference to a state of 'neutrality' if one of the two contracting parties was attacked. Similarly, article 2 stipulated that the two countries would 're-examine' the situation if a non-preventable

> *Box 3.3*   Key Provisions of the Greco-Turkish Additional Treaty, 27 April 1938
>
> *Article 1*
>
> Should one of the High Contracting Parties become the object of an unprovoked act of aggression on the part of one or more Powers, the other High Contracting Party undertakes to safeguard its neutrality by opposing, if necessary by arms, the use of its territory by the said Power or Powers for the passage of troops, arms or ammunitions of war or for the supply of provisions, cattle, etc., or for the passage of retreating troops or for purposes of military reconnaissance in such territory.
>
> *Article 2*
>
> Should one of the two High Contracting Parties be the object of an act of hostility on the part of one or more third Powers, the other High Contracting Party shall exert every effort to remedy the situation. If war becomes an accomplished fact notwithstanding such efforts, the two High Contracting Parties shall undertake to re-examine the situation with care and in a friendly spirit with the object of reaching a settlement in conformity with their higher interests.
>
> *Article 3*
>
> The two High Contracting Parties shall undertake not to allow in their territory the formation or the residence of organisations or groups whose object is to disturb the peace and security of the other country or to change its Government, or the residence of persons or groups planning to conduct a compaign by propaganda or by any other means against the other country.
>
> *Article 4*
>
> The High Contracting Parties agree that the mutual engagements, bilateral or plurilateral, which they have contracted and which are in force shall continue to produce their full effect irrespective of the provisions of the present Treaty.
> [...]
>
> *Source*: League of Nations 1934b: 176–179.

war broke out. Much, it seems, was left open to interpretation and future diplomatic manoeuvring.

In the meantime, Italy's ambitions in the Mediterranean and the expansionism of Nazi Germany continued to ring alarm bells in both Athens and Ankara. In an attempt to win over Bulgaria, Greece and Turkey, along with the other Balkan Pact signatories, signed the Thessaloniki Agreement on 31 July 1938. The agreement recognised Bulgaria's right to re-arm which had been restricted under the Treaty of Neuilly (1919). In exchange for this, previous agreements for the demilitarisation of the Thracian frontiers were annulled and Greece and Turkey were free to re-deploy troops in the area, thus making it easier for both to enforce their mutual security guarantees (Alexandris 1982: 169–170; Toynbee 1953: 417, Vol. III). As Ankara and Athens became increasingly dependent on each other for their respective defence, issues of minority protection nearly disappeared from their bilateral diplomatic agenda.

Internationally, developments in London boosted hopes for the preservation of the territorial status quo in the Balkans. The British Prime Minister,
Neville Chamberlain, shortly after the Italian-sponsored coup in Albania,
announced a unilateral guarantee of the borders of Romania and Greece,
declaring in the House of Commons on 13 April 1939 that:

> In the event of any action being taken which clearly threatened the
> independence of Greece or Romania, and which the Greek or Romanian
> government respectively considered it vital to resist with their national
> forces, HM's Government would feel themselves bound at once to lend
> the Greek or Romanian Government...all the support in their power.
> (Papagos 1995: 64–66; Toynbee 1953: 111, Vol. III)

At the same time, Turkey was drawn further into defence agreements with
the West European Allies. Negotiations between Britain, France and Turkey
resulted in a Treaty of Mutual Assistance, on 19 October 1939, providing
that in case of war in the Mediterranean due to aggression of a European
power, the three countries would cooperate and lend each other all aid
and assistance in their power. The same would apply if Britain and France
entered into hostilities in fulfilment of their guarantees towards Greece and
Romania. Both London and Paris undertook to aid Turkey if it was attacked
by a European power (Toynbee 1953: 120–122, 137–145, Vol. III; Alexandris
1982: 170–171).

Consistent with the spirit of the above agreements, when Mussolini
attacked Greece in October 1940 Turkey deployed its troops along its Thracian
borders, as a deterrent to Bulgaria. According to the British Ambassador in
Ankara, Sir Hugh Knatchbull-Hugessen:

> It would be impossible for Turkey to weaken its defences by sending a
> military mission in Greece. It would be also impossible for us to offer
> naval support or participate in operations in the Dodecanese...When we
> examined these problems we preferred not to invite Turkey to assume
> military action before we could secure more support, but we believed
> that it could follow a positive stance without being in danger of being
> attacked. Indeed, the Turkish Government could offer something for
> Greece assuring the Greek government that it could safely withdraw
> its army from the eastern borders of Thrace. The Turkish government
> was ready to block Bulgaria and the Prime Minister informed the Greek
> Ambassador...that his country could count on Turkish help in the event
> of a Bulgarian attack. (Knatchbull-Hugessen 2000: 188)

Moreover, the Turkish government encouraged volunteers from among
the Greek-Orthodox community of Turkey to join the Greek Army to fight
the Italians. Their path was eased by the efforts of the Hellenic Union of
Constantinopolitans (*Ελληνική Ένωσις Κωνσταντινοπολιτών*), with official

Turkish approval (Tsouderos 1950: 203; Alexandris 1982: 175–179; Exarchou 1999: 154). When the German Army reached Komotini, the Evros Brigade of the Greek Army, with 100 officers and 2000 soldiers, was able to escape to Turkey (8 April 1941), after an agreement between the two governments. The Brigade's commander, Major-General Ioannis Zisis, had received the order to preserve his unit and cross the border. On arrival, the Greek military personnel, officers included, were disarmed (Papagos 1995: 401). Subsequently, Zisis committed suicide. The men of the Evros Brigade were then given the choice to be dispatched to the Middle East or to be sent back to Greece. All the officers and 1200 soldiers chose to join the Greek Army in the Middle East, where they arrived in early summer 1941. The rest of the brigade's soldiers were repatriated to Greece in February 1942.

Some reports, however, suggest that Turkey's treatment of the Greek soldiers was not so positive. A brigade member recalled that the conditions of their stay in Turkey were similar to those of prisoners of war and that the behaviour of the Turkish personnel was rather brutal (Lipordezis 2002: 28–36).[6] Another issue of contention emerged after the end of the war in relation to members of the Greek-Orthodox community in Istanbul who had fought with the Greek forces in the Middle East and were later denied re-entry having been stripped of their Turkish nationality (for having fought alongside the armed forces of another country).[7] Similar complaints appeared in Greek military reports towards the end of the war with regard to the treatment of Greeks who fled the Axis occupation zone through the Turkish borders. Each of these accounts were received by Greek diplomats with some frustration and scepticism over Turkey's ambivalent position vis-à-vis Allied forces in general and Greece in particular.[8]

Nevertheless, the spirit of Greco-Turkish understanding survived for much of the period of Greece's occupation by the Axis. Throughout this period many Greek officers were permitted to cross the Turkish borders and join the Allied forces in the Middle East. In addition, during the famine of winter of 1941–1942, the Turkish Government facilitated the collection and dispatch of supplies to the Greek population, which was organised by the Allies, the American Greek War Relief Association (GWRA), the International Red Cross and the Swedish-Swiss Relief Committee. Moreover, a committee of prominent Turks, Greeks and Armenians was created in Istanbul in order to collect subscriptions for the Greek Red Cross Fund and several events were held for the support of the Fund. Indicatively, the Committee of the Istanbul Ladies, headed by the spouse of the Mayor of Istanbul collected

---

[6] On this see AYE/1948/56.4, The Equipment of the Evros Brigade, March 1948.

[7] For more details on this incident see FO/371/58868, British Embassy Ankara, to Southern Department, FO, 22 July 1946. See also FO/371/58868, Southern Department to British Embassy, Ankara, 7 July 1946.

[8] See indicatively AYE/1945/21.3, Greek Embassy in Turkey, Naval Attaché, to the Naval Ministry, 10 August 1944. For similar comments also see Tsouderos 1950: 203.

and dispatched to the Greek troops 15,000 boxes with Turkish delights and other sweets through the Turkish Red Crescent (*Kizilay*) and the famous *Haci Bekir* patisserie of Istanbul offered many boxes of confectionery (Exarchou 1999: 154). Similarly, the Red Crescent collected and dispatched packages from Istanbul Greeks who had relatives in Greece, whilst professional associations in Turkey mobilised to send their own aid to their Greek colleagues (Macar 2008). However, the main operation of humanitarian aid was mainly funded by the GWRA and the 'Hellenic Union of Constantinopolitans'. The much needed food supplies were dispatched to Greece with the Turkish steamers *Kurtuluş* and (later) *Dumplupinar*. The shipments of supplies took place between October 1941 and August 1942, when they were terminated by the new Turkish Government of Şükrü Saraçoğlu, whose foreign minister Numan Menemencioğlu had pro-German sympathies. Hence, less than one third[9] of the originally scheduled 50,000 tons of grain were sent to Greece (Kazamias 2008; Kyrou 2008; Macar 2008).

Despite these manifestations of support, however, Turkey was deftly stepping aside from its earlier security commitments to Greece (and the Allies) and avoiding conflict with the Axis Powers (Kitsikis 1990: 140; Türkeş 1994: 139; Pikros 1996: 87). The earlier rapprochement with Greece had come up against its limits. Turkey re-interpreted its security interests and concluded that a separate strategy of some ambiguity would serve it best. A very large factor in its shift was the fear – prior to Hitler's attack on the Soviet Union – that Germany might launch an invasion of its territory (Deringil 2004: 112–122). This fear of Germany also meant that Ankara would avoid provoking Bulgaria and that it would say little about the treatment of its kindred minority in Western Thrace. The pendulum had swung away from supporting the security of Greece. The Turkish press published very few articles and made few comments about the German attack on Greece.[10] Domestic public opinion should not be stirred; no upset should be caused to Berlin.

For their part, the Allies asked whether Turkey was willing to assist them according to their earlier agreements. The Foreign Office instructed its Ambassador to Turkey, Sir Hughe Knatchbull-Hugessen, that:

> If the Allies implement their guarantees to Greece as a result of an Italian attack on Greece a state of war will exist between the Allies and Italy, and it's essential that in these circumstances a state of war should also exist between Italy and Turkey. Turkey should adopt the same attitude as the Allies with regard to any formal declaration to be made. (Deringil 1982: 40)

---

[9] Estimates vary between 6500 and 17,000 tons.
[10] AYE/1941/26.B/4/T, Greek Consulate, Izmir, to the Foreign Ministry, Department of Turkey, 8 April 1941.

Turkey, however, preached a strategy of caution, avoiding precipitous acts. On 26 June 1940 the Turkish Government issued a statement claiming that:

> [It] has considered the situation which has arisen from Italy's entry into the war and have decided on the application of Protocol 2...Turkey will preserve her present attitude of non-belligerency for the security and defence of our country. While continuing on one side with military preparations, we also have to remain more vigilant than ever. We hope that by this position of watchfulness and by avoiding any provocation, we shall preserve the maintenance of peace for our country and for those who are around us. (quoted in Deringil 1982: 40)

Turkey was also very concerned at the Soviet Union's involvement, given past historical conflicts. According to the German Ambassador in Turkey, Franz Von Papen:

> The British desire to establish a new order in Europe with Soviet assistance greatly disturbed the Turks. They had no wish to see Germany ruin the British Empire – but nor did they relish the prospect of too close cooperation between the Soviets and Britain. The ideal for them was...to find the possibility of a compromise. (Deringil 1992: 46)

Von Papen also mentioned that, in the eyes of Turkish Foreign Minister Menemencioğlu:

> Turkey needed a balanced situation in Europe. It also needed a strong Germany in the middle of Europe to counterbalance the imperialist aspirations of the Soviet Union and the Russian plans in the Dardanelles. (Von Papen 2000: 30)

The British appeared to accept the nature of Turkey's diplomatic predicament. Its Ambassador in Ankara, Knatchbull-Hugessen (2000: 164–165, 181–188, 209–210), agreed that Turkey was in a weak position, although he also identified signs of evasiveness. He preferred that it remain neutral, acting as a buffer to German expansion in the Balkans (Kuniholm 1980: 23–24; Pikros 1996: 106–110; Denniston 1997: 53, 58). In an overall assessment of British policy towards Turkey, the British Foreign Secretary, Sir Anthony Eden was to later conclude that:

> Whatever soft words may be employed on both sides, the fact remains that the [Anglo-Franco-Turkish] Treaty [of Mutual Assistance] has not in practice worked out as was intended; for we have, in fact, been fighting Germany and Italy in the Mediterranean for several years and Turkey has

not lifted a finger to assist us. In these circumstances we can hardly be expected to continue to be bound by our obligations to Turkey.[11]

Thus, prior to the outbreak of war, the balance of strategic interests had swung rapidly. Earlier talk of Greco-Turkish mutual security guarantees had been abandoned by Ankara, fearing for its own safety. The possibility of a Bulgarian invasion – threatening Western Thrace – had brought Athens and Ankara together and then its realisation had blown them asunder. The Allies had tried to draw Turkey in to their alliance only to find that, with the Axis on the doorstep, Turkey was recalculating its interests. It had decided to adopt a stance of ambiguity in the guise of neutrality. Turkey feared both Germany and the Soviet Union. The legacy of rapprochement with Greece and the later reality of endeavouring not to provoke the Axis both meant that Turkey was inhibited from making any significant initiatives with respect to the Muslim community in Western Thrace. Turkey had withdrawn strategically and felt obliged to be silent. The fate of the minority would be determined locally. As Western Thrace prepared for war, it was the threat from Bulgaria that disturbed the region.

3.3   Western Thrace prepares for war

Under the Metaxas regime, the imminent threat had undoubtedly been identified as Bulgaria and this had direct consequences for the situation in Western Thrace. Greece was concerned about the defence gaps that the area presented along the borders with Bulgaria, especially in the northern areas of the districts of Xanthi and Rhodope. When General Alexandros Papagos was appointed Chief of Staff of the Greek Army in August 1936, he set about reorganising and modernising the Greek military in terms of its logistics, equipment and tactics. An essential part of that project was the reinforcement of Greece's northern defence by building a series of fortifications along the border with Bulgaria. Papagos made little effort to disguise his suspicions towards the various minority populations across Macedonia and Western Thrace. His specific arguments affecting Western Thrace are summarised in Box 3.4.

Indeed, the immediate border areas with Bulgaria had a population density of less than seven inhabitants per sq. km. Similarly in the areas north of Xanthi and Komotini population densities were 21 and 11.5 inhabitants per sq. km respectively, still well below the Greek average of 52 inhabitants per sq. km.[12] In another report on the level military preparedness in the area,

---

[11] CAB/66/48/36, War Cabinet, 'Policy towards Turkey', Memorandum of the Secretary of State for Foreign Affairs, 4 April 1944.

[12] GAK (Athens), K65/92, Metaxas Archive, GES, 3rd Office, 'Table of population density of the frontier regions', 8 December 1937.

Box 3.4 Papagos' Memorandum on the Settlement of Border Regions and the Removal of Suspected Populations, 8 December 1937

"[the] border regions of the country and particularly those north and east of River Nestos, i.e. north of Papades, north of Paranestion and north of Komotini, until the borders are very sparsely populated. The situation, from a military point of view, is very precarious. Due to the lack of villages and the subsequent scarce deployment of defence forces, bands from the neighbouring sovereignty [Bulgaria] enter our territory easily in order to steal and maybe spy, but in the event of conflict with Bulgaria they could infiltrate in order to destroy essential infrastructure. There are many such defence gaps in the areas of Papades and Paranestion in particular.

[...]

We need to increase the population of those areas with the settlement of families with undoubtedly Greek sentiments and consciousness.

[...]

It is known that in sensitive, from a military point of view, areas there are populations with questionable national feelings. On the eve of war, such populations not only cannot be used for supporting the defence forces, but they may also provide assistance to the enemy.

The properties of the suspected populations in the restricted zones near the defence fortifications have been expropriated or are about to be expropriated in accordance to the law on the safety of fortifications and these populations will be resettled elsewhere. Yet, this settlement should be in the mainland and not in border regions".

Source: GAK (Athens), K65/92, Metaxas Archive.

Papagos proposed the mobilisation of the local population, with frequent training sessions and the creation of local reserve units.[13]

His references to those with 'questionable national feelings', however, were often ambiguous. Hence, although the Turkish speaking population in the lowlands was not identified as a reason for concern (Papagos 1997: 169–172), the Pomak villages of Northern Xanthi and Rhodope (near the border fortifications) were explicitly included in the areas under surveillance. The Bulgarian dialect spoken by the Pomaks in the Rhodope Mountains was regarded by the Greek authorities as a sign of ambiguity over their 'national loyalty'. Whatever Papagos' plans for the 'Hellenisation' of Northern Greece, however, the truth remained that, on the eve of the war, the process of 're-settlement' he had envisaged had made little progress.[14]

---

[13] GAK (Athens), K65/93, Metaxas Archive, GES, 3rd Office, Papagos, 'Report on the military preparation and coordination of the frontier populations', 14 December 1937.

[14] GAK (Athens), K65/93, Metaxas Archive, 'Memorandum of the Minister of Agriculture on the submitted report of the Agricultural Bank of Greece by H. Vasmatzidis on the Colonisation of the Frontier Regions', 14 February 1940.

The Greek authorities made better progress with the construction of the 'Metaxas line', a Maginot-inspired network of 21 well-armed fortifications and bunkers built across the length of the 300 km Greco-Bulgarian border. Two such forts were built in Western Thrace. The first was in Echinos, north of Xanthi, the second in Nymfaia, north of Komotini. Similarly, new roads connecting Xanthi to Echinos (and from there to the Bulgarian borders), and Komotini to Nymfaia were constructed in order to serve the needs of the Greek war machine (Papagos 1997: 326–327, 345–347). Western Thrace would be difficult to defend from invasion. The rather narrow strip of land between the Bulgarian border and the Aegean Sea (which, at its narrowest point, is just 30 km), the lack of fast and secure communications, the difficult mountainous terrain; and, the scarcity of compact populations along the borders with Bulgaria preoccupied Papagos. He paid a great deal of attention to secrecy while building the Metaxas line. The design of the fortifications was top secret and the workers used in the construction were non-Thracians.

In a further military measure, new restricted zones were established (Law 376/1936) all along the northern borders of the country, to reinforce security and prevent espionage.[15] Military and police controls within these areas were tight, with a number of checkpoints on key roads and viaducts (Papagos 1997: 313; Lipordezis, 2002: 27). At the time, special identity cards were given to the people who lived inside the zones and civilians wishing to travel in and out of the area had to apply for a special permit to the nearest police or military authority, giving a full account of their journey and its purpose (Papagos, 1997: 313). Notably, in Western Thrace, the areas that were designated as 'restricted' were almost exclusively occupied by Pomaks.[16] The designation of restricted zones had a profound and negative effect upon the Muslim minority as a whole and especially the mountainous Pomak communities. It resulted in their further economic and social isolation and put an additional barrier to their communication with the cities of Komotini and Xanthi and the Turkish communities in the lowlands.

In order to add to the manpower of the Greek military, Papagos ordered an increase in the length of national service. In 1936, it was increased from 18 to 21 months for combatant soldiers and from five to eight months for those who were exempted from combatant duties. These changes also affected Muslim soldiers. Until then, Muslims served a shorter service and enjoyed a series of benefits (exemptions, leaves, etc.). This preferential treatment,

---

[15] The restricted zone along the Yugoslav border was abolished in 1990 and the Thracian one in 1995.

[16] In the Xanthi region the restricted areas included a number of villages to the north such as Oraion, Miki, Echinos, Pachni, Thermes, Medousa and in the Komotini region the villages of Nymfaia, Asomatoi, Symvola, Gratini, Pandrosos, Folea, Ano Mytikas, Kato Mytikas, Arriana, Sappes and others (*Proodeutiki*, 11 September 1939).

however, ended and Muslim men were obliged to serve the full 21 months of their service. Later on, Papagos ordered a further increase of military service to 24 months for every combatant soldier regardless of religion (Papagos, 1997: 353).

For Greek society at home, the onset of the Metaxas dictatorship had brought a series of repressive measures. New policies were enacted restricting the freedom of the press, political activity and education. Many of these restrictions also affected the Muslim community in Western Thrace which, in addition to tighter controls over education and the minority press, experienced a *de facto* ban on property transactions.[17] Yet, the regime remained conscious of the need to maintain good relations with Turkey. In this context the modernist (Kemalist) wing of the Muslim community in Western Thrace became a preferential interlocutor with the Greek authorities (Tsioumis 1997: 60–61). It is significant that both the 'Association of Turkish Youth' of Komotini and the 'Association of the Turkish Teachers of Western Thrace' were first recognised by Greece's Court of First Instance during this period (Kourtovik 1997: 252).

For the implementation of the regime's strategy in the area, Metaxas appointed his close confidant, Evangelos Kalantzis,[18] as Governor-General of Thrace.[19] After the war, Kalantzis developed impeccable right wing credentials when he was appointed as Minister of Public Order by Papagos in 1954 (Kalantzis 1969: 107–110). In the 1930s, however, his brief on handling the minority was a more moderate one. This accommodating spirit was also evident in Metaxas' surprising gesture towards Turkey. During his visit to Ankara in October 1937, he proposed a comprehensive and reciprocal

---

[17] The regime remained highly suspicious of all minority groups in the country. The Muslim minority of Western Thrace was no exception, although the Slavs and the Chams of Northern Greece were identified as a more serious threat. For an insight into the regime's thinking on minorities see the 'Report on the Situation of Northern Greece from a National Perspective', prepared by the Director of the Greek security services, Georgios Fessopoulos (in Skordylis 1994).

[18] During Kalantzis' term in office, a new settlement was created on the outskirts of Komotini, in order to relocate a number of Roma families that previously resided in the centre of Komotini. The plans for such relocation were supported by the municipal authorities of Komotini in the context of redeveloping the city's centre. The new settlement was called *Kalaintzeia* or *Kalantzia* (Καλαϊτζεία – Καλάντζεια) in honour of Kalantzis. In the language of the Roma the name was changed through time into Kalkanca, and today it is officially known as *Hephestus* (Ήφαιστος). See Mavrommatis 2004: 83–84; Zenginis 1994: 58.

[19] Another indication of Metaxas' interest in the minority, was the creation, in 1936, of the Directorate for Political Affairs (within the Administration-General of Thrace) and of the position of the Inspector-General for Foreign and Minority Schools. See, respectively, Emergency Ordinance (Αναγκαστικός Νόμος) 132/1936, FEK A'/419, 25 September 1936 and Emergency Ordinance (Αναγκαστικός Νόμος) 248/1936, FEK A'/460, 17 October 1936.

solution of all minority issues affecting Greco-Turkish relations within the framework of the Lausanne Treaty. The Turkish side responded by emphasising that all minorities in Turkey enjoyed their full rights and that it had no specific concern over the treatment of the Muslims in Western Thrace.[20]

Unstable tectonic plates below Greece and Turkey became an occasion for a further expression of mutual support. In January 1940 a catastrophic earthquake that coincided with heavy storms caused many deaths and more than 145,000 were left homeless in Turkey. The Greek government offered humanitarian aid to Turkey and in a letter published in Xanthi's local newspaper *Proodeutiki*, Prime Minister Ioannis Metaxas stated:

> It is with great sorrow and regret all Greeks heard about the disaster that struck the noble Turkish nation, with which we are bound with unbreakable friendship and close alliance. Earthquakes, storms, floods and catastrophe brought the loss of many thousands of human beings and devastated prosperous cities and towns. I am confident that not a single Greek heart can remain unmoved towards such a disaster. The Government has done its duty. However, I am asking for every Greek's contribution towards a nation which is so closely connected with ours. I am confident that every Greek will contribute as if this disaster had struck fellow Greeks.[21]

The Greek government launched a well-organised nationwide humanitarian aid campaign by mobilising local authorities. In Western Thrace, the local prefectures and municipalities formed fund-raising committees with cross-community participation. They comprised Greek-Orthodox bank directors, officials from the local associations and unions, the Muftis and Muslim community leaders. The campaign in Western Thrace was indeed very successful and both communities showed a great deal of generosity. For example, the trade union of the tobacco industry workers in Xanthi offered 1000 Drachmas during a period of extreme crisis for the industry (caused by the effects of the 1929 world economic crisis). In Xanthi alone, the amount raised reached 267,000 drachmas (then $1793), a quite substantial amount for that time.[22]

3.4   The Muslim community of Western Thrace and the outbreak of war

In the summer of 1939, days before Hitler invaded Poland, Western Thrace was put on a war footing. Local newspapers bombarded the population with

---

[20] AYE/1940/8.A/3/2, Greek Embassy in Ankara, Raphael, to the Foreign Ministry, Directorate of Political Affairs, Department of Turkey, 29 October 1937.

[21] *Proodeutiki*,15 January 1940.

[22] *Proodeutiki*, 26 February 1940 and 15 January 1940.

press releases and orders by the local Gendarmerie Command and the military on issues of civil defence and protection. Instructions were given to the public on how to react in case of air-raids and on how to build air-defence shelters.[23] Moreover, the *Proodeutiki* newspaper of Xanthi published daily on its first page an order by the local Gendarmerie Command according to which 'any conversation on military issues is forbidden'.[24] Papagos ordered the tightening of security within the restricted areas with stricter procedures for the issuing of permits and more intensive controls at the checkpoints. In an attempt to boost the morale of the local population and the troops stationed in Western Thrace, King George II toured the local units during July 1939. By September 1939 people had started gathering food and other necessities, creating serious shortages in the local market.[25] Everyone in Western Thrace was preparing for war.

Despite Metaxas' policy of neutrality, Greece soon found itself at the receiving end of Mussolini's expansionist plans. On 15 August 1940, the Greek naval vessel *Elli* was torpedoed outside Tinos harbour in an apparent act of aggression by Italian forces. A few weeks later, on 28 October 1940, the Italian Ambassador Emanuele Grazzi presented Metaxas with a three-hour ultimatum, demanding free passage for Mussolini's troops to occupy unspecified strategic sites within Greece. Metaxas rejected the ultimatum. Even before Mussolini's ultimatum had expired, Italian troops began their attack on Greece, through Albania. The main Italian attacks were in the Pindus Mountains, near Ioannina, later crossing the Kalamas River in Epirus. With Mussolini committing too few forces and underestimating the effects of the weather his army was soon in trouble. Within three weeks, the Greek Army had cleared its territory of the invading forces and launched a counter-attack, pushing the Italians well back into southern Albania. The Italians launched a full-scale counter-attack on 9 March 1941 which also failed, despite their superior forces. After one week and 12,000 casualties, Mussolini called off the counter-attack and his troops retreated.

When Mussolini launched his attack on Greece, the first contribution of the Muslim community to the war effort was the participation of Muslim conscripts in the Greek Army, fighting on the Albanian front. There were many reported incidents of bravery and, inevitably, of fatalities. At least one interviewee (now residing in Izmir, Turkey) recalled that her father had fought and died in the Albanian campaign – a source of apparent pride despite her subsequent loss of Greek citizenship and a long legal saga with the Greek authorities over his war pension.[26] There are only a

---

[23] *Proodeutiki*, 28 August 1939, Exarhou 1999: 50.
[24] *Proodeutiki*, 4 September 1939.
[25] *Proodeutiki*, 18 September 1939.
[26] Interview 51.

few known cases of Muslim deserters. A report from the Greek Consul of Edirne to the Ministry of Foreign Affairs in March 1941 made reference to ten Muslim deserters during the first ten days of that month.[27] A few months later, a report from the Bulgarian authorities in Western Thrace referred to 63 Muslim deserters from the Greek Army.[28] A local resident also recalled:

> We left in April 1941, when I was five. We left to escape the war. I remember the sound of German planes dropping bombs. My father had been called up for the Greek Army, but his father-in-law told him he'd better 'go home' and serve in the Turkish army.[29]

In Western Thrace, all males who belonged to the conscription cohorts of 1917 to 1940 were called to join-up. Along with them thousands of male Muslims were called to enlist in the local units that were stationed in the region.[30] Within their units, Muslim soldiers fought in the battles of the Albanian front, and the Macedonian-Thracian fronts. In total, 46 Muslim soldiers were killed and another ten were missing in action. Out of these casualties, 30 (24 dead and six missing) belonged to the 29th Regiment of Komotini, one of the units that suffered the most in the bloody battles of Kalpaki and Boubesi (see Tables 3.1 and 3.2). The 56 casualties represented 0.04 per cent of the total Muslim population of Western Thrace according to the 1940 census. By comparison, the Greek-Orthodox causalities from the same area were 334 or 0.09 per cent of the respective population. The Directorate of Army History also makes reference to six Armenian and two Jewish casualties from the area (GES/DIS 1990). These formed part of the total of 15,572 Greek soldiers who died or went missing during WWII (see Table 3.3).

---

[27] AYE/1941/14.3, Greek Consul of Adrianople to Greek Ministry of Foreign Affairs, 15 March 1941.

[28] CSA/264/1/185, No. 2200, Secretary-General of the Administration-General of Belomorie, Angelov to the Secretary-General of the Foreign Ministry, 1 October 1941.

CSA/264/1/185, Secretary-General of the Administration-General of Belomorie, Aggelov to the Secretary-General of the Foreign Ministry No. 1728, 9 September 1941.

[29] Interview 42.

[30] These units were the XII Division in Komotini that included the active 29th Infantry Regiment of Komotini, the 81st of Alexandroupoli and the newly formed 80th, 82nd, 83rd, 84th, 86th, and 87th Reserve Regiments, a Regiment of mountain artillery, two squadrons and two despatch companies. The XIV Division in Xanthi, that included the active 37th Regiment of Infantry of Stavroupolis and the newly formed 41st and 93rd Reserve Regiments, a Regiment of mountainous artillery, one squadron and one despatch company.

Table 3.1 Muslim Soldiers Killed during the Greek-Italian and Greek-German War

Name/ Surname	Father's Name	Birthplace	Year of Birth	Unit	Date/ Circumstances of death
Ahmet Oğlü Sadik	Ahmet	Sykorrachi, Alexandro- upolis	1920	33rd Infantry Regiment	Killed in Kako Oros, Heraklion (battle of Crete), May 1941
Ahmet OğlüOsman	Ahmet	Orestiada, Evros	1910	n/a	Drowned in Porto Lagos, Komotini, 14.5.41
Ahmet Osman Oğlü Ahmet	Osman	Ano Vyrsini, Komotini	1916	29th Infantry Regiment	Killed in South Kozani, 4.41
Ali Oğlü Hasan	Ali	Komotini	1916	29th Infantry Regiment	Killed in Psari village of Kleisoura, 11.3.41
Ali Oğlü Mümin	Ali	Polyanthos Komotini	1917	29th Infantry Regiment	Died in Kozani hospital, 28.12.40
Ali Oğlü Raef	Ali	Pagouria, Komotini	1917	29th Infantry Regiment	Killed in Tepeleni, 17.3.41
Ardaylı Hasan	Mehmet	Oraion, Xanthi	1909	6th Mountain Artillery Regiment	Killed in Rovitsa, 13.3.41
Bayram Oğlü Elmasim	Bayram	Amvrosia Komotini	1913	29th Infantry Regiment	Died in the Alexandroupoli Military Hospital, 3.1.41
Günüç Ali Hüseyin	Ali	Lykeio Sappes, Rhodope	1917	29th Infantry Regiment	Killed on the Senteli Hill North-East of Tepeleni, 10.3.41
Haci Mümin Oğlü Mustafa	Haci Mümin	Evmoiro, Rhodope	1912	37th Infantry Regiment	Committed suicide in Evmoiron, Rhodope, 7.1140

Continued

Table 3.1 Continued

Name/ Surname	Father's Name	Birthplace	Year of Birth	Unit	Date/ Circumstances of death
Hafuzoğlu Hüseyin	Memet	Kalhas Komotini	1919	29th Infantry Regiment	Died in Boubesi (North-West of Kleisoura), 6.4.41
Hasan Oğlü Mehmet	Hasan	Komotini	1919	840th Unit	Killed on the Albanian front, 13.12.40
Hasan Oğlü Nazim	Hasan	Sostis Komotini	1907	81st Infantry Regiment	Died in the Sidirokastro Military Hospital, 6.1.41
Hasan Pasha Hüseyin	Ayşe	Paterma Gratini	1917	29th Infantry Regiment	Killed on the Senteli Hill, 11.3.41
Hasan Oğlü Sadik (Corporal)	Hasan	Komotini	1919	29th Infantry Regiment	Killed on the 1211 Hill, West of Pogradets, 10.12.40
Hüseyin Oğlü Şerafettin (Corporal)	Hüseyin	Komotini	1919	29th Infantry Regiment	Killed in battle North-West of Pogradets, 9.12.40
Hüseyin Daout	Ayşe	Stylari, Rhodope	1919	29th Infantry Regiment	Killed on the Senteli Hill, 13.3.41
Hüseyin Oğlü	Mustafa	Kalhas Komotini	1908	29th Infantry Regiment	Killed on the Senteli Hill, 10.3.41
Hüseyin Oğlü Memet	n/a	n/a	n/a	n/a	Killed in Nikaia, Athens, 19.3.41
Hüseyin Raef	Memet	Satres, Xanthi	1919	37th Infantry Regiment	Killed in Paradeisos, Kavala, 9.4.41
Ibrahim Oglou Giousouf	Ibrahim	Gratini, Rhodope	1916	29th Infantry Regiment	Killed on the Senteli Hill North-East of Tepeleni, 10.3.41

Continued

Table 3.1   Continued

Name/ Surname	Father's Name	Birthplace	Year of Birth	Unit	Date/ Circumstances of death
Ibrahim Oğlü Mustafa	Ibrahim	Komotini	1918	29th Infantry Regiment	Died in the XVIIa Military surgical unit (Pogradets), 6.12.40
Ispoğlu Mehmet Ali Mehmet	Mehmet Ali	Arisvi, Komotini	1908	Supply Unit, Xanthi	Died in Xanthi Military Hospital, 17.1.41
Kel Mehmet Oğlü Ali	Mehmet	Arisvi, Rhodope	1907	81st Infantry Regiment	Died in the Alexandroupoli Military Hospital, 2.11.40
Kuruci Ahmet	Hüseyin	Didimoteicho, Evros	1920	Training Centre, Nafphlion	Killed in Heraclion, Crete, 23.5.41
Kukri Oğlü	Sakki	Komotini	1907	15th Infantry Regiment	Died in the 2nd Military Hospital in Ioannina, 5.2.41
Mehmet Oğlü Amet	Mehmet	Velkio Sappes, Rhodope	1905	87th Infantry Regiment	Killed in Vermio during an air-raid, 13.4.41
Mehmet Oğlü Hüseyin	Mehmet	Sarakini Kalhantas, Rhodope	1917	29th Infantry Regiment	Killed at the Tria Avga Hill, 30.3.41
Mehmet Oğlü Ibrahim	Mehmet	Kosmio, Komotini	1916	XII Defence Sector	Died in the Komotini Military Hospital, 28.1.41
Muço Sali	Hüseyin	Kotilo [sic. Kotyli or Kotino] Xanthi	1909	41st Infantry Regiment	Died in the Xanthi Military Hospital, 11.11.40

Continued

Table 3.1 Continued

Name/ Surname	Father's Name	Birthplace	Year of Birth	Unit	Date/ Circumstances of death
Mustafa Haik	Mustafa	Kallyntirio Gratini, Komotini	n/a	n/a	Died in the provisional Military Hospital of Korytsa, 29.3.41
Osman Oğlü Ahmet	Osman	Palladio Komotini	1919	29th Infantry Regiment	Killed in Pogradets, 6.12.40
Osman Oğlü Hasan	Osman	Komotini	1916	82nd Infantry Regiment	Killed in Siatista, Kozani, 15.4.41
Pekir Yusuf	Hasan	Symvola Rhodope	1919	29th Infantry Regiment	Killed in Tria Auga, 28.3.41
Şakir Oğlü	Şakir	Sostis Komotini	1916	29th Infantry Regiment	Killed on the Senteli Hill, 14.3.41
Sali Oğlü	Sarba	Komotini	1905	80th Infantry Regiment	Died in the S1 Medical Hospital Unit, 29.3.41
Sali Şerif	Osman	Amaranta Komotini	1918	29th Infantry Regiment	Died in the 1st Military Hospital in Ioannina, 22.3.41
Salim Alim	Salim	Amaxades Komotini	1917	29th Infantry Regiment	Killed in Pogradets, 9.12.40
Selim Oğlü Ferat	Selim	Evlalo Xanthi	1914	S 23 Company of workers	Died in the Koritsa Provisional Military Hospital, 5.3.41
Şerif Oğlü	Mehmet	Archontika Sappes	1916	29th Infantry Regiment	Died in Archontika, 31.12.40

Continued

Table 3.1   Continued

Name/ Surname	Father's Name	Birthplace	Year of Birth	Unit	Date/ Circumstances of death
Tahsinoğlü Reşat	Tahsin	Komotini	1905	87th Infantry Regiment	Killed in Kleisoura, 10.3.41
Tevfik Oğlü Nevres	Tevfik	Komotini	1915	29th Infantry Regiment	Killed on the Mpali Hill, Trembesina, 8.3.41
Topal Sali Ahmet (Corporal)	Sali	Organi Komotini	1917	29th Infantry Regiment	Killed on the Senteli Hill, 10.3.41
Yakupoğlu Mehmet	Yakup	Didimoteicho, Evros	1910	n/a	Died 11.3.41
Yusuf Kiazim	Yusuf	Komara, Evros	1912	XIII Artillery Regiment	Killed on the 1292 Hill in Kleisoura, 3.12.40
Yusuf Oğlü Osman	Giousouf	Komotini	1918	29th Infantry Regiment	Killed in Pogradets, 6.12.40

Source: GES/DIS 1990.

Table 3.2   List of Missing Muslim Soldiers in the Greek-Italian and Greek-German War

Name/ Surname	Father's Name	Birthplace	Year of Birth	Unit	Circumstances of disappearance
Ali Oğlü Ali	Ali	Komotini	1905	87th Infantry Regiment	Reported as missing in Kleisoura, Kastoria, 4.41
Ali Oğlü Hasan	Ali	Iasmos, Komotini	1912	29th Infantry Regiment	Reported as missing in Pogradets, 1.12.40
Ahmet Kehaya Houssein	Ismail	Anonyma, Komotini	1919	29th Infantry Regiment	Reported as missing in Boubesi hill in Kleisoura, 10.4.41
Edirneli Hüseyin	Memet	Pelagia, Komotini	1915	29th Infantry Regiment	Reported as missing in Grevena during an air-raid, 8.4.41

Continued

Table 3.2 Continued

Name/ Surname	Father's Name	Birthplace	Year of Birth	Unit	Circumstances of disappearance
Mümin Oğlü Mehmet	Mümin	Sostis, Komotini	1917	29th Infantry Regiment	Reported as missing in Erseka, Kleisoura, 2.41
Bayram Ali Oğlü Şakir	Bayram Ali	Evlalo, Xanthi	1916	Motorcycle Platoon of Kavalla	Reported as missing (drowned) in river Nestos, 10.4.41
Osman Hüseyin Hüseyin	Hüseyin	Isalos, Amaranta, Komotini		29th Infantry Regiment	Reported as missing in Tria Auga, Beratio, 1.4.41
Şakir Oğlü Osman	Şakir	Xanthi	1906	2nd Calvary Centre	Reported as missing in the Military Hospital of Kastoria, 6.4.41
Hüseyin Efenti Hoca Zeki	Hüseyin	Vrysika, Didimoteiho, Evros	1919	81st Infantry Regiment	Reported as missing in the Roupel fort during an air-raid, 8.4.41
Hüseyin Oğlü Mehmet	Hüseyin	Komotini	1915	29th Infantry Regiment	Reported as missing in Kleisoura, 3.41

Source: GES/DIS, *Struggles and Casualties of the Greek Army during World War II*, Athens 1990.

Table 3.3 Greek Military Casualties in WWII

	Officers	Soldiers	Total
Dead 1940–41	713	12.636	13.349
Missing 1940–41	29	1.785	1.814
Dead, Middle East 1944–45	49	351	400
Missing, Middle East 1944–45	7	2	9

Source: GES/DIS, *Struggles and Casualties of the Greek Army during World War II*, Athens 1990.

Statistics aside, it is impossible to evaluate the contribution of Muslim combatants during the War, particularly as many of them were often regarded as 'second class soldiers' and hence assigned to auxiliary duties by their commanders. That said, there is evidence to suggest that many Muslim soldiers shared a feeling that the 1940–1941 War was also 'their' conflict and fought bravely alongside fellow Greek combatants. One of the very few known facts about their contribution is that, among the first 16 wounded soldiers from Xanthi, nine were Muslims (Exarhou 1999: 147, 159).

Interviewees who had been called up recalled that Greek officers during the War behaved in an exemplary fashion, treating everybody under
their command equally. Some Muslim soldiers became non-commissioned
officers.[31] Moreover, inhabitants from Echinos repeatedly referred with
pride to the existence of the Metaxas fortification in their village and the
battles that took place during the German attack. The fortification not only
became a reference point for the village; it is also now an improvised play-
ground for children, a communal heritage.[32] The loyalty shown by many
young members of the Muslim community at the time is revealed in the
testimony of one particular soldier from the village of Koptero (West of
Komotini), who after many adventures returned to Greece in 1948 and told
his story to the military authorities:

> During the Albanian war in 1940–41 I fought as a soldier in the
> Greek Army. I was in the 28th transport battalion. After the end of
> the Albanian war I returned to my village, which in the meantime,
> had been occupied by the Bulgarians, who arrested me and sent to
> prison in Iasmos, near Komotini. A Pomak called [...] betrayed me to the
> Bulgarians, accusing me of being a friend of the Greeks and as a fighter
> of the Albanian front. This Pomak was executed three months ago [in
> 1948] in Xanthi for being a spy for the Bulgarians. I managed to escape
> from the prison of Iasmos where I was locked up by the Bulgarians and
> I fled to the Middle East in 1941, where I joined the 1st brigade (3rd
> Battalion) of the Greek Army.[33]

The declaration of war had caused a strong sense of unity among Greeks.
That sense was also shared by members of the Muslim community in
Western Thrace, with many local veterans taking pride in their participation in the war and receiving widespread recognition form their community
peers. This sense of unity is apparent in the article (written in 1946) of the
local Turkish-language newspaper *Trakya* about the 1940–1941 war. Despite
the fact that *Trakya* was considered by many Greeks as a mouth piece of
Turkish nationalism with an anti-Greek agenda, its article on the 1940–1941
war offered a rather different perspective (see Box 3.5).

In addition to the military contribution of minority members, Muslim
civilians had also shared the burden of supporting those fighting with the
Greek Army. As elsewhere in Greece, the local authorities in Western Thrace
together with community associations were mobilised in order to collect

---

[31] Interview 18. During our discussion a number of locals from Sminthi joined our
conversation and confirmed this information. Also interviews 4 and 12.

[32] Interviews 4 and 12.

[33] AYE/1948/105.6, Administration-General of Thrace, Xirotyris, to the Foreign
Ministry, Department of Turkey, Report on witness' statement, (Orestiada, 12 July
1948), Komotini, 30 July 1948.

Box 3.5   Extract from *Trakya* on the 1940–41 War, December 1946

28 October 1940

Today is a day of celebration for Greece. There is no one in our country, young or old, who does not feel proud today. All around the world, people remember 28 October 1940 a day where a mighty nation of eight million spears submitted in front of a small nation.

In the night of 28 October 1940, the Greek Prime Minister, in full confidence of the Greek people's patriotism and unity, said NO. Greece would re-live Thermopylae and Miltiades' invitation to the Persians for battle. [.....]

Six whole years have passed since the 28th of October 1940 and today we celebrate that glorious day. For us and for all nations who love their homeland and who want to live free and independent this is a day of pride. This day is a shining example which reminds us all that even the most powerful enemy and the most advanced weapons of destruction are doomed to fail against a glorious nation that loves its country.

On 28 October 1940 every Greek heart was beating as one. This unity made all of us a single fist that defeated the 8 million spears army of charlatan Mussolini. We the Turks of Western Thrace as citizens of Greece got our share of glory.

We salute the heroes of the 29th Regiment who were crippled. We salute every hero who fought this war.

Source: *Trakya*, 9 December 1946.

---

clothes, food, cigarettes and money for the troops. Locally, the results of that campaign were impressive. In just five days, more than 3000 packages were prepared in Komotini and sent to the soldiers of the 29th Regiment, whereas throughout Western Thrace more than 22,000 packages were prepared within a month (Kalantzis 1969: 57). The Muslim community took an active role in the campaign. This is evident from the fact that, throughout the Greco-Italian war, local newspapers published regular lists of individuals who made donations. Within these lists, there are many Muslim names of donors. Indicatively, two of these lists are given in Tables 3.4 and 3.5.

After the Italian campaign came the reality of German invasion and then life under occupation. With Mussolini's troops failing, Hitler decided to save the face of the Axis Powers and attacked Greece on 6 April 1941. Nazi forces launched Operation Marita with the 12th German Army Corps invading Greece through Bulgaria, following an earlier agreement of military cooperation between Field-Marshal Von List and the Bulgarian General Staff (Van Creveld 1973).[34] Within a week of the agreement, German troops were deployed along the Greco-Bulgarian border. With defeat certain, Papagos decided to 'maintain the focus of the Greek Army's effort on the Albanian theatre of operations, even in the event of a German attack and regardless of its outcome on the Bulgarian front, in order for the Greek Army to keep its

---

[34] Bulgaria officially joined the Axis on 1 March 1941 by signing the Tripartite Pact.

Table 3.4 Contributions of Xanthi Villages to the Greek Army, February 1941

Name/Surname	Residence	Donation
Cemali Oğlu Hussain	Mikro Evmoiro	1 Calf
Mümin Oğlu Raif	Mikro Evmoiro	2 Rams
Idriz Oğlu Hasan	Vaniano Gizela	1 Ox.
Halil Oğlu Husain	Vaniano Gizela	1 Calf
Georgios Deligiorgis	Leyki Gizela	1 Calf
Dimitris Ntontsios	Leyki Mikro Evmoiro	1 Calf
Demos Tsakiris	Leyki Mikro Evmoiro	1 Calf
Argyris Hatzioannou	Leyki Mikro Evmoiro	1 Calf
Diamanto Athanaseli	Leyki Mikro Evmoiro	1 Calf
Georgios Prastanis	Leyki Mikro Evmoiro	1 Ox.
Georgios Lampidis	Leyki Mikro Evmoiro	1 Ox.
Ibrahim Oğlu Iliaz	Lambrino Mikro Evmoiro	1 Ox.
Mümin Oğlu Siampan	Lambrino Mikro Evmoiro	1 Calf
Halil Oğlu Aziz	Kyrnos Evlalo	1 Calf
Ramadan Oğlu Mustafa	Kremasti Evlalo	1 Ox.
Dimitris Alexiadis	Polysito	1 Calf
Alexandros Alexiadis	Polysito	1 Calf
Polyvios Dagas	Polysito	1 Ox.
Haci Mestan Ömer Husain	Mikro Evmoiro	849 Drachma

Source: *Proodeutiki*, 9 February 1941.

Table 3.5 Contributions of Farmers from Western Thrace to the Greek Army, November 1940

Village/town	Donors
Sydini	35 Greeks
Erasmion	30 Greeks, 6 Muslims
Kentiti	11 Muslims
Iliopetra	7 Muslims
Avaton	25 Greeks, 9 Muslims
Genisea	1 Greek
Potamia	1 Greek
Magana	15 Greeks
Ziloti	1 Greek, 2 Muslins
Orfanon	6 Muslims
Evlalon	2 Muslim

Source: *Proodeutiki*, 8 November 1940.

gains against the Italians' (Papagos, 1995: 335). Papagos had already embarked on the further reinforcement of the fronts of Albania and Central and Eastern Macedonia, by transferring many units from Western Thrace to these areas. That meant that the only units defending Western Thrace were the garrisons of the forts of Echinos (with 26 officers and 806 soldiers) and Nymfaia (with 14 officers and 464 soldiers), along with a few more detachments, many of which contained several Muslim soldiers (Papagos, 1995: 385). Facing an overwhelmingly superior enemy (in both numbers and equipment), the Greek Army stood little chance: Western Thrace was doomed to fall.

With the advance of the Axis troops imminent, Western Thrace was gripped by fatalism. According to the Governor-General of Thrace, Evangelos Kalantzis, 'the prospect of a Bulgarian occupation had crushed everyone's morale. Fear and terror ruled everywhere' (Kalantzis 1969: 62). The first to flee Western Thrace were state officials, Kalantzis included. Regional and municipal officials, judges, bankers and much of the clergy abandoned the region without making any provision for the preservation of order and some basic form of state administration (Kalantzis 1969: 62–63; Mekos 2002: 121). The vast majority of those officials had come from 'Old Greece' and had settled in the region in the 1920s and 1930s. In the eyes of the collaborationist Greek Prime Minister, Georgios Tsolakoglou, they were 'either incompetent, or intentionally unproductive, since they considered themselves as underprivileged for being transferred to Thrace' (Tsolakoglou, 1959: 177), a region that was – and still is – considered an undesirable transfer for Greek civil servants. A resistance fighter from Rhodope, also confirmed that:

> The local authorities, including the Governor-General of Thrace, Evangelos Kalantzis, left the area the day before the German attack. Only the Metropolitan (the head of the local clergy) remained in situ and spoke in public meetings in order to encourage the dispirited population. He was later expelled by the Bulgarians.[35]

Greek authorities in the area reported that members of the Muslim community tried to get out of Western Thrace by any means possible, leaving behind their shops and houses.[36] This is how a former Muslim resident of Komotini recalled these events:

> The Greek Government and its authorities all dissolved in one night. There was general chaos. The jails were opened by the Germans. The

---

[35] Interview 29. The same events are also described in.ELIA/47, Bulgarian Occupation in Macedonia and Thrace, 'Report of the Metropolitan of Maroneia and Thasos on the situation of his Metropolitan diocese after the German military occupation', Chalkida, 26 June 1941.

[36] AYE/1944/1.1, Xanthi Prefecture, to Administration-General of Thrace, Interior Directorate, 21 July 1945.

offices of the Greek public administration were plundered by the locals, who took everything... The Germans took the city in about two hours. There was no defence. We packed and left with a horse and carriage. My family escaped soon after the occupation started. We carried papers saying that we were going to harvest, but we actually continued to the border. We went with the Greeks driving our carts. There were about ten carts in a convoy. We Turks were not allowed to drive the carts. At the Maritsa [Evros] River, we came across a terrible sight. A whole crowd of Turkish refugees were huddled together with whatever possessions they'd been able to take with them. We crossed the river as officially "Greek", but with no identification papers of any kind. Small rowing boats took one family across at a time. I remember we kissed the ground on our arrival into Turkey![37]

Another former Muslim resident of Medousa remembered:

We escaped to Turkey in April 1941, after we learnt that the Bulgarians were going to kill my father. We left at midnight, with none of our possessions, all huddled on the back of an open lorry. At first, the Turkish borders were not open. We arrived at the crossing point with no water and no food. We drank the river water. A friend of my father's mediated with the guards. We all crossed in a rowing boat that was meant for just two.[38]

According to Kotzageorgi-Zymari (2002: 154–155), more than 2000 Muslims fled to Turkey shortly before the German attack of April 1941, whilst by September 1941 this number had risen to 12,483 – though an unknown number of them returned later (Daskalov 1992a: 33)[39] – putting huge pressure on the Turkish Inspector-General of Eastern Thrace to accommodate the newly arrived refugees.[40] The refugees faced much danger and hardship. Subsequently many more Muslims fled the Bulgarian occupation of Western Thrace and the hardships of the Greek civil war (see Chapters 4 and 8). A good number of them faced an uncertain reaction once settled in Turkey, as

---

[37] Interview 37.

[38] Interview 34.

[39] Many refugees were 'trapped' in the buffer zone of Evros and remained there until the end of the war, as they were settled by the German authorities in abandoned properties. The Germans provided them with medical care (vaccines) and food supplies. According to Batıbey, relations between Muslim refugees and the local Greek Orthodox majority were very good (1976: 34–40).

[40] AYE 1941/14/A/3/3, Foreign Ministry, Political Affairs, Balkans, Director D. Gafos, to Ministry of Public Security, 15 April 1941.

well as major obstacles to returning to Western Thrace when peace came. They were again the peoples 'in-between'.

The Germans launched their attack against the fort of Nymfaia (North of Komotini) on 6 April 1941. The fort received a barrage of artillery fire and the next day the garrison surrendered. Likewise, following two days of heavy fighting, the garrison of Echinos also surrendered and, by 8 April, the Germans had captured all the main cities of Western Thrace (Komotini, Xanthi and Alexandoupolis). In the immediate aftermath of the collapse of the two Greek forts the German Army remained in command of the whole of Western Thrace. This changed on 21 April 1941 when the Bulgarian Army entered Eastern Macedonia and Western Thrace, opening up a new (and highly traumatic) chapter for the lives of the local population (Kotzageorgi-Zymari 2002: 38–42).

In the meantime, the map of Greece had been transformed: by 30 April 1941, the Greek mainland was under Axis control. The fall of Crete on 1 June, left the Greek government seeking refuge in Cairo. The Axis occupation divided Greece between German, Italian and Bulgarian zones of control. Hitler took control of the strategically important areas – Athens, Thessaloniki, Central Macedonia, several Aegean islands and most of Crete. Some two-thirds of Greece was occupied by Italian forces, until the overthrow of Mussolini in September 1943 (when they were replaced by German and Bulgarian forces). Of greatest relevance here is that north-eastern Greece, including Eastern Macedonia and Western Thrace came under Bulgarian administration, with the exception of a narrow strip along the Greco-Turkish border near River Evros, which remained under German control (for more details see Map 2 and Chapter 4). This satisfied Bulgaria's long-held claims on these territories for a 'Greater Bulgaria' which had been shattered in the aftermath of WWI.

The arrival of Bulgarian troops in Western Thrace brought significant misfortunes to both the Greek-Orthodox and the Muslim communities. In Athens, a puppet government was established with General Georgios Tsolakoglou as Prime Minister under the full control of the Nazis.

3.5   Changing loyalties: the battle(s) for Turkey's neutrality

When Germany invaded Greece and Yugoslavia in April 1941, Athens saw Turkey as distancing itself from its pre-war commitments to come to its aid. President İsmet İnönü refused to take risks on their behalf (Deringil 2004: 109–116). Turkey even declined to appoint an Ambassador to the Greek government in Cairo until 1943. Leitz (2000: 91) argues that Ankara's change of strategy (towards appeasement of the Axis) was already agreed one month earlier (March 1941) when Hitler's troops marched into Bulgaria. Hitler had written to İnönü to reassure him that the move was not directed at Turkey.

Indeed, the spokesman of the German High Command in Bulgaria declared that:

> In view of the respect in which the German Army holds Turkey, they see no reason whatever for any military move against that country. The only troops on the Turkish border were Bulgarian frontier troops.[41]

Moreover, weeks before the fall of Athens, Greek diplomats reported that:

> According to the Turkish Ambassador, the letter from Hitler which Von Papen handed to President İnönü contained assurances that Germany would respect Turkish independence. In the President's reply, which the Turkish Ambassador handed to the Führer on 20 March, the President declared, in a friendly but unambiguous tone, the determination of Turkey to resist any attempt on a part of a third power to [missing word] her territory.[42]

Turkey remained wary of the Nazis, but this now meant avoiding provoking them. Since the previous year, Berlin had in fact considered Turkey as a possible military target (Deringil 2004: 115–120). Admiral Raeder in September 1940 had suggested this as part of a strategy to push Britain out of the Mediterranean. German options included moving from Bulgaria to Turkey and on to the Suez Canal or proceeding from Libya to the Suez Canal and on to Syria and Turkey. When İnönü had shown reluctance to allow German troops free transit through his country, Von Ribbentrop had reportedly fumed about wiping out Turkey within a week (Leitz 2000: 91). But any designs on Turkey were shelved whilst the attack on the Soviet Union was planned and pursued.

Turkish foreign policy was now one of 'active neutrality', a term that belied much ambiguity of posture but followed clear strategic interests. On 18 June 1941, a ten-year Treaty of Friendship was signed between Germany and Turkey which provided that:

> The Third Reich and the Turkish Republic undertake to respect the integrity and the inviolability of their respective territories and to abstain from taking any measures directed in any way against each other.
>
> The Third Reich and the Turkish Republic undertake to discuss all issues of mutual interest in a spirit of friendship, in order to achieve a compromise.
>
> This Pact is valid for ten years from the day of its conclusion. (Von Papen 2000: 71)

---

[41] HW/12/263, Turkish Military Attaché, Berlin, to Defence Minister, Ankara, No. 089644, 10 April 1941.

[42] HW/12/263, Mavroudis, Athens, to Greek Legation, London, No. 089341, 2 April 1941.

With this Treaty, Turkey was now in the peculiar position of being bound to Germany via a benevolent neutrality, whilst it still acknowledged its mutual assistance treaty with Britain (Leitz 2000: 86). The new policy was communicated by the Foreign Minister Numan Menemencioğlu to all Turkish embassies abroad:

> According to this Treaty [of Friendship] our policy is declared to be as follows:

- Turkey will preserve her neutrality between the belligerents around her.
- Turkey has resolved to oppose by force of arms any kind of attack which is made upon her territory. She will refuse at all times any interference with her independence of action.
- Turkey is the ally of Great Britain and cannot become an instrument of any movements directed against her.
- As there exists no actual subject of disagreement between Turkey and Germany, Turkey will be the friend of Germany, and will abstain from any act against her.
- Turkey continues to maintain her present close and permanent ties and relations with England as before.[43]

The Turkish policy of engagement with Germany and, particularly, the supply of Turkish chrome to the German war machine, frustrated the British. Winston Churchill wrote to the US President Franklin Roosevelt, in March 1944, that:

> We are already studying how best to induce Turks to limit the supply of chrome to Germany. Question is very complicated one owing to existing Turco-German agreements, and I doubt whether personal appeal to Turkish President would help at present stage. As you know, Turks are at present in a very selfish and obstinate mood and an appeal to their better feelings might have the opposite effect to what we desire... Above all there is danger that they will regard so friendly a message at this juncture as a sign of weakening on our part.[44]

Anthony Eden also referred to the Turkish attitude, as well as the strategic priorities of Britain with respect to Turkey's position in the conflict (see Box 3.6).

---

[43] HW/12/265, Foreign Minister, Ankara, to Turkish Minister, Madrid, 'Turco-German Treaty: Turkish Declaration to Diplomatic Representatives', No. 092441, 22 June 1941.

[44] CAB/120/715, Prime Minister Churchill, to President Roosevelt, 19 March 1944. Generally on the Turkish wartime position see Weber 1983.

Box 3.6   Anthony Eden's Assessment of Turkish Policy in World War II, April 1944

During the war our immediate interests in Turkey is to obtain from her the maximum help possible against Germany. The help we required from her in the early part of the war was of a passive sort, namely, to act as a barrier against German penetration in the Middle East. Since the collapse of Italy, however, we have wanted something more, namely, the use of Turkish air bases and eventual active participation by Turkey in the war.

In recent months British policy in Turley has been directed to obtaining these immediate interests, but we have in the face of Turkish recalcitrance failed entirely to achieve our object. At the end of January we decided therefore to abandon our efforts and withdrew our military mission and cut off armament supplies to Turkey without notification or explanation, and in conjunction with the Soviet and United States Governments adopted an attitude of aloofness [...]

It was not expected that the reactions of the Turks to this policy would be spectacular, nor have they been. Indeed, it might even be said that our action has been a relief to them, because it has also resulted in the cessation of political pressure on them.

Source: CAB/66/48/36, War Cabinet, 'Policy towards Turkey', 4 April 1944.

The Turkish policy of 'active neutrality' was met with suspicion by Greek officials who feared that Turkey also nursed plans for the acquisition of territories that belonged to or were likely to be claimed by Greece in a post-war settlement. Since May 1941, Germany had proposed the cession of two or three Aegean islands to Turkey, in combination with the promotion of Turkish interests in Syria and Iraq, while İnönü had made a proposal for a 'reconstructed' Balkan peninsula, if Germany won the war (Alexandris 1982: 183; Deringil 1992: 50; Pikros 1996: 133–134; Denniston 1997: 73).

The Greek government-in-exile was equally alarmed by Turkey's negotiations with the Allies and rumours that Britain had, on several occasions, offered Lesvos, Lemnos, Chios and the Dodecanese to Turkey in exchange for its participation in the war. Additionally, the Turkish government offered to send troops to the Balkans as a police force to restore order during the Axis retreat.[45] The Turkish offer met with British reluctance:

> Turkish intervention in the Balkans must principally be for the purpose of helping us to clear the Germans out of the area. It must be out of the question that we should use Turkish troops to enter Greek or Yugoslav territory merely to keep order after German withdrawal.[46]

---

[45] CAB/120/710, From Ankara to Foreign Office, 5 September 1943. FO/12/292, Greek Embassy, Raphael, Ankara to Greek Embassy, London, No. 122391, 10 September 1943. CAB/120/710, From Foreign Office to Ankara, 14 September 1943.

[46] CAB/120/710, From Foreign Office to Ankara, No. 1303, 14 September 1943.

Box 3.7 Report of the Greek Embassy in Ankara on the Turkish Position during the War, August 1944

Turkey refused to fulfil the terms of its alliance with England [...]
  [Turkey] refused to fulfil in practice the terms of the Greco-Turkish alliance.
  Before the war, Greece proceeded with many acts of goodwill in the context of an honest friendship towards Turkey: it banned nationalist instruction, it erased from Greek poems and folk songs any phrase harming this friendship and prohibited any eventual action that would oppose the spirit of Greek-Turkish friendship. Moreover special funds were raised and material help was sent to the victims of the earthquake in Turkey.
  By contrast, when Greece was conducting a desperate military struggle against two empires, Turkey found the opportunity to show its true sentiments towards Greece and achieve small material gains against Hellenism. Hence ... new persecutions were initiated against the Greek element and the Church [refers to the Capital Tax].*

Note: *For more details on the Capital Tax (*Varlık Vergisi*) imposed on minorities in Turkey see Akar (1992) and Ökte (1987).

Source: AYE/1945/21.3, Greek Embassy in Ankara, 'Report on Turkey', 10 August 1944.

The British reassurances, however, did not calm the suspicions of the Greek Prime Minister-in-exile, Emmanuel Tsouderos, who dismissed outright the prospect of Turkey placing troops on the Greek islands or appearing as the 'liberator' of Greece after the war (Tsouderos 1950: 79–81, 180–182).[47] Not surprisingly, Greek diplomatic reports prepared in the later stages of the war recorded a deep resentment of Turkey, which, they claimed, had moved away from the pre-war spirit of Greco-Turkish friendship (see Box 3.7).

As Germany's prospects in the war waned, new security dilemmas emerged. Indeed, Turkey's participation in the war on the side of the Allies was discussed and bargained for in several Allied conferences.[48] Finally,

---

[47] For the Greek concerns, complains and representations indicatively see FO/195/2486, No. 1237, 21 September 1944, Foreign Office to Helm, Ankara. FO/195/2486, No. 1132, 1 September 1944, Foreign Office to Helm, Ankara. FO/195/2486, No. 1213, 16 September 1944, Foreign Office to Helm, Ankara. FO/371/37179, Minutes, 23 February 1943.
During 1941–42, the Soviet Union – at the peak of its 'Great Patriotic War' was also positive towards similar concessions to Turkey FO/195/2478, British Embassy, Ankara, Knatchbull-Hugessen, to the Foreign Office, Eden, 29 January 1943.

[48] In Moscow (December 1941), Casablanca (January 1943), Adana (January 1943), Quebec (August 1943), Moscow (October 1943), Cairo (November 1943) and Teheran (December 1943). For Churchill's efforts to bring Turkey into the conflict see Denniston 1997. A large memorandum on Turkish foreign policy until 1942 can be found in FO/195/2478, Knatchbull-Hugessen, British Embassy, Ankara, to Foreign Office, 29 January 1943. Also see FO/371/37465, 'Turkey and the War', 15 January 1943.

without actively joining the war, Turkey severed its economic relations with Germany on 2 August 1944, and then declared war on her (on 23 February 1945) shortly before Germany's surrender in May 1945.[49] As early as April 1943, the Greek Ambassador in London, Athanasios Agnides, recorded a conversation with his Turkish counterpart on future developments, where the latter was reported as having commented:

> Let us see what you and we shall find when the war ends. Europe will be menaced by disease and revolution, and Greeks and Turks must be in the closest friendship so as to restore some sort of order. To this end we shall perhaps have to tighten the bonds of our friendship even to the point of federation. We are both threatened by the Slav peril, and we can face it if we are united. The present leaders of Turkey, Inonu, -, - [two missing names] and I myself, realise the value of Greco-Turkish friendship and the advantages which it can confer on us both if we exploit it, not merely between our two selves but also in collaboration with Britain. No other policy is open on us [...]
>
> Finally, the Ambassador spoke of Bulgaria, abusing her and ending with the words, "Bulgaria has incurred the hatred of all her neighbours, even of Russia".[50]

The comments of the Turkish Ambassador revealed deep rooted Turkish fears over the revival of Bulgarian revisionism. During the early stages of the war Turkey had sought to come to an understanding with Bulgaria through the signing of a Non-Aggression Pact on 17 February 1941, in which both countries agreed to maintain good neighbourly relations.[51] In the spirit of the Pact both Ankara and Sofia agreed to reduce the number of armed forces along their border.[52] Indeed, throughout the war, leaders

---

[49] FO/371/48764, Turkish Foreign Minister, H. Saka, Ankara, to the British Ambassador, M. Peterson, Ankara, 'Turkish Declaration of War upon Germany and Japan', 23 February 1945. According to the Russian General Biryusov, 'Turkish help to the Allies at this stage of the war would be about as much use as a dose of medicine to a dead man'. British sources perceived that 'the Turkish declaration may have rather annoyed the Russians'. FO/371/48764, From Sofia to Foreign Office, 28 February 1945.

[50] HW/12/287, Agnides, London, to Greek legation, Cairo, 'Greco-Turkish relations: Greek Ambassador, London, reports conversation with M. Orbay, No. 116901, 27 April 1943.

[51] HW/12/261, Foreign Minister, Ankara, to All Stations, No. 087979, 'Turco-Bulgarian Declaration', 22 February 1941. HW/12/262, Greek Embassy, Washington, Diamantopoulos, to Foreign Ministry, Athens, No. 088271, 3 March 1941.

[52] HW/12/264, Italian Embassy, Magistrati, Sofia, to the Foreign Ministry, Rome, No. 090808, 11 May 1941. HW/12/264, Italian Embassy, Magistrati, Sofia, to the Foreign Ministry, Rome, No. 090881, 13 May 1941.

in both Bulgaria and Turkey affirmed their willingness to preserve the bilateral status quo and committed themselves to abstain from acts of aggression.[53]

There was an important connection between these diplomatic moves by Turkey during the occupation and the position of the Muslim community in Western Thrace. With these diplomatic constraints, Turkey was obliged to put the fate of the Muslim community on the backburner. According to British intelligence, during the course of the war, Turkish officials received 'many reports of Bulgarian ill-treatment of the Turkish minority, and of the Pomaks...The Turks in Bulgaria fear that this ill-treatment, which is a comparatively recent development, is a prelude to war against Turkey'.[54] Turkish diplomacy responded with caution. British sources remarked that:

> Turkish opinion is watching with increasing interest the development of events in Bulgaria and is paying special attention to the Bulgarian authorities' treatment of the Turkish-Moslem minority. In spite of the strict censorship, reports are received here from time to time from which it appears that, having driven the Greek population out of Western Thrace, the Bulgarians are now using the same methods towards the Turks. (*The Times* 25 February 1943)[55]

The Turkish Premier, Şükrü Saraçoğlu, however, appeared to dismiss reports about the persecution of Turkish minorities abroad. A British diplomatic note of a meeting between Saraçoğlu and the British Ambassador reported him as having said that:

> There was no ill-treatment. Some Turks may have been moved out of their villages, but so had Bulgarians. The [British] Ambassador mentioned the reports of massacres, and he replied that it was the Bulgarian habit to massacre. He seemed perfectly calm about the matter and said that the Bulgarian Government continued to send friendly messages.[56]

---

[53] FO/371/37158, British Embassy, Ankara, to Eden, Foreign Minister, London, 25 September 1943.

[54] HS/5/185, 'Information on Bulgaria', 9 March 1943.

[55] The article makes further references to displacements, forced conversions and propaganda regarding the Slav character of the Muslim population.

[56] FO/371/37158, British Embassy, Ankara, to Southern Department, Foreign Office, 5 March 1943.

In a similar fashion, the Assistant Secretary-General of the Turkish Foreign
Ministry agreed, according to the same British sources, that:

> Although there were occasional incidents, the matter was certainly not of
> major importance...Minorities of all kinds always exaggerated their case
> and the Turks in Bulgaria were not an exception.[57]

In this context, the Turkish press was discouraged from publishing details
on the treatment of the Muslim communities under Bulgarian rule. Turkey
had, once again, chosen to tread carefully. Not that this reassured the British
who suspected that, despite its constraints, Turkey could potentially use the
minority issue as a pretext 'with which ultimately she can, if necessary, pick
a quarrel with Bulgaria'.[58] For the moment, however, no quarrel was picked.
Bulgarian dominance in Western Thrace was there to stay.

3.6   Conclusion

Rather than being some kind of side-show, Western Thrace was very much
at the centre of Greece's invasion by the Axis in 1941. Greece had recognised
it as its prime area of vulnerability, but then proved unable to defend it.
The imminent threat of invasion through the same corridor led Turkey to
distance itself for its pre-war security commitments to Greece. The Germans
marched in and the Bulgarians then (mostly) took it over. Placating the Axis
meant that Turkey was in no position to take up the cause of the Muslims
of Western Thrace.

The sequence of events meant that the conditions seemingly established
in the pre-war period were ripped asunder. Mussolini's surprise attack
disrupted Greece's military planning; the threat of the Nazi advance left
Turkey to step aside and proclaim its neutrality; and, the terms of the
Lausanne Treaty became an irrelevance. The Greek government was forced
into exile. Geo-politically, nothing was the same.

In all of this, the Muslims in Western Thrace faced conditions they were
unable to influence. Local young Muslims had joined the fight against
Mussolini and a good number had died. Now, Greece's collapse and Turkey's
abandonment left the community to face the new rule of the Bulgarians –
a regime that would soon bring many horrors. How the minority would
respond to occupation was to be shaped by the local conditions and
inheritance outlined in this and the preceding Chapter.

---

[57] FO/371/37158, British Embassy, Ankara, to Southern Department, Foreign Office,
5 March 1943.

[58] FO/195/2478, From P.C.O. Istanbul to Knatchbull-Hugessen, Ankara, 1 February
1943.

4
Belomorie

4.1 Introduction

With the invasion complete, the occupation of Western Thrace created new challenges to the local society. How would the authorities deal with the various socio-ethnic groups? What favour/discrimination would be shown and how would the communities respond? How would the new policies affect the demographic mix of the area and the relations between the various components? What might be the longer-term consequences? Initially, though, the question was how would the Muslim community respond to the invaders: as friends or foes?

This chapter addresses the realities of life in Western Thrace under the occupation. It highlights the contrasting responses of the local Muslims to the Germans and to the Bulgarians. It examines the extent to which the misery of the Bulgarian rule was shared by the Greek Orthodox and Muslim populations. The occupation meant a system of severe rationing, but it also tolerated soldiers looting farms and terrorising the locals. More particularly, the Chapter explores the strategy and impact of the enforced cultural assimilation – 'Bulgarisation' – of the region. With the influx of Bulgarian officials and professionals, the demographic balance was changed. Moreover, something close to one-in-ten Muslims from Western Thrace escaped the deprivations of the occupation by fleeing to Turkey. For those that remained, the fate of the various minority groups proved to be different: between the mountainous Pomaks and the lowland Turks, for example, and even more starkly between the collaborationist Armenians and the annihilated Jews. These experiences would leave their mark on the region. Yet, ultimately, the impact of the occupation would be more a matter of Western Thrace being shaken to its foundations rather than being prompted into widespread resistance or inter-communal strife.

4.2 The arrival of the Bulgarian administration

Following the successful completion of the German offensive against the Greek Army, the north-east region of Greece was carved-up by the Axis

Powers. Bulgaria controlled the area extending from Eastern Macedonia (the districts of Drama and Kavalla and almost all of Serres) to Western Thrace (the districts of Xanthi and Rhodope), the islands of Thasos and Samothrace, and about a third of the district of Evros [see Map 2]. Evros, on the eastern border with Turkey, was made an exception, however. Here, the Germans maintained under their control a strip of land, of about 2800 sq. km, stretching from the village of Antheia (east of Alexandroupoli) to the south up to the village of Dikaia to the north (immediately west of the Greek-Bulgarian-Turkish border) (Bravos 2001/2003: 147).

This is how the Turkish Ministry of Interior reported the arrival of the Axis forces to the Turkish Prime Minister:

> According to reports, a German force of 60 troops entered into Altunkaraağaç [Orestiada], after requests made by the population who feared the Bulgarians, and it was said that the Germans ordered the Bulgarians to deploy 30km away from the Turkish borders... According to the declaration of the German invasion forces of 3 May 1941 there will not be any Bulgarian troops in the villages from Filibe [Provdiv], near Sivilivgrat [Svilengrad], to Dedeagaç [Alexandroupolis], and that area will be controlled by the Germans.[1]

Didimoteicho was the administrative centre of this border-zone and the Germans appointed a 'puppet' Greek Prefect to administer non-military affairs.[2] The German presence served to control important railway junctions that connected Bulgaria, Greece and Turkey and to prevent the possibility of a Bulgarian-Turkish clash (Turkey had pressed for such a buffer zone).[3] The stationing of German troops so near the Turkish border was also intended, no doubt, to be a reminder to Turkey that alliance with the Axis was not necessarily such a bad idea.

As for the new Bulgarian-controlled areas, they were annexed by Bulgaria and became the Province of *Belomorie* (in Bulgarian; 'White Sea').[4] *Belomorie* was part of the 4th Administrative Region of the Bulgarian State (along with Stara Zagora and Plovdiv). Western Thrace was divided into the administrative centres of Dedeagach (Alexandroupolis), Gumuldjina (Komotini) and Ksanti (Xanthi), with the latter being the capital (Kotzageorgi 2002: 52).[5]

---

[1] BCA/77D80/301000/7348113, 'Ministry of Interior to the Prime Minister', 6 May 1941.

[2] WO/252/800, 'Greece, Zone Book, No. 8, Macedonia and Thrace, Part 1, People and Administration', 29 February 1944.

[3] WO/252/800, 'Greece, Zone Book, No. 8, Macedonia and Thrace, Part 1, People and Administration', 29 February 1944.

[4] Decision of Bulgarian Government of 3 May 1941.

[5] The other administrative centres of *Belomorie* in Eastern Macedonia were Kavalla, Drama, Serres, Sidirokastro, Zihni, Thassos, Eleftheroupoli and Chrysoupoli.

The Bulgarians lost no time: at a plenary session of the Bulgarian Parliament (*Sobranje*) in Sofia on 14 May 1941, the union of the new acquisitions with the rest of the nation was proclaimed, amidst scenes of great patriotic fervour (Daskalov 1992b: 104–105). Bulgaria had achieved its long standing national objective: access to the Aegean and the annexation of a region over which it harboured historical claims. *Belomorie* had been born.

The pre-war Greek administration was uprooted completely: a task that was facilitated by the fact that most of the civil servants had already abandoned the area in panic. The administration was soon entirely 'Bulgarised' as thousands of military staff, policemen, prefects, mayors, bankers, lawyers, doctors, tax officials, teachers and other civil servants arrived in the area to take control of local and regional authorities, public services, hospitals, banks and schools (Daskalov 1992b). The ousted Greek military authorities reported on the arrival of the new Bulgarian administration with predictable horror:

> The cities of Western Thrace, Komotini and Xanthi appear (in late October 1941), according to eye witnesses, to be a wilderness. The inhabitants avoid going out on the streets, while the few that dare to appear on their doorsteps look frightened. Everybody wishes to leave the area with their families, even if they have to abandon everything else behind. They only want to save their lives.[6]

In the months to come the new Bulgarian authorities would do nothing to dispel Greek prejudices. Indeed the intensity and extent of the Bulgarian brutality in Western Thrace would soon turn all sections of the local population (Orthodox Greek, Turkish, Pomak) against their new masters.

4.3   Accounts of Bulgarian repression

Bulgarian rule in the new *Belomorie* came to show some differentiation. The Orthodox Greeks were identified as the main barrier to the consolidation of the new regime owing to the large presence of the Greek element in the area since the 1920s and the dominance of the local Orthodox Church. At the same time, the Muslim population was the target of separate treatment. In particular, the authorities sought to 'Bulgarise' the Pomaks, asserting what they saw as their lapsed national identity. Across the different groups, however, the Bulgarians faced a near-total lack of support and, whenever possible, passive resistance. Not unrelated to this response, moreover, in the general pattern of life under the occupation, was an air of some lawlessness.

---

[6] Greek Defence Ministry report on 'The Greek Territories of Eastern Macedonia and Western Thrace under Bulgarian Occupation since 6 April 1941' in GES/DIS 1998: 259.

Though policies were determined in Sofia, on the ground implementation displayed much discretion.

The worst Bulgarian atrocity across the wider region involved a massacre in Drama (Eastern Macedonia) on 28–29 September 1941, costing the lives of some 2140 people (Paschalidis and Chatziannastasiou 2003: 315). News of this repression spread further afield, stoking fear. Whilst in Western Thrace there was no comparable incident, the authorities did maintain a reign of terror with threats of heavy retaliation should incidents occur. Bulgarian officials and settlers were often violent towards the local population and they were encouraged to do so by the army. The climate was to be one of fear and terror. Moreover, Brigadier Sirakov, Commander-in-Chief of the 2nd Bulgarian Army Corps, issued orders stressing that 'spying is a duty of all the Bulgarians living in the area of the Aegean'.[7]

The Muslim community in Western Thrace had a very early taste of what life might be like under the occupation. Immediately after the arrival of the Bulgarian army in Komotini, Bulgarian troops penetrated into the Muslim quarters of the city and looted many shops and houses. On 25 April 1941, they attacked those standing in their way and stole whatever valuables they could find. These attacks lasted for three days. By, then, on the third night, the Muslims adopted a new defensive tactic. They banged cutlery as loud as they could in order to warn their neighbours that Bulgarian soldiers were approaching. That night has survived in the memory of the Komotini Muslims as the *Teneke ile Alarm* (the Cutlery Alarm) (Batıbey 1976: 7–8).[8] One Komotini resident remembered that:

> People from the minority were climbing on the big fig trees to see and alert the rest of us when the Bulgarians would come towards our neigh-bourhoods. When they saw them, they banged the cutlery to scare them. People from the minority officially complained to the Germans who forbade the Bulgarians to approach the minority quarters.[9]

According to Batıbey (1976: 26–31), this tactic was adopted following the instructions of the Turkish Consul (on this see also Chapter 5). The latter, seeing that the raids during the night had not ceased, decided to send an aide to Sofia in order to inform the Turkish Embassy there. Batıbey claims that the intervention of the Turkish Ambassador with the Bulgarian gov-ernment brought these raids to an end after a week. The (Greek-Orthodox)

---

[7] CSA/177/3/2665, Commander-in-Chief of the 2nd Bulgarian Army Corps, No. 25/657, 'Orders related to the struggle against the guerrillas', Drama, 25 May 1944.

[8] Some interviewees also referred to this incident, whether they witnessed it or just heard about it. Interview 25; Interview 26; Interview 28.

[9] Interview 43.

Metropolitan of Maroneia and Thasos, Vassileios, also confirmed these events, recalling that:

On the 25 April between 10pm and 4am shots were continuously being fired in the Turkish quarter of the city. For the raids, the break-ins that occurred in shops, the shooting and other arbitrary acts we made many representations to the Bulgarian military Commander who always expressed his ignorance and that he would take all the necessary measures, although he never issued any such order.[10]

A post-war report on Bulgarian atrocities compiled by Greek university professors also referred to these events:

When the invaders entered Komotini the pillage of Turkish houses lasted for three whole days. The unfortunate Turks – to whom the violation of their house is an insult done to their religion – began to sound the alarm by means of beating on cans. Bulgarian officers wearing soldiers' uniforms took part in the pillage. The memory of these frightful events is still kept alive among the Turks of Komotini. They call them *Teneke bayram*. The Bulgarian Military Governor summoned the heads of the Moslem community before his presence and asked what all this noise meant; on hearing what had happened he displayed great indignation at this alleged vilification of the Bulgarian Army.[11]

The local Muslim community soon contrasted their plight under the German and the Bulgarian soldiers. The Germans were seen as more self-disciplined and more likely to make polite, friendly gestures. At the same time, more everyday contact was experienced with the Bulgarians, who ruled and policed Western Thrace. Two residents of Komotini recalled:

[The Germans] did not harm anyone from the local population. When they arrived in Komotini, they camped in an area near the Muslim neighbourhood and they took many of the supplies they needed from us, paying for everything they took [note: with 'occupation *Deutschmarks*' that carried very little value]. Moreover, when there was surplus food, it was distributed to the children. Germans from the Administration passed our area frequently. In fact in the German zone in Evros – we called it the 'free

---

[10] ELIA/47 (Thessaloniki), 'Report of the Metropolitan of Maroneia and Thasos for the conditions in the area since the Bulgarian occupation', 25 June 1941.

[11] A report of Professors of the Universities of Athens and Salonica, 1945: 46. A senior Muslim clergy in Komotini also recalled these events as *Teneke gecesi* ('The Nights of the Cutlery'). Interview 8.

zone' – there was no oppression and the conditions were much better in Alexandroupolis. When news came that the Bulgarians are coming, in 1941, many people tried to go to Turkey, but Turkey did not accept them and they remained, somehow like refugees, for four years in Feres that belonged to the German zone.[12]

During the early period of the Bulgarian occupation, my father did not even dare to go out for our basic shopping as he was afraid that the Bulgarians might take him to labour camps in Bulgaria. I was therefore told to do the shopping. In this early period when Bulgarian raids were a frequent phenomenon many families tried to move towards more central areas, where there was still some German presence that prevented any arbitrary actions on behalf of the Bulgarian troops.[13]

Similarly positive memories of the Germans were recalled by an interviewee from Komotini, who was a young child in 1941. 'The Germans were very friendly and the soldiers were giving chocolates to the kids'.[14] Another interviewee from Komotini remembered:

When the Germans came the people were very cautious. The young ones went out to see the German Army parading. I was out too and because I had blonde hair and looked like a German, the soldiers approached me and gave me money, chocolates and other goodies. I also remember well the special printing machines that the Germans brought with them in order to issue 'occupation *Deutschmarks*.[15]

This latter remark is indicative as several interviewees stressed that the Germans always paid for the produce or material they took. As a former resident of Mega Piston (Rhodope) commented:

The Germans took what they needed – milk, eggs, etc. – but they paid for these things. The Bulgarians exploited everyone who lived in the area, be they Greeks or Turks. They took sheep, the crops, all sorts of things – perhaps more than half of our produce. And they didn't pay a thing for it all.[16]

Whilst the memories of the German soldiers were positive, the contact with them was relatively limited. Moreover, there is no evidence that the Muslims saw the German invaders as 'liberators' or that they collaborated with them

---

[12] Interview 25.
[13] Interview 26.
[14] Interview 36.
[15] Interview 37.
[16] Interview 46.

in order to advance their position vis-à-vis other parts of the local society. One interviewee commented that 'the Germans seemed to sympathise with the Turks',[17] but a former resident of Komotini put matters in context:

> When I look back, I still think well of the German soldiers. But I can't recall anyone liking them more than we did the Greeks. That's not the point. We saw the Germans as more likely to protect us, that's all.[18]

In other words, German troops were seen as a restraint on the excesses of the Bulgarians. As noted in Chapter 3, the German High Command had larger strategic reasons not to provoke Turkey at this time and the local treatment of the Muslim community appeared consistent with this imperative.

The Bulgarians had neither the incentive nor the discipline to exercise similar restraint. Members of the Muslim community were punished by the Bulgarian gendarmes and ordinary settlers simply because they spoke Turkish in public or because they wore the fez or for no identifiable reason other than they were Muslim. Muslim women were attacked for wearing the veil. One former resident of Komotini recalled:

> One day I went with my grandma to a well to get water. A Bulgarian soldier approached her, took her scarf and was swearing at her. A German soldier happened to pass by on a horse and when he saw the incident he rushed towards our side, hit the Bulgarian and took care of my grandma. The Germans often offered us chocolates and other sweets. I liked the Germans. They protected us.[19]

Another interviewee from Xanthi remembered:

> Two Bulgarians had put sand and glass in rationed bread. The Germans condemned them to death. The whole community turned out to witness the killing.[20]

The brutality and ill-discipline of the Bulgarian occupation awoke deeply-engrained historical memories. One interviewee placed his own recollections in the context of the stories passed down to him from his grandfather:

> One of my grandfathers fought in the Balkan Wars and in Palestine during World War I. My grandfathers and grandmothers saw very bad

---

[17] Interview 36.
[18] Interview 45.
[19] Interview 45.
[20] Interview 35.

things caused by the Bulgarians at that time. My grandfather had told me that the Turks had two enemies: the Bulgarians and the Arabs. He also told me that they did not face any problems with the advancing Greek soldiers at the time. On the other hand the Bulgarians were insulting them on many occasions like when checking their papers at road blocks etc. The Turkish community has a reason to hate the Bulgarians on a racial base for what happened in 1913. Those memories were revived in 1941.[21]

Others recalled a similarly brutal treatment against both Muslims and Orthodox Greeks:

Both the Greeks and ourselves feared the Bulgarian soldiers attacking us. When we Turks went to the wheat fields and to the tobacco fields, our parents said we had to go together in groups for safety. I remember a Greek girl having been attacked and raped by a Bulgarian soldier.[22]

Owning to a lack of discipline in the Bulgarian army and the presence of many nationalist paramilitaries in the area, Bulgarian rule was often arbitrary. The local gendarmes and police, tax collectors, municipal officers, as well as ordinary Bulgarian citizens regularly took upon themselves to resolve personal grievances against both Orthodox Greeks and Muslims. Many of these crimes went without punishment. The sense of subjugation was overwhelming: as one interviewee recalled: 'The Bulgarians were barbarians: just too scary'.[23] With the repression of the occupation also came torture. Many Muslims were tortured in order to force confessions or extract information. After the war, Greek security services recorded the testament of an Orthodox Greek who was imprisoned in Alexandroupolis:

During the five days that I remained imprisoned, I witnessed all the cruelties committed against young Greeks and Turks, whose screams and cries every night broke the hearts of us all.[24]

A particular measure that led to widespread violence against both the Muslim and the Christian population was the new Bulgarian law on nationality. The law was introduced in April 1942 and, provided that all Greek nationals of non-Bulgarian origin residing in *Belomorie* had to accept Bulgarian citizenship by submitting a personal declaration to the authorities before

---

[21] Interview 47.

[22] Interview 50.

[23] Interview 43.

[24] AYE/1944/6.1 Request of Komotini resident, industrialist P.N. Exarchos to the Administration-General of Thrace, Thessaloniki 25 August 1941.

1 April 1943. The authorities attributed much importance to the implementation of this measure (which was instrumental to the 'Bulgarisation' of the area) and used all means at their disposal to convince the local population to apply for Bulgarian nationality. According to Greek refugees who fled Macedonia and Western Thrace, a series of privileges were offered to those who would accept such as extra food supplies, the right to remain in their houses and their exemption from the locally imposed curfew.[25] For those who refused, the authorities introduced a number of penalties, the most important of which was the stripping of their professional licences (on this see below).[26]

When the Bulgarians realised that this measure was not delivering the expected results (for example, only 1604 Orthodox Greeks requested Bulgarian citizenship in the region of Komotini),[27] they pressed on with more heavy handed practices. The Pomaks, in particular, became targets of such violence. Given the fact that the Pomak community spoke a Bulgarian dialect, the authorities considered them as potentially more receptive (than either the Greeks or the Turks) to their assimilation policy. Although there have been no reports of forceful conversions to Christianity (a practise that was widespread during the period 1912–1919), Foteas maintains that the Bulgarian authorities demanded from Imams in Pomak villages to sign declarations that 'their ancestors were Bulgarian by race who had been forcefully proselytised to Islam by the Ottoman conquerors' (1978: 10–11). Those who failed to do so, such as the Imam of the village of Oraion, faced punishment and torture. According to Foteas, the authorities also obliged all Pomak parents to register their babies with a Bulgarian name within eight days of their birth.

Yet the Pomaks remained attached to the religious self-identification, reluctant to subscribe to a nationally-inspired collective identity. This cautious reaction enraged the Bulgarian administration. According to a post-war report by Greek university professors:

> In order [for the Bulgarians] to frighten them [the Pomaks] into accepting Bulgarian citizenship, they hanged head down the Pomak Imam Hassan, who had refused Bulgarian citizenship. He was left in that position all

---

[25] See reports of refugees given to the Gendarmerie authorities in Athens and Thessaloniki, in AYE/1944/4.4. Indicatively see 'Report on witness examination', 7 August 1942.

[26] AYE/1944/4.1, Inspectorate-General of the Prefectures, Region of the Administration-General of Macedonia, to the Administration-General of Macedonia, Interior Department, Thessaloniki, 8 March 1944.

[27] AYE/1947/111.1, Commander of Rhodope Gendarmerie, 'Report on active propaganda and Public safety in the district of the Rhodope Gendarmerie Command', 13 September 1947.

through the night. On the following day his tormentors exhibited him to the villagers threatening that they would be dealt with in the same manner unless they changed their names and became Bulgarians. On the same day they killed another villager allegedly for the theft of sheep in Bulgarian territory. After these incidents, the inhabitants seized by terror hastened to hand their applications for the acquisition of Bulgarian citizenship. In the same way, other Pomaks, the inhabitants of Medousa in Thermae, were forced to apply for Bulgarian citizenship.[28]

Eventually, the Bulgarian tactics bore fruit: there was a considerable increase in the number of Pomaks who opted for Bulgarian citizenship, some of whom assisted or collaborated with the occupation authorities (Kotzageorgi 2002: 63).[29] According to oral testimonies from the area, some people changed their names to Bulgarian ones on their own will in order to obtain privileges and access to much-needed food supplies.[30]

The Bulgarian administration also sought to conscript the local population into their military effort. A compulsory drafting of *Belomorie*'s men into the Bulgarian Army began in April 1942, when there was a call to duty for all men born between 1920 and 1921. These men constituted the cohort of 1941 that would have otherwise been due to complete national service in the Greek Army that year. Later, in 1943, the Bulgarian administration decided to draft older cohorts that had served in the Greek Army in 1940–1941. Many resisted joining the Bulgarian Army. Some Christians tried to escape to the German-controlled areas, or they joined the resistance, whilst a number of Muslims fled to Turkey. Those who did accept conscription found that the allocation of duties within the Bulgarian Army brought with it a number of points of distinction.

From the few existing written and oral sources, it appears that the Christians were all included in the Labour Battalions of the Bulgarian Army, the so-called *trourdouvakia*.[31] The Labour Battalions were organised along military lines (companies, battalions, regiments), but their soldiers carried no armour. Living conditions in the battalions were extremely harsh. The conscripts worked for more than ten hours per day from spring to autumn in quarries or in public works for the construction of road and railway networks in Bulgaria or the recently acquired territories of Yugoslavia and Greece.[32] The daily food rations were very poor: 400 grams of maize or corn bread and boiled beans. Daily life was marked by frequent arbitrary beatings and

---

[28] A report of Professors of the Universities of Athens and Salonica: 1945: 70.

[29] Interview 27.

[30] Interview 18.

[31] The word comes from the Bulgarian word *truda*, meaning 'labour'. It also appears as *Dourdouvakia*. Interview 14; Interview 29.

[32] Interview 29.

accidents of fallen rocks and explosions (Stolingas 2006: 162–166; Exarchou 2002). According to an Orthodox Greek veteran, the conscripts of 1942 were taken to Kumanovo (Bulgaria) and those of 1943 to Petrich (Bulgaria) while those of 1944 were sent to infrastructure projects built by the Bulgarian Army in Nymphaia, north of Komotini.[33]

A number of Pomaks were enlisted in the Labour Battalions, whilst others served in the fighting units within the Bulgarian Army, usually inside Bulgaria. The conscription of Turks from Western Thrace into the Bulgarian forces, by comparison, was far more limited. Oral testimonies suggest that only very few Turks served in the Labour Battalions whereas there is no evidence of any Western Thracian Turk having served in a fighting Bulgarian army unit.[34] In 1946, those who served in the Labour Battalions from Xanthi, created an association for the moral reinstatement and financial compensation of all those who enlisted. A total of 2185 persons submitted applications for their official recognition as war prisoners. Almost all such applications were approved by the Greek state which also provided a very small compensation fund (drawn from post war Bulgarian reparations to Greece). Of those eligible for compensation 1434 were Orthodox Greeks, 702 Muslims (both Turks and Pomaks), six Armenians and one Jewish (Exarchou 2002: 116).

During their time of supremacy in Western Thrace, the Bulgarians were able to exert almost total control, but commanded little local support. The extremely harsh occupation regime played to far-right nationalist fervour at home, but it was too crude and insensitive to win local hearts and minds. Within an overall atmosphere of repression, the Muslim community received variegated attention. The Pomaks were subject to special 'Bulgarisation' measures, but they showed very little support and responded to them only when forced. The Turks of Western Thrace were relatively less affected, but still subjected to punitive measures and random attacks. Whilst all ethnic groups suffered hunger and deprivation; none collaborated to any significant extent (with the exception of the Armenian community, see below). In the short run, a regime of fear might have stifled large scale local resistance. In the long run, however, the Bulgarian presence was de-legitimised by its own brutality and the long memory of the local communities who seemed reluctant to lend their support for the consolidation of Bulgaria's power in *Belomorie*.

4.4   The economic impact of the Bulgarian occupation

Economically, the newly-occupied areas offered many gains to the Bulgarians and they sought to take advantage of them as rapidly as possible.

---

[33] Interview 29. The accuracy of this information has not been confirmed.
[34] Interview 8; Interview 13; Interview 18.

The strategic ports of Alexandroupolis and Kavalla secured the long-sought outlet to the Aegean Sea, thus strengthening significantly Bulgaria's economic and commercial position in the region. The area also possessed rich tobacco production and gave Bulgaria a near-monopoly in the Balkans.[35] More generally, the new areas offered rich agricultural resources, since they comprised large and fertile plains.

At the same time, the economic effects of the occupation were to reduce the local population – whether Christian or Muslim – to utter poverty, dependent on the vicissitudes of Bulgarian rule. Harsh economic measures prevailed. The Greek currency, the *Drachma*, was abolished and substituted by the Bulgarian *Leva*. However, in this exchange, the banks returned only 60 per cent of the monetary value to the rightful owners, while the remainder was returned in Bulgarian bonds (which could not be cashed for a number of years). All bank deposits and liabilities were assumed by the Bulgarian state. The occupation authorities also confiscated factories, housing, land, agricultural machinery, cattle, vehicles, household effects and personal objects, many of which were distributed to the new Bulgarian settlers. Transactions of both movable and immovable property between the local population were banned, except in cases that the buyer was a Bulgarian citizen. Moreover, the Bulgarian authorities imposed heavy taxes, the value of which changed constantly. Non-Bulgarians were banned from serving in a number of professions, such as doctors and lawyers, with many Orthodox Greeks and Muslims deprived of their professional licences. Similarly, the local population was banned from employment in the public services and construction projects. Most businesses, particularly the more profitable ones, had to accept a Bulgarian partner, who, in many cases, managed to eventually acquire control of the business.[36]

According to Kotzageorgi and Kazamias (2002: 107–128) half of the cultivated land and one quarter of free land – along with machinery, cattle, and cattle feed – were given to the Bulgarian settlers. Local farmers who had their land expropriated by the Bulgarian administration were forced to remain *in situ* as agricultural workers. Tobacco crops were purchased at extremely low prices by Bulgarian firms and cooperatives. Producers were allowed to keep only small proportions of their produce: for example, olive oil producers could retain ten kilos of olive oil and 20 kilos of olives with five more kilos of olive oil for every additional member of their family. Local Bulgarian administrators kept a vigilant eye on the processes of sowing,

---

[35] In the pre-war period, Western Thrace provided some 50 per cent of the total tobacco production of Greece. During the occupation period *Belomorie* provided one third of the Bulgaria's tobacco production.

[36] AYE/1944/1.1, Xanthi Prefecture, to the Administration-General of Thrace, 'Damages inflicted on Greece during the Occupation', 21 July 1945.

cultivation and harvesting of all the agricultural production. Bulgarian soldiers were charged with the protection of the production on the farms until the final products were safely stored in Bulgarian facilities.[37] Bread was also prepared in the army-guarded mills and was subsequently distributed to the local population through vouchers.[38]

Looting was a common occurrence, usually under the pretext of searches for weapons. Bulgarian gendarmes and soldiers raided Muslim houses, stealing food and other objects they found of use, despite the depleted provisions. Such pillage did not go unnoticed by the Bulgarian Ministry of Interior which warned local officials and governors in August 1944:

> Certain members of staff have confiscated on some occasions personal property belonging to the foreign population and particularly to Bulgarian Muslims. Such incidents are being used as propaganda by the Greek guerrillas.[39]

In the concluding part of this communication, the relevant local authorities were urged to 'assume all necessary measures' to remedy the situation, but, it seems, they did so with little success.

The Bulgarians took the greater share of the local produce and livestock. A number of interviewees confirmed this: estimates of the proportion taken ranged between 60 and 70 per cent.[40] A Muslim interviewee from the village of Mega Piston (Rhodope) recalled:

> During the Bulgarian occupation there was repression for all the population, the country was exploited, the Bulgarians took all the animals, flour, 60% of all agricultural production and did not pay for anything. My father hid and "stole" part of our production, which was supposed to be taken by the Bulgarians. If we were caught hiding our crops we were beaten and paid heavy fines. We were very hungry as we had no flour and bread. At least we had some supplies, however poor, unlike in the cities.[41]

---

[37] ELIA/47 (Thessaloniki), 'Archive of Bulgarian Occupation in Macedonia and Thrace'. Ministry of Public Security, Aliens' Directorate, to the Premier's office, 'Memorandum of a Greek refugee from Bulgarian-occupied Thrace 26 August 1942.

[38] According to a Greek resistance veteran, the mills in the mountainous areas were still operated by the local Pomaks. By contrast in the Turkish-populated lowlands, bread making facilities were taken over by the Bulgarians. Interview 14.

[39] CSA/662/1/9, Interior Ministry, Administration of Belomorie, to the local commanders and mayors of Belomorie, No. 7826, 10 August 1944.

[40] Interview 29. Two Muslim residents of Komotini also agreed that the Bulgarians collected three-quarters of all production. Interview 25 and Interview 26.

[41] Interview 46.

Several interviewees told stories of Bulgarian soldiers coming and lifting up the floors to check for hidden food and wheat. One such vivid account follows:

> Our farm was occupied by the Bulgarians. We produced vegetables and the Bulgarians sent them to Bulgaria. They came and took anything they liked whenever they liked it. They put their guns on the people's heads and with their bayonets they cut the food bags. My father was whipped because he reacted and the soldiers started swearing at my mother, because she took a kitchen knife and threatened them. We had 200 sheep and other animals (horses, cows) which were taken by the Bulgarians. One day twelve soldiers came and the one in charge said: "bring out every sack of food or I will lock you up". Years later my father managed to get back the cows under the armistice terms, but not the horses. The Bulgarians inspected the wheat harvesting in order to collect the production. My father was offering spirits to the soldiers, getting them drunk so that he could hide a bit of our production. Our farm was quite known to the Bulgarians and they often "preferred" to visit it. We had a mill controlled by the Bulgarians, where my father used the same tactic with the drinks. The Bulgarians even took the foodstuff that was used to feed the animals.[42]

Despite official Bulgarian statements to the contrary, both the local Greek Orthodox and Muslim populations were desperate for food. In response to questions raised by the Germans about the economic measures applied by the Bulgarians, the latter replied:

> The existence of certain economic problems is a feature that appears in all the countries as a result of the war and the new economic and social order in Europe.[43]

According to Greek diplomats in Ankara, Bogdan Filov, the Bulgarian Prime Minister, during his tour of Western Thrace felt obliged to reassure the local population:

> There will be no discrimination in the provision and distribution of food supplies among the population.[44]

---

[42] Interview 38.

[43] CSA/662/1/51, Administration-General of Belomorie, to the Interior Minister, Xanthi, August 1942.

[44] AYE/1944/22.2 Greek Embassy, Ankara, to the Greek Foreign Ministry, 8 July 1943.

Despite Bulgarian reassurances, however, the economic situation in Western Thrace was desperate. One of the oldest interviewees from Komotini spoke for many when he said: 'my chief memory of the Bulgarian occupation can be simply put: hunger'.[45]

The food allocation system differentiated between the various local populations. According to a post-war report written by Greek academics:

> Ration-cards were of a different colour for the Bulgarians and the Greeks and Muslims; the cards for the latter two bore the word *Inoriti* (alien nationals). Greeks and Muslims were forbidden to buy food on the free market. Even for the sick, milk and meat could not be obtained. Bulgarian storekeepers were obliged to post up on their doors the notice *Samo za Balgarote* (only for Bulgarians). Those who did not comply with this order and sold food to Greeks and Muslims were punished.[46]

Non-Bulgarians could only obtain bread through bread coupons. According to an association formed by Macedonian and Thracian refugees, the daily ration for Bulgarians was 300 grams of wheat bread, whilst Orthodox Greeks and Muslims had to accept 200 grams of bad quality maize and corn bread, often mixed with other ingredients.[47] Moreover, non-Bulgarians were not allowed to buy a series of basic supplies like fish, petrol and soap.[48] Under these circumstances black-marketing was rife. If the Bulgarian authorities found supplies in Greek Orthodox or Muslim households that exceeded rationing quotas the owners were punished with heavy fines, imprisonment and heavy beatings. Bulgarian police and the army made successive raids on Greek Orthodox and Muslim houses looking for 'illegally' acquired supplies, which provided an additional pretext for looting these households.[49]

Although economic deprivation and malnutrition were widespread among the Muslim community, it appears that the Pomaks suffered more from the economic policies of the Bulgarian authorities. According to one interviewee from the village of Kechros (Rhodope):

> The first two months of the Bulgarian occupation in the mountainous areas, were quite smooth, they were an "adaptation period", but after this initial period the Bulgarian authorities started looking for food supplies

---

[45] Interview 43.

[46] A report of Professors of the Universities of Athens and Salonica (1945: 38).

[47] AYE/1944/1.3 Committee of Macedonians and Thracians to the Representative of the 3rd Reich in Greece, May 1943.

[48] AYE 1944/1/3 Committee of Macedonians and Thracians to the Representative of the 3rd Reich in Greece, May 1943. (Day unknown)

[49] ELIA/47 (Thessaloniki), 'Report of the Metropolitan of Maroneia and Thasos for the conditions in the area since the Bulgarian occupation', 25 June 1941.

and livestock. The people used hand-mills secretly and if they were found with wheat they were sent to prison in Komotini for six months, where they were being beaten and tortured.[50]

The misfortune of the Pomaks might well have been related to geography. Given the seclusion and isolation of their communities, it was even harder to reach them with essential supplies. The occupation had also disturbed their trading networks, leading to further poverty. The braver of the Pomak farmers defied the restrictions and entered into Bulgaria proper in order to purchase or beg for some food supplies – mainly beans and corn – from neighbouring Bulgarian Pomaks to smuggle back to their villages.[51] There are credible oral testimonies that many Pomaks died of hunger in Echinos and other villages in the Rhodope Mountains, particularly during the winter of 1941–42, when the local crop was extremely poor due to the severe frost and heavy rain.[52]

By comparison to the Pomaks, the condition of the Turks of Komotini and the villages in the lowlands was better. This was probably due to the fact that the exercise of Bulgarian control in the larger villages of the lowlands and the urban centres of the Western Thrace was naturally more difficult. Exchanges 'in kind' or smuggling of agricultural products under the nose of the Bulgarians were easier in the larger (and more fertile) fields of the lowlands. In addition many Turks had in their possession Turkish *Lira*, a much stronger currency than the *Leva*. This provided the Turks with greater spending power and some additional defence against the very high inflation experienced in the area during the war. In late 1941, for example, the exchange rate of the *Lira* against the *Leva* was 1:3. By 1943 the rate had fallen to 1:8000 and in 1944 it stood at 1:14,000.[53] The financial position of the lowland Turks (particularly in Komotini) often provided the pretext for Greek nationalists to imply a 'privileged' treatment of the Turks by the Bulgarian authorities.[54] This, however, was far from the truth. The Metropolitan of Maroneia and Thassos, Vassileios, for example, confirmed

---

[50] Interview 30. Another interviewee claimed to have heard that in the lowlands, there were road blocks of the Bulgarian Army when people returned from the fields in order to prevent them from hiding wheat that could be used to prepare flour. One of these road blocks was staffed by a local Pomak who was very strict and violent. Interview 27.

[51] Interview 17, Interview 18.

[52] Interview 4, Interview 12, Interview 13, Interview 18.

[53] A report of Professors of the Universities of Athens and Salonica 1945: 35.

[54] GAK Kavalla, 'Archive of Foreign and Minority Schools', F.95B, Ministry of Interior, Aliens' Directorate-General, II Office, D. Vlastaris, 'Report of the Muslims living in Greece', July 1952.

that the 'Turkish element' had suffered equally as the Orthodox Greeks from Bulgarian measures.[55]

A post war report on the experiences of the Bulgarian occupation compiled by Greek University professors offered an even more sombre account:

> The Turks were denied the right to work and suffered from hunger. Mortality among the Turks rose from two to three weekly deaths to forty deaths a day. The imams had hardly the time to bury the dead. In one of the four Turkish districts of Xanthi only 150 out of 400 Turkish families survive to-day. A true picture of the extent of starvation will be conveyed by the fact that the Moslems were reduced to eating tortoises although this is forbidden by their religion.[56]

The pattern of economic suffering in Western Thrace during the occupation reveals both ethnic/national and geographical cleavages. The Bulgarian strategy of linking legitimate economic activity to the (Bulgarian) Citizenship Law brought immediate hardship to all those who chose not to comply. Those most hurt by such practices were the middle class communities (such as professionals and shop keepers) in the towns and the large villages in the lowlands. Amongst them Greeks and Turks suffered the most. For the Greeks, in particular (the pre-war economic elite), the impact was immense adding more destitution to those who had already lost their jobs in the public administration following the arrival of Bulgarian settlers. A similar fate also awaited the few middle class Turks of Komotini and Xanthi, whose access to Turkish *Lira* had, in some few cases, provided a lifeline. The Turkish farmers in the lowlands suffered badly from the punitive taxation and rationing practices of the Bulgarian administration, but their access to food was somewhat facilitated by the weakness of the Bulgarian forces to police effectively their economic activity. The Pomaks in the Rhodope Mountains had no such luck. Their centuries-long practices of subsistence agriculture and local market-based exchanges were severely affected by the occupation. Having infrequent access to the markets of the lowlands and enduring much tighter forms of Bulgarian control, the Pomak mountain villages were doomed. Ironically, the only community in Western Thrace able to speak the same language as the newly arrived Bulgarian masters was left to suffer the most. As so often in the decades preceding the war, there was little affection and much acrimony between the Bulgarians and the Pomaks.

---

[55] ELIA/47 (Thessaloniki), 'Report of the Metropolitan of Maroneia and Thasos for the conditions in the area since the Bulgarian occupation', 25 June 1941.

[56] A report of Professors of the Universities of Athens and Salonica 1945: 46–47.

4.5   Wartime population movements

An enduring unwritten law of Balkan nationalism asserts that the numerical superiority of an ethnic group in a region constitutes the basis for a solid claim of sovereignty over that area. Throughout the 1910s and 1920s, Greece and Turkey had each forced respective minority populations in the wider Thrace region out of areas they had controlled. Loyal to this doctrine, the Bulgarians now tried to alter the population composition in *Belomorie*, creating a demographic superiority over the local population by virtue of immigrants from Bulgaria proper. They met with some success.

The Bulgarian authorities sought large-scale expulsions of Orthodox Greeks from the area with a parallel influx of Western Thracian Bulgarian émigrés (who had left the area in the 1920s) as well as (Bulgarian) settlers from south-west Macedonia, Romania and Russia.[57] Such a dramatic change would provide the Bulgarians with a very strong argument that would help to guarantee the permanent inclusion of the area in Bulgaria after the end of the war. A Bulgarian report of 1941 on the 'strengthening of Bulgarisation and the Bulgarian administration in the Aegean', prepared by a Committee that included officials of the Foreign Ministry, the Academic Geographical Institute and the Thracian Research Institute, noted that this area:

> ...is the most important newly-liberated Bulgarian region. But as the majority of the Bulgarian population was [previously] expelled, it is now ethnically weak. Our rule will only be strengthened if Bulgarians become more than 50% of the overall population...We must first displace at least half of the Greek population, especially the refugees...Soon at least 100,000 Greeks must be expelled and the land that they will leave behind must be handed over to Bulgarian emigrants...The number of the Bulgarian settlers that will arrive in the area must be analogous to the number of Greeks and Turks that will leave the area.[58]

The Bulgarians sought to lure four particular social groups from Bulgaria: civil servants, professionals, businessmen and the landless poor. All four groups were offered several types of inducement and economic benefits to settle in *Belomorie*. The strategy delivered its objectives: by mid-1943 a total of 92,523 Bulgarians had settled in Western Thrace (Kotzageorgi 2002: 189). The arrival of Bulgarians in the area was followed by the expulsion (and in some few cases voluntary departure) of the local population. The US Office of Strategic Studies (OSS) referred to the Bulgarian policies

---

[57] CSA/284/3/62, 'Report on the strengthening of Bulgarisation and the Bulgarian administration in the Aegean', 29 April 1941.
[58] CSA/284/3/62, 'Report on the strengthening of Bulgarisation and the Bulgarian administration in the Aegean', 29 April 1941.

as 'colonisation under the guise of repatriation'.[59] Of the tens of thousands who left the area (Kotzageorgi 2002: 191), a significant portion were members of the Muslim community who chose to seek better fortune in Turkey, rather than follow those (i.e. the Greek Orthodox majority) who fled to other parts of Greece.

For the Muslims of Western Thrace (particularly the Turks in the lowlands), Turkey was the 'motherland' (*anavatan*). Turkey's neutrality and the many Thracian Muslims who had emigrated to Turkey during the inter-war period, had created a sense of familiarity and security which provided a way out of the misery of wartime Western Thrace. The estimates of the number of Muslims who emigrated to Turkey at that time vary. Öksüz (2003: 272) and Papadimitriou (2003: 149) put that number at 10–12,500, a figure close to that offered by the Greek government (10–15,000) at the time.[60] The estimate of the Bulgarian administration of the period referred to 12,500 'Turks' having left the area (Daskalov 1992a: 33). Archival material from the Greek Ministry of Foreign Affairs suggests that the Turkish government at the time put the number of Muslims emigrating to Turkey at 30,000.[61] Whatever the exact figure of this emigration wave, the truth remains that it was significant – at least one Western Thracian Muslim out of ten left the area. There are reports that during the very first days of the arrival of the Bulgarians in the area and even before, more than 2000 Muslims fled to Turkey (Kotzageorgi 2002: 154–155, Batıbey 1976: 34–40).

The continuous influx of the Muslims from Western Thrace caused great concern to the Turkish government, since a basic pillar of its policy towards the minority was the preservation of its presence in Western Thrace. Thus, the Turkish government decided to ban the entry of more refugees in to the country. Indeed, according to Kotzageorgi (2002: 154–155) the Turkish government negotiated with the Bulgarian authorities for the return of the first 2000 refugees. The latter, however, remained in the German zone in Evros, as the Bulgarians posed further restrictions on their passage. Most of the refugees were gathered in Alexandroupolis, and Feres while waiting for the permission of the Turkish authorities to enter Turkey or the permission of the Bulgarian authorities to return home. Bulgarian authorities at the time suggested that 63 of those immigrants were soldiers of the Greek Army who had deserted when the war begun. Eventually they were allowed to return

---

[59] NARA/M1221/1174, Office of Strategic Studies, Research and Analysis Branch, 'Population Movements in Greece'. Undated (but containing information for the period up to July 1943).

[60] AYE/1944/21.6 Foreign Ministry, Directorate of Political Affairs, 'Emigration of the population from the Bulgarian-occupied Macedonia and Thrace', 30 November 1944.

[61] AYE/1944/21.6 Foreign Ministry, Directorate of Political Affairs, 'Emigration of the population from the Bulgarian-occupied Macedonia and Thrace', 30 November 1944.

to their homes.[62] The Governor-General of Belomorie accused the Turkish Consulate in Komotini of encouraging this emigration.[63] There is also a Greek military source confirming that:

> ... in contrast to the Greeks, the Turks were not forced to depart, but it is one and a half months now that with the encouragement of the Turkish Consulate, they leave in haste to Turkey, abandoning all their properties behind.[64]

The Bulgarian and Greek allegations over the role of the Consulate (in encouraging emigration) seem, on the face of it, rather misplaced. In April 1945 the Turkish Foreign Ministry in its instructions to the Turkish Embassy in Athens was rather forthcoming with regards to the policy on Muslim emigration from Western Thrace:

> At every opportunity we instructed our Consulate in Gumuljina to make the necessary suggestions to the effect that the best course they could take to help our country would be to remain where they were... It is in accordance with the high interests of our country that our racial brothers should be left where they are.[65]

The Turkish Embassy in Sofia too protested to the Bulgarian authorities that members of the Muslim community were forced to leave Western Thrace and it announced that Turkey would stop accepting them. Still, a number of Muslim immigrants managed to cross the Turkish border in secret. Those who did not were eventually returned to their homes (in Western Thrace) following the intervention of the Bulgarian government which instructed the *Belomorie* authorities to consent 'for political reasons' to the Turkish demands.[66]

Diplomatic manoeuvring aside, oral testimonies from Muslim refugees paint a dire picture of escape:

> We heard that the Bulgarians wanted to kill my father due to his relations with the Greeks, therefore we left immediately and went to Xanthi, taking

---

[62] CSA/264/1/185, No. 2200, Secretary-General of the Administration-General of Belomorie, Angelov to the Secretary-General of the Foreign Ministry, 1 October 1941.

[63] CSA/264/1/185, Secretary-General of the Administration-General of Belomorie, Aggelov to the Secretary-General of the Foreign Ministry No. 1728, 9 September 1941.

[64] ELIA/47 (Thessaloniki), 'Bulgarian Occupation in Macedonia and Thrace', Note by Captain A. Sirbopoulos, 13 January 1942.

[65] HW/12/315 Turkish Foreign Ministry to Turkish Ambassador in Athens, 'Regarding emigration from Western Thrace', 28 April 1945.

[66] For more on this see CSA files 264/1/497; 264/1/185.

only our clothes. The Bulgarians were already in Xanthi. We stayed there for ten days hiding. We tried to prepare our immigration documents and we left for Komotini at night on the back of a truck. We stayed there for one night and the following night we went to Alexandroupolis and then to Feres with a cart. In Feres it was the German zone, it was like a border. Hundreds and thousands from the minority were there trying to go to Turkey. The Turks did not open the borders to the first immigrants. My family was caught there with no food or water. We suffered for days. My father got in contact with Fuat Balkan [Ali Fuat Cebesoy] – an MP in Turkey – who was his friend asking if he could intervene with the authorities in order to let us in Turkey. Balkan managed to get us permission. There was only a small boat for everybody to cross the river and we suffered from the mosquitoes. In Uzunköprü we found some time to wash our clothes. We then went to Ipsala and a day later to Keşan. We then moved to Malkara, Tekirdağ, took a ferry to Erdek, and went to Bandirma. From there we took a train. Forty coaches packed with immigrants. In every station they left a coach there. My family went to Tire. We stayed in a motel for two months. We were not settled there. My father preferred to move to Istanbul and settle there because he knew the place well. The Turkish people were hospitable towards the immigrants but the authorities did not provide employment and I started working from an early age.[67]

Another refugee from Komotini remembered:

We left in 1941 at the time of the German invasion. We decided to leave because there was no Greek state any more, the civil services had left in one night. The prisons were opened and the people were raiding and looting the public buildings. My family obtained documents that we were going for harvesting to Evros and we crossed the borders. At the time you needed special documents in order to approach the borders. We then crossed illegally. We went to the borders with a convoy of horsecarts (around ten). There were many people at the borders and there was only one small boat. A Turkish soldier was in charge of this boat.[68]

Other refugee stories recalled forceful expulsions by the Bulgarian authorities:

The educated from Xanthi and Komotini were exiled twice by the Bulgarians. My father was exiled in 1941 to Gabrovo for a year. In 1943 he was exiled again for 6 months. He was 43 years old and when he

---

[67] Interview 34.
[68] Interview 37.

Table 4.1   Population Statistics for Western Thrace, March 1942

District	Total	Greeks	Bulgarians	Turks	Others	Departure of Greek families	Settlement of Bulgarian families
Xanthi	86,843	33,620	24,426	27,358	1489	2,300	655
Komotini	101,825	39,699	16.010	42,528	3588	571	545
Alexandroupolis	20,452	15,273	2890	1355	934	1053	752
Western Thrace	216,920	96,092	43,526	71,301	6001	3956	1992

Source: Kotzageorgi, quoting Jaranov (2002: 190).

returned his hair had turned grey. They were digging roads, they had nowhere to wash; people got injured and died. Rations were set at 100 grams of maize. Bulgarian Mohammedans [i.e. the term used by the Bulgarian authorities to identify Pomaks in Bulgaria] on the other hand were given white bread. Some people from the minority signed declarations becoming Bulgarian Mohammedan.[69]

The exact impact of the Bulgarian occupation on the population mix of Western Thrace remains a matter of uncertainty. Statistics prepared by the Bulgarian authorities in 1942 provided data on the area (see Table 4.1).

The picture presented in the Bulgarian statistics, however, makes for a difficult comparison with the pre-1941 situation. For a start the total population (216,920) of Western Thrace in Bulgarian statistics appears to contain nearly 140,000 fewer people than the last Greek census of 1940 where the total population appeared as 355,940 (see Chapter 2). Only part of this discrepancy may be explained by the number of Orthodox Greeks that fled the area on the eve of the Bulgarian occupation. It is not unreasonable to assume that both the numbers of 'Greeks' and 'Turks' in the Bulgarian statistics fell 'victims' of the Bulgarian agenda of colonising Western Thrace and the imperatives to show that this strategy was actually working. It is also significant that the number of 'Bulgarians' listed in the census included all Pomaks from the Rhodope Mountains who, according to the 1920 Allied census (the last one to make specific reference to 'Pomaks'), numbered nearly 12,000 (see Chapter 2). The origin of the remaining 30,000 'Bulgarians' appearing in the 1942 census might have been diverse. A large majority of them would have been returning Bulgarian refugees who were evicted from the area in the aftermath of the Greco-Bulgarian population exchange in the 1920s, whilst a good number of administrators from Bulgaria proper would have arrived in

---

[69] Interview 36.

the area to staff the new authorities of *Belomorie*. The number of Western Thracians (particularly Greeks) who agreed to register as 'Bulgarian' in order to benefit from the new regime is more difficult to estimate, albeit not completely insignificant.

Of more direct relevance here is the number of registered 'Turks' in the Bulgarian statistics. If the Bulgarian-provided number of 71,300 is taken at face value, then the number of 'Muslims' (that is the combined number of Pomaks and Turks) between the Greek census of 1940 and the Bulgarian census of 1942 had decreased by nearly 26,000 (see Chapter 2).[70] This number is closer to the 30,000 estimate of the Turkish government. If the Bulgarian statistics are assumed to be under-representing the number of 'Turks' in 1942 (for the purpose of boosting the proportion of Bulgarians in the area), then the size of wartime Muslim migration to Turkey comes closer to the estimates of Oksüz (2003) and Papadimitriou (2003) who put it at 10,000–12,500. This figure is also consistent with the view of the Bulgarian (and, later, the Greek) authorities at the time. As is so often the case with Balkan historiography, research into the fate of minority populations confronts issues of definition and the accuracy of data.

4.6   Education and religion as vehicles of Bulgarian nationalism

The alternative to compulsory population movements has been, in the Balkans, to assert control via forced assimilation in education and cultural policies. The agents of 'new' nationalisms have long considered them as the most efficient means of constructing – or deconstructing – national identity. The perception of education as a national instrument and not just a social commodity has repeatedly transformed it into a means of manipulation and coercion, especially with respect to the position of minority populations.

The educational policy of the Bulgarians during the occupation constitutes another example of the connection between education and nationalist expediency. The Bulgarians sought to 'Bulgarise' the populations within their occupation zone and promote Bulgarian national ideals. In doing so, they made notable distinctions between the Orthodox Greeks, the Turks and the Pomaks. In May 1941, the Bulgarian Ministry of Education organised *Belomorie* as a single educational region and established a Regional Inspectoral Council, based in Xanthi, which was responsible for the regulation and management of all educational matters in the new areas (Daskalov 1992b: 111–112; Kotzageorgi 2002: 84). All Greek schools at each level were shut down and all Greek Orthodox staff were replaced by new Bulgarian staff.

---

[70] 112,171 'Muslims' in 1940 as opposed to 71,301 'Turks' plus 15,000 'assumed' (based on the 1940 Greek census) 'Pomaks' in 1942.

Box 4.1 Extract from *Zora* on the Opening of a Bulgarian School in Komotini

Komotini, 7 June.

Today the flag of the re-constructed Gymnasium of Komotini received the official inauguration and blessing. The school received the names of our great proto-Apostles Saints Cyril and Methodius. The flag was blessed by the Metropolitan of Plovdiv, Cyril, supervising the district of Maroneia, along with father Gorazd and others. Representative of the Minister for Public Education and bearer of the flag was the regional Education Inspector, Mr. G. Nalbadov. The Metropolitan delivered a very moving speech referring to the civilizing and educational achievements of the Bulgarian people. Mr Nalbadov spoke about the potential of the Bulgarian spirit and intellect. Additional speeches were given by the Director of the school A. Popov, Stoiko Stoikov representative of the Gymnasium of Targoviste, which offered as a gift the flag and the flag bearers Liuben Karadimov for Targoviste and Sergio Dimitrov from Komotini. In the ceremony, which took place in the courtyard of the Gymnasium, there were also present representatives of all the state authorities and cultural associations, as well as the whole of the Bulgarian population of the city.

Source: *Zora*, 11 June 1942.

The Bulgarian language became the only official language of instruction, whilst the use, either in speech or in writing, of the Greek language within schools was completely banned. Schools were re-organised according to the Bulgarian system and curriculum into primary schools (1–4 grade), middle schools (5–8 grade) and secondary schools (9–11). School buildings were stripped of anything related to Greece (inscriptions, books, maps, etc.). They were also given names of Bulgarian national heroes, Bulgarian saints, as well as contemporary German personalities, such as the *Adolf Hitler* primary school in Xanthi.[71]

The Bulgarian newspaper *Zora* described the opening of such a school in June 1942 (see Box 4.1).

---

[71] CSA/177/7/189, To the Minister of National Education, No. 37, 5 January 1942. According to Kotzageorgi (2002: 86–87) at the end of the academic year 1941–2 in Eastern Macedonia and Western Thrace there were 128 primary schools with 9647 pupils and 252 teachers and 24 middle schools with 1374 pupils and 48 teachers. For the 1942–1943 academic year, the Bulgarian authorities sought to increase the number of primary schools to 173 with 390 teachers and to 36 for middle schools (with 64 teachers). In addition, six mixed-gender secondary schools were planned, one in each district capital. All minority schools operated privately. During the academic year 1941–1942, there were 13 primary and one middle Turkish schools. There were also, two Armenian primary kindergartens and four Armenian primary schools. The following year there were 20 Turkish primary schools, two Armenian kindergartens and four Armenian primary schools.

Morning Prayer assumed a national character as students sang:

I am Bulgarian. I love Bulgaria. May I work all my life for the greatness of my people! My God, be my guide![72]

The daily curriculum was filled with Bulgarian history, language, literature and geography. In order for the Bulgarian schools to attract non-Bulgarian students, the authorities provided daily lunch to the students and food supplies for their families. Moreover, during vacation time, the students were sent to summer camps in Bulgaria, while scholarships and other economic incentives for higher education studies in Bulgarian universities were offered in order to strengthen the students' relations with the 'motherland'.

In parallel to the 'Bulgarisation' of education, the new administration gave particular emphasis to the destruction of the cultural heritage of the local population and the subsequent import of new Bulgarian cultural models. Greek-language signs were banned and were replaced by Bulgarian ones. All cities, towns and villages received new Bulgarian names. Every publication in Greek was confiscated. All public monuments and statues were destroyed and in their place new ones were erected commemorating events and heroes from Bulgarian history. All radios, receivers and records were seized. Bulgarian flags were distributed to all citizens who were obliged to raise them during every religious or national Bulgarian celebration. Bulgarian cultural associations, choirs and reading rooms were created, while in Komotini a Bulgarian theatre, performing Bulgarian-language plays, was established. A number of Bulgarian nationalist youth organisations were instrumental to the 'Bulgarisation' of Western Thrace, such as *Otech Paissiy* (Father Paissiy), *Brannik* (Defenders), *Sborni* (Unionists), *Orlovi* (Eagles) and others. These were organised under the auspices of the Bulgarian state and engaged in cultural activities, the instruction of the Bulgarian language, and military training.[73] The task of the cultural assimilation of the Pomaks was under-taken by the nationalist organisation *Rodina* (Motherland), which, with the Bulgarian-appointed Mufti of Xanthi, Arif Beyski (Kamen Bolyarski), as its head engaged in nationalist propaganda towards the Pomaks, seeking to enlist them in the register as Bulgarians and to remove the veil and their traditional clothes (Daskalov 1992b: 118–120; Kotzageorgi 2002: 58–60).[74]

---

[72] CSA/798/2/48, Protocols of the Educational Administration-General of Belomorie, Minutes No. 1, Inspectorate Committee for Education in Xanthi, 10 June 1941.

[73] There were several other nationalist organizations, not established by the Bulgarian authorities, headed by old *Komitadjis*. Some of these had clear fascist and pro-German sympathies.

[74] CSA/284/3/62, 'Report on the strengthening of Bulgarisation and the Bulgarian administration in the Aegean', 29 April 1943.

The Bulgarian administration adopted a more relaxed attitude towards the education of the Turks in the lowlands of Western Thrace. Turkish students were treated as a separate educational group and there was no aggressive attempt to integrate them into the system of Bulgarian education. Turkish private schools and the religious *Medrese* were allowed to continue their operation under the jurisdiction of Bulgarian-appointed Muftis.[75] Although all subjects previously taught in Greek were replaced by a Bulgarian-language curriculum, minority schools in the lowlands were allowed to teach the Turkish language and religious instruction continued. Chronic shortages of staff, however, severely restricted the provision of minority education in the area.[76] The Bulgarian administration also took active measures to counter the advance of Turkish nationalism amongst the minority. Batıbey argues (1976: 52) that all minority teachers with alleged sympathies for Kemalist ideas were replaced by conservatives. The circulation of Turkish books was restricted across Western Thrace whilst the authorities also banned the (until then frequent) travel of local students to Turkey for basic education or higher studies in Turkish universities.[77]

In the more isolated villages of the Rhodope Mountains, however, the educational policy of the Bulgarian administration produced an intensive assimilation campaign for the local Pomaks. Bulgarian planners urged 'coordinated and organised cultural and educational action in order to promote their [the Pomaks'] national consciousness that was buried centuries ago'.[78] Lower-ranking Bulgarian administrators were encouraged to treat Pomaks as any other Bulgarian citizen.[79] Pomak students were regarded as children of Bulgarian descent, 'Mohammedan Bulgarians', a label given to them in official state correspondence. In the Pomak villages north of Xanthi, for example, only the Bulgarian language was used in minority schools (with the exception of the instruction of the Koran in Arabic). However, it appears that in some Pomak villages north of Komotini, the teaching of Turkish was not always forbidden – a *de facto* recognition by the Bulgarian authorities that some of these communities had already been 'Turkified'.

Particular emphasis was put on the education of Pomak women and their emancipation. They were not allowed to wear the veil in public. In the 1942–1943 *Plan for the Educational and Cultural-Social Action of the Teachers*

---

[75] CSA/471/1/1311, Regulation for the operation of the religious school *Medrese i-Alie* in Komotini.

[76] Interview 13; Interview 14; Interview 25; Interview 26; Interview 30.

[77] GAK Kavalla, 'Archive of Foreign and Minority Schools', F.95B, Ministry of Interior, Aliens' Directorate-General, II Office, D. Vlastaris, 'Report of the Muslims living in Greece', July 1952.

[78] CSA/798/2/48, Protocols of the Educational Administration-General of Belomorie, Minutes No. 1, Inspectorate Committee for Education in Xanthi, 10 June 1941.

[79] CSA/177/5/83, Regional School Inspector, Komotini, to the Minister of Education, 'Report for March and April 1944', No. 398, 26 April 1944.

in Belomorie, the Bulgarian Ministry of Education issued particular instructions for teacher activity in the 'Mohammedan-Bulgarian Communities'. According to the circular, 'particular attention should be given to the Mohammedan-Bulgarian woman', in order to 'emancipate her from being secluded and shy'. The instrument for that would be the female Bulgarian teachers who:

> Ought to pay frequent visits to the houses of all their students, in order to get to know their parents well, especially their mothers and older sisters, and develop a close relationship with them... Through such attention, affection and spontaneous talk about their everyday life in the farms and their houses... teachers should gain the trust of the Mohammedan-Bulgarian woman, in order to offer first aid and medical advice when needed and create seminars for girls on practical household matters.[80]

However, these ambitious Bulgarian projects met with rather limited success. In official correspondence, Bulgarian officials appeared disappointed at the results of their educational policies towards the Pomaks, complaining that their plans were disorganised and uncoordinated.[81] The fact that 'the teachers in the Mohammedan-Bulgarian schools [had] not received any additional pedagogical training' was identified as one of the main reasons for this failure.[82] Although the Bulgarian Ministry of Education introduced a series of incentives for secondment to the new territories (amongst them appointment without exams, 5000 *Leva* additional pay and free books) many Bulgarian teachers were displeased with their transfer and soon abandoned their positions and asked for their return to Bulgaria proper (Kotzageorgi 2002: 94). Kotzageorgi (2002: 106) also asserts that the Bulgarian administration recruited just 390 teachers to the primary schools of Eastern Macedonia and Western Thrace, whereas in the pre-war period there were 2060 Greek teachers in the same area.

As Bulgarian teachers faced major obstacles in their deployment and working conditions, their commitment began to wane. According to the recollections of Pomak students, Bulgarian teachers were indifferent towards their duties and often violent to their students. In a report of the Regional School Inspector of Komotini it was noted that in 1941–1942, five of the 20 schools situated in the Pomak villages of Rhodope did not operate at all, as their teachers were either drafted into the Bulgarian Army or they never appeared

---

[80] CSA/798/2/48, Protocols of the Educational Administration-General of Belomorie, Minutes No. 1, Inspectorate Committee for Education in Xanthi, 10 June 1941.

[81] CSA/177/7/170, Regional School Inspector of Komotini, to the Regional School Inspector of Xanthi, No. 465, 26 June 1942.

[82] CSA/177/7/170, Regional School Inspector of Komotini, to the Regional School Inspector of Xanthi, No. 465, 26 June 1942.

in their posts.[83] Moreover, the Bulgarian authorities believed that the poor economic condition of many Pomak families was an additional reason that prevented the students from attending their classes on a daily basis (an issue that has changed little since).[84]

In fact, the Bulgarian educational programme for the Pomaks failed to meet its objectives not simply because of its organisational deficiencies, but mainly because it faced the persistent, albeit passive, resistance of the Pomak community itself. According to data that was available to the Regional School Inspector of Rhodope, in 1941–1942 only 845 Pomaks attended classes in Bulgarian schools.[85] It is possible that the number of those actually attending school regularly was even lower, considering that school attendance was (and still is) heavily affected by the farming cycle. As economic conditions worsened after 1942, it is also probable that the number of Pomak students declined further. The ambitious Bulgarian plans for the emancipation of women were also counter-productive, as many Pomaks reacted to the ban on the veil by forbidding the female members of their families to leave their houses. Hence the aggressive practices of the Bulgarian authorities for the cultural assimilation of the Pomaks had met with extremely unfavourable local conditions; most notably a strong commitment to Islamic values and 'closed' family structures that had shaped the outlook of the Pomak communities for centuries.

In parallel to the 'Bulgarisation' of Eastern Macedonia and Western Thrace, the Bulgarian authorities launched a widespread offensive against the Greek Orthodox Church, perceived to be the most serious obstacle to their plans. The threat of Greeks rallying around 'their' church led the authorities to expel all Greek Orthodox clergy and replace them with Bulgarians (Daskalov 1992b: 116–117). All religious ceremonies were now to be conducted in Bulgarian and all inscriptions, including tombstones and icons in Greek were replaced by Bulgarian ones. Churches and religious properties were looted while, during the occupation, some 46 priests were executed.[86]

In religious matters too, the Bulgarians showed greater tolerance towards Muslims. This was in stark contrast to the experience of the local Muslim population during the last period of Bulgarian control (1913–1919). The

---

[83] CSA/177/7/170, Regional School Inspector of Komotini, to the Regional School Inspector of Xanthi, No. 465, 26 June 1942.

[84] CSA/177/8/13, Inspectorate-General of Education, to the Governor-General of Belomorie, Uundated (but reports on the academic year 1942–1943).

[85] CSA/177/7/170, Regional School Inspector of Komotini, to the Regional School Inspector of Xanthi, No. 465, 26 June 1942.

[86] AYE/1950/32/1, Ministry of Information and Press 'Greece's Human Sacrifices' 17 October 1949. It is significant to highlight that according to the same source in the rest of Greece 21 priests were executed by the Germans and five by the Italians.

Muslim religious institutions continued to operate, albeit under centralised Bulgarian control (Daskalov 1992: 117). The Muslim communities and the Muftis of Western Thrace were placed under the jurisdiction of the Mufti of Sofia. The Bulgarians took control of the Mufti offices, the communal Muslim property and the *Medreses*, replacing all administrators and committee members with Muslims they trusted, whether Thracian Muslims or Bulgarian Pomaks. Many Muslim associations were dissolved and new Muslim community centres and school committees were established.[87] The Bulgarian authorities, particularly in the villages, monitored closely the activities of imams. Despite the profound implications for the everyday lives of local Muslim communities, there is no evidence to suggest that the actions of the new Bulgarian administration attracted significant (public) opposition by Muslim leaders in Western Thrace.

The pattern of religious control also appears to have been inconsistent. In the Pomak areas, some mosques were closed whilst others remained open.[88] In Kechros, a Pomak village, the local Imam remained in place. At the same time, many mosques were looted by the Bulgarians for anything of value.[89] The most well-known incident was the arson of the Çarşi Mosque in Xanthi, where, according to local accounts, the Bulgarians had stolen its expensive carpets and set it on fire in order to cover their traces. Additionally, the Bulgarians expelled the Mufti of Xanthi, Galip Bey, whom they charged with plotting against their rule – a claim that a post-war Greek investigation found to be untrue.[90] Galip Bey was summarily replaced by a young Pomak from Bulgaria, Arif Beyski, who allegedly 'wore a hat, knew no Turkish and his conduct was that of an enemy of the Turks'.[91]

The arbitrary and violent nature of the Bulgarian occupation provided incentives for the Muslim population to seek support from the Turkish Consulate of Komotini, as the only counter-veiling source of protection. This was indeed a remarkable change of fortunes for the Consulate, which, a few years earlier, had been regarded with considerable suspicion, not only by the Greek state but also by the (then, significant) traditionalist element within the minority itself which distrusted the modernist ideals of Kemalism. Chapter 5 will discuss the role of the Consulate during the Bulgarian occupation in more detail.

---

[87] Relevant correspondence can be found in CSA/471/1/1082.

[88] Statements by interviewees appear contradictory on this point.

[89] Interview 8; Interview 13; Interview 18; Interview 25; Interview 26; Interview 30.

[90] Allegedly, during their investigation the Bulgarian gendarmes also stripped the unlucky Mufti of the 1,200 *Leva* he carried with him. See, A report of Professors of the Universities of Athens and Salonica 1945: 69.

[91] A report of Professors of the Universities of Athens and Salonica 1945: 72.

4.7   Smaller minority groups in wartime Western Thrace

The severity of wartime occupation confronted the various ethnic groups of Western Thrace with stark choices, often forcing them to balance their own survival instincts against those of their neighbours as well as against the demands of their newly-arrived Bulgarian masters. Collaboration with the occupying forces promised safety and survival. Non-compliance, even in its most passive form, threatened expulsion and, often, death. Of the smaller communities in the area, the Armenians were the only ones to develop close relations with the Bulgarian administration. The Roma community, on the other hand, locked in its own marginalisation, was subjected to widespread violence by the Bulgarian forces, but escaped the systematic extermination campaign suffered by its kin elsewhere in Europe. The Jews of Western Thrace had no such luck as their centuries-old communities were almost entirely wiped off the local map.

The Armenian community

During the Axis occupation several Armenian communities around Greece suffered a similar plight to that of the rest of the Greek population with reports that approximately 2000 Armenians perished during that period (Hassiotis 2002: 97). In particular, the Armenian community in the neighbourhood of Dourgouti in Athens took active part in the local EAM-ELAS movement (Ghazarosyan 1998: 286–287). In Western Thrace, however, the local Armenian community followed a rather different path, collaborating closely with the occupation authorities. According to a report submitted to the (collaborationist) Greek authorities in Thessaloniki by an Orthodox Greek who fled Western Thrace in 1942:

> Immediately after the invasion, the Armenians assumed a very hostile attitude towards Greece. Very few Armenians appeared to be friendly to the Greeks. The Bulgarians seem to trust only the Armenian element. With Armenians as mediators, you could easily resolve any matter with the Bulgarian authorities.[92]

A report by the Administration-General of Thrace in November 1941 painted a similar picture of Armenian collaboration, noting that:

> Since the establishment of Bulgarian rule in Western Thrace, and especially since 29 September,[1941] the Armenian element has supported

---

[92] ELIA/47 (Thessaloniki), 'Archive of Bulgarian Occupation in Macedonia and Thrace'. Ministry of Public Order, Aliens' Directorate, to the Premier's office, 'Memorandum of a Greek refugee from Bulgarian-occupied Thrace', 26 August 1942.

their efforts, providing false information against the Greek population, aiming to contribute to the elimination of Greeks and thus concentrate and control all the trade in its hands, which constitutes its ultimate aim.[93]

Evidence in the archives of the Greek Ministry of Foreign Affairs suggests that the Armenian community collaborated closely with the Bulgarians at all levels.[94] As a reward for such support, the Bulgarians granted the Armenians the same privileges enjoyed by Bulgarian settlers and spared them from the oppressive measures imposed on the rest of the population. The Armenian school of Alexandroupolis, for example, which had 80 students, was allowed to continue its operation with Bulgarian logistical support, while the community was free to practice its religious services without Bulgarian interference (Daskalov 1992: 126).[95] Significantly, the Armenian community continued unhindered its commercial activities, accumulating significant wealth in its hands.

Relations between the Armenian and the Muslim communities, both prior and during the Bulgarian occupation, were strained. During the inter-war period there had been a number of violent incidents involving gangs of Armenians – often aided by their Greek Orthodox peers – attacking Muslims (see Chapter 2). These incidents had created an atmosphere of mistrust, but had not escalated into an all out conflict. As a Muslim interviewee recalled:

> Our relations with the Armenians were mainly commercial. We had more relations with the Greeks. I remember my parents saying that we should be careful when dealing with the Armenians.[96]

Armenian collaborationism during the occupation period put further pressure on inter-communal relations. The accounts of local Turks claimed that the Bulgarians regularly used Armenian informants to collect information on minority teachers, particularly on those suspected to embrace Kemalist ideas (Batıbey 1976: 52).

---

[93] GES/DIS 1998: 312–333.

[94] AYE/1947/111.1, Commander of Rhodope Gendarmerie, 'Report on active propaganda and Public safety in the district of the Rhodope Gendarmerie Command', 13 September 1947.

[95] AYE/1950/70.1, Aliens' Centre-General of Macedonia-Thrace, to Aliens' Directorate-General, 29 March 1950. GAK Kavalla, 'Archive of Foreign and Minority Schools', F.95B, Ministry of Interior, Aliens' Directorate-General, II Office, D. Vlastaris, 'Report of the Muslims living in Greece', July 1952.

[96] Interview 33. Others depicted a more benign picture: 'we didn't have any problems with the Armenians. My father went hunting and he often did that with Armenians friends'. Interview 42.

The extent of Armenian collaborationism with the Axis forces during the war is difficult to establish. After liberation, Alexandroupolis' newspaper *Eleftheri Thraki* published a list of those who 'made fortunes during the occupation'. Out of a total of 28 names listed, nine were Armenians – a number that was hugely disproportionate to the size of their community.[97] Another list prepared by informants reporting to the collaborationist Greek authorities in Thessaloniki in 1942 refers to 11 Armenians as leading figures of anti-Greek activity and collaboration with the Bulgarians in Xanthi.[98] Evidence from the Greek Ministry of Foreign Affairs also suggest that during the retreat of the Bulgarian forces in September/October 1944, more than 140 suspected collaborators (along with their families) fled the district of Komotini for Bulgaria. Of these, 41 were Armenians.[99]

The widespread reports of Armenian collaboration, prompted Greek and British officials to recommend the expulsion of the community from the area after the War. A report of the Municipality of Xanthi in the summer of 1944 made clear the feelings of the Greek authorities towards the Armenians:

Despite the undisputed reality that the Armenians are favourably attached to the Bulgarians, after the Asia Minor Catastrophe unfortunately we did not take the necessary precautions and this anti-Greek element was allowed and encouraged to settle in the regions near the borders. Although the Armenians of Xanthi have no ground for complaints against the Greek administration, since under its auspices they enjoyed equal rights and worked to their prosperity, they still welcomed with apparent satisfaction and enthusiasm the presence of the Bulgarians in the area. They did not confine their feelings only to platonic moves of goodwill, such as the dispatch of messages on behalf of the Armenian Community congratulating the Bulgarian government and the offer of a very expensive sword to the King of Bulgaria, but many of them actively participated in the economic persecution of the Greeks. In the present report we cannot refer to actions of individual members of the Armenian population, but it must be stressed that in general they appeared surprisingly ungrateful and assumed an anti-Greek position, while at the same time they openly expressed a very strong pro-Bulgarian attitude. These

---

[97] *Eleftheri Thraki*, 26 February 1946.

[98] ELIA/47 (Thessaloniki), 'Bulgarian Occupation in Macedonia and Thrace', Thessaloniki Aliens' Department, to Athens Aliens' Department, 'Anti-Greek activities of the Armenians in Xanthi', 26 June 1942.

[99] For more details see name-lists in AYE/1947/111.1, 14/2/1947.

are the reasons for which this population should not have a place in this region any more.[100]

The British Ambassador in Athens concurred:

The Armenians, largely refugees of 1922 from Asia Minor, have behaved very badly towards the country that sheltered them by co-operating with the Axis authorities. It would seem highly desirable that they should be removed to Soviet Armenia. [...] Since 1930 several thousands have been transferred to Soviet Armenia, by arrangement with the Government, which sent ships to Salonica and Kavalla for the purpose. Those remaining ... have in many cases been completely captured by German propaganda, giving this group by far the worst record, for production of German agents and informers, of all sections of the population of Greece. The desirability of further emigration seems to be indicated.[101]

Thus, after the War, the Armenian population of Greece (and of Western Thrace in particular) dwindled. During 1946–47 a Soviet-inspired plan for the repatriation of all Armenian Diaspora to the Soviet Armenian Republic led many Armenians to leave civil war-torn Greece (Hassiotis 2002: 97). From the 55,000 Armenians who arrived in Greece after the Greco-Turkish population exchange of 1923, only 9000 remained in the country by the late 1940s.[102] In Western Thrace, the 1951 census registered just 549 Armenians, down from a total of 2268 in 1940 (see Table 2.1).

The Roma community

Information about the condition of the Roma population during the course of WWII is much more scattered. The organisation of their communities (structured around patriarchical families or *faras*) has left very little written evidence of collective action, whilst their low life expectancy has depleted the potential pool of first-hand oral testimonies. There are indications that a number of Roma from Western Thrace fought alongside the Greek Army in the 1940–1941 Greco-Italian War. Following the onset of the Axis occupation in the area, the local Roma community was not subjected to a systematic campaign of extermination, similar to those reported in other parts

---

[100] AYE/1944/1.1, Xanthi Municipality, to the Administration-General of Thrace, 'Armenian activities and propaganda', 21 July 1944.

[101] FO/371/43775, Leeper to Eden, 29 May 1944.

[102] Hassiotis 2002: 97–98, 105–106; www.armenians.gr/index1024.html (accessed on 30 October 2008).

of Axis-controlled Europe.[103] This is all the more surprising considering that the eastern part of the region of Evros (populated by a significant number of Roma) was occupied by German forces. Yet, Roma families experienced the Bulgarian reign of terror. A Roma resident of the village of Drosero recalled:

> There was a lot of tyranny and hunger during the Bulgarian occupation. The situation then was much worse compared to the later period of the civil war, as the Bulgarians were beating and terrorising us. There was no way to negotiate or communicate with them and the people could not sleep at night because they were afraid of night raids by the army.[104]

Indeed there is evidence to suggest that the Roma community suffered extensively from malnutrition and was ravaged by contagious diseases.[105] Tsonidis (1980: 214), for example, makes reference to a major outbreak of smallpox – affecting overwhelmingly the local Roma community – in German-occupied Orestiada that obliged the German forces to immunise a significant part of the local population in 1943.

Oral testimonies suggest that local Roma were subjected to major levels of violence by the Bulgarian forces who often 'recruited' them for anything ranging for menial jobs to hard labour.[106] There are also accounts of regular Bulgarian raids in Roma settlements with the purpose of dispersing their residents.[107] A number of interviewees also recalled frequent incidents of rape against young Roma women by Bulgarian soldiers.[108] Such practices stood in sharp contrast to the experience of either Turkish or Pomak women for whom no evidence of such incidents were uncovered. The memory of wartime occupation still induces attitudes of hostility against the Bulgarians by many local Roma.[109]

No clear pattern of reaction to the occupation is apparent across the different geographical areas or religious sub-groups (i.e. Muslim or Christian) of local Roma. There is some evidence of collaboration with the occupying

---

[103] There are some (as yet undocumented) reports that, in other areas of Greece, the Germans had prepared for the transportation of significant numbers of Greek Roma to Auschwitz, but the plan was aborted following the intervention of Archbishop Damaskinos and (collaborationist) Prime Minister Ioannis Rallis. For more details see European Roma Rights Centre 2003: 33–34. For a different view, see Politou (2008: 143).

[104] Interview 22.

[105] Interview 20; Interview 21; Interview 22.

[106] Interview 21.

[107] Interview 20; Interview 21.

[108] Interview 19; Interview 21; Interview 23.

[109] Interview 21.

forces, but these tend to be rather isolated incidents. Terzoudis (1985: 40), for example, argues that a number of Roma participated in an irregular group of German collaborators in the area of Didimoteicho/Orestiada, under the leadership of a Belorussian named Turboi. The engagement of the Roma community with the local anti-Axis resistance was non-existent. This may be related to the fact that in the areas inhabited by Roma, there was minimal resistance activity in general. On the other hand, there are accounts that a degree of self-organisation did exist in Roma settlements where local men set up patrols to warn others about imminent attacks.[110]

Yet, if life for the Roma community in Western Thrace was ridden with dangers, the fate of the Roma community in Bulgaria proper appeared to have been even worse. There are reports of two major waves of emigration of 'Bulgarian Roma' to Western Thrace. According to Kotzageorgi (2002: 176), the first took place in late 1942 where a number of Roma settled in the area without the prior agreement of the Bulgarian forces. The second wave appeared to have taken place shortly after the end of the War, either to escape persecution in Bulgaria or to seek better employment prospects in Greece (Trubeta 2001: 165).

Thus, it seems that the local Roma community remained at the margins of the wartime conflict in Western Thrace. Clearly none of the key players in this conflict anticipated strategic benefits from their collaboration. The local resistance groups (dominated by the Greeks) ignored them completely. The Muslim community too considered them as a rather marginal and, largely, unwelcome kin. The Bulgarian forces did not attempt to use the Roma in the context of a wider plan for their administration in the area, opting, instead, to victimise them in a brutal and inconsistent way. In the end, the social and economic marginalisation of the Roma community in Western Thrace known before and since the 1940s remained the case under the occupation.

The Jewish community

The onset of the Bulgarian occupation sealed the fate of the Jewish community in Western Thrace. In February 1943, the Bulgarian Commissioner for Jewish Affairs, Alexander Belev, signed an agreement with the SS official, Teodor Daneker, for the rounding up of all Jewish population within the Bulgarian occupation zone. Ten days later, on the night of 3 March 1943 – Bulgarian Independence Day – the Bulgarian Army, with a well-coordinated but secret operation, rounded up the Jewish population from all the towns within the whole of Bulgarian occupation zone (including Western Thrace and Eastern Macedonia), a total of 4200 persons (Fleischer 1988: 318–319

---

[110] Interview 21.

Table 4.2 The Loss of Jewish Life in Western Thrace during WWII

	Population	Perished	Escaped/ Survived
Komotini	818	790	28
Xanthi	550	544	6
Alexandroupolis	140	133	4
Orestiada	197	194	3
Didimoteicho	900	897	33
Total	2605	2558	74

Source: Enepekidis (1969: 170).

Vol. 2; Exarchou 2001: 99–100). The age-old Jewish communities of Western Thrace were effectively wiped out overnight. As one Muslim interviewee recalled:

> The authorities gathered the Jews in just one night. The night before the Bulgarians had marked Jewish houses with a "J" and stood guard outside so that no Jew could escape. Only 3–4 Jewish families were not touched because they had Turkish nationality. After they gathered the Jews, they took them to the area of Machaira, it's like a small canyon near the borders with Bulgaria. From there they continued into Bulgaria. We all felt sorry for what was happening. We did not understand what was happening. The properties of those Jews disappeared.[111]

Most captured Jews suffered terribly in the hands of their captors, before they were eventually handed over to the Nazis. The vast majority of them were to later perish in the Treblinka concentration camp in occupied Poland. Of the 4200, very few survived. According to data from the Central Jewish Council presented by Enepekides (1969), the annihilation of the Thracian Jews was almost complete (see Table 4.2).

It is not entirely clear what motivated the pogrom against the Jews in the area. After the war the then Communist government of Bulgaria was eager to remind the Allies that (unlike almost everywhere else in Europe) there was no extermination policy against Bulgarian Jews (Miller 1975: 93–106). In a propaganda publication targeting the US government in 1946, the Bulgarian Political Mission in Washington argued that Bulgaria had thwarted the extermination policy (see Box 4.2).

---

[111] Interview 43.

Box 4.2 Extract from *The Truth About Bulgaria*, May 1946

The real Bulgarian spirit manifested itself in many and diverse ways. Probably nothing speaks more eloquently of the effect of this passive but stubborn resistance than the fact that it frustrated – effectively and definitely – the Nazi imposed Anti-Semitic policy of the Boris government. This policy brought discrimination – yea. But throughout all these years even though the Nazis applied insensent pressure, no Bulgarian Jew was murdered – not a single one was shipped off to the extermination centres of Poland.

The net result of this resistance is, as Michael L. Hoffman pointed out in the New York *Times* of 4 March 1946, that 'Bulgaria is the only country in Europe with a Jewish population more numerous (today) than before the war'. One could add to this that the Jews again enjoy, to fullest extent, the equality of opportunity and expression, which was always theirs in their Bulgarian homeland. The Jews seek no exodus from Bulgaria now.

Source: Bulgarian Political Mission to Washington, *The Truth About Bulgaria*, May 1946.

Indeed, the fate of Jews in Bulgaria proper contrasts sharply with their experience in Western Thrace. The military orders for the rounding up of Jews in the area seem to have little connection to pre-war animosities. There is no evidence that relations between the Bulgarian and Jewish communities prior to 1920s (i.e. before Bulgarians were evicted from Western Thrace) were strained. It is plausible that the extermination of Jews in Western Thrace was an act of good service by the Bulgarians to their German masters in exchange of the latter's 'understanding' on the issue of Bulgarian Jews (Miller 1975: 99–101). Fleischer (1988: 318, Vol. II) argues that the eradication of the Jewish population served long-term Bulgarian aspirations for an ethnically 'pure' Western Thrace. A more mundane explanation may also suggest that the removal of Western Thracian Jews simply provided an excellent pretext to take over Jewish businesses and property in the area.

The reaction of the Greek Orthodox community to the plight of the Jews appears to have been one of muted sympathy, although there are claims that some Orthodox Greeks sought to make financial gains along the way (Enepekidis, 1969: 180; Papastratis 2001: 66; Exarchou 2001: 105). There is also evidence that some Orthodox Greeks resented the presence of Jews in their areas. According to one of them:

There are official orders from the central authorities for their persecution. Hence, that's the reason why they appear to approach the Greeks. There are however among them agents that work for the Bulgarians. If the authorities had left them unharmed, they would have followed the same stance as the Armenians [i.e. collaborationism].[112]

---

[112] ELIA/47 (Thessaloniki), 'Archive of Bulgarian Occupation in Macedonia and Thrace'. Ministry of Public Order, Aliens' Directorate, to the Premier's office,

On the other hand there is little evidence with regard to the feelings of the Muslim minority towards the Jewish community. The recollections of interviewees today suggest a similar feeling of empathy mixed with an overriding fear of getting too involved. One Muslim interviewee recalled:

> We Turks tried to help. We were childhood friends; we'd play together. But we couldn't do anything. We couldn't understand what was happening. Then one morning we realised the Synagogue was empty and that the objects and possessions inside had been taken away by the Bulgarians.[113]

The experience of the Bulgarian occupation unleashed different challenges for all ethnic groups of Western Thrace prompting each of them to seek, where possible, their own survival strategies. The reaction of the Muslim community to this new reality is discussed in detail in the next chapter. The fate of the Armenian and Jewish communities in wartime Western Thrace, offered two contrasting examples. By the end of the War both of these communities were all but erased from the local map, each for different reasons. The two largest communities (the Muslims and the Greek Orthodox) watched the suffering of the Jews from a safe distance with the latter occasionally profiting from their misfortunes. Armenian collaboration with the Bulgarian forces was indeed extensive. A significant number of Armenian collaborators featured in post-War court-martials organised by the Greek administration, while the vast majority of the local Armenian community migrated to the Soviet Union after the War. The Muslim community – itself a victim of Armenian collaborationism – shed few tears about this departure. On the other hand, the Roma community continued its own marginalised existence. The Roma suffered much arbitrary violence at the hands of the Bulgarians, but their community in Western Thrace escaped the horrors inflicted upon the local Jews (or, indeed, other Roma communities across Europe) by the Axis forces. As so often before (and since), the fate of the local Roma appeared to attract little attention by either the Muslim or the Greek Orthodox communities. In sum, the reaction of the different ethnic groups to the occupation experience in Western Thrace had produced neither a total breakdown of relations nor major incidents of inter-communal solidarity. This was, indeed, consistent with the pattern of inter-communal relations during the inter-war period.

'Memorandum of a Greek refugee from Bulgarian-occupied Thrace', 26 August 1942.

[113] Interview 43.

4.8   Conclusions

The collapse of the local Greek state and the arrival of the Axis forces in Western Thrace brought chaos and then brutality, lawlessness, and economic suffering. The disciplined conduct of the German forces contrasted sharply, in the minds of the local Muslims, with the unruliness of the Bulgarians who took over. The new *Belomorie* regime had set out with extensive aims, but the reality was of insufficient resources, unreliable personnel, corruption, wanton violence, disorder, and local mistrust. This was a regime that lacked the capacity to win support and, instead, had to rely on fear and repression to maintain compliance. The cruelty and suffering it imparted invited only animosity and rejection.

The pattern of political repression instigated by the new *Belomorie* regime differentiated both between the different ethnic groups in area, but also between the different elements of the Muslim community. The law on Bulgarian citizenship was the key vehicle for 'undoing' the authority of the Greek state in the area. Its effects were felt by all communities, but hurt the Orthodox Greeks the hardest. The latter also bore the main brunt of the religious and educational policies of the new regime. The Turks of the lowlands might have been spared the worst Bulgarian excesses in religious and educational terms, but did not escape frequent violent attacks and looting. The Pomaks of the Rhodope Mountains, by comparison, suffered a much harder fate. Their cultural proximity to Bulgaria (particularly in linguistic terms) separated them out for a special Bulgarisation campaign; a remedy for their 'lapsed' Bulgarian identity. This was, perhaps, the greatest irony of *Belomorie*: a regime that sought to assimilate them let them endure the worst of any of those remaining in the region. The results of this assimilation campaign, thus, failed to achieve its anticipated results as the Pomaks stuck to their old Ottoman ways.

The economic results of the Bulgarian occupation were also diverse. Once again the Pomaks came out worst as their isolated villages were the only areas in Western Thrace where incidents of famine were reported. Economic conditions in the main towns of the area were better, but not much. Punitive taxation, expropriations and frequent looting hit Orthodox Greeks and Muslims alike. Large parts of the pre-war middle classes were also hit by the law on Bulgarian citizenship which severely restricted the scope for legitimate work. Those with access to the hard currency of the period – the Turkish *Lira* – were provided with a lifeline, but not for long. Those who could, fled the area either to German/Italian-occupied Greece or Turkey. Indeed large numbers of both Orthodox Greeks and Muslims chose to do so; possibly over 10 per cent of the latter escaped to Turkey. This exodus, combined with the arrival of nearly 100,000 Bulgarian settlers, transformed the demographic mix of Western Thrace. Those fleeing to Turkey had chosen their survival strategy; for those that remained in Western Thrace, they confronted the question of survival on a daily basis.

The greatest contrasts occurred in the experiences, not of the Greek Orthodox and the Muslims, but between the smaller ethnic groups of Western Thrace. The Armenians collaborated; the Roma were brutally treated; and the Jews were wiped out. Many locals witnessed the preparations for what became the deportation of the Jews, some heard their violent removal during the night, whilst a number sought to quickly profit from their disappearance. Then, as before and later, the Roma were largely ignored by the rest.

The Bulgarians brutalised and repressed both the Greek Orthodox, the previous majority, and the Muslims, the largest minority. Their forces established full military control. The suffering was immense and widespread. The question that arises, therefore, is precisely how did the local population react: in particular, how did the Muslims respond to the occupation? The evidence of local strategies for survival will be examined in the next chapter.

5
Strategies for Survival

5.1 Introduction

With the extent of control exercised by the new Bulgarian authorities in Western Thrace, the local Muslim population (as indeed all other ethnic groups) was forced to adapt and to learn how to survive. Most starkly, they were confronted by strategic choices: resistance, collaboration, or passivity? This chapter explores the evidence as to how the Muslim community reacted.

Initially, it seemed that the region might prove to be conducive for resistance activity. Yet, an early act of resistance – one of the very first uprisings in occupied Europe – was brutally crushed and this dampened subsequent activity until the eve of the Allies' victory. More generally, the scope for resistance activity was structured by the prevailing political climate of the 'Greek' organisations, which was highly polarised politically. The main resistance force – EAM (*Εθνικό Απελευθερωτικό Μέτωπο* – National Liberation Front), dominated by the Communists – sustained a contradiction between a rhetoric of engaging the Muslim community and the reality of their neglect. A nationalist resistance grouping, EAO (*Εθνικές Αντάρτικες Ομάδες* – National Guerrilla Groups), garnered greater support and involvement from the Muslim population, but this was at the end of the conflict in 1944.

In his study of Greece in the later civil war period Kalyvas developed a theoretical frame with implications for when resistance and collaboration may occur (Kalyvas 2006). Thus, the higher degree of control exercised by the authorities, the greater the level of collaboration (Kalyvas, 2006: 111). In Western Thrace, the Bulgarian forces certainly established a high level of control, but the evidence of Western Thrace suggests minimal collaboration in general (the Armenians were the exception) and on the part of the Muslims, in particular. Alternatively, the relevance of the local ethnic mix of population is only lightly touched upon in the Kalyvas study, when he examines Almopia, part of Pella in Macedonia, Greece. Here he concludes that ethnic polarisation was not a factor in stimulating violence (2006: 314). This is a parallel to the Western Thrace case: the existence of ethnic minorities did not stimulate resistance or insurgency – if anything, it acted to dampen the level of such activity – nor did it lead to inter-communal strife between Muslims and the Greek Orthodox majority.

Into this discussion of resistance or collaboration falls the special position of the Turkish Consulate in Komotini which, since the Treaty of Lausanne and the politics of the inter-war period, had developed a self-ascribed role of guardian to the local Muslim population. The reality of the Axis invasion and the 'active neutrality' of Turkey, however, placed the Consulate in an extremely delicate position with respect to 'protecting' its kindred community.

5.2   The onset of resistance activity in occupied Greece

On 27 April 1941 German troops entered Athens. A few days before King George II and the Greek government under Prime Minister Emmanuel Tsouderos fled the capital for Crete and from there sought refuge in Cairo where they pledged their support to the Allied struggle against the Axis. The power vacuum in Athens was quickly filled by the appointment of a collaborationist Prime Minister, Lt. General Georgios Tsolakoglou, by the German authorities.[1] Just a few days later on the night of 30 May 1941, two young students from Athens, Manolis Glezos and Apostolos Santas, climbed the Acropolis and, under the nose of German guards, brought down the flag of Nazi Germany. This act was to prove hugely symbolic for Greek resistance to the Axis. Indeed, from the beginning the occupying forces of Greece experienced signs of resistance that were soon to spread across many parts of the country.

The widespread resentment against the foreign invaders – combined with conflicting ideological designs over the post-war future of the country – gave rise to a dynamic and highly politicised domestic resistance movement. This fractious mosaic was the result of the earlier divisions within Greek politics. It emerged from a number of diverse sources: pro-Venizelist army officers who had been removed by the Metaxas dictatorship, ambitious representatives of the pre-War political establishment and the underground network of the (outlawed) KKE. By far the largest and most dynamic of any of these resistance groups was EAM and its military wing ELAS (Greek People's Liberation Army – *Ελληνικός Λαϊκός Απελευθερωτικός Στρατός*) which remained largely under the control of the KKE and its Secretary General, Giorgos Siandos. EAM, seeking to act as a political umbrella organisation,

---

[1] Tsolakoglou was succeeded, in December 1942, by Konstantinos Logothetopoulos who was, in turn, replaced by Ioannis Rallis in April 1943.

succeeded in mobilising large numbers of volunteers, both in urban centres and, particularly, the countryside and was able to spread its influence to most parts of Greece. On the other hand, ELAS, as a resistance army, remained under the leadership of Aris Velouchiotis and Stefanos Sarafis, engaging in a wide range of military operations against the occupying forces and soon developed into a well-organised and large force.

The dominance of EAM/ELAS in the resistance movement was challenged by a number of Republican and Royalist groups which, nevertheless, never managed to converge around a single leadership structure. Many of these groups operated independently and maintained a strong regional outlook. The largest such group (and EAM/ELAS' main adversary) was EDES (National Republican Greek League – *Εθνικός Δημοκρατικός Ελληνικός Σύνδεσμος*), an initially Republican and subsequently Royalist outfit under the leadership of Napoleon Zervas, who operated mainly in Epirus (North-West Greece). A smaller Republican group with its powerbase in Central Greece was EKKA-5/42, (National and Social Liberation – *Εθνική και Κοινωνική Απελευθέρωση*), under the military command of the pro-Venizelist Colonel, Dimitrios Psarros. In Macedonia, the largest Republican/Royalist resistance groups were ΕΛΟ under the leadership of Antonis Fostiridis (see below for more on this) and YVE-PAO (Defenders of Northern Greece/ *Υπερασπιστές Βορείου Ελλάδος* – Pan-Hellenic Liberation Organisation/ *Πανελλήνιος Απελευθερωτική Οργάνωση*) under the leadership of Ioannis Papathanasiou.

Many Greek resistance groups operated under the guidance and logistical support of the British. The Special Operations Executive (SOE) found fertile ground in Greece to fulfil Churchill's ambition to 'set Europe ablaze' in order to harass Axis troops across occupied Europe.[2] The engagement of SOE in Greece started with a spectacular act of sabotage at the Gorgopotamos viaduct in November 1942; an operation that was executed jointly with the two main resistance groups, ELAS and EDES. From that point onwards, the British mission, under the command of Colonel Eddie Myers and, later, Christopher 'Monty' Woodhouse,[3] developed a leading influence over the Greek resistance movement. British Liaison Officers were eventually deployed in most regions of Greece (but not Western Thrace) assuming the key responsibility of co-ordinating the activities of disparate armed groups. The British involvement, depending on the expediencies of the day, involved the mediation (but, often, the exacerbation) of the disputes that plagued relations between the various resistance groups in Greece. In

---

[2] For more about the purpose and role of the SOE in Greece see Clogg (1975, 1981). More widely on the SOE see Foot 1999.

[3] Both gave their personal accounts on their participation in the events in Myers 1975 and Woodhouse 1976.

the region of Eastern Macedonia, this delicate task[4] was entrusted to Major Guy Micklethwait, or *Major Miller*, as he became known to the local Greek guerrillas.

Western Thrace, in particular, also attracted the attention of the United States that, in late 1943, despatched to the area a small group of OSS agents, under the Greek-American Major Alexandros Georgiadis. Their aim was 'to cooperate with the [joint] British Greek intelligence operating out of the Greek Consulate [of Edirne, Turkey]',[5] in order to expand the Allied apparatus in the area For this objective, Georgiadis collaborated closely with the Edirne Consulate, but also developed close links with ELAS forces in Evros where they commanded significant strength (see below).

Elsewhere in Greece, as most urban centres and lowlands came under the tight control of the occupying forces, the heartlands of the Greek resistance were inevitably located in the mountainous countryside which provided the guerrillas with greater operational freedom and relative safety. The mountainous communities thus became the main sources of recruitment and provisions for the guerrillas, but they also paid the heaviest price from Axis reprisals. The same communities were to be later brought to the forefront of the Greek civil war following the breakdown in relations between the main resistance groups.

Despite the fact that all resistance organisations maintained that their sole objective was the liberation of Greece, their competition over the direction of the country after the War was intense. The motives behind this competition and the instruments used for fulfilling each side's ambitions were neither clear nor always openly articulated. EAM proclaimed that its main post-war ambition was the postponement of the King's return to Greece pending a referendum. Its opponents, however, maintained that EAM's true agenda was the creation of a Soviet-style 'People's Republic'. On the other side, many Republican and Royalist groups presented themselves as defenders of the parliamentary, Western-style, nature of Greek democracy. In the eyes of EAM/ELAS, these groups were simply the pretext for the establishment of a repressive dictatorial regime. Both sides soon challenged each other's patriotism and accused the other for collaborating with the enemy. Many Republican and Royalist sympathisers were branded as profiteers and German collaborationists. To its opponents, EAM/ELAS encapsulated the threat of Communist expansionism and stood accused of encouraging Bulgaria's aspirations for the secession of Macedonia and Western Thrace from Greece.

---

[4] See, indicatively, HS/5/317, H.Q. Force 133, Top Secret (ref. B2.INT 8/14), 'A History of the Triatic Mission', 8 November 1944.

[5] Personal letter of Alexandros Gregoriadis to Dr John Iatrides, 7 February 1973. Dr Iatrides' personal archive.

The suspicion between the two sides soon escalated into a full scale civil war (see Chapters 7 and 8), the first signs of which became apparent as early as 1943 during the occupation. ELAS, by far the most powerful force at that time, was able to eliminate most of its opponents and, on the eve of Greece's liberation, was militarily dominant across most of the Greek countryside.

In Macedonia and Western Thrace the Greek resistance movements followed a rather different trajectory, however. In both regions the extent and intensity of resistance activity was more limited than elsewhere in Greece (see below). In addition, the multi-ethnic character of Macedonia and Western Thrace added further complications to the political and military conflict between EAM/ELAS and its opponents. The KKE's controversial policy on minorities was also significant in this respect. In January 1942, for example, the 8th Plenary Session had maintained that:

> Our Party must focus all its activities in order to enlighten the national minorities, especially the Slavophone Macedonians, so as to avoid being taken over by the hatred of the national oppression of the Greek capitalists and the ongoing demagogy of the conquerors, particularly of Bulgarian imperialism and chauvinism, which is a satellite of Hitler and Mussolini. (KKE 1981a: 65)

A similar commitment on the emancipation of national minorities was repeated in the Party's Pan-Hellenic Conference at the end (December) of the same year:

> Our Party, which struggles for full equality of the national minorities that live in Greece, must undergo every pain to enlighten them against the threat posed by the fascist Axis operations and use them as its [the KKE's] instruments. The national minorities must be organised on the basis of the anti-Axis struggle and the common brotherly anti-fascist effort along with the Greek people for the victory of the Soviet Union and its Allies, which constitutes the guarantee of the free and brotherly coexistence of all peoples. (KKE 1981a: 93)

KKE's wartime rhetoric on these issues revealed apparent similarities with its pre-war line. Although references to 'independence' were now notably dropped, the discourse on forging strong alliances with all minority groups remained strong. At the forefront of this discourse stood the Macedonian Slavs, for whom both the Bulgarian and Yugoslav Communist parties had maintained a strong interest. However, the same was not to be the case for the Muslims of Western Thrace. Contrary to KKE's resolutions, little energy was invested in organising local support networks in the area. Neither did the Bulgarian or (the much weaker) Turkish Communists seek to claim the soul of the local Muslim communities. Again, key regional wartime players neglected the Western Thracian Muslims, with the effect that their position towards the occupiers and resistance fighters alike would be determined from within and not from without.

5.3   The activity of EAM-ELAS in Western Thrace

The first signs of resistance activity in Eastern Macedonia and Western Thrace developed very soon after the consolidation of Bulgarian forces in the area. The first major incident – locally celebrated as the 'first uprising in occupied Europe' – took place on 28–29 September 1941 near the city of Drama – just under 50 km east of Xanthi. The revolt targeted a range of Bulgarian authorities in the vicinity of Doxato – army positions, the police, the public administration and local authority offices – both in the city of Drama and the surrounding areas. The operation involved over a thousand men recruited and organised by the local KKE branch and members of the Party's Macedonian Office. Some 35 Bulgarians died as a result of the operation, mainly police officers and civil officials. A number of suspected collaborators were also targeted (Paschalidis and Chatzianastasiou 2003: 263). Afterwards, the swift Bulgarian response brought fulsome retribution: at least 2140 people were executed including many women and children.[6]

The severity of the Bulgarian response in Drama had a huge restraining impact on the development of the resistance movement in both Eastern Macedonia and Western Thrace. The operation had been badly coordinated and its timing was premature. In many respects, the local resistance groups never managed to get over the Drama events. The Bulgarian retributions also dealt a massive blow to the morale of the local population, shaking popular faith in the benefits of armed resistance. The immediate consequence of the executions can be seen in the almost total destruction of the local KKE apparatus, with many leading local party cadres amongst those killed or imprisoned. Furthermore, false rumours suggested that the uprising had actually been an act of connivance between the Bulgarians and the KKE. The number of suspected dead was also hugely inflated at the time – some even suggesting that over 15,000 people had perished. The effect was to distil distrust and disunity amongst the Greek Orthodox community. In such an atmosphere of terror and insecurity, many of the local cadres decided to leave for the German-controlled areas, while the ones who stayed behind kept a very low profile and remained passive. The impact of

---

[6] The number of 2140 is the more reliable estimate put forward by Paschalidis and Chatzianastasiou (2003: 263). Antonovski (1961: 67) estimates the number of casualties in Drama and its outskirts to 2500–3000. Kotzageorgi-Zymari and Kazamias (1994:103) refer to 2000–3000 in Drama and 5000–6000 throughout the district. Others have estimated the number of casualties to over 4000 (see Konstantaras 1964: 47; Chysochoou, 1949: 31; Fleischer 1988:97, Vol. I).

the suppression made the resistance leadership hesitant to engage in further substantial initiatives. Thus, from this very early point onwards, Western Thrace appeared to be a 'lost cause', while other regions of the country, such as Roumeli (Central Greece), offered better prospects for a successful guerrilla struggle.

This was a view certainly shared by Chrysa Chatzivassileiou, a member of the Central Committee of the KKE in Athens. She had arrived in Thessaloniki just a few days after the events of Drama in order to appraise the situation and draft the future strategy of the Party in Eastern Macedonia and Western Thrace. Chatzivassileiou criticised the operation and urged KKE cadres to leave the area. She also ordered all existing resistance groups to dissolve or at least suspend their armed struggle until further notice. In a stark u-turn of strategy, Chatzivassileiou's orders were later overturned by Markos Vafiadis who arrived in Thessaloniki in December 1941 and demanded that all communist organisations and guerrilla groups should resume their activities in the area (Chatzis 1983: 179, Vol. I). Much of the damage, however, was already done. The resistance activity in Western Thrace never really recovered until the dying days of the Bulgarian occupation. For most of the intervening period, Western Thrace was effectively ignored by the leadership of EAM-ELAS.

Indicative of the weakness of KKE in Eastern Macedonia and Western Thrace was the fact that during the crucial Pan-Hellenic Conference of the KKE in December 1942 (in which Giorgos Siandos was elected Secretary-General), no delegates for these two regions (alongside the Greek islands and Crete) were present 'due to technical reasons' (KKE 1981a: 77). Further evidence that Western Thrace did not feature on KKE's 'radar' can also be found in the detailed *Report of the EAM Committee of Macedonia for the three year-long national liberation struggle of the people of Macedonia*. The report was drafted in August 1944 and presented in much detail all the activities of EAM during the occupation period, but contained no references to EAM/ELAS' presence in Western Thrace (KKE 1981b: 82–106, Vol. I). Geography also, no doubt, played a significant role in Western Thrace's isolation from the rest of resistance activity in occupied Greece. The severe difficulties in the physical crossing of the three different occupation zones (Italian, German and Bulgarian) and the technological limitations in communications between the 'hubs' of the resistance in Athens and Thessaloniki and local organisations in Western Thrace would have encouraged the latter's introversion and isolation.

Despite these adverse conditions, two resistance cells were eventually established in Western Thrace. The first cell, dominated by EAM/ELAS, was formed in the German-controlled area of Evros. In the summer of 1941, the Regional Committee of Evros was created on the individual initiative of local KKE cadres. Its fate was sealed by the succession of leaders sent from the national EAM/ELAS leadership or those who, rather bizarrely, claimed to represent it. The first such leader was Argyris Dalkaranis (also known as

Aris) who arrived in Evros in October 1941 and presented himself to the Regional Committee, claiming to carry orders from the Party to assume its political guidance. Rather surprisingly, the members of the Committee, completely isolated from the party hubs in Athens and Macedonia, consented to Aris' proposal. Aris soon managed to concentrate all power in his hands and impose his personal views on the outlook of local EAM/ELAS, its policy and military strategy. The self-proclaimed leader – who, in fact, had not received any such orders from KKE – was a typical Communist of his era. According to the memoirs of his fellow fighter, Vaggelis Kasapis, at the onset of the Greco-Italian war, Aris had attempted to flee Greece, through Bulgaria, in order to fight for the Soviet Union. A fervent supporter of armed resistance, Aris regarded the formation of each guerrilla unit as very important; a distraction at the rear of the German Army which could benefit the struggle for the defence of the Soviet 'motherland'. According to Kasapis:

> The Soviet Union was the country of his youthful dreams. Lenin's country was the country where the damned of this world had risen. The country of the red May 1st, where the humble of the earth are free to celebrate that day; the country where after having broken their chains, they were building a new world of their own, a world of comrades and brothers. (Kasapis 1977: 56, Vol. I)

Aris' rule ended in April 1943 when he was arrested by the Bulgarians in Komotini and was handed over to the Germans, who shot him dead while he was attempting to escape. The leadership of the Regional Committee of Evros was now assumed by another self-proclaimed 'instructor', claiming – again falsely, as it turned out – to have received authorization by the Party, Lefteris Galiadis (known as Odysseas). According to Mazower, his 'reign of terror' was 'the most chilling illustration of the revolutionary mentality at work within ELAS' (Mazower 2001: 318).

Aided by their geographical isolation, both Aris and Odysseas were able to develop their strategies free from the political interference of the official KKE. The most significant divergences appeared over the ideological and political framework of EAM and the role of the KKE within it, as well as the propaganda methods and recruitment practices they adopted. Throughout the occupation period, even during flashpoints of conflict within the resistance movement itself, EAM sought to position itself as an inclusive, diverse and politically neutral organisation, whose sole objective was the liberation of the country and the free expression of the popular will after the war. Consistent with this objective, there was the conscious effort to downgrade the relationship between KKE and EAM. Unlike KKE, the 'official' EAM never sough to cultivate and police the ideological 'purity' of its members.

In Evros, the situation on the ground was rather different. Not only was there no effort to downplay the Communist identity of the Regional

Committee and of its military wing, but on the contrary this identity was widely pronounced both privately and in public. It was also frequently used during the Committee's negotiations with local notables and officials. For example, in correspondence with the Greek Consulate of Edirne, Odysseas asked for their cooperation and exclaimed:

> We are being told that we are Communists; yes, 98% of us are Communists, as they say, but it is an honour that it was the Communists from our district who first went to the mountains and fought against fascism and after the liberation, our People will judge the deeds of each one of us.[7]

The Regional Committee of Evros and its military wing did, indeed, resemble a revolutionary army. Their men bore the Communist insignia of hammer and sickle and the Soviet star on their uniforms and wore red silken scarves on their necks. During their public meetings they sang the hymn of the Comintern with their fists in the air. The propaganda leaflets of the Regional Committee of Evros, *Popular Guard* (*Λαϊκός Φρουρός*), and the Communist Party branch of Komotini, *Red Guard* (*Ερυθροφρουρός*) were well-versed in the Marxist-Leninist rhetoric and they threatened the representatives of the pre-war bourgeois establishment.[8] Moreover, EAM in Evros chose to create a recruitment network from within familiar circles, confining its contacts almost exclusively to members of local trade unions and cadres or sympathisers of the Party. Aris, for example, had given strict orders banning any cooperation with republican personalities or representatives of the pre-war political elite. As a result, all members of the group maintained strong bonds of trust, built upon reputations of Communist orthodoxy (Kasapis 1977: 226, Vol. II). The Committee resembled more a closed group of conspirators and bore no resemblance to the wide and open front that the Central Committee of EAM in Athens aspired to become.

The situation in Evros changed fundamentally in February 1944, when EAM despatched to the region an experienced party member from Athens, Athenodoros Katsavounidis, in order to assume the leadership of party organisations and guerrilla groups there. With his arrival, the EAM of Evros was officially incorporated into EAM proper and its armed groups became the 81st regiment of ELAS. Katsavounidis proceeded to the full reorganisation of the local force, forming armed groups according to established ELAS guidelines.[9] He also made significant efforts to discourage local

---

[7] AYE/1944/11.3, 'National Guerrilla Band of Evros district', to the Edirne Greek Consulate, 7 October 1943.

[8] AYE/1944/10.3, Directorate of Special War Services, to the Premier, Cairo, 8 January 1944; Chatzianastasiou 2003: 63.

[9] Each unit included a Military Commander responsible for strategic planning, a Captain (*Kapetanios*) in charge of the guerrillas and a Political Commissar responsible for the 'ideological enlightenment' of the unit's men.

ELAS units from displaying their Communist sympathies. All party insignia were now removed from the guerrillas' uniforms.[10] The former local leader, Odysseas, was court-martialled and executed shortly afterwards (Kasapis, 1977: 128–130, Vol. II). A number of other members of the group suspected of brutality and improper conduct were also court-martialled, while all outstanding capital punishments of those convicted in absentia by Odysseas were annulled.[11]

Katsavounidis seemed determined to exercise-self restraint towards EAM/ELAS' domestic adversaries and intensify the group's struggle against the German forces that controlled this part of Western Thrace. His strategy delivered positive results on both counts. During August-September 1944, when the German forces started to withdraw from Evros, ELAS forces launched a series of attacks against them across a wide area of Western Thrace, killing, according to EAM sources, 150 Germans and capturing more than 200 prisoners and substantial war material.[12] The guerrillas also managed to obtain the control of the strategically important local railway network. In addition to his significant military successes, Katsavounidis contributed greatly to the relative stability of Evros, particularly as relations between ELAS and its local adversaries became less tense.

The second main resistance cell of EAM/ELAS operated on the border between Western Thrace and Eastern Macedonia, in the districts of Drama, Kavalla and Serres, extending to the northwest corner of the district of Xanthi. Following the catastrophic events in Drama in 1941, KKE began slowly to re-emerge in the area and, by May 1942, a new Area Office of Eastern Macedonia-Thrace was set-up (partly to act as a conduit to EAM). Its main organisational centre was in Kavalla, since the Party's network in Drama was still severely weakened. Several months later, in early 1943, the first ELAS groups made their presence felt in Eastern Macedonia in the Lekani (Çal-dağ) Mountain and engaged in a series of skirmishes with Bulgarian forces. ELAS activity acquired a more concrete form by late September 1943, with the formation of the 26th ELAS regiment in Paggaion Mountain between Drama, Kavalla and Serres, which numbered around 170 fighters (Chatzianastasiou 2003: 95). The regiment was re-organised in early 1944 when Kostas Konstantaras became Commander and, by the summer of the same year, its membership reached 1100 men (Konstantaras 1964: 165). Although the 26th regiment enjoyed some success in harassing the occupation forces, it never really managed to inflict great damage on them or to sustain continuous activity in the area. Its best moment was the battle of Platamonas in Kavalla, on 29 July 1944, when a Bulgarian unit of 150 men was attacked, sustaining casualties that ranged, according to different sources, between six and 50 (Chatzianastasiou 2003: 206).

---

[10] AYE/1944/10.3, Edirne Consulate, to the Ankara Embassy, 9 March 1944.

[11] AYE/1944/10.3, Edirne Consulate, to the Ankara Embassy, 3 March 1944.

[12] AYE/1944/10.3, Ankara Greek Embassy, to the Foreign Ministry, 5 September 1944.

The impact of EAM/ELAS in Xanthi was rather poor. The news of the brutal suppression of the Drama revolt followed by a wave of arrests of local KKE cadres by the Bulgarian forces undermined the development of a strong EAM resistance movement locally. Some organisational groundwork began in late 1942, when KKE's Macedonian Office sent Spyros (or Takis) Liapakis to the city of Xanthi. A few months later (in February 1943), however, Liapakis was arrested by the Bulgarians and was forced to confess precious details about the Party apparatus in the wider area. As result, a new wave of arrests and executions ensued in the areas of Xanthi, Kavalla and Serres (Chatzianastasiou 2003: 62, 90). The Party in Xanthi was reorganised a year later, when, in February 1944, the first guerrilla groups were formed and afterwards they became part of the 26th ELAS regiment (Chatzianastasiou 2003: 90, 184). Yet again, however, the Bulgarians were able to 'decapitate' the movement following the arrest, torture and execution of the First-Secretary of KKE's local branch, Iosif Spartalis (Chatzianastasiou 2003: 197).

In Komotini, and Rhodope more generally, the local EAM/ELAS was even weaker than in Xanthi. After the Drama events, the Bulgarians launched a wide-scale operation against local Communist networks, leading to the arrest of six local cadres (Chatzianastasiou 2003: 62). A small nucleus of the party was preserved and distributed the news bulletin, *Red Guard*, without engaging in further significant political or military activity. In autumn 1941, an armed group was formed in Maroneia, under the leadership of the member of the Regional Committee of Xanthi, Lefteris Galiadis. This group, numbering no more than 20 men, did not engage in military action and retained a rather low profile (its members spent the night in their own houses).[13] By late 1943, most of the members of this group crossed to the German-controlled zone in Evros and joined the 81st regiment of ELAS.

EAM propaganda was similarly subdued in the districts of Rhodope and Xanthi. During the occupation, the local EAM branches in both districts are known to have issued and distributed only one publication (it is likely, but not confirmed, that they might have issued four more), when at the same time the branches in Kavalla, Serres and Drama issued 19 publications in total (and possibly eight more) (Kandylakis 2006: 17).

Hence, the pattern of EAM/ELAS' deployment in Western Thrace produced few opportunities for significant interaction with the Muslim community. The key ELAS-affiliated groups operated around the districts of Evros and Kavalla, both some distance from the main Muslim heartlands in the districts of Xanthi and Rhodope. For long periods of time, both units in Evros and Kavalla remained outside the control of the central ELAS command, which only managed to bring them fully in line as late as 1944. In particular, the locally-determined peculiarities that shaped the outlook of the Evros unit were bound to have restricted its appeal to the non-Communist constituency, let alone the insular and conservative communities of the Western Thracian Muslims.

---

[13] Interview 14.

Moreover, despite its earlier enthusiastic commitment to engage with all national minorities in Greece, KKE made no effort to penetrate the Muslim community in Western Thrace – a legacy that most certainly impacted adversely on EAM's ability to garner support among either the Pomak populations in the Rhodope Mountains or the Turks in the lowlands. The reasons behind KKE's failure to live up to its own agenda on this front can only be speculated upon. Its engagement with other minority groups such as the Slavs in Macedonia was both intense and successful. When the war broke out, a similar engagement in Western Thrace might have fallen victim to other, more pressing, imperatives of organising resistance activities in areas where the prospects for success looked greater. The Muslims were also likely to have been regarded as unreliable partners owning to their overtly conservative and religious disposition.

The Muslim community for its part viewed left-wing resistance groups with suspicion. Locally, EAM-ELAS was neither strong enough to protect nor popular enough to inspire. The instinctive identification of Communism as a 'godless' ideology was enough to deter many god-fearing members of the Muslim community from engaging with left-wing resistance. The link between Communism and the Soviet Union might have also played on historical memories of Russia's torment of the Ottoman Empire and the advance of Pan-Slavism in the Balkans which had contributed greatly to the uprooting of the vast majority of Muslims from the region. All in all the revolutionary and intensely secular undertone of EAM/ELAS' campaign was simply not worth risking the wrath of Bulgarian retaliation. The realities of Axis occupation might have been very bleak for the Muslims of Western Thrace: the events of Drama, however, served as a poignant reminder that they could get a lot worse. Many interviewees recalled an intense atmosphere of fear.[14] As a former inhabitant of Komotini put it: 'no-one liked the Bulgarians, but that was it – we couldn't do anything about it'.[15]

Under these circumstances, evidence of Muslim sympathies towards EAM/ELAS are extremely limited. An Muslim interviewee from Megalo Dereio in Evros recalled that the headquarters of ELAS in his village enjoyed some degree of local support.[16] Another interviewee remembered that in the village of Sostis (in the district of Rhodope) German troops executed 20 local resistance fighters – amongst them 'four or five Turks'.[17] Similarly, a Greek-Orthodox resistance fighter maintained that:

> The population in Rhodope was rather conservative and the Muslim community there even more so. Few joined EAM and even fewer ELAS. I remember a Muslim recruit called Mustafa from Velkion and another

---

[14] Interview 43.
[15] Interview 48.
[16] Interview 5.
[17] Interview 43.

one from Komotini. A handful came from Sappes. In Xanthi, however, there were some Muslims who were members of the Party and did time in jail and in exile.[18]

But the emerging picture was clearly one of passivity. This was not a resistance struggle to liberate oppressed Muslims. No member of the local community or from a similar ethnic/cultural background emerged as a dominant figure within ELAS in the area. The limited 'Greek' resistance activity in the area forced no stark choices upon the Muslim community. As one interviewee from the village of Mischos recalled, 'during the occupation there was no Greek resistance in our area; there was nothing to join there'.[19] Another saw the ethnic mix of the area as significant: 'there was no Greek resistance in the region because Rhodope had a mixed population and the Greeks were not in the majority'.[20] It seems that EAM/ELAS never really traveled the distance to knock on the door of the Muslim community for support. Even if it did, few would have run to answer.

5.4   The activity of the nationalist resistance groups in Western Thrace

The nationalist resistance groups – known collectively as EAO – were a dynamic force in Eastern Macedonia.[21] They were fiercely conservative and consisted mainly of hardened Turkish-speaking, but Greek Orthodox, Pontians from the Black Sea who settled in Macedonia during the 1910s and mainly the 1920s. Nationalist groups also recruited volunteers from the edges of the Asia Minor (mostly Greek speaking) refugee community as well as from native Macedonians and Thracians. The nationalist guerrilla movement in the area started from a nucleus of small armed groups whose resistance against the occupying forces often descended into acts of banditry and looting, even against the very communities they were meant to protect. The structure of these groups was elementary: a Captain (*Kapetanios*), typically a village strong-man, followed by a few men (normally between five and 20) who, in most cases, were the relatives, friends or village compatriots of the *Kapetanios*. Their field of operations was also limited and revolved around village localities. For a long time, these groups had no political guidance or a clear military strategy; they lacked propaganda instruments, maintained no organised network of support or a clear allocation of duties (Marantzidis 2006b: 27–62). The central figure of the Nationalist resistance movement was Antonis Fostiridis, also

---

[18] Interview 29.
[19] Interview 48.
[20] Interview 46.
[21] By comparison to ELAS or EDES, the story of those groups is relatively under-researched. Two recent studies have shed more light on their history. See Marantzidis 2001 and 2006a. Also see Fostiridis 1959.

known as Anton Tsaous. He was born in Samsun[22] in the Black Sea (Pontus) and moved to Greece with the 1923 population exchange, where he worked as a rural guard around Kavalla. He had served as a sergeant in the Greek army where he acquired his nickname *Tsaous*.[23] Anton Tsaous rallied around him many of the guerrilla groups of the Turkish-speaking Pontians and eventually became the undisputed leader of the Nationalist guerrilla movement in Eastern Macedonia and Western Thrace.

The bringing together of these scattered Nationalist bands under a single military authority did not begin until towards the end of the war in January 1944, when a summit of all *Kapetanioi* on the mountains of Xanthi confirmed the position of Anton Tsaous as Commander-General and consented to the creation of local headquarters for the coordination of local resistance activity. From that moment on, EAO could count on the support of nearly 750 guerrillas (Chatzianastasiou 2003: 149), although individual groups continued to operate pretty much independently, obeying (if at all) a very loose chain of command towards the 'centre' (i.e. Anton Tsaous). In August 1944, negotiations between Anton Tsaous, the British liaison officer Major Miller and the leaders of the Republican resistance organisation PAO, which also operated in Macedonia, led to the incorporation of all scattered groups into better organised units. They also agreed to dispatch PAO officers to the various guerrilla groups in order to share command with existing *Kapetanios* and help to maintain discipline.

Owing much to their ideological differences and their natural competition for local control, the Nationalist guerrilla groups and ELAS regarded each other with suspicion. The vast majority of EAO members had strong Royalist sympathies and fiercely supported the return of the King after the War. ELAS' agenda was very different, with many of its members closely affiliated to KKE. Eventually, confrontation became inevitable. On New Year's day 1944, Fostiridis' men wiped out a unit of ELAS on the Lekani (Çaldağ) Mountain, a strategically important passage for access to the districts of Kavalla, Drama and Xanthi. Relations between the two groups never recovered. EAO, however, remained a powerful actor in the area, claiming some significant successes against the Bulgarian forces, notably the battle at the bridge of Papades (7–10 May 1944), where the Bulgarians suffered around 150 casualties (Chatzianastasiou 2003: 157).

Despite its relative success in the district of Drama, EAO's effort to extend its field of operations in the district of Rhodope met with insurmountable difficulties. In the village of Xylagani, near Komotini, a group of veterans of the Albanian front had formed a lightly armed guerrilla band and had tried to establish contact with the EAO. Their activities, however, were discovered

---

[22] Fostiridis 1959: 9. According to Chatzianastasiou (2006:304) he was born in the village of Erikli in the region of Bafra.

[23] From the Turkish word *çavuş*, meaning 'sergeant'.

by the Bulgarians who, in June 1944, attacked the village and killed almost all the participants, a total of 28 people (Chatzitheodoridis 2002: 450–453, Chatzianastasiou 2003: 163).

There are indications, however, that towards the end of the occupation, EAO recruitment had made some inroads into the Pomak communities of the Rhodope mountains. In May 1944, the British liaison officer Major Miller ordered EAO units to move towards the north-west of the Xanthi district, in the Haidou forest. This placed EAO at the heart of the Pomak region in Xanthi (Echinos, Sminthi, Thermes, Kotyli, etc.). EAO guerrillas and the local Pomak community soon developed mutual sympathy and established some cooperation. The Pomaks frequently cooperated with EAO as guides, informants and food suppliers on condition that EAO men operated in areas far away form Pomak villages so as to avoid Bulgarian reprisals (Chatzianastasiou 2003: 169). The sympathy of the local Pomaks towards EAO was also supported by oral testimonies collected from local interviewees.[24] That said, Fosteridis' memoirs (1959) makes no mention of Pomaks amongst his men. Chatzitheodoridis (2002: 264–6), on the other hand, claims that 89 Pomaks who collaborated with the EAO, later (1958) received official recognition by the Greek state as 'fighters of national resistance'.[25] A list of their names is provided in Table 5.1.

EAO was also very successful in developing close cooperation with many border Pomak communities in Bulgaria which allowed it to operate with relative safety along the Greco-Bulgarian border. On 28 October 1944, for example, three junior (Bulgarian) Pomak officers negotiated the surrender of 200 Pomak defectors from the Bulgarian Army to the EAO, while a whole unit of Bulgarian Pomaks joined the EAO headquarters in Falakro Mountain (Boz-dağ) near Drama (Chatzitheodoridis 2002: 263–268). The incident of the Pomak defectors supplements further evidence with regards to the porous nature of the Greco-Bulgarian border in the area during the War and the interaction between Pomak communities on either side of the border.[26]

---

[24] Interview 12.

[25] There is some uncertainty as to whether all those named in Chatzitheodoridis' list resided on the Greek side of the border in 1944. The list contains no birthplaces for those named. It is possible that some of those who collaborated with EAO were actually Bulgarian Pomaks (i.e. Pomaks residing on the Bulgarian side of the border) who, after the end of the war, decided to move to Greece.

[26] In 1941 a group of approximately 2500 Bulgarian Pomaks fled their homes as a result of racial harassment and attempted to cross the borders to Turkey, but were refused entry. The Bulgarian authorities in Western Thrace allowed them to settle in the area. After the end of the War the Greek authorities demanded their resettlement. Having resisted strongly the prospect of their repatriation, this group of Bulgarian Pomaks was eventually allowed to emigrate to Turkey. For more details see GAK (Kavalla), 'Archive of Foreign and Minority Schools', F.95B, Ministry of Interior,

Table 5.1   Pomaks Recognised as 'Fighters of National Resistance'

1. Abdullah Recep of Yusuf (1938)	31. Kazepaci Halil of Hasan (1943)	61. Katioğlu Mustafa of Ismail (1916)
2. Ayanoğlu Hasan of Mehmet (1942)	32. Apazoğlu Apif of Ahmet (1937)	62. Apazoğlu Cavet of Ahmet (1927)
3. Cavdaroğlu Osman of Hasan (1940)	33. Cegeloğlu Ibrahim of Omer (1940)	63. Havanoğlu Tahir of Tahir (1922)
4. Çavusoğlu Mustafa of Osman (1937)	34. Çausoğlu Cemal of Hussein (1928)	64. Çesuroğlu Ibraim of Siper (1915)
5. Çavuşoğlu Sapan of Hasan (1938)	35. Çavuşoğlu Mehmet of Hasan (1942)	65. Çaloğlu Ussein of Murat (1926)
6. Çeferoğlu Ahmet of Mustafa (1946)	36. Çahiroğlu Serket of Tahar (1942)	66. Çinoğlu Ismail of Bayram (1943)
7. Çolakoğlu Hüseyin of Ussein (1944)	37. Hasanoğlu Ali of Hasan (1932)	67. Hacioğlu Raif of Hussein (1929)
8. Haliloğlu Zaimis of Yusuf (1942)	38. Karadağ Hasan of Hussein (1937)	68. Karakuşoğlu Issein of Azhmet (1922)
9. Karahasan Şaban of Hasan (1950)	39. Karamustafaoğlu Mustafa of Ru. (1918)	69. Karakuşoğlu Mustafa of Ahmet (1901)
10. Karahasan Hasan of Hasan (1926)	40. Kapsanoğlu Hussein of Ismail (1937)	70. Kavan Zali of Hasan (1925)
11. Kagioğlu Faik of Ali (1912)	41. Kaskos Ahmet of Ramasan (1916)	71. Kehagiaoğlu Hussein of Murat (1938)
12. Kehaya Abdullah of Muşat (1925)	42. Kokkinov Atem of Yaonp (1921)	72. Kehagiaoğlu Zeinin of Ismail (1937)
13. Kehayaoğlu Irin of Iris (1946)	43. Kehagiaoğlu Ismail of Tahir (1926)	73. Kekoğlu Ali of Talia (1940)
14. Keleşoğlu Mustafa of Necip (1898)	44. Kehagiaoğlu Ali Riza of Ismail (1933)	74. Keletzekos Mehmet of Şerif (1936)
15. Kugurukoğlu Ussein of Mehmet (1933)	45. Payramoğlu Osman of Ismail (1937)	75. Koroğlu Ali of Hussein (1940)
16. Kuritosmanoğlu Hussein of Şekir (1941)	46. Kuritosmanoğlu Osman of Şekir (1930)	76. Kutoğlu Ali of Sali (1926)
17. Kostekoğlu Ali of Issein (1949)	47. Molla Oğlu Ahmet of Işli (1949)	77. Molla Oğlu Sali of Mustafa (1939)
18. Merlev Hamit of Şahin (1938)	48. Burbaoğlu Mehmet of Ahmet (1932)	78. Oban Frani of Franz (1945)
19. Palioğlu Raif of Hasan (1926)	49. Paşoğlu Ahmat of Şavitin (1941)	79. Oğlu Aker Yusuf of Yusuf (1920)

Continued

Table 5.1 Continued

20. Uruçoğlu Rafat of Mehmet (1921)	50. Uzunoğlu Mehmet of Şaip (1943)	80. Papuçioğlu Mehmet of Iussein (1932)
21. Papuçioğlu Ali of Iussein (1937)	51. Rusianoğlu Halil of Rusian (1934)	81. Petkeroğlu Yussein of Osman (1911)
22. Tilekoğlu Hasan of Hussein (1941)	52. Puruçioğlu Mehmet of Ismail (1932)	82. Saidoğlu Osman of Hasan (1926)
23. Salioğlu Ali of Vali (1910)	53. Salioğlu Yefik of Küçük (1940)	83. Salioğlu Osman of Hasan (1940)
24. Salioğlu Osman of Sali (1940)	54. Semercoğlu Hussein of Refe (1943)	84. Sapanoğlu Ali of Isset (1945)
25. Şüleyman Hussein of Sali (1938)	55. Tosmanoğlu Sali of Hasan (1919)	85. Şapoğlu Ahmet of Ali (1941)
26. Şopoğlu Ibrahim of Mustafa (1940)	56. Suroğlu Ismail of Osman (1932)	86. Sufronoğlu Hasan of Osman (1910)
27. Soproğlu Şüleyman of Suleyman (1938)	57. Spyrov Uleyman of Sali (1924)	87. Terzoğlu Mehmet of Mustafa (1937)
28. Terov Aleti of Mustafa (1941)	58. Çavuşoğlu Ramzi of Ali (1937)	88. Yahian Mahmut of Azim (1917)
29. Delimanoğlu Osman of Hüseyin (1939)	59. Ziramoğlu Mehmet of Mustafa (1946)	89. Asnanoğlu Ali of Asan (1904)
30. Atemoğlu Şüleyman of Atem (1918)	60. Ahmetoğlu Cemal of Letif (1918)	

Source: Decision B5/87/1958 of the General Staff of National Defence quoted in Chatzitheodoridis (2002: 264–6).

The engagement of Western Thracian Pomaks with EAO stands in contrast to the failure of EAM/ELAS to gain significant inroads into the Muslim population in the area. Both cultural and ideological reasons may help to explain the greater affinity to the EAO. Most fundamentally, the Turkish speaking Pontians who formed the backbone of the groups loyal to Anton Tsaous, were naturally best placed to establish channels of communication with the Pomak

Aliens' Directorate-General, II Office, D. Vlastaris, 'Report of the Muslims living in Greece', July 1952; HW/12/315, Turkish Foreign Ministry, Ankara, to Turkish Embassy, Athens, No. 144321, 26 April 1945; HW/12/314, Turkish Ambassador, Athens, to Foreign Ministry, Ankara, No. 144198, 25 April 1945; HW/12/320, Turkish Ambassador, Athens, to Foreign Ministry, Ankara, No. 146302, 12 June 1945; FO/371/48784, British Embassy, Athens, 'Memorandum', 23 May 1945. For the Greek attempt to lay claim to Pomak-populated areas in Bulgaria after the war see Chapter 6.

communities in the Rhodope mountains, most of whom were able to converse in Turkish (in addition to their native Bulgarian dialect). Both Pomaks and Pontians were mountainous people, engaged in animal breeding and subsistence agriculture. Their isolated and introverted communities placed huge importance on issues of personal and family honour and resented outside intrusion. Committed to their (different) religious beliefs, the two groups shared an overtly conservative outlook and similarly masculine personal codes. The Pontians, who had lived alongside Muslim communities in the Black Sea for centuries, would have been in relatively familiar territory when they first established contact with the Pomaks. The same is not true about the intellectual instructors of EAM or the overwhelmingly 'Greek' membership of the local ELAS. Indeed many Pomaks around the village of Echinos confirmed their affinity towards the EAO in personal interviews.[27]

Evidence of Pomak sympathies towards the EAO, however, should not lead to misleading conclusions regarding the extent and intensity of Muslim resistance against the Bulgarian occupation within Western Thrace. The field of EAO operations in Western Thrace was limited. The organisation had almost no impact on the lowlands in either the Xanthi or Rhodope districts. Its engagement with the Turks in these areas was, thus, minimal. This reflected a regional pattern of subdued resistance activity across both sides of the ideological divide. When compared with other regions of Greece such as Roumeli (Central Greece) or Thessaly, EAM/ELAS' presence in Western Thrace was both weak and ill-coordinated. Similarly Nationalist resistance in the area did not match the organisational and numerical strength of EDES in Epirus. For the British too, who had sought early contact with resistance groups in Central Greece, Western Thrace never really became a primary field of engagement in their struggle against the Axis. Neither did the Muslim community feature in the British (and later the American) strategic planning in the area. Western Thrace, it seems, remained peripheral in the wider story of resistance in occupied Greece.

5.5   Muslim collaboration with the Bulgarian forces

Whilst the Muslims of Western Thrace kept most resistance groups at an arm's length, they seemed equally unenthusiastic to engage in active collaboration with the Bulgarian forces. Rather akin to the resistance organisations, it proved very difficult for the Bulgarians to penetrate and influence these insular and, often, remote communities. The latter held no sympathies for the new occupation regime, as a result of their previous bitter experiences of Bulgarian rule (1913–19), as well as the fear and oppression instigated by new authorities. Instead, the Muslim community simply endeavoured to

---

[27] Interview 4; Interview 12.

survive the occupation, a strategy that neither assisted nor disrupted the Bulgarian plans in the area.

The official correspondence of the new Bulgarian authorities in the area reveals significant difficulties in 'decoding' the attitude of local Muslims towards them. For example, a report by the Bulgarian School Inspector of Xanthi to the Ministry of Education, in October 1943, claimed that:

> The overall conduct of the Greek and the Turkish populations has been negative towards the Bulgarian authorities. The Communist and the British propaganda have only managed to exercise considerable influence on the Greeks, especially in the urban centres, where there is more stock of working-class population. The Turkish people are not interested in political affairs. They only care for matters related to Turkey. The Greeks are following the progress of the War and change their attitude in view of the way in which things develop. Many Turks wish for the victory of England. The Mohammedan Bulgarians [i.e. the Pomaks] are indifferent towards political matters.[28]

A rather similar tone was struck in a series of reports by the educational authorities of *Belomorie*, which argued that 'the Turks behave very well towards the authorities'[29] and that 'the Turkish population is not at all interested in political developments'.[30] Yet, a different report by the District Governor of Komotini to the Ministry of Interior underlined that 'the Turkish population is undertaking intense anti-Bulgarian propaganda'.[31] In his communication to the same Ministry a few months later (January 1944), the Governor-General of *Belomorie*, shared similar fears:

> Most intellectual young Kemalist Turks arrange meetings and they discuss political developments. They spread the rumour that in May 1944 Turkey will annex the area ranging from Alexandroupolis to Nestos, in exchange for its support for England during the war.[32]

Many Greek sources also present a rather benign picture with regards to the Western Thracian Muslims and often praise them for their positive

---

[28] CSA/662/1/26, Prefecture School Inspector, Xanthi, to the Ministry of Education, No. 3362, 1 October 1943.

[29] CSA/177/5/83, Regional School Inspector, to the Ministry of Education, 'Report for March and April 1944', No. 398, 26 April 1944.

[30] CSA/177/8/13, Inspectorate-General of Education, to the Governor-General of Education, Undated (but referring to the academic year 1942–43).

[31] CSA/264/7/848, District Governor, Komotini, to the Interior Ministry, No. 2546, 16 March 1943.

[32] CSA/662k/1/14, Governor-General of Belomorie, to Interior Ministry, No. 231, 10 January 1944.

predisposition towards the Greek community. In November 1941, for example, the Greek Inspector-General for Prefectures, Athanasios Chrysochoou,
suggested that 'the Turkish element has kept a rather favourable position
towards the Greeks'.[33] Similarly, the Rhodope Gendarmerie Command in
1947, referring to the wartime period, recalled that 'the Turks of Rhodope,
under the guidance of the Turkish Consulate of Komotini, did not proceed
to any obvious propagandist activities against the Greek element and our
national interests in general'.[34] The same attitude is verified by the British
War Office which, in February 1944, concluded that 'the present Turkish
population [in Western Thrace] is consistently philhellenic and hardly constitutes a minority problem at all'.[35]

There were, of course, exceptions. An unnamed report by the Greek secret
services in Western Thrace written in 1952 (at the height of anti-Communist
hysteria and just before the onset of the Greek-Turkish conflict over Cyprus)
painted a rather different picture:

> During the same [i.e. wartime] period, the Muslim Youth did not cease
> to move in secret for the preservation of its unity and its national con-
> sciousness, while some Muslims continued to provide the Bulgarians
> with malicious information against Greeks... During the rule of EAM,
> the Youth, and the Young Turks more general, made an attempt to
> assume the leadership of the community, because the then Communist
> administration appeared to offer some freedom with respect to the
> minority's administration, appointing the pro-EAM Osman Nuri,
> now a Member of the Greek Parliament, as Director of the Managing
> Committee of Xanthi, who, in a speech he delivered in Xanthi's
> central square, accused the Greek administration of mistreating the
> minority.[36]

Greek nationalist hysteria aside, the truth was that there were very few
instances of collaboration between members of the Muslim community and
the Bulgarians forces. Oral testimonies from the villages north of Xanthi

---

[33] See Administration-General of Macedonia, '4th Report of additional information collected until 30 November about events in Eastern Macedonia and Western
Thrace against the Greek element', in DIS/GES 1998: 312–333.

[34] AYE/1947/111.1, Commander of Rhodope Gendarmerie, 'Report on active propaganda and Public safety in the district of the Rhodope Gendarmerie Command', 13
September 1947.

[35] WO/252/800 Greece, Zone book No. 8 "Macedonia and Thrace", Part 1, People
and Administration, 29 February 1944.

[36] GAK (Kavalla), 'Archive of Foreign and Minority Schools', F.95B, Ministry of
Interior, Aliens' Directorate-General, II Office, D. Vlastaris, 'Report of the Muslims
living in Greece', July 1952.

confirmed that some local Pomaks cooperated with the 'Bulgarisation' campaign instigated by the occupying forces:

> [There were] people who changed their names to Bulgarian ones in order to obtain privileges and, as a result of the oppressive conditions, cooperated with the Bulgarians and assisted the occupation authorities.[37]

Perhaps the best known story of individual collaboration is the case of Hamdi Hüseyin Fehmi. Papadimitriou (2003: 150) argues that Fehmi, who had been President of the Xanthi Committees for the Management of Muslim Properties collaborated openly with the Bulgarians, to the extent that he chose to wear a Bulgarian military uniform. In a somewhat bizarre turn of fortunes, Fehmi was later recruited by the post-war Greek authorities in order to undermine Bulgaria's sovereignty along the Kresna-Harmanli corridor (see Chapter 6). Another case was that of Mehmet Arnaous, a 30-year old barber from Xanthi, who in 1946 received the death penalty by the Special Collaborators' Tribunal of Komotini for being 'a traitor of the nation and a collaborator of the Germans', whose reprisals in Didimoteicho, on Arnaous' advice, resulted in the execution of four local people.[38] The third best known incident involved Neir Bey from Orestiada. According to the testimony of a local Greek resistance fighter:

> [Neir Bay was] an agent of German intelligence, who established his own network of informants and provided the Germans with reliable information. Neir himself did not hesitate to send his own son to prison in order to monitor the conversations between members of the resistance who had been arrested. The latter soon realized his motives and took extra precautions. The future of Neir Bey's son proved ill-fated. In his effort to flee to Turkey, he was arrested by the Greek guerrillas and paid with his life for his good services to the invaders. (Terzoudis 1985: 40)

Further isolated incidents of Muslim collaboration are reported in the memoirs of ELAS fighters such as Kasapis (1977: 63) and Terzoudis (1985: 254–255), who, nevertheless, present no specific evidence or particular names in relation to these activities.[39]

Whatever few instances of collaboration between the Muslim community and the Axis forces existed, it is certain that these never assumed a mass

---

[37] Interview 18; Interview 27.

[38] *Eleftheri Thraki,* 26 February 1946.

[39] There was another individual case of a Turkish national from Ioannina, named Hasan Pas(ch)enta, who had allegedly collaborated with the Axis forces. He was arrested by Greek guerrillas on 21 October 1944 and was imprisoned. According to the Turkish embassy in Athens he was mistreated and the Embassy questioned the circumstances of his arrest by the Greek authorities. AYE/1947/28.5.

character or an organised form. In most cases they involved individuals (as indeed was the case with Greek Orthodox collaboration in the area), rather than organised groups (but see the Armenian case in Chapter 4). There is only one notable exception to this pattern: a rather peculiar case of 'cross-community' collaboration. According to Terzoudis (1985: 40, 135), it involved a Belorussian, named Turboi, from Orestiada who, under German instructions, led a 65-strong group of collaborators, which included 15–20 Greeks and a number of 'non-Christian Gypsies, Turks, one Armenian and some other opportunist inhabitants from the areas of Didimoteicho and Orestiada'. Turboi's group took part in joint operations with the Germans in the wider area of Evros, but was later liquidated by local ELAS forces. Terzoudis' story can, in all likelihood, be cross-referenced with an O.S.S. report which makes reference to the nucleus of a Security Battalion that was formed in Evros on 28 March 1944. According to the Americans, the group consisted of 43 men, of which 13 were Greeks and 30 'Gypsies or Turks'.[40]

5.6   The Turkish Consulate of Komotini

The onset of the Bulgarian occupation of Western Thrace placed the Turkish Consulate in Komotini in an extremely delicate position. Ever since its establishment in the aftermath of the Lausanne Treaty (1923), the Consulate was regarded as the natural 'protector' of the local Muslim community as well as the main vehicle for the propagation of Kemalist ideals to the traditionalist communities in the area. By itself this was a rather hazardous task. The diplomatic imperatives of the War complicated matters further. During the early stages, Turkey's ambiguous policy of neutrality necessitated a very careful balancing act vis-à-vis the German troops who were stationed along the Greco-Turkish border and the Bulgarian forces who occupied the rest of Western Thrace where the main body of the Muslim communities resided (for more on this see Chapter 3). The Turkish Consulate, headed by a former veteran of the Turkish campaign in Asia Minor against the Greeks, Tevfik Türker, faced a nearly impossible task: on the one hand not to offend the Axis forces on the ground, whilst at the same time trying to minimise the worst Bulgarian excesses against its kin communities and halt the wave of emigration of local Muslims to Turkey that was gathering pace in the meantime.

Similarly, according to Batıbey (1976: 7–8, 12–15), the first days of the Bulgarian occupation were rife with rumours that a massive pogrom against the Muslim population was imminent. This plan was allegedly averted following the intervention by the Turkish Consul with the Bulgarian authorities on 8 May 1941. The meeting between Türker and the Bulgarians is also confirmed by Minaidis (1984: 124) who claims that the Turkish Consul was mistakenly arrested by a Bulgarian patrol on the way, only to be released

---

[40] NARA/RG 59/R&A 2165, OSS Research and Analysis Branch Reports, 'The Greek Security Battalions', 18 May 1944.

subsequently with a Bulgarian apology. The Greek Ambassador in Ankara, Raphael Raphael, also referred to the above incidents:

> All that has come through is a report depicting in the blackest colours the Bulgarian occupation. The Turkish Consul was obliged to protest to the Bulgarians [...] but without result. As the Turkish Government does not recognize the Bulgarian occupation of Thrace, a demarche protesting against Bulgaria [...] was made yesterday in Berlin and the return of the German ambassador is being awaited in order that a similar protest may be made to him.[41]

Oral testimonies suggested that Türker held subsequent meetings with the German authorities where he asked for their assistance to bring the Bulgarians to reason.[42]

Batıbey (1976: 13) further recalls that soon after their arrival in Komotini, Bulgarian soldiers attempted to bring down the Turkish flag from the building of the Turkish Consulate, but were confronted by the Turkish Consul who threatened them with his pistol. Such an act of defiance must have certainly impressed the locals. Yet, under the diplomatic imperatives it faced, the Consulate's power to exercise influence over the local Muslim community was severely restricted. Indeed, the treatment of the Pomak communities in the Rhodope Mountains as 'lapsed' Bulgarians made their connection to the Consulate unacceptable in the eyes of the occupying forces. The influence of the Consulate over the Turks of the lowlands was certainly greater, but there too a significant hard core of 'traditionalists' who resented Kemalist modernity were likely to have been reluctant to engage with it.

As the local conditions worsened, the incentives of local Mulsims to seek the protection of the Consulate increased. The latter was delighted to oblige. Throughout the occupation period, local Turkish officials worked tirelessly to enhance the presence of Kemalist teachers in minority schools. The Turkish Consul, for example, provided regular financial support to Kemalist teachers who were fired by the Bulgarian administration for promoting nationalist views. According to Batıbey, this is how one such teacher recalled his first contact with the Consulate:

> It was a few days before Kurban Bayram [a Muslim religious celebration]. The money I had in my pocket was not enough to buy "coupon bread" [i.e. ration-bread]. I had a family of six. My kids were hungry. Dark thoughts filled my head as to what I could do. My friends had no money either. During that time I was shivering from being destitute, a Consulate official came and sat next to me as I lay in a corner outside my

---

[41] HW/12/264, Raphael, Ankara, to Foreign Affairs, Canea [Chania], No. 090556, 1 May 1941.
[42] See, for example, Interview 8.

house. He took an envelope out of his pocket: "this is from the Consul, Mr. Tevfik Türker" he said. And he walked away. I opened the envelope. And what did I see? It was full of money. I went into my house immediately. I started counting. There was six hundred *levas* exactly. At that time the value of the *leva* was high. With this money I could buy Bulgarian "coupon bread" for more than three months. Without wasting any time I went to buy the corn bread they gave us. I fed my family. We praised Allah. We prayed to Allah to give many years to the Consul. This assistance continued. Mr. Tevfik saved us from starvation. As I found out later, such assistance was given to teachers with many children, like me. May Allah give him what he wishes for. (Batibey 1976: 52–3)

On the other hand, the Bulgarian-appointed traditionalist teachers became the target of a systematic smear campaign by the Consulate. The efforts of the Turkish government to reshape the content of minority education in Western Thrace towards the ideals of Turkish nationalism had already begun in earnest in the 1930s, assisted by the spirit of rapprochement with the Greek government (on this see also Chapter 2).[43] The Pomak communities in Eastern Thrace were also targeted for similar 'enlightenment'. According to the local Turkish inspector:

In the region of Thrace there exists a kin population, called Pomaks, who are ill-fortuned to be deprived of the Turkish language and, as a result, of our national culture and feelings too...there are 76 Pomak villages in Edirne, 53 in Kirklareli, 19 in Tekirdağ and 27 in Çanakkale...81 such villages do not have a school...In the villages with schools the new generations regained their mother tongue and national culture.[44]

The cleavage between Kemalist and traditionalist elements within the Muslim community and its impact on the occupying forces is also confirmed by Bulgarian sources. According to Daskalov (1992b:125–126):

Around 69%[45] of the Turkish people were Kemalists and the rest Old Turks. Their supporters were actively and openly involved in propaganda activities against the attempts of the Bulgarian authorities to include the

---

[43] During a visit to Greece, in April 1938, the Turkish Premier Celal Bayar offered £220 for the repair of the central minority school on Komotini. The Komotini community leader, Ismail Mestanoğlu expressed his gratitude stressing that "this high favour...gave the Western Thrace Turks the courage to hang on to the Grand Revolution that they always believe in". BCA/14532/301000/144292, Ismail Mestanoğlu. Community leader to the Prime Minister, 9 May 1938.

[44] BCA/14530/301000/1432811, Public Inspectorate of Thrace to the Prime Minister, 22 April 1937.

[45] The derivation of the figure 69 per cent is not known to us.

children of the Bulgarian Mohammedans [i.e. Pomaks] in the Bulgarian schools. [...] The Turkish intelligence service recruited collaborators from among this opposition. The Turkish Consulate of Gumuldjina [Komotini] was the centre of the anti-Bulgarian opposition of the Turkish population. Hafız Galip, Osman Mehmet, Kitapçi Mustafa were the leaders of the opposition of the Gumuldjina Turks against the Bulgarian authorities. Hasan Demir, Serday Bey, Rashid Bey and others were the leaders of the opposition of the Xanthi Turks.

Indeed, official Turkish correspondence confirms regular meetings between Consulate staff and local minority youth, both during the period of the Bulgarian occupation and in the immediate aftermath of Western Thrace's liberation.[46] By that time the strategy of the Turkish Consulate to use minority education as a vehicle for defeating the traditionalist element within the minority and promoting nationalist ideals had started to pay dividends. In his official correspondence to the Turkish Foreign Ministry in December 1944, the Turkish Consul of Komotini reported:

> I visited one of the newly opened Turkish minority schools. Despite three years of Bulgarian occupation, I witnessed with amazement the achievements of the little Turkish pupils in such a small period of time...I am touched by their expression of loyalty and respect towards our national leader İsmet İnönü, by their commemoration of Atatürk, by the flowers in red and white colours that were offered to us and by the sorrowful songs they sung for Rumelia, which were composed after the Balkan Wars. I knew that if these songs were heard by any of the Greek administrators they would not be allowed and the teacher told me that such kind of performances are hidden from foreign eyes and they are very careful to share these sad memories only with friends.[47]

The Consulate's strategy of containment vis-à-vis the Bulgarians had also improved its profile in the local Muslim community. Writing in late 1944, on the occasion of the religious celebration of Kurban Bayram, the Turkish Consul in Komotini had every reason to be joyful (see Box 5.1).

Hence, by the end of the War, the Turkish Consulate had seen a remarkable reversal of fortunes. A few years previously, a large section of the minority (namely the old-Muslim traditionalists) regarded it with suspicion as a rather unwelcome vehicle of Kemalist secularism that threatened the traditional power structures within the Muslim community. The Bulgarian

---

[46] BCA/433591/301000/25672512, Turkish Consul. Komotini to Turkish Foreign Ministry, 2 December 1944.

[47] BCA/433592/301000/25672513, Turkish Consul, Komotini, to Turkish Foreign Ministry, 16 December 1944.

Box 5.1 Communication of the Turkish Consul of Komotini to the Turkish
Foreign Ministry, December 1944

Around 4,000 of our kin population from all around the district of Western
Thrace came to the Consulate and competed with each other in expressing
their loyalty to their motherland. The leaders and members of the Muslim
Communities of İskeçe [Xanthi] and Gümülcine [Komotini], the local Muftis,
the leaders and members from the Turkish Youth Unions of the two towns and
some from the other towns, and people from every class and occupation, farmers and villagers came to visit me for the four days of the Bayram ... Among these
visitors were people coming from the Hodja and Hadji groups who are remnants
of the Ottoman Empire ... and who, due to their mistaken beliefs and ignorance,
remain foreign to our land ... I understand that this flow does not have a sincere
interest in approaching Turkey or ourselves, but it suggests that their mentality
is changing and becomes more receptive to new ideas. With few exceptions, it
appears that most people are not offended by the new ideas and join the intel-
lectuals that keep pace with the current reform movements in our land.

Source: BCA/433591/301000/25672512, Turkish Consul. Komotini to Turkish Foreign
Ministry, 2 December 1944.

occupation, however, had introduced new realities on the ground that made
old intra-minority divisions increasingly obsolete. In the words of Öksüz
(2003: 273) the wartime experience had allowed 'the Turkish Consulate
in Komotini [to pay] close attention to the problems of Western Thracian
Turks, and [play] an important role in keeping them loyal to Turkey, in
indentifying them with the basic principles of the Turkish Revolution and
in building strong bonds with the Turkish state'. At the same time, diplomatic and logistical wartime imperatives had restricted the sphere of the
Consulate's influence to its core kin, namely the Turks of Western Thrace's
lowlands. Both the Pomaks (who were subjected to a more intense assimilation campaign by the Bulgarians) and the Roma (who remained locked in
their own marginalisation) retained a significant degree of independence
from the entreaties of the Consulate. This variegated pattern of patronage would also impact on the nature of violence experienced by the local
Muslim communities during the approaching civil war (see Chapters 7
and 8).

5.7   Conclusions

As the Muslims of Western Thrace faced up to the dilemmas of life under
the Bulgarian occupation, overwhelmingly they chose disengagement and
passivity rather than resistance or collaboration. In this reaction, they were
served by a number of wider contextual factors that inhibited an organised
resistance on their part.

The general level of resistance activity in Eastern Macedonia and Western Thrace was to prove lower than that witnessed in other parts of Greece. The wider region had experienced one of the first uprisings against the Axis anywhere in Europe, but the brutality of the Bulgarians' response stifled further activity thereafter. Locally, EAM was neither strong enough to protect nor sufficiently popular to inspire support. Bizarrely, EAM was affected by two episodes of new leaders arriving to falsely claim authority from the national command. The fact that this could occur reflected the geographic isolation of the region and the limitations of the force. The lack of engagement of EAM with the local Muslims contradicted previous Communist rhetoric on forging alliances with them. By contrast, the EAO grouping did make some inroads into the Muslim community – a contrast affected by both a greater linguistic and ideological proximity – but this was not until the end of the War.

At the same time, there is very little evidence of collaboration on the part of the Muslim community with the Bulgarian authorities. The *Belomorie* regime found the Muslim community difficult to penetrate, but its policies also repelled them. The most telling case – the Pomaks – rejected the attempted 'Bulgarisation' of their community and suffered badly in the hands of the occupying Bulgarian forces. In the lowlands the Turkish Consulate in Komotini, as the 'natural' protector of the local Muslim community, was placed in a very difficult position. There were episodes in which the Consul was able to intervene with the Bulgarians and achieve some limited gains. Yet, the Consulate could do little for the Pomaks, given their isolation and their 'special' treatment by the Bulgarians. Overall, the attempted guardianship of the Consulate for the Muslims of the region probably served to boost the latter's Kemalist rather than Ottoman orientation. With the rejection of both the Bulgarians and the Greek Communists, the Muslim community, particularly in the lowlands, experienced a 'Turkification' by default.

Many of these themes were to recur during the period of the civil war. The 'puzzle' of the Muslims' passivity and disengagement is thus a two-part one and the study now turns to the period of liberation in 1944 and the descent into civil war. The explanation of the puzzle will be brought together in Chapter 9.

6

In-Between Two Wars

6.1 Introduction

As WWII entered its closing stages, the power struggle for control of Western Thrace assumed a renewed urgency, both internationally and locally. With the advance of the Red Army, the Fascist Bulgarian regime at home collapsed. Subsequent Bulgarian attempts to re-write the history of Sofia's entanglement with the Axis forces and maintain access to the Aegean Sea met with stiff opposition by both Greece and Turkey. Behind their reaction – and those of their allies in London – laid fears that Bulgaria's ambitions could facilitate Soviet expansionism and disturb regional security. In Athens, the approaching end of the war encouraged territorial revisionism against Bulgaria through the deployment of the 'Pomak card'. The claim of the Greek government to southern Bulgaria, however, lacked credibility and was eventually swept away by the wider geo-political bargain of the post-War settlement.

Locally, the collapse of the *Belomorie* regime left behind it scenes of economic devastation and an explosive political mix. Remarkably, the Bulgarian army remained *in situ* proclaiming their allegiance to the Communist cause. EAM/ELAS entered into a *de facto* power-sharing arrangement with the Bulgarian army until the latter left in late October 1944. Following their withdrawal, local scores were settled between ELAS and EAO and the former emerged as the effective administration across Western Thrace. When the 'official' Greek state returned to the area during the spring of 1945, its authority was both limited and contested. Although the civil war was still some months away, the main battle-lines of the conflict to come were already visible.

Amidst this fluidity, the Muslim community in the region faced a series of new challenges. Economic hardship and deteriorating security forced many to seek better fortune in the lowlands of Western Thrace or, more typically, to emigrate to Turkey. In the meantime, the process of the minority's own political and cultural transformation continued. A new generation of minority leaders and the results of the 1946 election confirmed the ascendance of the pro-Kemalist fraction. With the Bulgarian threat now in retreat, Ankara found a more fertile ground to reassert its position as the protector of all Western Thracian Muslims. Here, too, the terms of the later diplomatic contest between Greece and Turkey began to take shape.

6.2   The fall of the Bulgarian empire

The Allies advance

By mid-1944 the clear prospect of defeat for Nazi Germany prompted many within the Axis camp to turn their back on Hitler in a desperate effort to disassociate themselves. For Bulgaria, the approaching defeat of the German forces posed a mortal danger for its aspirations to consolidate its control over Macedonia and Western Thrace and ensure the long-term sustainability of the post-1941 status quo. The impending arrival of the Red Army in the southern Balkans and the prospect of Bulgaria losing its prized possessions along the Aegean coast triggered a political crisis in the country. The unexpected death, in August 1943, of the pro-Nazi King Boris III had already created a power vacuum that was only partially filled by the Regency Council set up to advise Simeon II, Boris' six-year-old son and heir. Although some ill-fated secret contacts between Bulgarian officials and the Allies on negotiating a treaty of surrender did take place in January 1944 (Miller 1975),[1] Bulgaria's attachment to the Axis remained strong throughout the premiership of Dobri Bozhilov.

With the advance of the Red Army in the Balkans, the more conciliatory Ivan Bagrianov became Prime Minister of Bulgaria (in May 1944). Next door, in Romania, the collaborationist regime of Ion Antonescu collapsed on 23 August, following a coup by King Michael. Within a day Romania changed sides and allied with the Soviet Union which quickly overran the whole country. The 3rd Soviet Army under General Fyodor Tolbukhin continued its march towards Bulgaria. On 26 August the Bulgarian Government in an attempt to appease the Soviets declared its neutrality in the war between the Soviet Union and Germany. The Soviets were not impressed. Their advance towards Sofia continued uninterrupted.

The imminent arrival of the Red Army in Bulgaria produced shockwaves throughout Macedonia and Western Thrace. The news lifted the morale of the local ELAS forces which carried out a large scale campaign of sabotage

---

[1] Bulgaria had declared war on Great Britain and the United States at the end of 1941. The first military engagement between the two sides, however, came at the end of 1943 when British and American aircraft launched a series of bomb raids against the Bulgarian capital, Sofia. Despite its Axis affiliation, however, Bulgaria never declared war on the Soviet Union. The two countries maintained diplomatic relations throughout the war.

and attacks against the retreating German troops. The resolve of the German troops was badly shaken and a number of German garrisons surrendered to ELAS or fled to Turkey (Kasapis 1977: 196–230, Vol. II). From late August 1944, ELAS' 81st regiment controlled several towns within the German occupation zone such as Feres, Didimoteicho and Soufli. A string of successful raids against fleeing German troops brought plenty of military supplies to ELAS' forces who soon secured their complete control over the German occupation zone. By 4 September all German forces had evacuated Evros for fear of being cut off, while Bulgarian forces also retreated from central Macedonia. Significantly, however, Bulgarian troops did not retreat from Eastern Macedonia and the rest of Western Thrace – areas which Bulgaria still considered its own territory.

In the meantime, German forces had begun a rapid withdrawal from Bulgaria. In some cases, Bulgarian forces attacked small and isolated German units in their attempt to display some anti-Axis activity (Miller 1975). On the diplomatic front, events moved at an astonishing pace. On 5 September, the Soviet Union declared war on Bulgaria. Six hours later, Bulgaria declared war on Germany, while the German retreat from Bulgaria had almost been completed. For a few hours Bulgaria was at war with both the Axis and the Allies. Eventually, the six-hour Bulgarian-Soviet war ended with no casualties when the Bulgarian Ambassador in Ankara proposed an armistice with the Soviets. On 8 September, Tolbukhin's troops invaded Bulgaria facing no resistance since the Bulgarian Army was ordered not to oppose the Soviets. The next day, a coup organised by the 'Fatherland Front', a coalition of Bulgarian opposition parties dominated by the Communist Party of Bulgaria, overthrew the government of Konstantin Muraviev (who had replaced Bagrianov as Prime Minister on 2 September 1944) and formed a pro-Soviet administration under Kimon Georgiev. Within a day Bulgaria had moved from the Axis to the Allies and from fascism to communism. Having performed an astonishing u-turn, the new Bulgarian government sought to exercise leverage and to maintain control over Eastern Macedonia and Western Thrace.

Bulgaria tries to stay

While the diplomatic endgame for the post-war settlement remained some way off, the tactics of the Bulgarian government focused on delaying their troops' retreat from the occupied areas. Taking advantage of the conflict between feuding Greek resistance troops (particularly ELAS and EAO) in Macedonia, the Bulgarians tried to justify their military presence in occupied Greece as a guarantee for maintaining law and order. In addition, the Bulgarian government continued to insist that its troops remained stationed in the area with the objective of carrying out a full scale campaign against the Germans (Kotzageorgi-Zymari and Kazamias 2002: 255–256). These arguments served a dual purpose. On the one hand they enabled Bulgaria to maintain control of Eastern Macedonia and Western Thrace, and, on the other, to reinvent the role of the Bulgarian army in the Greek territories, not as forces of occupation, but rather as friendly Allied troops. The Bulgarian government made exhaustive efforts to underline that Bulgaria was now an Allied country.[2] It emphasised that after the country was occupied by the Red Army, the Bulgarian Army was under the command of Soviet General Tolbukhin. Indeed, later on the Bulgarian 1st Army, led by the Soviets, followed the Soviet campaign against Hungary and Austria (Crampton 1997: 181–183).

Bulgarian expectations of maintaining their status in Macedonia and Western Thrace met with stiff opposition by the British. London made clear that the retreat of the Bulgarian forces was the necessary condition for an armistice between Bulgaria and the Allies (Kazamias 2002: 251). The demand stipulated that the evacuation of Bulgarian troops should be completed within 15 days, while it was also suggested that a high ranking British liaison officer should be sent to the area to supervise the evacuation. Initially, British aspirations were met with hesitation by both the US and the USSR, but eventually both Allies accepted the British proposals (Baev 1997: 60–64).[3]

In the meantime, the changing constellations of power produced chaotic scenes in Western Thrace. Bulgaria had kept an army of 50,000 in the area under the command of General Asen Sirakov.[4] After its consolidation in

---

[2] Very enlightening in that respect was the lengthy memorandum, prepared by the Fatherland Front, presenting Bulgaria's case to the Allies. The memorandum included a number of tables outlining Bulgaria's contribution to the 'war against Germany'. The memorandum also claimed that 'the Greeks fail to mention the enormous sacrifices made by the Bulgarian State in order to help the population of this province and to improve general conditions there. ...These and other constructive and social activities and lasting improvements should be taken into consideration when the Bulgarian occupation of Thrace and Eastern Macedonia is being appreciated'. For more details see 'The Truth about the Greek Reparation Claims against Bulgaria' (1 February 1946), attached to FO/371/58537, British Military Mission to Bulgaria, to the Under-secretary of State and the War Office, 'Greek Claims against Bulgaria', 18 May 1946. This was a Bulgarian reply to the Kingdom of Greece, Ministry of Foreign Affairs, Tables of Damage done to Greeks by the Bulgarians, Athens, 1 October 1945, in FO/371/58535. The British regarded these Bulgarian claims as an 'essay in exaggeration and misinterpretation'. WO/178/50, War Diary of Allied Control Commission (Bulgaria), British Mission, 1 June 1945 to 30 June 1945.

[3] On the armistice terms and Britain's attitude on the withdrawal of the Bulgarian army from Thrace see: WO/201/1606A, Foreign Office to Caserta, Tel. 3314, 20 September 1944; FO/195/2483, Foreign Office, to Leeper, Caserta, Tel. 20, 20 September 1944; WO/204/360, Allied Force Headquarters, Joint Planning Staff, 'Armistice Terms', 27 February 1944.

[4] WO/201/1606A, Ankara to Foreign Office, Tel. 611, 2 October 1944. FO/195/2483, Helm, Ankara, to Foreign Office, Tel. 1733, 2 October 1944.

Box 6.1   Declaration of Fatherland Front Ministers over Macedonia and Thrace, October 1944

We, the Ministers of the Fatherland Front, have abolished Bulgarian rule of Macedonia and Thrace, we reconstituted the rights and freedoms of the people, and we have given all power to the local people's organisation EAM.

After a long period of darkness, the sun of freedom rises for Macedonia and Thrace. Fascism and oppression against the people – who have been robbed, tortured and slaughtered with no reason other than defending their freedom – are over. In full brotherly agreement with EAM, the Bulgarian army remains at its posts within Macedonia and Thrace in order to serve the people, to fight the German troops that remain on Macedonian territory and to smash Bulgarian and Greek fascists. The existing Bulgarian institutions, except the fascist ones, will remain in place in order to assist the military, the new authorities and the population. Representatives of EAM will be accepted in the post offices, the telegraph offices and the railways. These public servants, either Bulgarian or Greek, will be on the payroll of the local government.

Secret agents of the enemy tried to undermine the relations between Bulgarian civil servants and the Bulgarian population. Instead of serving the public, directors and employees of the public administration abandoned their posts causing disorder. They must return immediately to their posts and serve the Bulgarian military and the Greek authorities until they are granted official permission to return to Bulgaria with their families. The directors of the public administration will have to deposit their previous salaries, as well as pre-deposit their next ones.

Thracian Bulgarians will remain in their homes. Their safety is guaranteed by the Greek authorities and the Bulgarian army. Moreover, Bulgarian immigrants will not be transferred until the necessary measures are taken. Today, more than ever before the life of Bulgarian employees and immigrants is guaranteed because the administration of Macedonia and Thrace is under the people's authority, while the Bulgarian army is ready to cooperate with the administrative authorities and the antartes [i.e. guerrillas] for the rooting of democracy and the annihilation of the enemies

We express our gratitude to the glorious Bulgarian army and its leaders for their support in achieving our mission. We also salute the Greek antartes [i.e. guerrillas] of EAM and the Greek people who proved their trust to us from the first moment we arrived and who worked alongside us in establishing the new authorities.

We call all nationalities of Macedonia and Thrace to rally around the new Greek authorities in order to maintain order and to defend freedom.

Source: AYE/1944/10.1, Greek Embassy, Ankara to Foreign Ministry, 10 October 1944.

---

power, the Fatherland Front sent officials loyal to the new regime to undertake the command of Thracian troops and relieve those who had supported the previous administration. That transition was by no means smooth. In Alexandroupolis, for example, there were clashes between Bulgarian naval officers and officers of the territorial army loyal to the Fatherland Front. At the same time, the new regime dispatched a delegation of two cabinet ministers, Terpesev and Neikov, to Eastern Macedonia and Western Thrace in order to tour the area and to propagandise (see Box 6.1) the intentions of the Fatherland Front to the local population (Baev 1997: 57–60).

Bulgarian troops started to evacuate Eastern Macedonia and Western Thrace on 13 September 1944. The following day ELAS entered Komotini and Xanthi. The circumstances of the Bulgarian retreat however remained complex.[5] Although the Bulgarians handed over political authority to EAM, a number of Bulgarian troops remained stationed in the area for a number of weeks. In the main cities controlled by ELAS, militia groups were formed by members of EAM in order to maintain order.[6] All prisoners and hostages taken by the Bulgarians during the occupation were released and in many cases as happened in Komotini-Bulgarian officials were executed in public by ELAS court-martials. Both EAM and the Bulgarians jointly set up local administration committees (notably for public health and food distribution) in order to face the dramatic problem of food shortages in the area. Amidst this uncertainty, the Bulgarians maintained that Soviet General Tolbukhin himself had given the order that the administration of Western Thrace be undertaken by a four-member administrative committee composed of two Greeks, one Bulgarian and one Turk. In Komotini, the Fatherland Front formed a revolutionary committee with the joint participation of Greeks, Muslims, Armenians and mostly Bulgarians. The committee issued a declaration asking citizens to obey its decisions (see Box 6.2).

In the end, all Bulgarian ambitions and all Greek fears as to the future of Eastern Macedonia and Western Thrace were resolved by the 'percentages agreement' between Churchill and Stalin during their meeting in Moscow on 9th October 1944 (Mazower 2001: 368; Xydis 1963: 57–58). Two days later, the United States, Britain and the Soviet Union in a common declaration to Bulgaria clearly stated that the retreat of the Bulgarian forces from the occupied Greek territories was the necessary prerequisite for an armistice. Bulgaria adhered immediately to the declaration and on 25 October, a day before the expiration of the deadline given to Bulgaria, all Bulgarian troops were withdrawn from Eastern Macedonia and Western Thrace. Bulgaria finally signed a truce with the Soviet Union and the Allies on 28 October 1944, exactly four years after the Greco-Italian War had broken out.

The persistence of the British regarding the retreat of the Bulgarians from Eastern Macedonia and Western Thrace and their anxiety to safeguard

---

[5] WO/178/48, War Diary of Allied Control Commission (Bulgaria)-British Delegation, From 1 November 1944, to 30 November 1944, Report by Maj-Gen. W.H. Oxley, Head of the British Mission to Bulgaria, 'The Evacuation of Bulgarian Armed Forces and Civil Authorities from Thrace'.

[6] HS/5/152, 'Greece, Political, Developments in Drama Area', 25 September 1944; HS/5/152, Greece: Political, 'EAM-ELAS cooperation with Bulgarians', 11 October 1944.

Box 6.2   Declaration of the Provisional Committee of the Fatherland Front in Gumuljina, 11 September 1944

People of Belomorie,

The end of the fratricidal war between Balkan nations is over. The undefeated Red Army of the great Russian nation is marching through the Balkans. The Bulgarian people are welcoming them with joy and submit themselves under its flag. From this day the Bulgarian army gives its right hand to the Red Army and puts itself under the service of the enslaved Balkan nations.

  We make an appeal to the whole of the people in Gumuldjina [Komotini] regardless of ethnicity to have full trust towards the Bulgarian army which is ready to defend the eternal brotherhood of Balkan nations. We appeal to put the undefeated red flag with the hammer and sickle on your houses and put down any other national flag of the deluded Bulgarian and Greek patriots. Maintain order until tomorrow when general assemblies between Bulgarian and Greek freedom fighters will determine the peaceful coexistence of Balkan nations.

Long live the brotherhood between Bulgarians, Greeks, Armenians and Turks!
Long live the comradeship between the red Bulgarian army and the red units!
Long live the free Balkan states!
Long live the freedom bearer Soviet Union and its undefeated Red Army!
Long live Stalin!
Death to Fascism!

On behalf of the Fatherland Front committee in Gumuldjina.

Philip Georgiev, Doctor	Alexander Nitzev	Georg Belev,
Stefan Solakov	Cyril Begaev	Petar Misev
Milous Tsakalov	Vasil Mainov	Cyril Tsernokolev, teacher
Agel Karaivanov	Oto Kakarelis	Atanas Platsidis
Emil Gerasimou	Nikolas Nikolaidis	Kostas Simopoulos
(Unreadable) Yusuf	Şevket Osman	Akvor Kevorkian
Bedros Berberian	Hajic Masianian	

Source: AYE/1947/111.1.

Greek sovereignty over these territories had as much to do with the pursuit of their own interests in Greece as with the settlement of British-Soviet relations in the Balkans (Kuniholm 1980: 126–130).[7] The retreat of the Bulgarian forces was meant to stabilise a devastated Allied country in which Churchill had invested a lot of political capital. The prospect of Greece's

---

[7] This increased British interest was expressed in several British documents. Indicatively see: WO/201/1606A, From Foreign Office to Moscow. Tel. 102, 27 September 1944; WO/201/1606B, Minister Resident Cairo, to Foreign Office, Tel. 2185, 18 September 1944; FO/195/2483, Leeper, Caserta, to Foreign Office, Tel. 1238, 20 September 1944; WO/178/48, War Diary of Allied Control Commission (Bulgaria)-British Delegation, From 1 November 1944, to 30 November 1944, Report by Maj.-Gen. W.H. Oxley, Head of the British Mission to Bulgaria, 'The Evacuation of Bulgarian Armed Forces and Civil Authorities from Thrace'.

northern neighbours being engulfed by the Soviet empire was, at that point, both clear and imminent. The return of Macedonia and Western Thrace to Greece would be an excellent gift by the British to George Papandreou, the Anglophile and staunchly anti-communist Greek politician who was about to return to Greece and to lead a national unity government in Athens. For the British, the consolidation of Papandreou in power was the best guarantee that the ever-increasing influence of EAM would be checked.

On a different level, the retreat of the Bulgarians from Eastern Macedonia and Western Thrace secured common Greco-Turkish borders; a key geopolitical aim of the British in order to safeguard uninterrupted channels of communication in the British empire (Kotzageorgi-Zymari and Kazamias 2002: 266–267). Indeed, Western Thrace was a vital link for the consolidation of British interests in Southeast Europe and the Middle East. Access by the Bulgarians (and, by extension, the Soviet Union) to the Aegean would pose a serious risk for these interests. The British chose Macedonia and Western Thrace as the borderline between the 'Free World' and the 'Iron Curtain' in the Balkans. At the same time, they avoided the Soviet navy dominating the eastern Mediterranean.

On the grand scale of things, the existence of the Muslim minority in the region, made very little difference to how the Allies viewed the post-war settlement there. Thus a wartime British Foreign Office report noted that:

> There is no evidence that under Greek rule they [the Muslims] were in any way a discontented minority, or that the Turkish government is dissatisfied at the way the Greek Government has treated them. In any case, Greece and Turkey have recognized the Treaty of Lausanne as final.[8]

The Americans shared a similar perception. This is evident in a State Department survey of National Minorities in Foreign countries written in January 1947 which reported that: 'the Macedonian Slavs and the Moslem Albanians constituted the two primary minority problems in Greece in the interwar period and seem most likely to raise the minority issue in Greece at the present time'.[9] The report focused on these two minorities in two separate chapters, whereas it failed to make a single reference for the Muslim minority of Western Thrace.

Bulgaria's surrender, however, did not bring an end to its aspirations in Macedonia and Western Thrace. After the war, the new Bulgarian (Fatherland

---

[8] FO/371/33211, The Royal Institute of International Affairs, Foreign Research and Press Service, to Howard, Southern Department, Foreign Office, 'Minorities in Greece', 28 August 1942.

[9] NARA/M1221/4209, 'Department of State, Intelligence Research Report: A Survey on National Minorities in Foreign Countries', 2 January 1947.

Front-dominated) government launched an international campaign aiming at persuading international public opinion that not only had the country become a victim of Nazi ferocity, but it had also paid a heavy price resisting it. A typical example of Bulgaria's argumentation is reflected in the report prepared by the Bulgarian Political Mission in Washington to the United States (see Box 6.3).

Other Bulgarian sentiments went further, as with the publications of the 'Justice for Bulgaria Committee' which stressed that 'Bulgaria has always striven and will always strive for an expedient solution of the question for an actual territorial outlet to a free sea, by achieving the return of Western Thrace, so unjustly taken from her'.[10]

Bulgarian proclamations to that effect, were met with hostility by the Greek government, but also by a number of Greek publications in the area.[11] Similar concerns were also raised by the Turkish press that reported regularly on developments in Western Thrace following the end of the occupation.[12] The vast majority of them fiercely criticized the Bulgarian government and its opportunism and asked for Bulgaria's exemplary punishment for its role in WWII. According to Turkish journalist Hasan Kumcay:

> Instead of contemplating what to do in order to improve their position and to reduce their sentences as war criminals, Bulgarian politicians claim Western Thrace and speak as if they represent a country that made great sacrifices fighting side by side with the Allies during the war. Now, that's an absurd misinterpretation![13]

Shortly before the end of the War, the Bulgarian Ambassador had responded with considerable sarcasm to Turkish demands for the withdrawal of the Bulgarian forces from Western Thrace, informing Ankara that 'if our presence in Thrace causes such a reaction because we have split you from your so beloved Greeks, you can calm down because in a very short while we will evacuate Greece'.[14]

Playing the 'Pomak Card'

The Greek government under Prime Minister Konstantinos Tsaldaris (April 1946–January 1947) responded angrily to the Bulgarian claims. Pursuing its own geo-strategic interests, Athens demanded not only that Western

---

[10] Justice for Bulgaria Committee 1946: 10. For a similar discourse articulated by Bulgarian refugee associations (of those who had left Western Thrace since Neuilly) see Aarbakke (2004).

[11] See indicatively, *Proia*, 6 December 1946.

[12] See, indicatively, the review of Turkish press by the Greek Ministry of Foreign Affairs. AYE/1944/10.1.

[13] See translated article by the Greek Ministry of Foreign Affairs, AYE/1946/42.3.

[14] AYE/1944/8.5, Raphael, Ankara, to Foreign Ministry, 30 September 1944.

Box 6.3   Extracts from *The Truth About Bulgaria*, May 1946

Record as Axis satellite

Bulgaria's role in World War II as an ally of the Axis never really materialized. Despite the persistent demands of Hitler that Bulgaria provide at least several divisions for the Eastern Front – with the promise of Crimea and an interest in the Caucasian oil-fields as inducements – no Bulgarian troops were ever sent against the USSR.

King Boris could not satisfy Hitler in this regard as he well knew that such a move would bring open revolt. But he compensated the Fuehrer by declaring war on England and the United States – another fateful act, of which the Bulgarian people learned over the radio only after it had been made.

[....]

There has been much misrepresentation about the Bulgarian "occupation" of Thrace and Macedonia. The Bulgarian army units entered these areas long after they had been conquered by the Germans; they took no part in the invasion.

[....]

Bulgaria's real war effort

The Bulgarians wasted no time in assuming the offensive against the Wehrmacht. Having already forced the German army of occupation to evacuate their territory, a rejuvenated Bulgarian army left the country's frontiers in the early days of September '44 to make their modest contribution to the Allied cause.

There followed eight months of the only real fighting that the Bulgarian Army did in World War II.

The Germans had taken special precautions in the natural fortresses of the Macedonian mountains in order to maintain contact with their forces in Greece. It took many weeks of the stiffest fighting before the Germans were forced to abandon their entrenched positions at Pirot, Bela Palanka, Niš, Leskovac, Stratsin, Kumanovo, Scopje – the Macedonian Capital, Podujevo, Mitrovica, Raška, Novi Pazar...

By the end of November, however all of Macedonia, much of Serbia and other parts of Yugoslavia had been liberated by the Bulgarian troops and the entire Vardar Valley had been blocked for the retreating Germans.

Not the least result of this campaign was the fact that the Germans were forced to evacuate Greece in such a haste that they had to abandon there, and especially on the Aegean islands, huge quantities of men and materials.

[....]

Retribution

The war that was forced upon Bulgaria did not only cost the lives of untold numbers of innocent people. It caused physical and acute mental pain to most Bulgarians. It brought destruction to their cities and it upset the economic life of their country. It divided the people into warring camps and estranged the nation from the rest of the world. It finally brought the Bulgarian State to the brink of still another national catastrophe.

The Bulgarian people at large were obviously not a voluntary party to the events that led to this disastrous climax. They were carried away by an unfortunate set of circumstances over which they had no control, and by the strength of a small group of political mercenaries who were backed to the fullest extent by the resources and the resourcefulness of the Third Reich.

Punishment for these crimes had to be meted out sooner or later. And the Bulgarians have already held their own trials, and they have meted out punishment against their own war-criminals, against those who acted "as instruments of Hitler" and in utter disregard of the sentiments of the Bulgarian people against those who had the impudence to identify their own petty, egoistic interests with the interests of their nation.

This – probably the most distasteful- chapter in the recent Bulgarian history has already been closed.

Source: Bulgarian Political Mission to Washington, *The Truth About Bulgaria*, May 1946.

Thrace remain under Greek sovereignty, but that the Greek borders be expanded at the expense of Bulgaria. More specifically, Greece demanded the shifting of the Greco-Bulgarian border almost 36 miles to the north and the annexation of a long strip of Bulgarian land, stretching from Kresna to the west towards Harmanli to the east, populated by approximately 300,000 people, of whom almost 150,000 were Bulgarian Pomaks (Thrax 1944: 58–59; Naltsas 1946: 44–50; Kondis 1986: 160; Popovic 1986: 96–98; Eminov 2007). The official Greek objective was to double the distance between the Bulgarian borders and the shores of the Aegean so that Greece could reinforce its strategic defence against a possible Bulgarian invasion in the future. In April 1946, the Greek Ambassador in Washington submitted two written proposals to the US State Department asking for renegotiation of the Greco-Albanian and the Greco-Bulgarian borders. According to Kondis (1986: 160–161) the Greek reasoning was that this had to be done in order for Greece to reinforce its defence against its northern neighbours, to ensure the safety of Greek speaking minorities and to strengthen its strategic role in the Balkans and the Eastern Mediterranean. The State Department asked for the advice of the US Joint Chiefs of Staffs which concluded that the Greek demands both against Albania and Bulgaria were not feasible and could easily lead the Balkans to a new conflict. Later in April-May during the proceedings of the Council of the Allied Ministers of Foreign Affairs in Paris, Greece repeated its claims but it again encountered a negative reaction (Kondis 1986: 162–163).

The last Greek attempt to claim Bulgarian territory took place at the Paris Peace Conference (29 July–11 October 1946)[15] where Allied countries negotiated the details of the peace treaties with Italy, Finland, Romania, Hungary and Bulgaria. The Greek delegation, under Premier Tsaldaris,

[15] Prior to the Paris peace conference, two meetings of the Council of Ministers of Foreign Affairs had taken place during which the annexation of the Dodecanese by Greece was approved.

Plate 1 Balkan Friendships . . . The Turkish Prime Minister, Celal Bayar, Visits Drama, 1938
© War Museum, Athens, Greece.

Plate 2   Before the storm: Greek soldiers pose in front of a Komotini Mosque, 1940
© War Museum, Athens, Greece

9ⁿ ΜΙΚΤΗ ΥΠΟΕΠΙΤΡΟΠΗ
ΑΝΤΑΛΛΑΓΗΣ ΕΛΛΗΝΟΤΟΥΡΚΙΚΩΝ
ΠΛΗΘΥΣΜΩΝ

ΠΙΣΤΟΠΟΙΗΤΙΚΟΝ ΕΤΑΜΠΛΙ (ΕΓΚΑΤΑΣΤΑΣΕΩΣ)

NEUVIEME SOUS-COMMISSION MIXTE
POUR L'ECHANGE

CERTIFICAT D'ETABLI
(DE NON - ECHANGEABILITE)

'Aρ. 78953.

'Επίθετον

Nom de famille

'Όνομα   Φαρμά
Prénom

'Όνομα πατρὸς   Χ⁀ Μεχμὶτ
Nom du père

'Όνομα μητρὸς   Νεφιά
Nom de la mère

Τόπος & ἡμερομηνία   Μίδουσα
γεννήσεως   1907.
Lieu et date
de naissance

Κατοικία   Μίδουσα
Domicile

Τόπος ἐγγραφῆς ἐς τὰ   Σίρραι
ληξιαρχικὰ μητρῷα   Ξάνθη
Lieu d'inscription
à l'état civil

'Επάγγελμα
Profession

Συμφώνως πρὸς ἀπόφασιν τῆς 9ης 'Υποεπι-
τροπῆς 'Ανταλλαγῆς 'Ελληνοτουρκικῶν πληθυσμῶν
'Ο κ. Φαρμά Χ⁀ Μεχμὶτ

Suivant décision de la Neuvième Sous-Commission
Mixte pour l'Echange des Populations Grecques et
Turques.

M

ἀναγνωρίζεται ὡς ἐταμπλί (μὴ ἀνταλλάξιμος)

est reconnu établi (non-échangeable)

Κομοτινῇ τῇ 26 Μαρτίου 1931

Comotini, le   193

'Ο Ἕλλην 'Αντιπρόσωπος
Le Membre Hellène

'Ο Πρόεδρος
Le Président

'Ο Τοῦρκος 'Αντιπρόσωπος
Le Membre Turc

Fuat

Plate 3   Those who stayed…an *Établi* certificate of non-exchangeability for a Western
Thracian Muslim, 1931
© Courtesy of Interviewee No. 34.

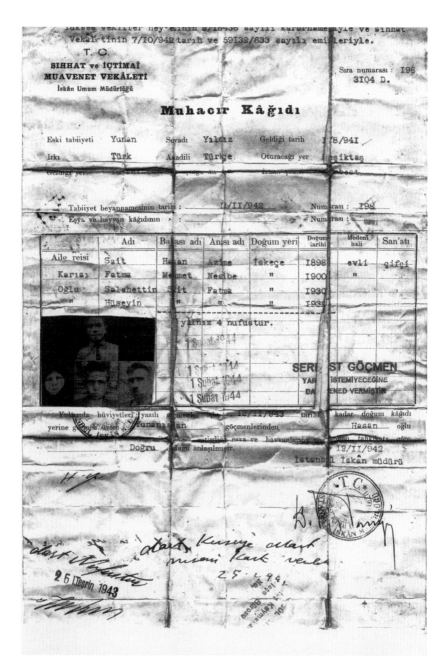

Plate 4 ...and those who left: an emigration document of Western Thracian Muslims arriving in Turkey, 1941
© Courtesy of Interviewee No. 34.

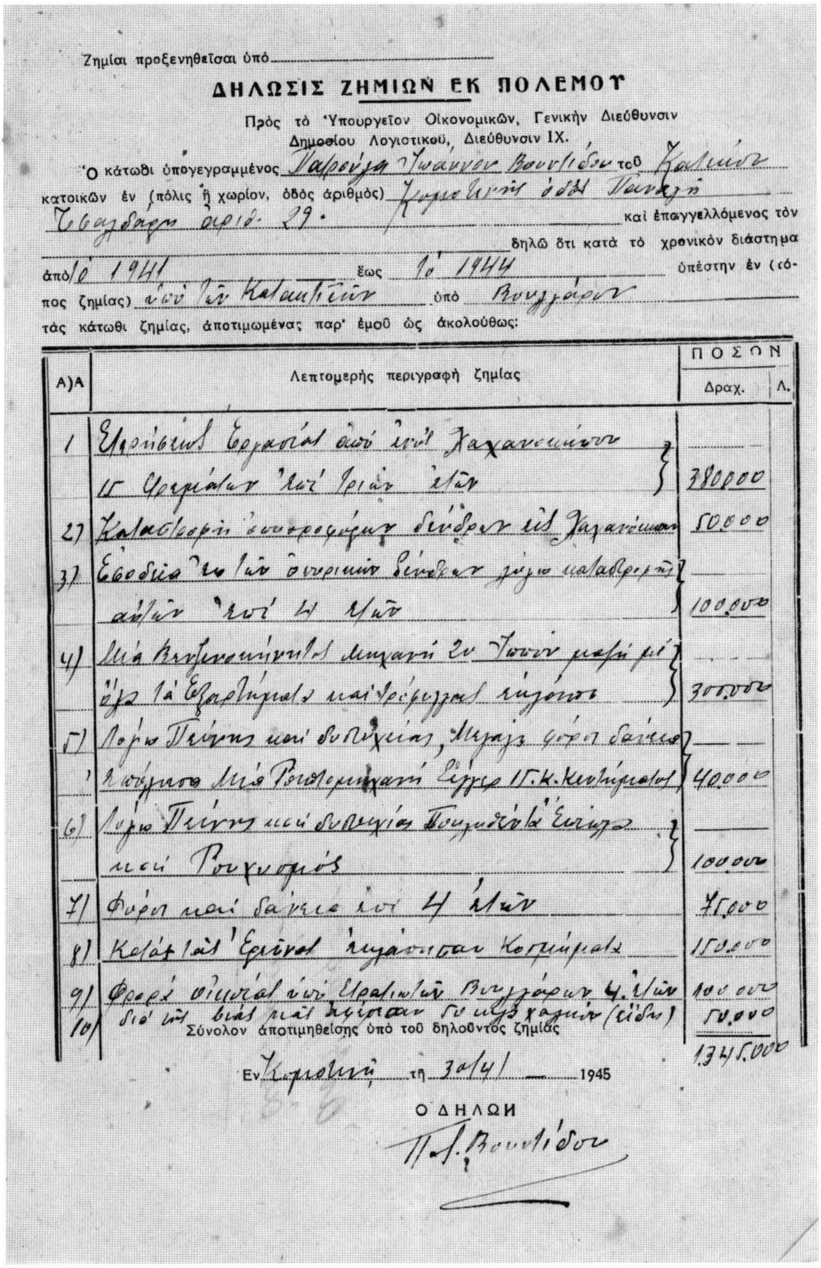

ΔΗΛΩΣΙΣ ΖΗΜΙΩΝ ΕΚ ΠΟΛΕΜΟΥ

Πρὸς τὸ Ὑπουργεῖον Οἰκονομικῶν, Γενικὴν Διεύθυνσιν
Δημοσίου Λογιστικοῦ, Διεύθυνσιν IX.

Ὁ κάτωθι ὑπογεγραμμένος _Παρούχα Ἰωάννου Βουλίδου_ τοῦ _Καλ..._ κατοικῶν ἐν (πόλις ἢ χωρίον, ὁδὸς ἀριθμός) _..._ _..._ _ἀριθ. 29._ καὶ ἐπαγγελλόμενος τὸν _..._ δηλῶ ὅτι κατὰ τὸ χρονικὸν διάστημα ἀπὸ _1941_ ἕως _10 1944_ ὑπέστην ἐν (τό- πος ζημίας) _..._ ὑπὸ _Βουλγάρων_ τὰς κάτωθι ζημίας, ἀποτιμωμένας παρ' ἐμοῦ ὡς ἀκολούθως:

A)A	Λεπτομερὴς περιγραφὴ ζημίας	ΠΟΣΟΝ Δραχ.	Λ.
1	_..._	380000	
2	_..._	50000	
3	_..._	100000	
4	_..._	300000	
5	_..._	40000	
6	_..._	100000	
7	_..._	75000	
8	_..._	150000	
9	_..._	100000	
10	_..._	50000	
	Σύνολον ἀποτιμηθείσης ὑπὸ τοῦ δηλοῦντος ζημίας	1345000	

Ἐν _..._ τῇ _30/4_ 1945

Ο ΔΗΛΩΝ

Π.Ι. Βουλίδου

Plate 5 War damages: a claim for compensation submitted by a Greek Orthodox inhabitant of Komotini in the aftermath of the Bulgarian occupation, 1945
© Courtesy of Patra Vondidou.

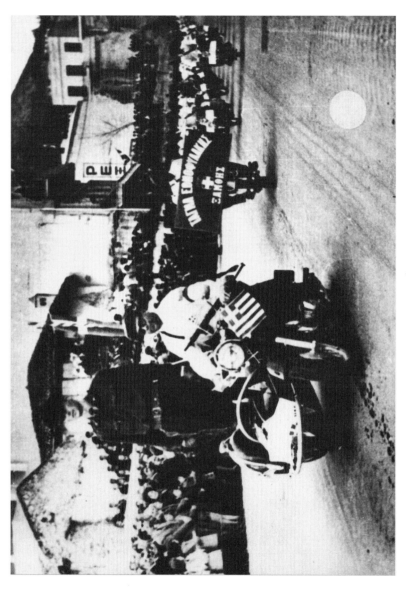

Plate 6 To the rescue? The National Guard parades in Xanthi, 1946
© War Museum, Athens, Greece.

Plate 7 The Fez and the Helmet: an Infantry parade of the National Greek Army in Komotini, 1947–49
© War Museum, Athens, Greece.

SAVAŞ

25 Kasım 194.

Serbest Yunanistan
Dağlarında Bir Yer

YUNANİSTAN CUMHURİYET ORDUSU
Doğu Makidonya ve Trakya
Komutanlığının Türk Dilinde Organıdır

Yıl I   Sayı 1
Fiyatı 500 Drahmi

Batı Trakya Türkleri Halkiki bir halk gazetesine kavuştu

İlk defa olarak Batı Trakya Türk azınlığı halkın menfaatını gütmekten gayri bir gayesi bulunmayan bir halk gazetesine kavuştu.

SAVAŞ size yurdumuzda, dünyada olup bitenleri olduğu gibi bildirecek, sizi ilgilendiren her meseleye sahifelerinde yer verecektir.

SAVAŞ Türk azlığının baş düşmanı olan kıralcı faşistlerin Türk ahalisini hile veya korkutma ile Cumhuriyet Ordusundan ayırmak ve mahvetmek için çevirdikleri oyunları size peşirden haber verecek ve düşmanın hilelerine kanmayın, korkutmalarından yılmayın, korkutmadan tutulacak en doğru yolun ne olduğunu gösterecektir.

SAVAŞ'ın başlıca vazifelerinden biri de bunca yıllar faşist baskısı altında ezilmiş, geri kalmış Türk azlığının uyanması, haklarını bilen ve arayan hür vatandaşlar olmalarında onlara her yardımı yapmaktır.

SAVAŞ Kudretli Cumhuriyet Ordusu tarafından kurtarılmış olan hür Yunanistan topraklarında serbestliğe, demokrasiye, kendikendini idare etme hakkına kavuşmuş olan halka, uğrunda bunca kanı döktüğümüz bu hakları anlaması onları kullanmayı öğrenmesi için gayret sarf edecektir.

SAVAŞ gerçekten bir halk gazetesidir, ve sahifeleri hepinize açıktır. Her vatandaş köyünde bölgesinde önemli saydığı her meseleyi, iyi olsun kötü olsun bize kısaca yazsın. Biz seve seve basacağız.

Biz öyle istiyoruz ki her Batı Trakyalı Türk kendisini SAVAŞ'ın sahibi, yazıcısı saysın ve ona göre hareket etsin.

Batı Trakyada başka bir Türkçe gazete de çıkıyor. İskeçede basılan Trakya gazetesi. Amerikan, İngiliz ve yerli faşist efendilerinin emirlerinden bir katre ayrılmayan bu gazete her sayısında Türk azlığının düşmanı kıralcı faşistler için medhiyeler okuyor; diğer taraftan Türk azlığı ile Yunan halkı arasında gerçek kardeşliğin sağlanması için cabalayan ve kurtardığı her karış toprakta bu kardeşliği gerçekleştiren, Türk azlığının en iyi dostu ve kurtarıcısı Cumhuriyet Ordusu hakkında Türk iftiralar savuruyor.

Dininize söven, kadınlarınızın namusuna tecavüz eden, masum Türk köylülerinin kanına giren, köylerinizi yağma eden ve yakan, binlerce Türk köylüsünü yurtlarından kovarak kasabalarda serseriliğe mahk m eden size her kötülüğü yapan kıralcı faşistlerin avu kalığını üzerine almış olan Trakya gazesine biz Türk adını yakıştıramıyoruz. Bu gazete olsa olsa Türk dilinde çıkan bir Amerikan uşağı Yunan Faşistlerinin gazetesidir.

Andartlar Gümülcüneye Girdi

12 Kasımda Cumhuriyet Ordusu birlikleri düşman müdafaalarını yararak Gümülcüne şehrine girdiler. Şehir içinde kıralcı faşistleri darmaduman eden andartlar 2 asker dolu kamyonu, 2 tankı, 1 zırhlı otomobili havaya uçurdular. Ayni gece başka cumhuriyetçi birlikler Şapçı, İrcan Hisar, Sirkeli, kozlu kebir, İrcan, polat, Susur ve Yanı köylerindeki düşman kuvvetlerine hücum ettiler. Düşmanın zayiatı pek büyüktür. Yalnız birliklerimizin saydıkları faşist ölüsü sayısı 10 dur. Cumhuriyetçiler bütün bu hareketlerde 6 ölü ve 10 hafif yaralı zayiat verdiler.

> Herkes Savaşa!
> Silah elde döğüşen kahraman Türk andartı, Cumhuriyet Ordusunun yardımına koşan Türk köylüsü, halkı cahillikten kurtarmağa cabalayan Türk öğretmeni hep demokrasi için savaşıyorlar.
> Sen de onlara katıl!

Saflarında bir çok kahraman Türk gönüllüsü barındıran, Türk aharisinin gerçek dostu olduğunu lafla değil her hareketi ile gösteren Cumhuriyet Ordusunun Batı Trakya Türkleri için yayınladığı SAVAŞ Gazetesi herinizi selâmlar.

El birliği ile SAVAŞI her tüten Türk ocağının ekmek, su kadar lâzım ve önemli bir ihtinacı yapacağız.

Plate 8 Communist enlightenment to the local Muslim unfaithful: the *Savaş* newspaper published by the DSE

demanded that Bulgaria cede the Kresna-Harmanli region to Greece and claimed the sum of $700 million as reparations. The Greek demands were met with the refusal of the Soviet envoy, who supported the Bulgarian claims for an outlet to the Aegean. The US envoy, in turn, also rejected the Greek demands. Eventually Greece secured $150 million as reparations from Bulgaria and Italy, whilst no border changes between Greece and Bulgaria were authorised. With the return to the pre-war territorial status quo now the preferred option of the big powers, both Greek and Bulgarian agendas for territorial expansion were severely undermined (Papadimitriou 2003: 153).

The Greeks, however, continued to undermine the legitimacy of Bulgarian authority over the north of the Greek border by playing the 'Pomak card'. The Greek strategy on this issue involved three key themes. First, to high-light the plight of the Pomaks under the Bulgarian occupation of Western Thrace during the war (but also during the 1870s and the 1910s when the area was under Bulgarian administration). Second, to draw attention to the oppressive measures of the new Bulgarian regime against the Pomaks of Bulgaria, many of whom had openly expressed their discontent. Third, to highlight the bonds of solidarity and ethnic identity that united the Pomak communities on either side of the border.[16]

The strategy to undermine Bulgarian authority in the area was put into operation as soon as the Greek governmental authorities were estab-lished in Western Thrace in October/November 1944. By order of the Greek Ministry of Foreign Affairs, Governor-General of Western Thrace, Charalambos Rouchotas, along with the local authorities started mobi-lising Bulgarian and Greek Pomak community leaders (Papadimitriou 2003: 153). Despite the very poor resources available to the new Greek administration at the time, the campaign to attract Pomak sympathies was well organised. A number of Bulgarian Pomak committees and associations were set up such as the 'Northern Thrace' association in Komotini which published testimonies of Bulgarian persecutions against the Pomaks and demanded the incorporation of the Bulgarian Pomak areas into Greece.

These associations were composed of Pomaks that had settled in Western Thrace during the occupation and now feared the prospect of returning to Communist Bulgaria (see Box 6.4).

Although it is reasonable to assume that Athens played a significant role in fostering such propaganda, the underlying suspicion of the Pomak population against the Bulgarians was indeed widespread. The prospect of sweeping changes to the status of the Pomaks (and other minorities) in post war Bulgaria had attracted the attention of the US State Department which

---

[16] For similar Greek attempts to play the 'Pomak card' at the Paris Peace Conference (1919) see Petsalis-Diomidis (1978).

Box 6.4 Memorandum of the Northern Thracian Turks in Komotini, 8 November 1944

ASSOCIATION 'NORTERN THRACE'
KOMOTINI (GUMULJINA)

Memorandum of the Northern Thracian Turks in Komotini, 8 November 1944
To: The Honourable Allied commission in Drama and Sofia (through the Greek government)

Esteemed gentlemen,

The subscribed Northern Thracian citizens of Komotini settled in the city three years ago (and later) have the honour to declare that:

Since the occupation of Greek Western Thrace three and a half years ago we came to Greece in the hope that this occupation would soon be over and that we would be at last free from the Bulgarian yoke. We were sure that after the end of the war we would be able to enjoy our freedom under the protection of Greece, the cradle of civilization, and the help of our great allies.

Northern Thrace is populated by 300,000 Turks. In the whole of that region there is not a single village of native Bulgarians. Bulgarians who have subsequently settled in the area represent less than 5% of the population. The situation of Turks in Bulgaria is pitiful. They were left in Bulgaria but they do not have any historical bond with the country. Only after the last war did everyone hear about the Bulgarian atrocities against us.

Northern Thrace is an integral part of Greek Thrace and is destined to be united with Greece. For this, we, the Northern Thracians who live in Komotini, have founded the 'Northern Thrace' association aiming at the annexation of Northern Thrace to Greece.

We believe that you have noticed the pitiful condition of hundred of thousands of people due to the inhumane and savage attitude of the Bulgarian government against every minority. It would not be fair for our people to be surrendered again to the claws of the beast to be mangled after the war is over. Having declared our will to be united with Greece and since we have founded this association, our return to Bulgaria would be impossible.

We appeal to you to use any means you deem appropriate in order to achieve the annexation of Western Thrace to Greece. This could allow those of us who already reside in Greece, but also our fellow Northern Thracians who still live under the Bulgarian yoke, to live.

We submit this appeal through our fellow Northern Thracian Izzet Mümin from Komotini. In the firm belief that your honourable commission will accept our just appeal, we express our gratitude.

The president   The secretary
Nuri Dürüt Oğlu   Ahmet Çolak Oğlu

Source: AYE/1944/10.1, Association 'Northern Thrace' to the Allied Commission in Drama, 8 November 1944.

---

commented that: 'the post-war Communist-controlled Fatherland Front is working towards abolition of special privileges for minorities and the extension of State control to economic, educational and social matters, as set forth in the new Constitution, thus establishing equality and uniformity of individual rights'.[17] Such a prospect would have troubled the conservative and anticommunist Bulgarian Pomaks, fearing that their fate in communist Bulgaria would be uncertain. Along with the Bulgarian Pomaks, the Greek Pomak communities mobilised in support of Greece, whilst at the same time seeking greater welfare provision (see Box 6.5).

The Bulgarians quickly became aware of the Greek efforts to entice the Bulgarian Pomaks and they launched their own 'charm' offensive. In Bulgarian Pomak villages proclamations were circulated, signed by community leaders which denounced Greek imperialism. In turn, pro-Greek Pomak associations argued that such memoranda were the outcome of harsh oppression by the Bulgarian police who coerced and harassed the Bulgarian Pomak communities in order to ensure loyalty to Bulgaria.[18]

In the meantime, the Greek government continued to raise the Pomak issue at various international fora. In September 1946 the Greek Pomak Hamdi Hüseyin Fehmi, a former Bulgarian collaborationist (see Chapter 5) and an ex-member of the Greek Parliament, together with the Pomak Bulgarian land owner Hakkı Süleyman, attended the Paris peace conference and requested the incorporation of Bulgarian territories inhabited by Pomaks into Greece.[19] The Pomak delegation was discretely organised by the Greek Ministry of Foreign Affairs.[20] The delegates, with the mediation of the Greek Minister of Foreign Affairs, contacted the envoys of the United States, New Zealand and India and submitted proposals with their requests.[21] Besides the Paris conference, memoranda by Pomak associations of Xanthi and Komotini were sent to the United Nations.[22] According to the State Department, the Greek Ministry of Foreign Affairs was planning to send a similar Pomak delegation to New York as "guests of the Greek UN mission, in view of their knowledge of the Pomak question".[23]

---

[17] NARA/M1221/4209, Department of State, Intelligence Research Report, 'A Survey on National Minorities in Foreign Countries', 2 January 1947.

[18] AYE/1947/111.1, General Association of the Muslims of Paşmakli [Smolyan] and the surrounding region, to the Foreign Ministries of Britain, USA, Russia and France, 8 April 1946.

[19] *Elliniko Aima*, 19 October 1946.

[20] NARA/M1221/4209, Department of State, 'Intelligence Research Report: A Survey on National Minorities in Foreign Countries', 2 January 1947.

[21] NARA/M1221/4209, Department of State, 'Intelligence Research Report: A Survey on National Minorities in Foreign Countries', 2 January 1947. According to the State Department source, the Indian delegate seemed to be positive towards the Pomak claim.

[22] AYE/1947/111.1, Memorandum of the Bulgarian Pomak refugees in Xanthi, to the honourable UN Committee, 13 February 1947. AYE/A947/111.1, Memorandum of the Bulgarian Pomaks, refugees in Komotini, to the honourable UN Committee, 14 February 1947.

[23] NARA/M1221/4209 Department of State, Intelligence Research Report, 'A Survey on National Minorities in Foreign Countries', 2 January 1947.

Box 6.5 Letter on Behalf of the Community of Miki to the Greek Authorities, September 1945

KINGDOM OF GREECE
PREFECTURE OF XANTHI
COMMUNITY OF MIKI   Miki 24 September
                                              To: Mr Rouchotas General
                                          Governor-General of Thrace

Our community is composed of 12 villages and numbers 4,000 people. The invasion of the Germans and Bulgarians in April 1941 found our people in prosperity, whereas their withdrawal found them pitiful, naked, sick and humiliated. Dear Sir, the suffering that the Bulgarian hordes have put us through in order to Bulgarise us or annihilate us are beyond imagination.

Since the first day the Bulgarian authorities were established, the destruction of anything that referred to the Greek state administration, even the public welfare infrastructure, was ordered. They banned the teaching of Turkish or any language other than Bulgarian in schools and they hired Bulgarian criminals as teachers. They changed our names and forced us to declare that we were Bulgarians to get food. They took our livestock, our food, our yearly provisions of butter and wool. They did not allow us to work, they harassed us and beat us for no reason. They forced us to deposit large amounts of our community taxes and many unjustifiable fines with no receipt. They forced us to work for months in public or military works or in logging our forests which were completely wiped out; they took everything. They gave every family just one kilo of flour per month.

Now that order, safety and justice -which is the main feature of the Greek Administration- has been restored, we would like to express to you, our gratitude and devotion to the government and the Greek state and our decision to fight for the harsh punishment of the murderous Bulgarians and for compensation of what we have suffered.

We are appealing to take the necessary steps towards the Greek Government and the Allied Governments of England, America and Russia for the fulfilment of our claims and for the protection and inclusion of all other desperate fellow Pomaks who suffer in Bulgaria.

We are appealing for the establishment of an allied committee in the Bulgarian Pomak territories in order to investigate Bulgarian vandalism, atrocity and pillage against the population.

Finally, since winter will find our people exhausted, naked, barefoot, sick with malaria and other epidemics, we appeal to you to order the distribution of clothes, shoes, medicine and especially Anteprin [i.e. antiseptic medication] which is running low. In addition to the food aid we have already received we are asking for the distribution of milk to the children which are in terrible condition. We have appealed for such aid to the prefecture of Xanthi two months ago.

With respect,

The President of the Community
On behalf of the community council and all community members
Topal Fahuz Hasan

Source: AYE/1947/11.1, Community of Miki to the Prefecture of Xanthi, 24 September 1945. (The file contains other similar memorandums.)

Ultimately, however, both the Pomak delegation in Paris and the memoranda to the UN failed to meet their objectives. The Pomak delegates were not heard in the official proceedings of the conference and their activity was confined to the fringes. The only concrete benefit for the Greek government in this respect was some favourable comments by a number of US newspapers (Tsioumis, 1997: 87–88). In addition to its limited impact in Paris, the Pomak delegation also received a hostile reception by the Greek Muslim MPs of Western Thrace Osman Nuri, Faik Engin, Osman Üstüner and Hüseyin Zeybek. In a joint declaration submitted to the Greek government (and the minority press in Western Thrace), they condemned the activities of the delegation:

> Two individuals, Hamdi Hüseyin Fehmi and Hakkı Süleyman, are in negotiations with Europe and America under the name "Pomak Committee" and discuss several minority issues. This has caused serious discontent on behalf of the Turkish minority. We declare that with the exception of the four Members of Parliament of Rhodope, no one else has the right to represent the minority. Moreover, we declare that we do not acknowledge Hamdi Hüseyin Fehmi as leader of the Muslim community of Xanthi. We declare that the minority of Thrace does not acknowledge this title and that we will take all the necessary steps to stop the activities of these individuals now and in the future.[24]

Then, as now, the Muslim MPs, and indeed most Turks in Western Thrace, did not acknowledge the Pomaks as a distinct ethnic community within the Muslim minority. They considered that the whole minority had a uniform Turkish ethnic identity.[25] Moreover, the incorporation of almost 150,000 more Pomaks (Popovic 1986: 96–98) – with a distinct set of customs and language as well as an overwhelmingly religious outlook – into Western Thrace would dramatically alter the ethnic composition of the area and disturb the pre-existing networks of authority upon which the minority leadership heavily relied.

Caught between an unfavourable international climate and a rather non-receptive local audience (particularly among the Turks of Western Thrace), the Greek attempt to play the 'Pomak card' during the aftermath of the WWII was a diplomatic manoeuvre that was, from the very outset, destined to failure. A change in the Greco-Bulgarian border would essentially run against the spirit of the 'percentages agreement' between Stalin and Churchill and pose an unnecessary complication to the emerging demarcation of zones of influence in post-war Europe. Moreover, the 'resurrection' of the 'Pomak issue' carried with it significant long-term risks for

[24] *Trakya,* 20 January 1947.
[25] *Trakya,* 13 January 1947.

Greek interests in the region. As the British Consul in Thessaloniki pointed out, the creation of a more than 400,000-strong Muslim minority in Greek Thrace, by changing the ethnic balance in the region, could give Turkey the opportunity to question Greek sovereignty there (see Box 6.6).

The Greek and Bulgarian Pomaks were clearly used by the Greek government in its conflict with Bulgaria in a rather opportunistic manner and the overall 'Pomak issue' was an attempt to confront Bulgarian expansionism by using the same means. This view is reinforced by the fact that, although the Pomak delegation was organised by the Greek government, the official Greek envoy in Paris did not try to secure 'official status' for them or put their demands high on the agenda. The 'Pomak issue', in other words, was used by the Greeks as a secondary line of defence/offence in a diplomatic 'dogfight' with Bulgaria (Tsioumis 1997: 87). The choice of the controversial Hamdi Hüseyin Fehmi (a confirmed collaborator of the Bulgarian occupation forces) as a figurehead of the Pomak delegation was indicative of the opportunism of the Greek Government. Evidently, the post-war expediencies had enabled Hamdi Hüseyin Fehmi to realise his own journey from the losing to the wining side; a pattern so frequently observed by a number of community leaders (from all sides of the ethnic divide in Western Thrace) during the 1940s.

6.3 A muted liberation

On the morning of 12 October 1944, the occupation of Athens by the Axis forces came to an end. Frantic crowds of Athenians watched the swastika disappear from the Acropolis and cheered as the German convoys evacuated Athens. The National Unity Government, formed as a result of the Lebanon Agreement on 17–20 May 1944 under Prime Minister Georgios Papandreou, arrived in Athens six days later (KKE 1981: 398–402; Clogg 1992: 135–136). On 23 October the new government, which included six Ministers of EAM, officially took office. The euphoria of liberation, however, did not last long. Divisions between EAM and its domestic opponents soon surfaced, sparking fears that a new round of conflict was unavoidable.

The spark that finally ignited the conflict was the terms of the disbandment of the various resistance groups and the formation of a regular Greek army. The government and the British demanded the disbandment of ELAS in order to eliminate what they thought was the main source of power for EAM. On the other hand EAM, enjoying a strong appeal among Greek public opinion, was not willing to give up its army which controlled almost the entire mainland. EAM also feared that by abolishing its military branch, it would make itself vulnerable to the demands of its domestic opponents. Negotiations between feuding fractions led to a deadlock and on 28 November KKE's Central Committee decided to withdraw all of EAM's Ministers from the government.

Box 6.6   Letter of the British Consul to Thessaloniki regarding the Pomaks of Thrace, September 1946

18th September 1946

British Consulate-General
Salonica

I see that the Greeks have put up at the Paris Conference a delegation of Pomaks to support the Greek case for the annexation of the southern part of Eastern Roumelia.

It may be interesting at this stage to give a brief summary of the present position as regards the Pomaks in Eastern Macedonia and Thrace. As you know, they are a border people of Bulgarian stock forcibly converted to Islam in the 17th century and now speaking both Bulgarian and Turkish, so that they pass from one side of the frontier to the other as easily as they change their national and political affiliations. As Moslems, those West of the Nestos [river] were subject to the compulsory exchange with Turkey in 1923, as Bulgarians they might also have come under the voluntary exchange of Bulgarians. The Pomaks East of the Nestos remained in Greece and up to 1941 were considered by the Greek authorities as forming parts of the official Turkish minority in Thrace. The Turkish Consul in Komotini also appeared to consider them as being under his wing, at least in their capacity of Moslem. The administrative unity of the two communities is shown by the fact that the head of the Turkish community in Xanthi before the war was Hamdi [Hüseyin] Fehmi, the present Pomak delegate at Paris.

Hamdi [Hüseyin] Fehmi is not at all a desirable representative for the Greeks to put up to present the Pomak case since he did not enjoy a very savoury reputation during the occupation. Pomaks during the Bulgarian annexation naturally found it to their advantage to call themselves Bulgarian and Hamdi quite openly and definitely collaborated with the Bulgars, being seen in Bulgarian uniform.

The effective differentiation between the Turkish minority and Pomaks appears to have begun in 1945 under the Governor-Generalship of Rouchotas who started the ball rolling by collecting petitions from Pomaks in his area alleging the persecution of fellow-Pomaks across the border in Bulgaria. These no doubt well-founded allegations of persecution have since received support from the number of Pomaks trickling across the frontier in flight from Bulgarian excesses.

While it is no doubt desirable that the Pomaks should be united under one government and while they would in present circumstances doubtless prefer Greek to Bulgarian rule, it seems very doubtful whether the Greeks will assist their claim to Southern Bulgaria by putting the case for uniting Moslem Pomaks. If such a union were to be effected the possibility of the Moslem population then in Greece east of the Nestos being in a majority over the Orthodox Greeks of the area, is not to be excluded. The Turks might then, assuming a different act of international circumstances, consider the possibilities of laying claim to the enlarged Western Thrace on the grounds that the population was predominantly Moslem. Reliable population figures are difficult to obtain but I will see if I can find some.

I am sending copies of this letter to the Political Representative at Sofia, to Ankara and the Southern Department.

Source: FO/371/58868.

On Sunday 3 December 1944 EAM defied an official government ban and organised a massive demonstration against the Papandreou government. While large crowds of EAM followers were demonstrating in the centre of Athens the police opened fire against them killing approximately 20 to 25 and injuring 100 to 120.[26] The next day EAM declared a general strike and organised a new demonstration demanding the resignation of the Papandreou government. That demonstration also met with police fire adding more dead and injured. The 33-day long conflict that went down in Greek history as *Dekemvriana* had begun. Fierce fighting soon spread all over Athens leaving hundreds of people dead. In total almost 13,000 ELAS guerrillas (mostly reservists) confronted a total of 10–15,000 men composed of regular government troops, the gendarmerie, the police, small nationalist resistance organisations, collaborationist groups and almost 10,000 British troops brought to Greece from the Italian front (Baerentzen and Close 1998: 101–128; Margaritis 2001: 67–78, Vol. I; Gerolymatos 2005: 147–206).

The battles lasted until early January resulting in a defeat for ELAS which withdrew its forces and sought a truce (which was eventually concluded on 11 January). A political agreement between EAM-ELAS and the government[27] was signed on 12 February 1945 in Varkiza. According to its terms, ELAS had to surrender its arms and disband within two weeks. The agreement also included a series of terms regarding the release of hostages and prisoners, the formation of a regular army, the protection of political liberties, the terms for the conduct of national elections and a referendum regarding the fate of the monarchy and the granting of amnesty (KKE 1981: 411–416; Richter 1981; Vlavianos 1992: 55–78).

Western Thrace also became a theatre of conflict during the December events. In fact, the conflict in Eastern Macedonia and Western Thrace had preceded the one in Athens. After the withdrawal of the Bulgarian and German troops from the area (October 1944), fighting between ELAS and EAO had broken out. In order to put an end to this conflict Colonel Stefanos Prokos, the government-appointed Military Commander in the area, proposed a plan according to which the whole of Eastern Macedonia and Western Thrace would be divided in two sections. EAO would occupy and control the 'VII frontier sector', a small area to the north of Drama, and ELAS forces which by far outnumbered EAO, would take control of the rest of Eastern Macedonia and Western Thrace. However, the two sides failed

---

[26] The exact number of casualties is debatable. For example Chatzis claims that the dead were 21 and the injured more than 140 (Chatzis 1983: 200, Vol. IV, whereas Rousos (1982: 327, Vol. II) claims that the total number of casualties was 54 dead and 70 injured.

[27] Papandreou resigned on 3 January 1945. A new government was formed under Nikolaos Plastiras.

to reach agreement on the proposed plan and a new armed confrontation broke out in November. On 1 December ELAS launched a large scale offensive against the weakened EAO. In the ten-day battle that followed, ELAS forces emerged victorious and gained control of the entire region of Western Thrace (Soilentakis 2004: 329–330, Vol. II).

Although the December conflict in Eastern Macedonia and Western Thrace was fierce, violence was limited to the combatant forces and it did not involve reprisals against civilians as it did in Athens. After the defeat of EAO, a conciliatory mood prevailed in the EAM-controlled areas. The Prefect of Xanthi – a government appointee and hence a natural opponent of EAM – reported that:

> ...during the rule of EAM, the people who were in charge did not persecute nationalists and the savage civil conflict did not spread in our region. Deep down they were also Greeks, they were also victimized by the Bulgarians. A spirit of national unity prevailed throughout the region and that was something extremely pleasant.[28]

Within this rather calm climate, relations between EAM and the Muslim minority remained good. In this context, EAM consented to the holding of elections (organised by the minority itself) for the Commissions for the Management of Muslim Properties, the first time this was allowed to happen since Lausanne (see also Chapter 2 and 8). The EAM administration also allowed the free distribution of school textbooks brought from Turkey by the Turkish Consul in Komotini. The circulation of Turkish textbooks as well as the election of the Kemalists Osman Nuri and Hafiz Ali Galip as Presidents of the Committees of Xanthi and Komotini respectively, were a triumph for the modernist fraction of the minority, which now had the upper hand in its power struggle against the conservative old-Muslims (Foteas 1978: 13; Tsioumis 1997: 80–81).

EAM remained in control of Western Thrace for several months until the end of March 1945, when large numbers of National Guard troops, together with British soldiers, came to the region in order to enforce the terms of the Varkiza agreement.[29]

Political tensions aside, the economic situation in the area remained dire. The Bulgarian occupation had left Western Thrace completely devastated with the local economic infrastructure all but destroyed. The tobacco trade

---

[28] GAK (Thessaloniki), 'Archive of Xanthi Prefecture', F.150 (B.10), Xanthi Prefecture to the Administration-General of Thrace, Directorate of Internal Affairs, 28 April 1945.

[29] For more details about this interim period, see ELIA/24/02, Archive of Epameinondas Vrettos.

had come to a standstill. Almost all factories in the region had closed down either because the Bulgarians had looted the machinery, or due to a lack of raw materials. Unemployment was extremely high and local traders faced severe shortages of capital. The lack of food coupled with the absence of a basic public health system posed serious threats for the lives of thousands, especially children.[30]

The newly established local authorities tried to cope with these enormous problems, including the need to elaborate a strategy towards the Muslim minority. The re-assertion of the authority of the Greek state over the minority population was underlined by a mixture of suspicion and neglect. Two, relatively minor, incidents highlighted this approach. The first was connected with an educational matter. In August 1945 the Inspector of Muslim Schools of Western Thrace, Minas Minaidis, wrote to his superior, the Inspector-General of Foreign and Minority Schools in Thessaloniki, reporting what he regarded as an important issue. According to Minaidis, throughout Komotini there had been a shortage of copies of the Koran and other religious and educational books. The only importer of books from Turkey was a Muslim bookseller in Komotini, who had submitted an application to get a passport which was, nevertheless, rejected. Minaidis asked his chief to inform Athens to issue a passport to the bookseller in order to travel to Turkey and purchase the necessary books.[31] Minaidis wrote:

> If the bookseller does not get permission to travel to Constantinople [Istanbul] within the next month, Young Turks may create a very unpleasant situation by accusing the Greek administration of obstructing the education of Muslim children in Western Thrace. The naive Muslim peasants of the countryside will be manipulated and convinced that we do not allow the reading of the Koran.[32]

The second incident had to do with boy scouting. During October-November 1945 the Head of the Muslim Community of Xanthi informed the Prefect of Xanthi, Anapliotis, that he wished to form a Boy Scout branch exclusively

---

[30] GAK (Thessaloniki), 'Archive of Xanthi Prefecture', F.150 (B.10), 'Prefect of Xanthi to General Administration of Thrace', 28 April 1945.

[31] Although there is no further evidence on whether the passport was issued, both subsequent issues of *Trakya* and the archives of the MFA suggested that Turkish textbooks were indeed sent from Turkey in 1947. *Trakya* 13 January 1947. GAK (Kavalla), 'Archive of Foreign and Minority Schools', F.95B, Ministry of Interior, Aliens' Directorate-General, II Office, D. Vlastaris, 'Report of the Muslims living in Greece', July 1952.

[32] AYE/1945/75.11, Inspector of Muslim Schools of Western Thrace to Inspector-General of Foreign and Minority Schools in Thessaloniki, 1 August 1945.

for Muslim children in the city. Addressing the Board of the Boy Scouts of Greece, the Prefect responded by arguing:

> Our opinion is against the formation of separate Muslim boy scout groups even if these are under the authority of the local branch. We support membership and dispersion [of Muslim children] in the existing groups, as it happens with the army, and, if necessary, the participation of two members of the Turkish minority in the board of the local branch.[33]

The Regent of Scouts of Greece agreed with the Prefect's views and sent him a letter to be communicated to the Head of the Muslim Community of Xanthi.

> We were informed with great joy that the Turkish brothers expressed their will to introduce their youth into scouting. They will be accepted with great enthusiasm. The principle of our organisation is that all Greeks regardless of race and religion are welcome. The separation of groups according to ethnicity or religion is beyond our principles because this could lead to segregation.[34]

The Prefect informed the Governor-General of Western Thrace, Rouchotas, about the whole incident. Rouchotas expressed his satisfaction about the way in which Anapliotis and the Scouts of Greece had dealt with the whole issue. However, Rouchotas was not entirely happy noting that 'it is the wish of this administration that in the future all issues regarding minorities and generally Western Thrace be reported by the Prefectures first to us or the centre [Athens] so that a single and uniform policy is followed'.[35] The mentality of control and of treating 'the minority' as a problem had re-emerged.

This aside, economic conditions in the area throughout 1945 showed little sign of improvement, with the Pomak communities in the Rhodope Mountains suffering the most. A report of the President of the Oraion village depicted their dramatic situation (see Box 6.7).

Given the relative absence of the Greek state in the Rhodope villages, the local population soon turned to forms of self-administration in order to ensure their survival. There were reports that the presidents of the

---

[33] AYE/1945/75.11, Xanthi Prefecture, to the Board of the Boy Scouts of Greece, 21 October 1945.

[34] AYE/1945/75.11, Communication of the Regent of Scouts of Greece to the Prefect of Xanthi, also copying to the Head of the Muslim Community of Xanthi, 29 October 1945.

[35] AYE/1945/75.11, Governor-General of Thrace, to the Prefect of Xanthi, 2 November 1945.

Box 6.7   Report on the Condition of the People in Oraion Village, April 1945

I am taking the liberty to describe to you Mr. Prefect the situation of the people in our village. As you know, the Oraion village is based exclusively on the cultivation of tobacco and stockbreeding. Our tobacco production before the war was 150,000 okas, [1oka=1,280grams] while the total number of our large and small stock was no less than 10,000.

Today, due to the barbaric Bulgarian occupation the production of tobacco fell to 70,000 okes, whereas stockbreeding is almost non-existent. The decrease in the production of tobacco in our area is due to three reasons.

1. Due to the fact that the barbaric raiders were buying our tobacco almost for free.
2. Due to the lack of fertilizers which are necessary for production in our mountainous soil.
3. Due to the fact that farmers during the occupation had to plant corn instead of tobacco in order to cope with the lack of bread.

The economic condition of the villagers is desperate since even bread is scarce and therefore 600 or more families are in danger of facing famine if no measures are taken.

The proposed measures for the relief of the villagers and the rescue of the production of tobacco and stockbreeding are the following:

1. Urgent provision of loans by the Agricultural Bank to the tobacco farmers based on their production.
2. Provision of loans for the 1945 production and the purchase of fertilizers since without them production falls to a third, while the tobacco quality falls from class A' to class B'.
3. Provision of livestock, small or big, but mainly animals that can draw ploughs since all of them were taken by the barbaric raiders.
4. Establishment of a gendarmerie station or a national force in order to safeguard order and the safety of the villagers as well as to lift their morale.

Oraion 9 April 1945

Source: GAK (Thessaloniki), 'Archive of Xanthi Prefecture', F.68, 9 April 1945.

---

mountainous villages resorted to the imposition of taxes and compulsory unpaid labour on the villagers in order to support the poorest families and to have community property (bridges, roads, etc.) repaired (Tsioumis 1997: 82).

The desperate economic situation in the area prompted the minority to turn to Turkey for help. Even before the Bulgarians evacuated Eastern Macedonia and Western Thrace the secretary-general of the Turkish Ministry of Foreign Affairs informed the Greek Ambassador in Ankara, Raphael Raphael, that a delegation of Western Thracian Muslims was planning to travel to Ankara and present the situation of the minority to the Turkish Grand National Assembly and ask the Turkish government to intervene for their relief. According to correspondence between the Greek ambassador and the Greek government-in-exile, Raphael told the Turkish secretary-general that he was unaware of developments in Western Thrace and assured him that he was going to do the utmost for the relief of the minority. The secretary-general showed understanding and assured Raphael that the Turkish government would not allow such a visit to take place.[36]

The Turkish interest in the minority intensified after the new Greek government was established, though it was expressed discreetly. Turkey stressed to Greek officials the hardship the minority had to endure and made complaints of ill-treatment against its members by EAM-ELAS. In a telegram sent on 20 April 1945 the Turkish embassy in Athens informed Ankara:

> I have drawn the attention of the Greek Foreign Minister, both orally and in an aide-memoire, to the position of the Turkish community in Western Thrace and I have asked that the necessary steps be taken to put an end to the assaults to which our racial brothers are exposed to. The Foreign Minister declared that he was shocked and distressed at my information and that if these incidents had taken place they had happened at a time when the authority of the local government had not yet been consolidated and that they had been committed by irresponsible organisations taking advantage of that situation. He added that there would be no question of further grievous incidents of this nature and that definite instructions would be given to the responsible authorities in Western Thrace.[37]

For the Pomaks, the harsh economic conditions facing them during the period between the liberation and the onset of the Greek civil war caused a new exodus (Öksüz 2003: 272–273). Many moved to Komotini, Xanthi and other cities of Western Thrace in order to find work. The extent of this movement is unknown, but in most cases it was occasional since the purpose of the Pomak workers was to support their families until the tobacco market recovered. Also, some Pomaks, especially those who lived near the Greco-Bulgarian border, chose to cross the border and look for labour in Bulgaria (Papadimitriou, 2003: 155). Others chose to emmigrate to Turkey. According to information given to the British consul of Thessaloniki by the Turkish Consul of Komotini, Muzaffer Görduysus (who had, in the meantime, succeeded Türker), the total number of Muslims who migrated to Turkey during that period was 3000.[38] This new wave of population movement was

---

[36] HW/12/305, Raphael, Ankara, to Greek Government Caserta, No. 137132, 10 October 1944.

[37] HW/12/314, Turkish Ambassador in Athens to Foreign Ministry Ankara, No. 144067, 20 April 1945.

[38] FO/371/58868, British Consulate-General Salonica, to Reilly, British Embassy Athens, 29 October 1946.

a cause of concern to both Greece and Turkey. The Turkish Ambassador in Athens, Enis Akaygen, reported the matter to the Turkish Ministry of Foreign Affairs and asked his consul in Komotini to monitor the situation carefully.[39] According to Ankara, the Greek Government encouraged the wave of immigration to Turkey. The Muslim MP in Greece, Osman Nuri, also believed that 'the Greek authorities were no doubt glad to see the Moslems go'.[40]

Such Turkish fears might not have been unfounded. The British Consul in Thessaloniki acknowledged that Greek border guards were, indeed, tolerant in allowing the departure of waves of Muslim immigrants from the country:

> The Greek authorities have been remarkably supine in the matter. As Osman Nuri observed, he could not understand a state allowing its nationals to melt away without passports or any other forms of control. The Greeks admit, perhaps with justice that their frontier guards are too thinly spaced to stop refugees. All they have done is to issue a circular to the presidents of the Turkish communities, telling them to urge their people to stay where they are and instructing them to make arrangements to safeguard property left behind.[41]

However, given the relative power vacuum that followed the immediate aftermath of Bulgaria's retreat from Western Thrace, it is extremely difficult to recover hard evidence (i.e. archival material) pointing to systematic harassment on behalf of the Greek authorities against the minority. A little later, in separate correspondence, however, the same British official wrote that Greece was not encouraging as exodus (see Box 6.8).

For its part, the Turkish government, on the other hand, tried to discourage immigration by mobilising its Consulate in Komotini (see Box 6.9).

The attitude of the two governments highlights some instinctive political and diplomatic reflexes. Amidst the uncertainties surrounding the consolidation of Greek authority in Western Thrace, the Greek government remained convinced that the minority, despite its placid attitude during the Bulgarian occupation, was a potential threat it could do without. Whether through choice or neglect, the exodus of the local Muslim population was never regarded as a problem that required urgent attention. Similarly, the plight of the Western Thracian Muslim was of interest to the Turkish

---

[39] HW/12/314, Turkish Ambassador, Athens to Foreign Ministry Ankara, No. 144160, 24 April 1945.

[40] FO/371/58868, British Consulate-General Salonica to Reilly, British Embassy Athens, 18 September 1946.

[41] FO/371/58868, British Consulate-General Salonica to Reilly, British Embassy Athens, 18 September 1946. On this see also FO/371/58868, British Consulate-General Salonica to Reilly, British Embassy Athens, 29 October 1946.

Box 6.8   Communication of the British Consul in Salonica to the British Embassy in Athens, November 1946

[...]
You have asked for our comments on the atrocity stories being spread by the Moslems who crossed the frontier into Turkey.

We have been able to confirm both through our own, through the Turkish sources in Thrace and through Greek official sources, that any allegations of persecution directed against Moslems are entirely untrue. The reasons for the recent Moslem immigration from Greece into Turkey were principally economic combined with a certain anxiety as to the [word missing] situation. The refugees come almost entirely from the Prefectures of Xanthi and Rodopi and not from that of Evros where armed bands are active.

We can only calculate that the tales of persecution are the product of a lively imagination on the part of both the refugees and the correspondent of the 'Son Telegraf' [i.e. Turkish Newspaper] who were no doubt glad to put together last year's tales of very real persecution of Moslems by Greek bands and this year's equally real atrocities practiced by Greek Communists on their fellow countrymen in Western and Central Macedonia. There is no reason at all to believe that Communists are at the moment practicing anything but propaganda fire against the Moslem population of Western Thrace.

We have in previous correspondence pointed out that economic difficulties lay behind this immigration which has now been stopped by the Greek authorities.

We are sending copies of this letter to Ankara Chancellery and to the Southern Department.

Source: FO/371/58868, 18 November 1946.

Box 6.9   Letter of the Turkish Foreign Ministry to the Turkish Ambassador in Athens regarding Emigration from Western Thrace, 26 April 1945

Under both the Bulgarian and the Greek EAM administrations our racial brothers in Western Thrace wished to emigrate to Turkey on account of the bad treatment they had experienced. At every opportunity we instructed our Consulate at Gumuljina to make the necessary suggestions to the effect that the best measure they could take to help our country would be to remain where they were. It was hoped that when the local Government authorities returned to Western Thrace the situation would revert to normal.

We learn however from dispatches received from our Consulate that since the beginning of April 1945 our racial brothers despairing of the future have begun to emigrate to Turkey, that some of the Greek inhabitants have stated with threats that the Turks will no longer be granted the right of living in these parts, that the Greek authorities are giving (? Underhand) encouragement to emigration to Turkey and that in consequence a state of panic has arisen. Again the Pomaks dwelling in the part of Western Thrace belonging to Bulgaria had settled in Greek Thrace in the year 1941 thinking that it would be easy to migrate to Turkey. About 2,500 of these have now been ordered by the Greek authorities to return to Bulgaria as being Axis nationals.

Our Consul at Gumuljina [Komotini] reports having taken steps to induce them to remain where they are but his action has been unavailing. We learnt from his dispatch of the 18th of April that some of these Pomaks (who are afraid of being punished in Bulgaria) had set out in order to migrate to Turkey. I accordingly summoned the Greek Ambassador to this Ministry and asked him to draw his Government's attention to the necessity of adopting measures to prevent the migration of our racial brothers living in Western Thrace. The Ambassador replied that it was in the interest of Greece that they remained where they were and in point of fact the Greek authorities had closed the frontier in order to prevent this migration. Referring to the 2.500 Pomaks mentioned above I asked the Ambassador that they too might be allowed to remain where they were until they return to Bulgaria in a regular manner. The necessary instructions have been issued to our frontier authorities not to admit refugees who wish to migrate to Turkey and to those who have already come. Among other things it has been decided by our Government to admit the aforesaid Pomaks.

The necessary instructions regarding these matters have been issued to our Consulate at Gumuljina [Komotini] and information about the above mentioned Pomaks has been sent to our Legation at Sofia. Please proceed along the same lines and when you obtain reliable information that our racial brothers in Western Thrace have been encouraged by the Greeks to migrate, please make representations to the Greek Government in whatever manner you think most suitable and that it is in accordance with high interests of our country that our racial brothers should be left where they are.

Source: HW/12/315, No.144321, 26 April 1945.

government only to the extent that the presence of their 'racial brothers' in Greece served future diplomatic calculations. In the middle of this power game stood a community that was used and abused and would soon be exposed to the ferocity of the approaching civil war.

6.4   From chaos to chaos

The Varkiza agreement might have succeeded in putting an end to the December conflict, but it proved to be a short-lived truce rather than a genuine peace agreement. A key term of the agreement was the disarmament of ELAS. Indeed, ELAS surrendered some 50,000 weapons, almost half the stock available in its arsenal. The vast majority of the surrendered weapons, however, were in poor condition with some beyond operational use (Averoff-Tositsas 1974: 167; Ioannidis 1979: 175–176). With a top secret order by the Headquarters-General of ELAS, the weapons which were in good condition were hidden in mountainous caves along with tons of ammunition and provisions that could maintain sufficient supplies for a month (Kasapis 1999: 37–47). Moreover, almost 4000 ELAS veterans had fled to the Bulkes camp in Yugoslavia or were scattered all along the Greco-Yugoslavian border. Almost 5000 former guerrillas kept their weapons across Greece and formed small networks of self-defence that remained inactive and cut off from each other. The reasons that led ELAS to hide its weapons remain contested and are beyond the explanatory scope of this book. For the Royalist camp this was considered as an act of treachery, whereas for the KKE camp it was a legitimate act of self-defence against the persecution of its members. Probably the most accurate interpretation came from Zachariadis himself: 'the Varkiza agreement was a pause, a chance to regroup and reconstruct the forces of the People's Republic towards the upcoming confrontation that was inevitable to come' (Zachariadis 1978: 15).

Another key term of the Varkiza agreement was the granting of amnesty for political crimes (Article 3). Accordingly:

> Amnesty is granted to all political crimes that occurred from 3 December 1944 until this agreement was signed. This does not apply to common crimes against life and property that were not necessary for the achievement of political goals. (KKE 1981: 413)

Consequently, amnesty did not cover political crimes that had been committed during the occupation, whereas the distinction between 'political' and 'non-political' crimes during the December events was open to wide-ranging discretion. Either way, the implementation of that particular article provided an opportunity to reopen old scores. Greece was swept by a wave of acts of revenge and the courts were flooded by thousands of indictment bills against members of EAM-ELAS. Republican and Royalist judges gladly sentenced the accused to lengthy sentences, often based on false accusations. In addition to 'official' state instruments, the persecution of the Left was effected through numerous paramilitary groups which cooperated closely with the gendarmerie and the police. These groups, often manned by common criminals, collaborationists and staunch Royalists launched a pogrom against members of EAM-ELAS, or anyone who was considered as sympathetic to their cause. For many veterans of EAM-ELAS these persecutions (labelled 'white terror') produced only one realistic option to safety: to escape to the mountains and to organise self-defence cells based on ELAS' previous resistance networks (Margaritis 2001: 173–187, Vol. I; Kalyvas 2003; Lymberatos 2006: 267–288).

By early 1946, many of these cells had become better coordinated under the umbrella of the KKE which intensified its anti-government polemic. In the meantime, much of the countryside remained effectively in a power vacuum, whilst the economic situation grew increasingly desperate. The British believed that a new centrist government would be able to get the country out of the economic and political crisis and safeguard their interests in Greece. Eventually national elections were announced for 31 March 1946. These elections, it was hoped, would allow the Communist Party and EAM to register their influence with the electorate and establish themselves as legitimate players in the domestic party political scene.

Zachariadis, however, had different ideas. Judging that this was the best time for KKE's outright confrontation with the government, he ordered KKE's members to boycott the election. On 30 March 1946, on the eve of the election, KKE forces launched their counterattack. On Zachariadis' orders, a well-armed Communist group attacked the gendarmerie station of Litochoro in Macedonia killing 12 gendarmes and national guards. From that point onwards, the descent into full scale conflict gathered an irreversible momentum.[42]

The Muslim community at the polls

The following day Greece went to the polls for the first time in more than a decade, monitored by the Allied Mission to Observe the Greek Elections, which, nevertheless, included no Soviet representatives (Mavrogordatos 1981: 191; Nikolakopoulos 2009: 56–57). The parliamentary elections were held on the basis of proportional representation and produced an overwhelming victory for the United Party of the Nationally-Minded (UPN, *Ηνωμένη Παράταξις Εθνικοφρόνων-ΗΠΕ*). This diverse, Royalist, coalition was dominated by the People's Party (PP, *Λαϊκό Κόμμα*) and included fragments of the Pro-Venizelist camp such as the Party of National Liberals (PNL, *Κόμμα Εθνικών Φιλελευθέρων*) and the Reformist Party (RP, *Μεταρρυθμιστικό Κόμμα*).[43] The UPN secured 55.12 per cent of the vote and 206 seats (out of a total 354). Second, with 19.28 per cent of the vote and 68 seats, came the National Political Union (NPU, *Εθνική Πολιτική Ένωσις-ΕΠΕ*), a coalition of centrist political parties which remained ambiguous on the issue of the Monarchy. Third was the Liberal Party (LP, *Κόμμα Φιλελευθέρων*), with 14.39 per cent of the vote and 48 seats (Ministry of National Economy 1947a; Nikolakopoulos 2009: 68–74).[44]

Nikolakopoulos has estimated that the national average of 'political abstention' (i.e. the percentage of votes attributed to KKE supporters) in the 1946 elections amounted to 25 per cent of the electorate (2009: 77–82). According to Nikolakopoulos, the districts of Xanthi and Rhodope had one of the lowest levels of 'political abstention' in the country (less than 15 per cent). Figures published by the KKE's official newspaper, *Rizospastis*, in April 1946 lead to a similar conclusion.[45] In the district of Evros, the level of abstention was considerably higher. *Rizospastis* put it at 44 per cent and

---

[42] For the importance of the attack of Litochoro see KKE 2001: 552.

[43] The coalition also included a number of other smaller parties.

[44] Parliamentary seats were also won by Napoleon Zervas' 'National Party of Greece' (*Εθνικό Κόμμα Ελλάδος*), the 'Union of Nationally-Minded' (*Ένωσις Εθνικοφρόνων*) and a number of smaller political formations.

[45] The abstention rate in Rhodope and Xanthi was estimated at 21.6 per cent, the second lowest in the country. See *Rizospastis*, 10 April 1946.

Table 6.1 Support for Minority Candidates in the 1946 Elections

	District	Party	No. of votes
Osman Üstüner	Rhodope	Liberal Party	7175
Faik Engin	Rhodope	Liberal Party	6450
Osman Nuri	Xanthi	National Political Union	2197
Hüseyin Zeybek	Xanthi	Union of Agrarian Parties	1410

Source: Nikolakopoulos 1990–1991: 186.

Nikolakopoulos between 15 per cent and 30 per cent.[46] As a general rule, abstention rates in the countryside were considerably lower than in the large cities and towns, possibly as a result of intense intimidation and the easier 'policing' of the voting process. Nikolakopoulos (2009: 81) estimates that in the town of Alexandroupolis 'political abstention' reached 33 per cent, compared to 31 per cent for Xanthi and less than 15 per cent for Komotini.

A total of four minority MPs were elected in Western Thrace in the 1946 elections: Osman Üstüner and Faik Engin in Rhodope and Osman Nuri and Hüseyin Zeybek in Xanthi (see Table 6.1).

The breakdown of the electoral results revealed the minority's strong support for pro- Venizelist leaders such as Themistocles Sofoulis (LP) and Georgios Papandreou (a coalition partner in the NPU). In the minority's heartlands in Komotini, support for the Liberal Party outpaced that of the People's Party by 3:1. In Xanthi, the People's Party gained an overall majority, but there too its dominance was challenged by the strength of the Union of Agrarian Parties which enjoyed considerable support from the Muslim community. Party politics aside, the electoral results of 1946 confirmed the significant empowerment of the pro-Kemalist element within the Muslim community in Western Thrace. In this context, the election of arch-modernists Osman Nuri (the editor of *Trakya*) and 32-year old Osman Üstüner (Chairman of the Turkish Youth of Komotini) provided a powerful reminder of shifting balances within the minority's power structures. Of the other two elected MPs, Faik Engin (the son of a local mufti from Komotini) was also sympathetic to the Kemalist cause, whilst the Pomak Hüseyin Zeybek (a member of the local Agricultural Co-operative) was the only representative of the traditionalist camp, enjoying widespread support across the Pomak villages north of Xanthi (Nikolakopoulos 1990–1991: 185–190; Aarbakke 2000: 109–110; Lymberatos 2006: 643–644).

[46] *Rizospastis*, 10 April 1946.

The Parliamentary election of March 1946 was followed by a plebiscite, on 1 September 1946, on the return to the throne of King George II. Sofoulis' Liberals campaigned actively against the restoration of the monarchy, whilst other pro-Venizelist leaders (such as Papandreou) remained ambiguous on that matter. On the other hand the UPN coalition was an arch supporter of the King's return, with the KKE urging its supporters to vote 'blank'.[47] Nationally, 68.4 per cent of the electorate voted in favour of the return of King George II and 31.5 per cent voted against. Xanthi and Evros followed the national pattern with the Royalist vote at 71 per cent and 70 per cent respectively. In Rhodope, however, Royalist support was considerably lower at 54.3 per cent.[48] The Muslim vote in the plebiscite appears somewhat differentiated from the pattern established in the Parliamentary election of March 1946. Detailed results from Muslim polling stations in the Prefecture of Rhodope revealed marginal support for the restoration of the monarchy despite the strong local appeal of the Liberals.[49] However, there were significant discrepancies. Organi, for example, returned an overwhelmingly Royalist vote (95.5 per cent), where as in next door Kechros less than 32 per cent of the electorate voted in favour of the King's return.[50] On the other hand, in the Pomak villages north of Xanthi Royalist support stood at an astonishing 98 per cent.[51] That said, the fundamentally flawed conduct of both the Parliamentary election and the plebiscite of 1946 does, indeed, minimise the scope for a more accurate interpretation of the minority's electoral behaviour during that period.

No turning back

In the aftermath of the March 1946 election a new government had been formed under Prime Minister Konstantinos Tsaldaris. In June that year, an anti-Communist bill (Γ' Ψήφισμα) was approved by parliament which instituted the death penalty and severe punishments against anyone implicated in subversive activities against the state. The bill provided for particularly draconian measures against the activities of armed groups in northern Greece, where suspects were court-martialled and, often, summarily executed. The government also launched an aggressive diplomatic campaign, accusing its northern (Communist) neighbours of threatening its territorial integrity.

---

[47] Those voting in the plebiscite were presented with a choice of three ballots: 'Monarchy', 'Democracy' and 'Blank'. In the official results published by the government, the anti-Monarchy vote was the combined total of the ballots labelled 'Democracy' and 'Blank'.

[48] For more details see, Ministry of National Economy (1947b) and Nikolakopoulos (2009: 88–93).

[49] *Proia*, 4 September 1946.

[50] Ministry of National Economy (1947b).

[51] *Proia*, 4 September 1946.

For its part, KKE continued to make its own war preparations in the belief that it could imminently mobilise a 40,000-strong army. Despite half-hearted messages of support from the Soviet Union, Zachariadis continued undeterred, turning instead to Balkan Communist parties for help. With Tito pledging support, Zachariadis instructed (in the summer of 1946) Markos Vafiadis to connect the scattered armed groups with each other and to coordinate their activity. Under Vafiadis' orders the Communist guerrillas attacked a string of gendarmerie stations and National Guard units. By December 1946, the Communist forces were reorganised along the lines of a regular army and the *Dimokratikos Stratos Ellados*, DSE, (Democratic Army of Greece) was born, with General Vafiades as its military leader. The DSE might have been the successor movement to EAM/ELAS, but the differences between the two were significant, particularly with regards to their organisation and mission. The DSE was an entirely ideologically-driven movement, under the total control of KKE and its leader Nikos Zachariades. By contrast, EAM/ELAS, despite KKE's hegemonic influence, maintained a broader ideological profile and included a significant number of non-communists in its ranks. The broader appeal of EAM/ELAS is also reflected on the size of its membership which was considerably larger to that of DSE, both in terms of fighters and civilian supporters.

While the civil conflict was spreading across Greece, the Turkish-language newspaper of Komotini, *Trakya*, wrote:

> In our country the most important issue these days is security. If there is no order and security in a country, there can be no state authority. All around our country there is conflict between brothers. Komotini and Xanthi are the most peaceful areas. We hope that this peace will not be disturbed. No brotherly blood has yet been spilled in our region.[52]

It is indeed true that when *Trakya* published this article the situation in Western Thrace was calm. This, however, was soon to change. The traditional isolation and introspection of the Muslim community did not spare them from the troubles of the Bulgarian occupation. The approaching civil war was to test their loyalties once again. Their response to the military conflict that soon engulfed them is the focus of the next two chapters.

6.5   Conclusion

The 'interregnum' between the end of the WWII and the outbreak of the Greek civil war was a period of much fluidity for Western Thrace. Moreover, the end of the War witnessed several surprising twists. With the Red Army on its doorstep and its wartime 'empire' in ruins, Sofia made desperate

---

[52] *Trakya*, 18 November 1946.

efforts to dissociate itself from its involvement with the Axis and re-position itself as a friend of the Allies. Few, however, were prepared to listen. As a result, Bulgaria's ambitions to retain some of the territory it gained during the war (particularly its coveted access to the Aegean) were doomed from the very start. The government in Athens now saw Bulgaria's misfortunes as an opportunity to pursue its own revisionist agenda. By using Bulgarian ill-treatment against the Pomaks (on either side of the Rhodope Mountains) as a pretext, the Greek government laid claim to the territories of southern Bulgaria. The Greek diplomatic offensive, however, was both shallow and opportunistic as was, indeed, the man chosen to 'front' it: Hadmi Hüseyin Fehmi, a former Bulgarian collaborator-turned-ally of Athens. By the end of the Paris Peace Conference, both Bulgaria and Greece had to contend with a return to the pre-1941 territorial status quo; a reminder that their respective irredentist ambitions had been swept aside by the strictures of Allied politics turning into the Cold War.

At the local level, the end of *Belomorie* had produced a power vacuum with an explosive potential. By late summer of 1944, the collapse of the Fascist regime in Bulgaria and the retreat of the German forces from Western Thrace had left EAM/ELAS in a dominant position. Whilst maintaining Bulgarian troops in the area, the new Fatherland Front-government in Sofia pledged support for its comrades in EAM. By the end of October 1944, at the demand of the Allies, all units of the Bulgarian Army were withdrawn from Western Thrace and ELAS had managed to defeat its local nationalist foes of EAO. Despite its dominance, however, the new EAM administration exercised power with relative restraint. During the same period, EAM also sought to extend a number of goodwill gestures to the Muslim community. The most important of these was the holding of direct elections for the Commissions for the Management of Muslim Properties (known as 'community elections'); the first time this had been allowed to happen since the signing of the Lausanne Treaty.

Yet, despite improved opportunities for political participation, the minority failed to register any significant level of support for EAM. Desperate economic hardship and poor security continued to feed Muslim waves of internal displacement (particularly of Pomaks converging to the large towns in the lowlands) and emigration to Turkey. The gradual return of the 'official' Greek state in Western Thrace must have raised hopes of greater security and prosperity, but these too were soon dashed by the deepening tension between EAM and those loyal to the government in Athens. For its part, the Muslim community witnessed the unfolding crisis through the prism of its own internal transformation. The results of the 'community elections' (held under EAM) confirmed the ascendance of the Kemalist elite within the minority. In the aftermath of the 1946 general election three out of four minority MPs claimed strong sympathies with Kemalism. Indeed, when Athens sought to play the 'Pomak card' against Bulgaria, all four Muslim MPs joined forces to remind the Greek government that only they could claim to be representatives of the 'Turkish minority' in Western Thrace. Implicit in this reminder was a refusal to recognise a distinct Pomak identity within the minority. The increasing activism of the minority's leadership on the ground mirrored the rekindling of Ankara's interest to resume its role as the protector of its kin in Western Thrace, now that the diplomatic constraints of the WWII had disappeared. For its part the regime in Athens soon rekindled its pre-war suspicions of the Muslim minority as an unreliable 'other' and Turkey's renewed interest would have reinforced such patriotic fears. Against the background of internal change within the minority and the reawakening of differences between Athens and Ankara, Western Thrace was to follow the rest of Greece into civil war.

7
Çekiç Ile Örs Arasinda (Between a Rock and a Hard Place)[1]

7.1 Introduction

Civil wars necessitate recruitment and propaganda to execute the conflict and gain supporters. The strategies deployed in these respects display how the conflict is conceived and who it embraces. This chapter explores the local operations of the conflict and considers how they were structured by the wider national context. In doing so, it locates the Muslims of Western Thrace in the strategies of both sides of the civil war and outlines how the Muslims responded to them.

The onset of the civil war in Western Thrace denied absolute control to either the Communist forces (the DSE) or the National Army (EES). The Muslim community was faced with adapting to a contest that saw both sides, in turn, demanding their compliance and help, then later raiding their resources and violently imposing their respective wills upon them. To explain how these actions occurred requires an analysis of the operational and strategic actions of the two warring parties in the region.

The Communist campaign of the civil war would display both continuity and change from the pattern established under the Axis occupation. The consolidation of Communist regimes to the north of Greece provided the Communist insurgents with additional resources and options. Yet, the decision of the KKE leadership to set-up a state-like apparatus (in both civilian and military terms) in the areas it controlled demanded a heavy price from the local population. In the Rhodope Mountains, few were prepared to pay it. KKE's efforts to appeal to local Muslims had been both inconsistent and late. The arrival of an 'imported' Muslim leader (Mihri Belli) and the creation of a DSE 'Ottoman Battalion' failed to galvanise widespread support. Soon, the DSE's contact with the Muslim community was engulfed in fear and intimidation.

---

[1] Editorial in *Trakya*, 23 June 1947.

For its part, the Greek government integrated the Muslim community into its anti-Communist campaign through a variety of means, including conscription to the EES and membership of paramilitary groups. As the conflict evolved, the compulsory evacuation of Muslim villages in the Rhodope Mountains also became a strategic asset in the hands of the government forces. Although at no point during the civil war did the Muslim community appear to embrace the conflict as 'its own', the government's anti-communist agenda found a naturally sympathetic audience among the conservative local Muslims, a community whose Ottoman inheritance contained fiercely anti-Russian historical narratives. At the same time, however, the local state authorities proved unable to resolve their own conflicts of attitude towards the Muslim community. To them, the minority continued to be treated as the 'other', warranting suspicion and caution.

7.2   Muslim soldiers of the Proletarian revolution

As the Greek civil war began, the principal strategic aim of the DSE became 'the creation of a free territory in the area of Macedonia and the liberation of the entire Macedonia-Thrace region with Thessaloniki at its centre' (Iliou 2005: 207). The realisation of this objective would enable the DSE and its patron KKE to build the foundations of 'new Greece' and assume the status of a legitimate government. In this context, the support pledged by Greece's Communist northern neighbours (Yugoslavia, Bulgaria and Albania), became an essential precondition for the insurgents' survival. Maintaining open channels with these countries ensured the uninterrupted supply of arms and ammunition to the Greek Communists as well as access to medical care for injured soldiers. Greece's northern neighbours also provided a safe haven during periods of protracted offensives by the Greek EES.

Between the spring and summer of 1947 there was a massive expansion of the DSE forces throughout the country, reaching an estimated manpower of 15,000 fighters (Margaritis 2001: 337, Vol. I). In response, the EES launched Operation Terminus (*Επιχείρηση Terminus*) in April 1947. For Eastern Macedonia and Western Thrace, in particular, the operation envisaged the total defeat of all DSE forces in the area by November 1947. In the meantime, the operation prioritised the cutting-off of Western Thracian communist insurgents from the main body of DSE forces in Eastern Macedonia. For this purpose, the EES conducted a series of mopping-up operations, in Evros (Operation Falakro/*Επιχείρηση Φαλακρό*, early June 1947) and northeast of Komotini (Operation Rhodope/*Επιχείρηση Ροδόπη*, early July 1947)[2] along with some additional activity in the area north of Xanthi. Despite its

---

[2] The main operations were conducted in the area Chloe-Smigada-Sarakini-Kato Drosini-Ragada.

ambitious targets, however, Operation Terminus failed to meet its objectives nationwide and, in July 1947, was abandoned altogether.[3]

The DSE had, by then, acquired significant operational capability and fighting experience, while its network of logistical support was much more developed than during the opening stages of the conflict. The DSE, though, had also not met its objective of securing large parts of the country under its constant and effective control. The range of DSE's dominance was restricted to mountainous, isolated and scarcely populated areas. This might have ensured some form of protection against governmental forces, but it did not provide for significant strategic advantages such as control of major transport routes or access to large pools of new recruits.

The military strategy of the DSE in Western Thrace

In September 1947 the leadership of DSE introduced Project Limnes (Σχέδιο Λίμνες) which became the core strategic plan for achieving military supremacy in Northern Greece (Margaritis 2001: 402–409, Vol. I). The DSE's forces in Western Thrace, according to the operation, were to assume an auxiliary role. They would be cut off from the main body of DSE in Macedonia and provide cover against a possible attack from the East. To this end, the majority of DSE forces in Western Thrace had to be moved to the mountainous area of Xanthi-Drama, in order to fortify the border with Macedonia. At the same time, the remaining DSE forces in the area would undertake a guerrilla campaign against government positions in Evros and Rhodope so as to engage as many units of the EES there as possible. In addition, Thracian units would also assume the responsibility of supplying the main body of DSE forces in Eastern Macedonia (Belli 2009: 59–60).

During the last months of 1946, DSE's forces in Western Thrace continued to grow. The centre of DSE's activities in the area was Evros where 5000 ELAS guns had been hidden in mountainous crypts in the run-up to the Varkiza agreement (Kasapis 1999: 38–41) The first guerrilla groups formed in the area consisted of former EAM-ELAS fighters who, in the aftermath of anti-Communist reprisals following Greece's liberation, had fled to the mountains or had returned from the DSE training camp in Bulkes (Yugoslavia). Nikos Kanakarides (or Lambros) became the Commander and Political Commissar of the DSE Headquarters of Eastern Macedonia and Thrace (HQ EMT). From there, a number of guerrilla units were moved to Rhodope and Xanthi and soon DSE established a presence throughout Western Thrace (Kasapis 1999: 171). The DSE units in the area were coordinated by three local headquarters in Evros, Rhodope and Xanthi. According to estimates of the Army Headquarters-General (GES – Γενικό Επιτελείο Στρατού, ΓΕΣ), loyal to the government, the strength of the DSE in Western Thrace at the

---

[3] DIS/GES 1976: 36–38, 46–52.

beginning of 1947 ranged between 1700 and 2100 men. A total of 800 to 1000 fighters operated in Evros, 500–600 in Rhodope and 400–500 in Xanthi.[4] Local DSE forces in the area operated with some success, capturing, in January 1947, a whole platoon of governmental troops near the village of Echinos (north of Xanthi).[5]

By the end of 1946, the flames of the civil war that had engulfed most of Greece seemed rather distant for the Muslim community in Western Thrace. Although a number of minor incidents and skirmishes had been reported in the area since 1945, the first major guerrilla attack against a Gendarmerie platoon took place on 26 June 1946 (Kasapis 1999: 79). Much of the early DSE activity centered on the mountainous areas of the Evros province. Here, although some of the Communist guerrillas' hideouts were located near Pomak villages on the Rhodope Mountains, contact with the locals was minimal. However, during the implementation of Operation Limnes, a large body of DSE guerrillas left Evros and moved towards the upland areas of Rhodope and Xanthi. Maintaining much larger numbers of guerrillas there increased the demand for food and logistical support. The local Muslim villages now came under tremendous pressure. According to articles published in the Turkish-language *Trakya* newspaper at the time, DSE divisions entered mountainous Muslim villages and started gathering food, clothes, animals, money and tobacco.[6] DSE did not follow a single pattern in the collection of supplies. In some cases guerrillas came into the villages, gathered all villagers and after a short propagandist speech, asked everybody for food contributions. In other cases the collection of food appeared to be more selective, targeting only particular wealthy villagers.[7]

These operations, however, were not always disciplined. According to reports in *Trakya*, Communist guerrillas often resorted to violence with DSE units raiding Muslim villages, usually during the night, in order to loot houses, pens and storehouses. Even the poorest peasants were targeted, with accounts that guerrillas confiscated everything that seemed valuable to them.[8] The reported violence perpetrated by DSE units was occasionally extreme. The DSE units, for example, took eminent community members such as the presidents of village councils as hostages, demanding that additional food was offered as ransom for their release. Anybody daring to oppose to these methods was stigmatised as a government informant and was publicly tortured. Such incidents were reported in the villages of Eranos and Livas.[9] There appears to be no ethnically-based differentiation

---

[4] GES/DIS 1976: 6.
[5] GES/DIS 1998: 315, Vol. 3.
[6] *Trakya*, 17 February 1947.
[7] *Trakya*, 20 January 1947.
[8] *Trakya*, 18 November 1946.
[9] *Trakya,* 16 June 1947 and 17 February 1947.

in the strategies employed by the DSE in this respect. Indeed when its units entered the mixed village Amaxades (near Iasmos), *Trakya* reported that similar demands were made of both the Muslim and Greek-Orthodox communities and both were handled in the same manner.[10]

Indeed, the gathering of supplies for the fighters of the DSE posed a difficult strategic dilemma. Access to small and mountainous (predominantly Pomak) villages was relatively safer, but supplies were poor as the local communities relied on subsistence agriculture produced on rocky and infertile land.[11] This is how a local Muslim villager from Ano Vyrsini (just south of the Greco-Bulgarian border) described his contact with the guerrillas to interrogators of the EES:

> Fifteen days ago 150–200 Communist bandits [συμμορίτες] came and stayed in my village, Ano Vyrsini, for six to seven days. One night they ordered us to stay in our houses, but I managed to go out and saw the guerrillas [αντάρτες] sending 5–6 mules towards the 66th Greek Border Guards post. As shepherds from my village told me, the mules went into Bulgarian territory and returned loaded, but I don't know what their load was. This was repeated 2–3 times during that night. I also know that many guerrillas spoke Bulgarian. I am not sure if they were Bulgarians, or if they just knew Bulgarian.[12]

Access to the larger villages in the lowlands, on the other hand, promised richer supplies for DSE fighters, but at a heavy security risk.[13] In many cases, guerrilla raids against Muslim villages were repelled by government forces, while in the ensuing battle a number of Muslim civilians died (e.g. as in the village of Selero in March 1947).[14]

DSE recruitment and violence in Muslim villages

Guerrilla activity in Western Thrace reached a peak in the winter of 1947–1948 as part of the implementation of the DSE's Operation Limnes (see above). At that time, a series of battles took place across the region. These included an attack on Alexandroupolis in August 1947,[15] frequent clashes on the outskirts of Komotini[16] and a major guerrilla offensive against the city of Komotini, in November 1947, which ended in failure.[17] The DSE demands

---

[10] *Trakya*, 20 January 1947.
[11] *Trakya*, 18 November 1946 and 21 July 1947.
[12] AYE/1947/111.1. 'Report on the Interrogation of A.O.E.', 4 February 1947.
[13] *Trakya*, 22 December 1946.
[14] *Trakya*, 10 March 1947.
[15] *Eleftheri Thraki*, 4 August 1947.
[16] *Proia*, 17 September 1947 and 6 November 1947.
[17] *Proia*, 13 November 1947.

on the Muslim communities in the Rhodope Mountains increased further. Operation Limnes had envisaged the recruitment of 10,000 men from the regions of Eastern Macedonia and Western Thrace. This target necessitated an increase of recruitment from Western Thrace by four to five times its 1947 level (Kasapis 1999: 214; Margaritis 2002: 390–392, Vol. II; Soilentakis 2004: 381, Vol. II; Iliou 2005: 204–211). Such pressing demands signalled the end of the Muslim community's cautious detachment from Greece's internal strife. The civil war had arrived in earnest in the Rhodope Mountains.

In mid-December 1947 the DSE's Headquarters-General despatched the Commander-in-Chief of Central and Western Macedonia, Lieutenant-General Giorgos Kikitsas, and a member of the KKE's Central Committee, Dimitris Vatousianos, to the headquarters for Eastern Macedonia-Thrace. Their brief was to gather information on the implementation of Operation Limnes in the area and adjust DSE's local strategy accordingly. A key issue when they met the Commanders of Eastern Macedonia-Thrace and Evros, Lambros and Kriton (Vaggelis Kasapis) respectively, was that of DSE recruitment from the local Muslim community. Kikitsas and Vatousianos envisaged that a successful campaign in this respect could add at least 2000 Muslims to DSE's forces. Their enthusiasm was reinforced as they toured Pomak villages, realising that 'each young Pomak was a Hercules who could carry a firearm on his back' (Kasapis 1999: 202).

Their plans were supported by Lambros, but not by Kriton who remained sceptical:

> The massive recruitment of mountainous Pomaks should not even be considered to become part of our plans. Their conservatism and their extremely religious primitive life make them unable to understand the struggle we are engaged in. And if today there is something that connects them with us, it is the fact that they fear us. It is to our advantage to continue our work and improve their usefulness to us. From the moment we will recruit them and place them in combatant divisions, everything will change for the worse. This is because they will desert *en masse* in order to avoid suffering the hardships of guerrilla life, constantly risking loosing their head over something they do not even understand. This means that, in addition to losing all the guns that we will give them, we will also lose the current services they provide. By deserting to the enemy they will reveal information about us and our moves, allowing them [the enemy] to acquire good knowledge of the mountainous territory where we dominate. (Kasapis 1999: 204–205)

Kriton's love for the Pomaks only stretched as far as assigning them auxiliary roles such as food suppliers and transportation mules: tasks, he thought, they would perform 'not because they want to, but because they cannot do otherwise' (Kasapis 1999: 205). Kriton's objections were eventually overruled by his superiors, whose main preoccupation continued to be the increase of DSE manpower in the area. This preoccupation was also shared by the DSE's Political Commissar for Evros, Giorgos Gagoulias:

> The Pomaks are a very clever people and they are very comfortable with their physical surroundings. But they do not adapt easily to new environments. They have strong family bonds and they do not like leaving members of their family on their own for long period of times. We respected that, but we were also in the middle of a war. The Headquarters issued orders for their recruitment. But given their [the Pomaks'] mentality the execution of this order was difficult. The guerrillas summoned the elderly [Pomaks] and discussed the order with them. They accepted it – what else could they do?[18]

In the meantime, the DSE's general recruitment plans for the Muslim community had received a significant boost with the arrival, in April 1947, of an unlikely revolutionary soldier in the Rhodope Mountains: Mihri Belli, also known as 'Captain Kemal'.

Mihri Belli's background was very different from those living in Rhodope. He had been born in Eastern Thrace in 1915, the child of a well-known and respected bourgeois family. His father was a judge and one of the leaders of the Turkish War of Independence (i.e. the campaign against the Greeks) in Eastern Thrace and, subsequently, a member of the Turkish Grand National Assembly (Belli 2009: 18). From an early age, Belli decided to follow a rather different path to that of his father. A committed supporter of the revolutionary Communist movement, Belli departed for academic studies in the US when he was 20, where he joined the Communist Party of America. During that time, he was actively involved in the student movement as well as the trade unions of black agricultural workers in Mississippi and the dockers of San Francisco (Belli 2009: 35–36).

Belli's first contact with Greece was in early 1933 when he visited Athens on a Greco-Turkish student exchange programme organised within the context of the 1930 Friendship Pact (see Chapter 3). The Turkish students were shown around Athens and visited Venizelos and the Mayor of Athens. This visit prompted his first philhellenic feelings. During his time in America he became friends with Greek immigrants and he chose to write his university thesis on the 1923 exchange of populations between Greece and Turkey (Belli 2009: 30–34). During the WWII, he had been inspired by the opposition of Greece to Hitler and Mussolini's forces and had admired the resistance movement of EAM-ELAS (Belli 2009: 17).

In the spring of 1940, while war raged in Europe, he returned to Turkey to contribute to the anti-fascist struggle. After travelling for five months

---

[18] Interview 24.

around the Far East, (since the crossing of the Atlantic was impossible during the War), he arrived in Turkey and now joined the illegal Communist
Party of Turkey. He undertook his military service in the Turkish Army for
three years and was appointed Lieutenant-Commander of a cavalry regiment (Belli 2009: 36–37). In the autumn of 1944 he was arrested for illegal
political activities and was sentenced to two years imprisonment and then
exile. He escaped to Bulgaria in 1946 where he came into contact with members of the BCP there as well as Greek Communists who regularly crossed
the border. Belli recalled that, at this point, 'Greek comrades from Eastern
Macedonia had started looking for a qualified Turk who could provide political guidance in these areas' (Belli 2009: 35). One of these members was
Thanasis Genios (also known as Lassanis) with whom he developed a personal friendship and close ideological sympathy.[19] Lassanis, in agreement
with Lambros and their superiors, asked Belli to enter Greece in order to
help with the recruitment of members of the Muslim community to the
DSE. Belli was only too happy to accept and, on 5 April 1947, he arrived in
Western Thrace full of revolutionary fervour (Belli 2009: 35–40).

During the initial stages of his mission, the policy of the DSE on Muslim
recruitment provided for the placement of individual Muslim fighters in
combatant units as this was regarded the best way of 'acclimatising' them
to life as Communist guerrillas (Kasapis 1999: 203). Captain Kemal was
appointed as political advisor and was authorised to organise the entire
operation of recruiting Muslim fighters. Subsequently, however, DSE policy changed and a new separate battalion manned exclusively by Muslims,
and led by Captain Kemal himself, was created (Kasapis 1999: 210). The
initial plan was to recruit solely on a voluntary basis, following tailored
propaganda. Lambros was optimistic that a 'campaign of enlightenment',
designed according to the mentality and customs of the Muslim community, would inspire support for the DSE's goals and lead to better recruitment results. His decision to give Belli the pseudo-name 'Captain Kemal'
was also an attempt to create positive connotations amongst local Muslims
to the cause of the DSE.

Kemal, together with a group of 4–5 experienced guerrillas, began touring
Muslim villages in order to attract new fighters. The appearance of Kemal
in the Muslim villages of Rhodope caused a great deal of surprise. The
following article of *Trakya* is indicative of local confusion:

> They say that the Turkish he speaks does not resemble either the accent
> of Xanthi or even the accent of Komotini. Some say he is a refugee from
> Turkey, others that he is a Greek from Istanbul, some others that he is
> Armenian and others that he came from Bulgaria. It is also said that he

---

[19] Lassanis was one of the first resistance fighters in Macedonia during the
occupation and a pioneer of the *Odysseas Androutsos* resistance group.

lived in Xanthi and that he moved to Komotini from where he fled to the mountains. They say that his name was Mustafa, but neither in Xanthi nor in Komotini people knew who he was.[20]

Despite his enthusiasm for, and frequent references to, Kemal Atatürk and the Turkish nation,[21] Captain Kemal's recruitment efforts bore little success. In July 1947, *Trakya* reported that he had barely managed to gather 30 Muslim guerrillas.[22]

While Kemal was busy recruiting fighters, the EES launched a purging operation to the north of Komotini. During a battle on 6 July 1947 Kemal was injured. A bullet destroyed his lower jaw, while a second bullet caught him on the shoulder. So severe was his injury that few believed that the new arrival would survive. He was immediately transported to Bulgaria for surgery in a Sofia hospital. The difficult operation was carried out by Bulgarian doctors, supervised by a top Russian surgeon and his team, who had apparently flown from Moscow for this purpose (Belli 2009: 62–74). Kemal remained hospitalised for nearly two months, but returned to the mountains of Western Thrace in the autumn of 1947. For a long time afterwards his speech was not clear, while his arm was bandaged (he later broke his arm again in an accident). Kemal's absence further impeded plans for Muslim recruitment to the DSE which was already well off target. Soon more drastic measures were taken. These included the compulsory recruitment of Muslim men together with an intensified propaganda effort.

During the first months of 1948, the DSE HQ EMT ordered the targeting of Muslims with proclamations printed in the Turkish language. The tone of these proclamations was not that of a revolutionary call inspired by the Communist principles of the DSE, but rather a strict order with a threatening undertone (see Box 7.1).

The tone of this proclamation was designed to appeal to the conservative and law-abiding nature of the local Muslim communities. No direct reference was made to Communism or the revolutionary aspirations of its domestic supporters. Instead the DSE was portrayed as the legitimate Greek army, answerable to the government of 'free Greece'. The emphasis was clearly on the need of citizens to fulfil their obligations towards the state, rather than on the revolutionary instincts of the Greek proletariat.

In a similar DSE proclamation, signed by Lassanis, in February 1948 the tone was now more threatening:

After the establishment of the Provisional Democratic Government of free Greece we have the right and the authority to call to arms every

---

[20] *Trakya*, 21 July 1947.
[21] Interview 1.
[22] *Trakya*, 21 July 1947.

> *Box 7.1* Proclamation of the DSE Addressed to the Muslims of Western Thrace, early 1948
>
> TO ARMS!
> To the Turkish Minority
>
> Comrades,
> The Democratic Army calls the youth of the cohort of 1938 to 1948 to arms. We are no longer a bunch of guerrillas [αντάρτες] who went up the mountains to fight for justice. Today there is a Democratic Government that is established in free Greece and its mighty Democratic Army brings death to the fascists. The Democratic Government is the only legitimate government in this country. Its authority comes from the people. The fascist government of pseudo-democrat Sofoulis is the puppet of the Americans and the English. That is why the Democratic Government, that is aware of its duties and responsibilities, calls the nation to arms to finish this disastrous civil war as soon as possible and lead the nation to freedom and peace [.....].
>
> Long live the Turkish Minority!
> Long live the brotherhood between the Turkish Minority and the Greek people!
> Long live the Democratic Government of Greece!
> Long live the Democratic Army!
>
> *Source*: AYE/1948/105.7.

patriot capable of fighting. That is why we call every Turkish patriot living either in the free Greek territory or in the enemy territory to serve in the ranks of the Democratic Army. Consequently, every one called to arms is obliged to present themselves to their nearest garrison or DSE unit in order to enlist. Those who do not present themselves by the date of enlistment will be considered as deserters and be punished by law.[23]

DSE propaganda in the area projected an idealised pictured regarding the compulsory recruitment of the Muslims (see Box 7.2).

Trakya, however, depicted a rather different picture arguing, in May 1948, that 'there was not a single Turk who willingly went up into the mountains'.[24]

Indeed, the overwhelming majority of oral testimonies and written sources point to the conclusion that the vast majority of Muslim men who enlisted in the DSE, were driven to do so by force. Yet the full truth behind the involuntary (or not) nature of the DSE's enlistment strategy is extremely difficult to establish. Most accounts of forced enlistment can be found in statements submitted by Muslim deserters of the DSE who were subsequently interrogated by the police and, hence, had an obvious incentive to underplay their own

---

[23] AYE/1948/105.7. DSE proclamation in Turkish translated in Greek.
[24] *Trakya*, 10 May 1948.

202 The Last Ottomans

Box 7.2 Proclamation of the DSE Addressed to the Muslims of Western Thrace, early 1948

Comrades,
Young Turks who have responded to the last order of the DSE are rushing to enlist in our ranks laughing, dancing and singing. They are well aware that they are doing their military service to pay a debt to their country. They know that the day the American-English invaders and their local representatives, the fascist royalists, will be forced to leave the country and a People's Republic will be established, a wind of total freedom will prevail. The people will enjoy the rewards for all their efforts by taking a breath of relief. These brave men know that democracy means complete equality among the people of this country. In the People's Republic of Greece, there will be no difference between Greeks and Turks and no discrimination.

Those who have joined the ranks of the DSE and those who know us well are aware that, for us, equality is not all words and no deeds. The young Turks in our ranks can see with their own eyes the Turkish officers who are chosen among them. They can see for themselves that it is possible for the Turks in the Democratic Army to rise to higher ranks.

On the other hand, they remember that in the army of the royal fascists the only job they could do was to take mules grazing and serve others. These young Turks are the witnesses of equality between Greeks and Turks, equality which we put into practice.

For that reason these brave young men called to join the army think like this: 'since our country is here, since we, along with the rest of the people, will benefit, then why not take part in the effort to establish the people's rule'.

Source: AYE/1948/105.7.

---

initiative in this respect. Not a single interrogation statement of a Muslim DSE fighter admitting that he had joined the DSE willingly was unearthed by this research. Another important source of information with regards to the DSE's recruitment of Muslims are the reports published by the *Trakya* newspaper. These provide a vivid ongoing account of the way in which members of the Muslim community were allegedly dragged into the civil war by the DSE. Yet their objectivity may also be questioned by the fact that *Trakya* maintained a consistently anti-Communist stance throughout the civil war, being published by Osman Nuri, a local MP for the centrist, but strongly anti-Communist, party National Political Union (NPU – *Εθνική Πολιτική Ένωσις*).

These provisos aside, the picture emerging from the available evidence with regard to the DSE's recruitment strategy in the Rhodope Mountains is one of intimidation and fear. In villages under the steady control of the DSE, the pressure for young men to enlist was enormous, often accompanied by threats against their life or the life of their families. In villages outside the steady control of the DSE, recruitment methods were even fiercer. *Trakya* records a number of cases where young Muslims were taken by force by DSE units, such as in the village of Lofarion where seven people were taken away.[25] In some cases, those taken were asked to perform auxiliary tasks for the DSE, before they were allowed to return home. Those who were considered capable fighters, however, stayed with DSE units for much longer. The testimonies submitted to UN observers by Muslim residents in the villages of Oraion (near Xanthi)[26] and Kardamos (in Evros),[27] offer typical stories of DSE recruitment during that period.

Captain Kemal, himself, acknowledged that very few Muslims joined the DSE voluntarily (Belli 2009: 84–85), but his memoirs provide few details on this key aspect of DSE's activities in the area. This is how he described his experiences:

> The antartes [guerrillas] unit would go into a village. If, for example, they found a villager at an appropriate age for recruitment working in the fields, they would say to him "Come join the DSE". The poor man responded "I have work to do, you can see that, I will be of more use to you if I carry on working". In most cases they were actually being honest. But no: "An order is an order" they [the guerrillas] would answer. So he would join them unwillingly. Many of those who joined involuntarily later became the bravest fighters of the Democratic Army (Belli 2009: 89).

Captain Kemal also makes references to Muslims who happily volunteered to join DSE units. One such case was thirty-year-old Irgat Mustafa, from a village near Sappes, who was one of the first to enlist. He was landless, completely illiterate and with no family. Kemal describes him as a worthy and good-hearted fighter, who was highly regarded by his comrades and was promoted to the rank of Platoon Commander. Other cases are those of Sari Ahmet, a poor shepherd, and the Roma Tahsin Karabing, an excellent shooter and tracker, who did not remain loyal to the DSE to the end (Belli 2009: 132–136). Captain Kemal's own descriptions suggest that the typical Muslim fighter of the DSE came from disadvantaged and marginalised backgrounds. If so, this was not inconsistent with typical DSE fighters in other parts of the country. Among the villagers in the Rhodope Mountains, however, the decision to join a revolutionary guerrilla force ran against deeply entrenched norms: those of a law-abiding Muslim and a committed family man. A 1947 report in *Trakya* reflected vividly these incompatibilities:

> Amongst them [i.e. Muslim guerrillas] there are a lot of people who had nowhere to stay and whose living conditions range from bad to dreadful. They are individuals who are not very well-known within the

---

[25] *Trakya*, 16 June 1947.
[26] AYE/1949/22.3, 'Witness Testimony to UN Observers', undated.
[27] AYE/1949/21.2, 'Witness Testimony to UN Observers', 26 August 1949.

community. Nobody, then, acknowledges their absence either in the town or the village.[28]

The Ottoman Battalion of the DSE

Captain Kemal's 'Ottoman Battalion' had been formed in early 1948 in the context of the new DSE policy of enforced recruitment.[29] The Battalion consisted mainly of Pomaks, but also comprised a number of Turks, Roma and Greek Orthodox Christians. Information about the Battalion's size is scarce and, often, contradictory. According to Kemal himself, and a number of oral testimonies, the Battalion consisted of approximately 300–500 men.[30] Government sources, however, put the number of those 'recruited' into the Battalion at 1,200.[31] This discrepancy runs against the grain of Greek civil war historiography where most DSE-affiliated sources have consistently overestimated their number of fighters. The 500 figure mentioned by Belli seems a more accurate estimate of the Battalion's average size over the course of its operation. Government sources most probably referred to the total number of recruited fighters, many of whom deserted the Battalion at various points and were replaced by new recruits.

The strongholds of the Battalion were the villages of Organi and nearby Smigada, where both the command post and the training camps for the new recruits were located. Training itself was basic, lasting only two weeks and mainly consisting of teaching new recruits how to use rifles (Belli 2009: 90). The Battalion did not have the appearance of a regular military formation and most guerrillas were dressed in their traditional (civilian) outfits. Both Greek Orthodox Christians and Muslims became officers. This is how a Muslim deserter from the village of Sidiron (Evros) described his experiences of joining the Ottoman Battalion under interrogation from governmental authorities:

I was recruited by the bandits [συμμορίτες] at the end of February 1948. I was brought to Smigada and from there along with another 250 Ottomans we were moved to the north of Papades where we worked on the opening of a road across the borders. On 25 March 1948 we were moved to the borders and after we walked for 500 metres we got into a car. We travelled for approximately 53 hours and we got off at lake. I asked where we were and I was told that we were in Kastoria. We stayed there for three

---

[28] *Trakya*, 21 July 1947.

[29] When Captain Kemal was injured again in 1948, the Ottoman Battalion was led by Major Dovris (a non-Muslim). See Interview 24.

[30] Belli refers to a manpower of 500, whilst Gagoulias to around 300. Interview 1; Interview 24.

[31] AYE/1948/105.7, Minister of Northern Greece Basiakos, to Foreign Ministry, Directorate of Political Affairs, 12 February 1948. The French-language edition of the Turkish newspaper *Cumhuriyet* (*Republique*, 14 February 1948) put the number of Muslim men in the DSE at 2000.

Box 7.3   *Trakya* Extract on the Progress of the Ottoman Battalion, May 1948

Guerrilla [Αντάρτες] activity

The two most important events this week were the surrender of Turks with their arms who were forcefully recruited [i.e. by the Battalion] and the bombardment of the Gökçepinar [Glafki] village in Xanthi.

As you all know, a few months ago the guerrillas started recruiting people from the villages that were under their control. At some point they even reached lowlands and surprised both the villagers and the government forces by taking some hundreds of people with them. Since then, the Turks started surrendering themselves with their weapons.

The number of those who surrendered is way over 500, while it is estimated that very few have not yet managed to escape. This week, the Turks who surrendered in the Papades village have returned to their homes in Komotini and Xanthi. In addition, another large group surrendered in Serres. In groups of three, four and five they keep surrendering themselves. These people have been through a lot and many of them are so skinny. They have been humiliated and they can hardly reach their homes in Komotini and Xanthi.

[...]

Source: *Trakya*, 5 May 1948.

---

months, where along with five more Ottomans we got into another car. We travelled for one day and two nights. And we reached the Greco-Bulgarian border near Haidou. We got out of the car at a place that was three hours away from the border and a Bulgarian soldier escorted us to the borders where we were picked up by a bandit [συμμορίτη] who escorted us to the Haidou Headquarters. There we joined the Ottoman Battalion which is commanded by someone named Kemal. Since then I served as a platoon leader in the Komotini area. I surrendered myself on 14 September 1949.[32]

In spring 1948, as the DSE's campaign in Macedonia was running into serious difficulty, the Battalion was ordered to move to the mountains of Drama (in the vicinity of Papades). The Battalion remained there for nine months and was involved in a series of battles. However, according to a local DSE commander, the commitment of Muslim fighters to the cause of the DSE was minimal.[33] The transfer of the Ottoman Battalion to Macedonia, in addition to the grave dangers it entailed, placed its Muslim fighters outside their 'natural' territory (the Rhodope Mountains) and demanded that they spent long periods of time away from their families. With many of the Battalion's fighters frustrated, a massive wave of desertions soon ensued. This is how *Trakya* reported on the progress of the Battalion in May 1948 (see Box 7.3).

---

[32] AYE/1949/25.1, 'Report from the 4th Group of Observers', 25 April 1949.
[33] Interview 24.

Given its ideological affiliation, *Trakya*'s report might have exaggerated the number of desertions, but there is little doubt that the Battalion's Macedonian expedition went disastrously wrong. In Kemal's memoirs, there is almost no reference to the campaign in Macedonia; perhaps an indication that the Battalion came very close to disbandment there. In fact, Kemal acknowledges that desertions became a major problem for the Battalion as the Greek EES started to evacuate civilians from the DSE's zone of control (on this see Chapter 8).

> The people who saw their families go, had two choices. Either to stay in the Democratic Army facing all the hardships and dangers of guerrilla warfare, leaving their women and children unprotected in the city, or join their family and get a job until they were able to return back to their village. For the mountainous villagers there was actually no dilemma. Desertion was, it seems, the most favoured solution. This explains the rise of the desertion rate during that period. (Belli 2009: 112)

Many of the deserters surrendered to units of the EES from where, after interrogation, they were set free. Those who left the Battalion and chose to return to their villages alone encountered mortal dangers. As yet an unidentified, but significant, number of Muslim fighters perished in the minefields of Nestos in their effort to escape from Macedonia into Western Thrace. Kemal's depiction of DSE's punishment for those attempting to desert appears rather too lenient. His memoirs recalled only one incident of execution. In most cases, according to Kemal:

> When we caught a deserter, we held him for a few days in poor conditions and when he repented and promised that he would fulfil his duties he was given permission to return to his unit. Despite the harsh circumstances of the war, we were as lenient as possible to those who were responsible for misconduct. (Belli 2009: 114)

By the summer of 1948 it was becoming apparent that the DSE's strategy of enlisting significant numbers of Muslim fighters in its ranks had failed. This failure was in fact confessed to Kriton by the Political Commissar of the DSE's General Headquarters, Vasilis Bartziotas, who conceded that:

> You were absolutely right about the Pomaks. As you predicted, not only did they not work for us, but they ran towards the enemy with the weapons we gave them. (Kasapis, 1999: 325)

The move to Macedonia had signalled the end of the 'Ottoman Battalion'.

In the meantime, the EES in Western Thrace focused on the containment of the DSE in that region, whilst government forces conducted their major operations against the Communist insurgents in Western Macedonia (see below). The EES' strategy also focussed on the protection of vital communications infrastructure from guerrilla attacks. In order to repel the strong DSE presence north of Komotini, the EES launched Operation Giona (*Επιχείρηση Γκιώνα*) in late May 1948. The operation resulted in the capture of Organi and Smigada – two of the main centres of the Ottoman Battalion in the Rhodope Mountains. Additional mopping-up operations were conducted in Evros, west of Didimoteichon (in August and September 1948) where a number of DSE strongholds fell and their facilities destroyed.[34] The victories of the EES in the mountainous villages of Komotini and Evros were followed by the compulsory evacuation of their inhabitants to safer locations in lowland villages or to the main towns of Western Thrace.[35] The strategy of compulsory evacuations by the EES had a devastating impact on the DSE units in the area. The zone of DSE's control shrunk dramatically and the insurgents were deprived of access to basic provisions and new recruits. Locally, the pro-government press, such as the *Proia* newspaper, had much cause for celebration:

> Hence, there remains a dead mountainous zone that was completely deserted and all the guerrillas' facilities, their forts, warehouses, observation posts were destroyed and blown away. Our Army now holds a strategic position that will not allow the guerrilla units in north-east Rhodope to regroup and become tactically operational as they had been for the last two years.[36]

The DSE, it seemed, had run out of both Muslim fighters and its local support network in the Rhodope Mountains. The campaign of the DSE in Western Thrace was soon to come to an end (see below).

Women recruitment in the Ottoman battalion

Gender equality and the emancipation of women were typically central features on the KKE agenda. A similar concern was also found in DSE literature; thus, 'the woman in liberated Greece works in the production process, takes part side by side with the man in the People's Rule administration and is a strong pillar for the Democratic Army'.[37] Through a series of legislative acts that were implemented in areas under its control, the DSE put much of its rhetoric into practice ensuring equal participation of women in the People's Committees and People's Courts (for more on these see Chapter 8). The DSE

---

[34] DIS/GES 1976:194, 287–291, 336–343.

[35] GAK (Thessaloniki), 'Xanthi Prefecture', File 623, Xanthi Health Centre, to the Health Ministry, 27 September 1948. See also Interview 18; Interview 25; Interview 26.

[36] *Proia*, 3 June 1948.

[37] *Demokratikos Stratos*, Issue 4, April 1949.

was even more zealous in the recruitment of women in its ranks. Indeed, as the areas under DSE control began to shrink during 1947, the female population became a precious resource for the Communist-led campaign. In February 1948, a decision of Provisional Democratic Government (the political arm of the DSE) issued an official endorsement of female recruitment, leading to a significant influx of women fighters in the DSE. By 1949, they accounted for over 15 per cent of its combatants.[38]

In order to reinforce and institutionalise the participation of women in the DSE, the Pan-Hellenic Democratic Union of Women was founded in October 1948. Members of the Union were both women fighters of the DSE and non-combatant women from the areas under its control. The Union's first President was Chrysa Chatzivassileiou, a member of KKE's Political Bureau, who was later replaced by Roula Koukoulou, the wife of KKE's leader Nikos Zachariadis. In addition to the Pan-Hellenic Union, DSE's 3000 Slav-Macedonian women established their own organisation, the Anti-Fascist Women's Front, AFZ (Antifasiste Front Zhena).[39]

In sharp contrast to the widespread participation of Slav-Macedonian women in the DSE, Muslim women from Western Thrace kept well clear of its ranks. Captain Kemal in his memoirs makes reference to just two Muslim women who joined the DSE, possibly the only two that existed. The first one was the wife of a DSE guerrilla named Hüseyin from Echinos. According to Kemal:

> This brave woman, a mother of several children, had joined voluntarily the Democratic Army along with her husband. She kept going from village to village wearing a military overcoat and explaining to women the cause that we were fighting for. (Belli 2009: 93)

The second was the wife of a local Roma, Tahsin Karambing, who took his entire family along with him in the DSE. His wife was a non-combatant.

The *Democratikis Stratos* Bulletin also makes a reference to a Muslim woman who was a member of the Provincial Council (*Επαρχιακού Συμβουλίου*) of the DSE. In March 1949, the Pan-Hellenic Democratic Union of Women held its first conference with the participation of 325 women from across Greece and seven foreign delegates. Among the delegates there was also a

---

[38] *Demokratikos Stratos*, Issue 11, November 1948; *Demokratikos Stratos*, Issue 3, March 1949. Vervenioti (2002:126) estimates that the overall participation of women in DSE reached nearly 50 per cent (approximately 30 per cent in the combatant units and 70 per cent in non-combatant services).

[39] *Dimokratikos Stratos*, Issue 4, April 1949.

woman representing the Muslim minority of Western Thrace. According to the bulletin:

> The strengthening and the expansion of our struggle is also proven by the participation of women from the Turkish minority in our confer-ence. The people's struggle left its mark there too. The Turkish representa-tive who is a member of the Provincial Council took the floor. This was the same woman for whom it would be natural to be locked in a room a few years ago.[40]

At its closing stages, the conference issued a call for more Muslim women from Western Thrace to join the DSE.[41]

Although there is very little evidence of Muslim women making an active contribution to the military campaign of the DSE in Western Thrace, their value as propaganda tools did not go unnoticed. *Savaş*, made a number of references to the rape of Muslim women by soldiers of the EES. Unusually, the names of these women were made public, pointing to the irony that their husbands had all enlisted to the EES.[42] The validity of such claims is, indeed, impossible to confirm. Yet, for the highly conserva-tive Muslim communities in the Rhodope Mountains, their use as propa-ganda instruments in order to deter Muslim enlistment in the Army had an apparent value.

At the political level too, the participation of Muslim women in the administrative structures created by the DSE also appears to have been disappointing. Captain Kemal himself acknowledged the incompatibilities between the Communist-driven agenda on women's emancipation and the conservative context in which the DSE had to operate in Western Thrace. In his words:

> This would go against the attitude of these traditionalist people who could not accept a woman as an equal citizen. Even amongst Muslim women, with very few exceptions, this inequality was considered normal. (Belli 2009: 93)

The timidity shown by the DSE in this respect was an implicit admission that much of its social programme would have to be compromised in order to maintain a minimum of support amongst the Muslim community. Similar

---

[40] *Dimokratikos Stratos*, Issue 4, April 1949.
[41] AYE/1949/21.2, 'Report on Pan-Hellenic Democratic Union of Women', Undated.
[42] *Savaş*, 25 November 1947 and 20 December 1947.

imperatives are also discussed in Chapter 8. The promise of 'social libera-tion' might have galvanised support for the DSE in other parts of Greece, but in Western Thrace it risked alienating further a local population that was already suspicious. In these circumstances, the (social) revolution in the Rhodope Mountains could wait a while.

The endgame of the civil war

Following the disappointing results of the EES's Operation Terminus, the US administration grew increasingly apprehensive about the apparent resilience of the DSE forces. In February 1948, James Van Fleet, a contro-versial US General, was appointed as Director of the Joint U.S. Military Advisory and Planning Group in Greece. Van Fleet's appointment brought the Greek Army under the increasing scrutiny of US officials who took centre stage in the organisation of military operations against the Communist forces. Boosted by US know-how and military assistance, the EES renewed its large-scale offensives against the DSE. Their main objec-tive was the removal of all Communist forces from central Greece and the gradual shifting of the main theatre of operations to the north-west of the country. Within months the success of the EES had pushed the main body of the DSE forces into the mountains of Grammos and Vitsi near Greece's border with Albania and Yugoslavia. Grammos, in particular, became a stronghold of the Communist forces with 5000–6000 committed and well-prepared fighters in the area (Zafeiropoulos, 1956: 360, Margaritis 2001: 24, Vol. II). In June 1948, the leadership of the EES decided to target Grammos with a massive offensive that struck at the heart of DSE's forces. Following two months of fierce battle, large parts of the DSE were forced to retreat and regroup in Vitsi.

The defeat at Grammos prompted a severe crisis within the DSE. Markos Vafiadis, its Commander-in-Chief, was discharged under mysterious cir-cumstances by the KKE leader, Nikos Zachariadis, who assumed overall command of the Communist forces. Vafiadis' dismissal was never officially announced and the leadership of KKE maintained that he had suffered a nervous breakdown and was flown to the USSR for treatment (Kousoulas 1965: 262; Vukmanovic 1985: 108–109). In addition to its own internal trou-bles, the DSE received another major blow as a result of dramatic develop-ments on the international scene. The Stalin-Tito split of June 1948 resulted in Yugoslavia's expulsion from Comintern and it re-shaped Communist alli-ances in the Balkans. Tito's search for new friends in the West came at a high price for the Greek Communists. Under severe pressure from Britain and the US, Tito announced in July 1949 the closure of the Greek-Yugoslav border and the ending of Yugoslav assistance to the DSE; a decision that was to prove decisive for the struggle of Zachariadis and his men (Kofos 1964: 161–163, 174–195; Vukmanovic 1985: 111–123; Barker 2002: 285–318; Pirjevec 2002; Papathanasiou 2004).

Despite its heavy defeat in Grammos, however, the DSE maintained control over large areas on the Albanian and Yugoslav borders. In Athens, the inability of the EES to deal the final blow to the Communist forces now caused its own problems. Exercised by what it regarded as widespread incompetence amongst its ranks, the US demanded far-reaching changes in the leadership of the EES. These calls led to the appointment, in January 1949, of Alexandros Papagos as Commander-in-Chief. Still feted after the laurels of the successful campaign against the Italian invaders in 1940, Papagos regained the confidence of the Americans and re-energised the Army's efforts against the DSE. Following sweeping operations, all Communist forces in Southern Greece were defeated by the summer of 1949. This allowed Papagos to concentrate all his efforts on the remaining 12,000–13,000 DSE forces in the mountains of Grammos (which had been re-captured by DSE in Spring 1949) and Vitsi. The ensuing Operation Pyrsos (*Επιχείρηση Πυρσός*) in August 1949 proceeded with a huge artillery and air assault and large number of troops on the ground. The ferocity of the attack, where napalm bombs were first used in action, overwhelmed the DSE forces in the area and forced Zachariadis to order the retreat of all of his troops to Communist Albania (GES/DIS 1951; Margaritis 2001: 511–558, Vol. II). The Greek civil war of 1946–1949 was over with a bitter defeat for the fighters of the DSE, many of whom were to spend decades in the countries of the Soviet Block as refugees.

The last year of the civil war was equally traumatic for the DSE forces in Western Thrace. The DSE there had failed to open a second front against the EEΣ, in what had been a plan to relieve the main body of the DSE forces that fought in Vitsi and Grammos. In its meeting on 3 September 1948, the Politburo of the KKE issued a damning statement with regards to the actions of its comrades:

> The Headquarters of Eastern Macedonia-Thrace has failed to fulfil its military objective which was to engage the largest possible number of enemy forces through a continuous military action and concentrated attacks against major enemy targets…The HQ EMT did not capitalise on the favourable environment created for this region by the battle of Grammos and, during that time, did almost nothing…The command of the HQ EMT did not fulfil the duties ascribed to it by the General Headquarters and it failed.[43]

The KKE's Politburo pointed the finger of blame at the Political Commissar of the HQ EMT and member of the KKE's Central Committee, Dimitris

---

[43] Decision of the Politburo of the Central Committee of the KKE regarding 'the Situation in the Headquarters of Eastern Macedonia and Thrace', 3 September 1948. Available in *Dimokratikos Stratos*, 10 October 1948.

Vatousianos, as the main culprit for this failure. Vatousianos was subsequently stripped of his rank. According to the same statement:

> The political work in the HQ EMT was minimal. The main benchmark on whether our political work in an HQ is going well must be our military performance. This is the main objective served by our political work… The weak and minimal political work in this [i.e. EMT] HQ is evident by: a) the fact that in the HQ EMT there is the largest number of desertions which exceed the combined total of all other HQs put together. It is worth noting that we don't see desertions only from newly-conscripted guerrillas, but from older ones too; b) the fact that there is an insufficient level of alert within the HQ. The enemy is omnipresent within our ranks, learns about our moves very quickly and surprises us and attacks us whenever it wants….[44]

The KKE's Politburo took drastic action to rectify these shortcomings. The HQ EMT was abolished in September and the new 7th Division was created in its place. In addition, a number of specific targets were introduced in order to improve the Division's fighting capabilities. These included, amongst others: the separation of the core fighting force from those performing auxiliary tasks within the Division; the conscription of 5000 new fighters; the liquidation of the nationalist forces of Anton Tsaous; the intensification of acts of sabotage against communication and transportation interchanges between Greece and Turkey; and the improvement of relations between the DSE forces and the local population.[45]

Following the announcement of these decisions Vatousianos, Lambros and Kriton, together with other commanders of the HQ EMT, were evacuated to Bucharest where they spent several months in Party-imposed exile. In March 1949, Lambros and Kriton received orders to return to their duties in order to implement the DSE's new strategy in the area. In addition, following a meeting between Kriton and Zachariadis (and other DSE commanders), the administration of Eastern Macedonia and Western Thrace was to be separated for all non-combatant matters (militarily the DSE forces in Western Thrace remained within 7th Division). The same meeting also decided that the DSE's main objective in Western Thrace would be the recruitment of new guerrillas (Kasapis, 1999: 345–347).

---

[44] Decision of the Politburo of the Central Committee of the KKE regarding 'the Situation in the Headquarters of Eastern Macedonia and Thrace', 3 September 1948. Available in *Dimokratikos Stratos*, 10 October 1948.

[45] Decision of the Politburo of the Central Committee of the KKE regarding 'the Situation in the Headquarters of Eastern Macedonia and Thrace', 3 September 1948. Available in *Dimokratikos Stratos*, 10 October 1948.

Even after the re-organisation, however, the military fortunes of the DSE in Western Thrace did not improve. The compulsory evacuation of the mountainous villages by the EES had severely depleted the potential pool of new recruits for the DSE whilst its fighters faced a desperate lack of provision. Desertions amongst the demoralised DSE forces continued to increase as the EES reinforced its defences and went on the offensive. More specifically, in April 1949, government forces launched a new mopping-up operation (Alma/Άλμα), this time in the region between the north of Alexandroupolis and the north-west of Komotini, where a large number of guerrillas had retreated to regroup. On 15–17 May the DSE guerrillas launched their last big offensive against EES positions in the village of Metaxades. Their purpose was the compulsory recruitment of approximately a thousand men from those who had been moved to the village as 'guerrilla-stricken' (for more on this, see Chapter 8) and remained under the close protection of the EES. DSE fighters from Western Thrace, assisted by those from Eastern Macedonia, engaged in a fierce battle with the government troops, but they faced total defeat. From a total of 1378 DSE fighters who participated in the operation, only 420–450 remained as the rest were killed, captured or deserted (Kasapis 1999: 385). Following the operation in Metaxades, less than 430 DSE fighters continued to operate in the entire region of Western Thrace (150 in Evros and Rhodope and 250 in Xanthi) (Kasapis 1999:391).

Frustrated and demoralised the remaining DSE forces in the area escalated their violence against Muslim villages which, by then, were regarded as a hostile terrain. One such incident was the slaughter in the village of Sminthi near Xanthi in 14 July 1949. Following the death of a DSE guerrilla in the area, DSE troops burned the village to the ground and executed 13 of its 19 remaining inhabitants (amongst which were four women and four children).[46] *Trakya* reported the incident (see Box 7.4).

Following its success at Metaxades, the EES launched a series of mopping-up operations in order to clear Western Thrace of all remaining DSE forces. The most important of these was Operation Elpis (Επιχείρηση Ελπίς) launched in early June in the area between the provinces of Xanthi and Rhodope. This was followed, a few days later, by Operation Lavi (Επιχείρηση Λαβή) near Xanthi.[47] In the aftermath of these operations the remnants of the DSE units in Western Thrace fled to Bulgaria where they surrendered their weapons, but they remained at the disposal of the KKE. There they were re-united with a number of Muslim recruits who, following the Ottoman

---

[46] GES/DIS 1976: 517. According to *Trakya* the number of victims was 15, see *Trakya* 18 July 1949. Dede (1980: 96–97) refers to 15 dead. An inhabitant of Sminthi also confirmed this incident arguing that the local communist forces executed 18 people because a guerrilla was found dead in the village. See Interview 18.

[47] DIS/GES 1976: 545–550.

Box 7.4   Trakya Report of the Sminthi Massacre, 18 July 1949

Guerrilla [αντάρτες] activity

To highlight the German atrocities during the war, one could use as an example [i.e. of reprisals] the killing of 50 locals for every dead German. All nations – the communists among them- had condemned such atrocities.

The atrocities committed by the antartes [guerrillas] against the people of the Southern Mahale in Moustaftsova [i.e the community of Miki of which the village of Sminthi is a part] on Thursday night caused a wave of rage all around the country and especially among Muslims. Such atrocities do not happen even amongst cannibal African tribes.

The antartes [guerrillas] secretly entered the village that is 18 kilometres north of Xanthi and slaughtered the women and children while they were sleeping. Some women were woken up and then mowed with machine gun fire. And, as if this was not enough, others were slaughtered with knives. Is it possible for those who committed such atrocities to be human?

At least the Germans killed adults, but they killed women, children, even infants. Just bear in mind that these women and children do not have the slightest idea of politics and most of them don't know how to read and write. This slaughter is inexplicable. It is not revenge or anything of this kind. Only a blood thirsty animal can do something like that.

They did that to show what communism is all about. They slaughtered 13 women and children, while from the 6 wounded women and children another two died later. They burned the houses. This is the Soviet administration which tries to give lectures about civilization.

Source: *Trakya*, 18 July 1949.

Battalion's demise in Macedonia, had been scattered to various countries of the Communist block (Tsekou 2007).[48] In Greece, the Communist leadership sought to explain the reasons behind the defeat at Metaxades by claiming that the 7th Division was infiltrated by enemy agents. The KKE, with the assistance of Bulgarian secret agents, conducted a series of investigations into this matter overseen by Dimitris Vlantas, a member of the KKE's Politburo. A number of leading figures of the DSE's 7th Division such as Kriton, Giorgos Gagoulias and many others were tortured and kept in Bulgarian custody, before they were set free in the early 1950s (Kasapis, 1999: 430–490; Gagoulias, 2004: 129–152).[49]

The fate of the exiled DSE leaders contrasted sharply with the exuberant mood of the winners of the conflict in Western Thrace. In October 1949 local commanders of the EES held a ceremony in the village of Gratini in order to celebrate the demobilisation of the last National Guard units.

---

[48] Tsekou makes reference to 56 'Ottoman' DSE fighters seeking refuge in Bulgaria. Gagoulias puts their number to 70. See Interview 24.

[49] For more on the fate of DSE refugees in Bulgaria see Tsekou (2007).

According to *Proia* this was the first peaceful celebration in the rural areas of Western Thrace since the end of WWII. In his message to the de-mobilised troops, Colonel Grammatikas stressed that:

> During a bleak period in which the whole of the countryside was brow-beaten and looted by the evils of Communism; at a time when the city of Komotini was assaulted by the guns of the [Communist] bandits and was subjected to repeated attacks; at a time when the entire population was terrified of the imminent danger of the destruction of anything Greek, but who was also inspired by the conviction of the just National struggle, you were called to protect freedom, Greece, yourselves and your fami-lies...The countryside now breaths freely, the farmers are returning to their villages and their fields and the very few remaining [Communist] bandits, full of fear and panic, are hiding in the forests, with their reek-ing flesh shivering...Long live the Nation! Long live the King! Long live the 36th Battalion![50]

The celebrations at Gratini signalled the end of military operations in Western Thrace and confirmed the victory of the government's forces in the Greek civil war. For the Muslim community in the area a precarious posi-tion of being stuck 'between a rock and a hard place' (*Çekiç Ile Örs Arasında*) had also come to an end. Few Muslims shed tears for the DSE's defeat. On the other hand, Muslim support for the government's campaign, whilst widespread during wartime, was soon to be marred by an increasing sus-picion towards the newly consolidated Greek authorities in the area. The war against Communism might have been won, but the battle for minority hearts and minds was still very much alive.

7.3 Good Muslim, bad Muslim

On the government side, the conduct of the anti-Communist campaign faced its own serious limitations. The outbreak of the civil war left no time for the country to recover from the ruins of the Axis occupation. The author-ities in Athens might have been recognised as the legitimate government of the country by the Allies, but, in military terms, their control had been confined largely to the big urban centres (and even there their authority was often fragile). As the ferocity of the unfolding civil conflict intensified, the government in Athens had struggled to rebuild the state apparatus and to re-construct the EES in order to repel the Communist threat.

During the first stages of the civil war, for example, the campaign against the Communist insurgents was undertaken by the Gendarmerie (Χωροφυλακή)

---

[50] *Proia*, 5 October 1949.

and the National Guard (*Εθνοφυλακή*) which was established immediately after Greece's liberation in late 1944. In October 1946 two more militias were established in order to assist the efforts of the government forces: MAY (Units for Rural Security – *Μονάδες Ασφάλειας Υπαίθρου, MAY*) and MAD (Units of Raiding Squads – *Μονάδες Αποσπασμάτων Διώξεως, MAΔ*). These militias consisted of volunteers from rural areas who were armed by the EES and commanded by reserve Army officers or former (right-wing) resistance fighters. Whatever their anti-Communist fervour, these militias had limited operational capacity and acted, in most cases, in an auxiliary role to that of the official government forces. Their volunteers kept their arms at home and were rewarded in kind, normally through the provision of food and clothing. Volunteers also kept their day-jobs and slept at home, but remained on stand by for duty at all times. The mission of MAY units was largely confined to the protection of local villages from Communist raids. The units of MAD had a more militarised outlook and they often participated in operations against guerrilla groups alongside the Gendarmerie and, later, the Army (Lymberatos 2006: 267–288).

The EES, at that time, was consumed with its own internal restructuring problems and was, in effect, operationally absent from the fight against the Communist guerrillas. The Army's weakness was the result of a combination of British miscalculations and lack of financial resources. Having underestimated the threat posed by the Communist insurgency, the British believed that 'civilian' security forces, alongside local militia groups, would be strong enough to respond effectively to the crisis. More fundamentally, the economic imperatives facing the British government at the time, limited its capacity to fund the Greek Army in order to transform it into a credible fighting force (Margaritis 2001: 231–239, Vol. I).

When Christmas arrived in 1946, the Greek Prime Minster, Konstantinos Tsaldaris, visited Washington amidst clear signs that the British government (under PM Clement Attlee) was seeking to minimise its involvement in Greece. The US President, Harry Truman, agreed to foot the bill for Greece's protection and pledged $250 million in military aid for the Greek government (the first manifestation of the so-called 'Truman Doctrine' for the containment of Communism which was to be implemented later in many other parts of the world). In addition, Greece was to become the recipient of over $1 billion of economic aid through the Marshall Plan, a significant part of which was channelled to financing the government's escalating conflict against the Communists. The onset of the implementation of the Truman Doctrine and the Marshall Plan, brought Greece under intense US patronage (Xydis 1963; Wittner 1982; Stathakis 2004; Vetsopoulos 2007). With the EES now at the forefront of the fight against the Communist insurgents, the Greek civil war was about to take another twist. The engagement of the Muslim community with the government-led forces warrants further attention in the next section.

Muslim recruitment in the Greek army
and government-sponsored militias

The contribution of the Muslim community to the war effort against the Communist forces was two-fold: through conscription to the EES and/or through enlistment in government-sponsored militias such as MAY. With regards to those conscripted into the EES no special army unit manned by Muslims (equivalent to the 'Ottoman Battalion' in the DSE) operated in the area of Western Thrace.[51] Instead all Muslim conscripts were dispersed in units across Greece, similarly to what would have happened to all other Greek citizens. According to the Greek Ministry of Press and Information, the total number of casualties (dead or missing) of the EES between 1 June 1946 and 10 September 1949 was 15,145, with 25,594 more soldiers injured.[52] The number of Muslim soldiers who died during this period is unknown. No equivalent list of named casualties similar to that published by the Greek Army for the 1940–1941 war against the Axis forces, exists for the period of the civil war. Hence, hard evidence as to Muslim casualties during that time remains limited. Indicative, but by no means conclusive, is the list displayed in the office of the Turkish Union of Xanthi which names 30 members of the local Muslim community who died during the civil war (see Table 7.1).

Irrespective of the exact number of causalities, the commitment of Muslim conscripts to the government's cause during the civil war is difficult to assess. Scattered evidence from Army reports on the conduct of Muslims soldiers at the time depicts an attitude of self-preservation, rather than one of conviction. It appears that some officers regarded the presence of Muslim soldiers in their units as a liability. In his report on the problems

---

[51] Operationally, Western Thrace (along Central and Eastern Macedonia) came under the competence of the 3rd Army Corps. In the early stages of the conflict, the area of Rhodope was assigned to a 400-strong Frontier Battalion (*Τάγμα Προκαλύψεως*) of the National Guard. In January 1947, GES dispatched to Thrace the 7th Army Division, which was based in Kavalla. The Division consisted of the 25th Brigade (stationed in Alexandroupolis), the 26th Brigade (alongside a Commando Unit, LOK/ΛΟΚ, *Λόχος Ορεινών Καταδρομών*) stationed in Komotini, and the 27th Brigade, stationed in Drama. The 7th Division also commanded the local Gendarmerie forces, the squads of Anton Tsaous and Psilogiannis (that were rearmed by the Army), two Raiding Squads of the Gendarmerie, and the Command of the National Guard Battalions of Thrace (*Διοίκηση Ταγμάτων Εθνοφρουράς Θράκης*) that consisted of the MAY and MAD units (later renamed into Military Command of Thrace/*Στρατιωτική Διοίκηση Θράκης*).

[52] The same report refers to 70,000 guerrilla 'casualties' with no distinction between dead, missing, injured or executed (by government forces). AYE/1950/32.1, 'Ministry of Press and Information, Directorate of Research; the sacrifices of Greece in manpower', Athens, 17 October 1949. Margaritis (2001: 50–51, Vol. I) estimates 13,839 (dead or missing) casualties for the EES and approximately 25,000 casualties for the DSE.

Table 7.1   Muslim Inhabitants of Xanthi Killed during the Greek
Civil War

Name	Fallen at	Date
Abdurrahim Ali	Konitsa	12.7.1948
Abdurrahim Hüseyin Derviş	Filyatra	5.3.1948
Ahmet Hasan Tomba	Beles	30.8.1948
Cemali Hüseyin Kabze	Kozani	3.10.1947
Cemali Arif Sadik	Didimoteicho	1947
Ahmet Halil Sari	Cupata	10.8.1949
Hasan Ahmet Alaca	Echinos	17.7.1949
Hasan Hüseyin Ciritli	Konitsa – Tambouri	13.8.1947
Hasan Elmas Abbas	Vapurda Himara	19.1.1948
Hasan Ahmet Zümre	Almopia	5.11.1946
Hasan Latif Deli	Pahni (Pasevik)	3.8.1949
Hasan Kadir Terzioğlu	Haidou	6.3.1947
Hasan Ahmet	Vapurda Himara	19.1.1948
Hüseyin Murat Koca	Mancarezavic	19.12.1950
Hüseyin Osman Topuz	Unknown	26.7.1945
Hüsnü Haci Mustafa	Memkova	5.7.1947
Ismail Ahmet Arslan	Pindos	26.11.1947
Kadir Hasan Onbaşi	Karpenisi	21.1.1949
Kamil Besim	Kastoria	10.10.1948
Mehmet Hüseyin Ciritli	Sinikova	12.7.1948
Mümün Hasan Oğlu	Dolaphan	2.8.1949
Mümün Hüseyin Cenç	Konitsa-Tamburi	13.8.1947
Osman Faik Adem	Almopia	15.11.1946
Osman Mehmet Ince	Mourgana	16.9.1948
Rahim Raşim Oğlu	Unknown	29.12.1949
Ramadan Hasan Demir Ali	Pindos	20.11.1947
Recep Hasan Sakalli	Konitsa-Tamburi	13.8.1947
Rifat Ahmet Çolak	Konitsa	8.8.1948
Riza Hasan	Portaria	30.8.1948
Salih Mümün	Aspro Valto	1948

Source: Turkish Union of Xanthi.

encountered by the 7th Division of the Territorial Army in its engagement
with DSE forces in December 1946, General Asimakopoulos, for example,
made reference to the presence among his men of '958 Ottoman conscripts
who constituted a liability and were useless for the conduct of guerrilla
warfare and probably for any kind of warfare'.[53] In a separate incident in
Kallithea (south of Komotini) on 27 November 1946, when the 555 Battalion

---

[53] DIS/GES 1998: 84, Vol. 3.

of Alexandroupolis was ambushed by DSE forces, it was reported that 13 Muslim soldiers surrendered to the guerrillas who took their weapons, stripped them of their clothes and let them go.[54]

A number of reports from the Administration-General of Thrace also suggested that many young Muslims fled Western Thrace and crossed the border into Turkey, in order to avoid conscription into the EES (see Chapter 8).[55] There were also reports that Muslim conscripts had sought to escape to Turkey during the course of their military service, prompting the Greek authorities to revoke their Greek nationality on the grounds of desertion.[56] On the other hand, some oral testimonies from Muslim veterans suggested much greater enthusiasm for fighting alongside the EES,[57] while some of those who had escaped to Turkey during the Bulgarian occupation of Western Thrace, asked to return to Greece in order to fight 'the common enemy [i.e. the Communists]'.[58]

Indeed, despite isolated complaints on the performance of Muslim soldiers on the ground, official civilian and army authorities appear to have gone out of their way to praise the contribution of Muslim conscripts to the war effort against the Communist forces. When a Muslim soldier was killed by a land mine in the Rhodope Mountains, for example, it was announced that his family would receive a substantial compensation of 1,000,000 drachmas. Many local dignitaries, including the Deputy Governor-General of Thrace, the Mayor of Komotini and the Commander of the 7th Division, announced that they would attend the funeral. In a letter to the soldier's family, published in the local *Proia* newspaper, General G. Kotsalos, the 7th Division Commander, wrote (see Box 7.5).

It is perhaps inevitable that each of the available sources on assessing the contribution of Muslim soldiers in the Greek Army may involve an inherent bias. Officials attending funerals during the civil war served as valuable propaganda instruments and important morale boosters for the local populations that had often little to do with the heroic deeds of the deceased soldier. Equally, Army compilations on the conduct of the 1946–1949 war that were published at a much later date (mostly in the 1960s and 1970s)

---

[54] GES/DIS 1971: 157.

[55] See, indicatively, AYE/1948/105.6, Administration-General of Thrace, Directorate of Political Affairs, Xirotyris, to the Foreign Ministry, Department of Turkey, 28 April 1948.

[56] AYE/1948/105.7, GES, 2nd Office, to Foreign Ministry, Directorate of Political Affiars, Department of Turkey, 30 January 1948. AYE/105.7, Directorate of Political Affairs, Department of Turkey and the Middle East, to GES, 13 February 1948.

[57] Interview 16.

[58] AYE/1948/27.1, Greek Embassy in Ankara, Skeferis, to Greek Ministry of Foreign Affairs, 14 February 1948.

Box 7.5   Letter to the Family of Dead Muslim Soldier Published in *Proia*, April 1949

Mrs Ayse,

We regret to announce to you that your husband was killed in action whilst serving the highest duty towards the motherland. His heroic death for the greatest gift in the world that is freedom became an example to our compatriots. He was another victim of the expansionist plans of the Slavs.

As a fellow comrade and co-combatant of the Greek soldiers, with his death he strengthens even further the Greco-Turkish bond, proving how fruitful this bond has been. The Greek motherland will never forget the sacrifices, of whatever kind, of the dear and brotherly Turkish element to the common struggle for the ideals of freedom. The General Commander of the Division, its officers and combatant units express their most sincere condolences.

General G. Kotsalos, Division Commander

Source: *Proia*, 27 April 1949.

---

would have most certainly been affected by subsequent Greek-Turkish animosity. It is also likely that contemporary accounts of these events by veterans themselves may be filtered through personal agendas and selective memory. What is certain, however, is that, within the highly polarised context of the civil war, decisions affecting collaboration with and/or resistance to either of the two warring parties became an extremely delicate task. This is particularly true for the isolated mountain communities where a significant part of the Muslim minority lived. In these areas, where control changed frequently between government forces and Communist insurgents, the option to remain 'neutral' disappeared. This predicament is expertly explored in Kalyvas's (2006) influential study of violence in civil wars.

As already noted, young Muslims faced the predicament of joining the government forces, but leave their families behind, vulnerable to Communist reprisals; or, instead, joining the DSE guerrillas, which might have ensured the safety of their families in the short run, but risked been stigmatised as 'Communist' with all the state-induced punishment (including death) that this often carried. Although similar security dilemmas faced many mountainous communities across Greece, their specific implications for the Muslims of Western Thrace (where the role of males as guardians of the family is of paramount importance) did not go entirely undetected by the Greek security forces. Indeed the Gendarmerie of Komotini acknowledged that:

As a result of the conscription of the classes of 1946, the guerrillas began terrorising Muslims during their raids to the villages, in order to prevent their enlistment to the ranks of the Army and remain in their villages instead. They also announced that anyone joining the Army should know that his property will be burnt down and his family be held hostage.[59]

Such reports must have certainly accelerated the implementation of compulsory evacuations of mountainous villages in Western Thrace. In the meantime, however, many Muslim families sought to escape their impossible situation by emigrating to Turkey (on this see also Chapter 8). As already noted, this option met with traditional Turkish sensitivities over the depopulation of the area by its Muslim inhabitants.[60] Embarrassed, the Greek state was keen to show that it had taken measures to thwart the exodus, but these led to very poor results. The government then suspended the enlistment of Muslims conscripts into the EES in mid-1948.[61]

Recruitment to the government-sponsored anti-Communist militias (such as MAY) appeared a much more attractive option for local Muslims. There is evidence (mostly provided by oral testimonies) that a significant number of Muslim men joined these groups as a means of protecting their villages from DSE raids. As already discussed, one of the key factors contributing to the widespread desertions amongst the ranks of the DSE's 'Ottoman Battalion' was the increasing demand for Muslim recruits to fight away from their locality, with no regular access to their families. The limited operational radius of MAY, on the other hand, offered no such hardship. In addition, recruitment to MAY units ensured access to food provisions as well as permission for local Muslim men to continue with their agricultural occupations.

The oral testimony of a villager from Chloe, near the headquarters of Captain Kemal's DSE forces in Smigada, offers some insights into the motives of joining government-sponsored militias:

I had no feelings at all for Communism and managed to escape from Bulkes [i.e. the DSE training camp in Yugoslavia]. I crossed the borders into Greece and gave myself up to the Army in Konitsa. I spoke to an officer/ interrogator about the conditions in Bulkes where 6 more Muslims were trained to become officers of the Ottoman Battalion. I decided to join the Army and stayed there for a period of 7–8 months. Initially I went to

---

[59] AYE/1947/28.4, Komotini Gendarmerie, Aliens' Centre, to Aliens' Centre-General of Macedonia-Thrace, 13 October 1947.

[60] AYE/1947/28.4, Aliens' Centre-General of Macedonia-Thrace, to Aliens' Department, Office II, 8 November 1947.

[61] AYE/1948/105.6, Greek Royal Gendarmerie, Aliens' Centre-General of Macedonia-Thrace, to the Department of Aliens, Thessaloniki, 2 January 1948. AYE/1948/105.6, Administration-General of Thrace, Directorate of Political Affairs, Xirotyris, to the Foreign Ministry, Department of Turkey, 28 April 1948.

the Municipality-Sponsored Battalions (*Δημοσυντήρητο Τάγμα*) for the protection of towns and then joined the MAY of Komotini. It was not unusual for a Muslim to volunteer to join the Army but no one wanted to join the guerrillas ... In the north, local Pomak [pro government] militias were formed, by villagers who were familiar with the ground conditions and knew the paths in the area between Chloe and Kechros.[62]

Another interviewee from Mega Dereio (Evros) confirmed the existence of local Muslim militias in the mountainous area adjacent to the Chloe-Kechros zone, recalling that:

In the area that was under the control of the guerrillas, there existed small groups of 4–5 persons that resisted the DSE and retaliated against its soldiers when there were acts of violence by the guerrillas against the minority population. The guerrillas "outlawed" those groups, but no one from the minority informed on them.[63]

Indeed, there is evidence that in the Muslim villages north of the Xanthi the operation of local MAY groups was both welcomed (by the locals) and effective. Interviewees in the village of Echinos named many local MAY recruits and recalled, with some pride, that DSE forces never set foot in their village.[64] This claim is convincing as Echinos stood at the border of the mountainous area that remained under the uninterrupted control of government forces for most of the duration of the civil war.

Evidence of state-induced violence against the Muslim community

During the course of the civil war, the Muslim community of Western Thrace frequently complained about the behaviour of the EES and the Gendarmerie. Many incidents of state violence apparently took place against Muslims in villages where control switched frequently between the guerrillas and government forces. In an article published in June 1947, *Trakya* articulated the predicament of the local population, particularly in the mountainous villages:

[These people are caught] between the devil and the deep blue sea. Because they are constantly under the control of the guerrillas they do whatever they are told to do in order to protect their lives. ... Quite frequently when the governmental troops cross those areas looking for guerrilla units, they behave as if they are the enemy. They press the villagers for information.

---

[62] Interview 16.
[63] Interview 5.
[64] Interview 4; Interview 12.

> *Box 7.6*   Extract from *Trakya* on the Plight of Muslim Villages during the Civil War, August 1947
>
> The war with the guerrillas should not be a reason for the annihilation of the few Turks that live in Thrace. The minority has committed no other sin other than to be faithful to the Government and the only thing we want is to continue living on our land and work our fields...But the Government has put this community in a corner as if it is responsible for Communism. And its [the government's] instruments are the soldiers, the gendarmes and the rural police. [Minority] people do not understand why this war is happening or why they are being persecuted by the Government. They start to believe that they are not wanted in this country...We have lost count of those killed by the guerrillas, in the same way that we have lost count of those who have been beaten by the governmental forces. The 40,000 Turks, who live in the mountains, will soon die of hunger. On the one side the guerrillas, on the other the governmental forces and then hunger. The guerrillas have rebelled against anything decent. It is futile to talk to them about humane behaviour, morality and the law...On the other hand there are villages that have remained under guerrilla occupation for more than eight months. The Army did not go there... If the State cannot protect their lives and properties, then who can? Is it right that the Army passes through these villages once a year and beat people up until they pass out?
>
> *Source*: *Trakya*, 4 August 1947.

The guerrillas, who see that the villagers are not on their side, do not trust them at all. The villagers cannot flee to the lowland areas, controlled by the Army, because they fear that their houses will be burnt. We believe that these people who have no problem at all with the State and are faithful should not be beaten and treated like animals.[65]

In a separate article in the same newspaper, the inability of the government to protect the Muslim villages in mountains was identified as a sign of neglect (see Box 7.6).

During the course of 1947 and well into 1948, there was a string of reports in *Trakya* regarding abuses by government forces against members of the Muslim community.[66] Many of these reports were frequently reproduced in the Turkish press which reported vivid stories of minority hardship and attempted escape from the horrors of Western Thrace.[67] Inevitably, some

---

[65] *Trakya*, 23 June 1947.
[66] See indicatively, the incident in Kremasti (Southwest of Xanthi) reported in *Trakya* on 30 June 1947.
[67] See indicatively AYE/1948/105.3 which contains many Turkish articles, from November 1947 to August 1948, from newspapers such as *Kör Kadı*, *Yeni Sabah*, *Memleket*, *Milliyet*, *Gece Postası*, *Son Saat*, *Vatan*, *Republique/Cumhurriet*, *Son Posta*, *Tasvir*, *Son Telegraf*, *Yeni Gazette*, *En Son Dakika*,and *Hürriyet*.

incidents of violence escalated into diplomatic rows where the Turkish authorities criticised the Greek security forces for not doing enough to protect mountainous villages against guerrilla attacks whilst beingn too heavy-handed during interrogations of Muslim villagers.[68] In one such case in the village of Amaxades, east of Xanthi, a group of Army soldiers stood accused of mistreating a group of Pomak elders, who, under interrogation, professed their ignorance as to the guerrillas' whereabouts. Following strong pressure by Turkish officials, the Greek authorities were forced to investigate the incident, before issuing an apology blaming the violence on over-enthusiastic members of the MAY militia.[69]

Indeed, accounts of state-induced violence during that time were also confirmed by oral testimonies. As one villager from Sminthi, North of Xanthi, recalled:

> During the civil war people suffered from both sides. During the day the Army came and questioned us as to why we accepted the guerrillas in our homes. When the sun set the guerrillas were breaking into our homes and took anything they needed. They hit and ran! People wanted to remain neutral, but we were in the middle, victims of both parties. Generally speaking though, we were against the guerrillas. We felt more secure and protected with the presence of the Army.[70]

In Komotini, the Army's decision to press local men into service for the construction of the town's defences also provoked complaints from members of the local Muslim community who were not convinced by official reassurances that this measure applied to all male citizens.[71] *Trakya's* reporting on this issue offers an interesting insight into Muslim perceptions of discrimination at this time:

> In the Turkish *mahalle* [neighbourhoods] compulsory work has already started, even though no official state or municipal order has been issued. Every morning at 5:30 a soldier comes to the house of a Turk who is then

[68] AYE/1948/105.3, Greek Embassy in Turkey, Skeferis, to the Foreign Ministry, Department of Turkey, 26 May 1948. AYE/1948/105.6, Greek Embassy in Turkey, Skeferis, to the Foreign Ministry, Department of Turkey, 26 March 1948.

[69] AYE/1948/105.7, Gendarmerie Higher Command of Thrace, to Administration-General of Thrace, Directorate of Political Affairs, 24 October 1947. AYE/1948/105.7, Foreign Ministry, Department of Turkey, to the Ankara Embassy, 3 December 1948. AYE/1948/105.7, Aliens' Centre-General of East Macedonia and Thrace, Director, A. Grevenitis, Tessaloniki, to Aliens' Department, Athens, 30 December 1948.

[70] Interview 18.

[71] AYE/1948/105.7, Governor-General of East Macedonia and Thrace, Office II, Grevenitis to Aliens' Department, Athens, 8 January 1948.

Box 7.7   *Trakya* Report on the Violent Incident Involving Officer Dimitris Ioannidis, February 1947

We have heard that in some places Army officers with a self-centred mentality find the opportunity to beat Turks up. The incident involving a noble member of the Xanthi community on 9 January [1947] offers such an example. Ferit Bey who was in business in Komotini bought a first class ticket for his return bus journey to Xanthi. Xanthi was the last stop of the journey. As the bus was about to depart, Mr Ferit Bey saw that somebody else was sitting in his seat and asked the bus company to make his seat available or refund him so that he could instead take the train that would depart in two hours.

The bus company asked the Army officer who occupied the seat to move so that Mr. Ferit could sit. When the bus stopped at the first road check and the Officer found out from the Gendarme who checked the ID cards that Ferit Bey was a Turk he turned to him and said "I will show you now" and forced him to move from his seat so that he could sit there instead. After some kilometres, the bus stopped again in Kalamokastro. The officer took Mr Bey out, beat him up and together with the Gendarme took him to the police station.

There he started to slap him again shouting "so you think that Turks should live here?". After the incident the officer went back to the bus and got off at Eggyro. The officer with such a mentality is Dimitrios V. Ioannidis. If a noble member of our community is treated in such manner, can you imagine what they will do to everyday citizens?

We believe that for the good of our country the officers, in particular, should change their mentality.

Source: *Trakya*, 17 February 1947.

compelled to work until 6 o'clock at night. This situation has been going on for two months now. And this measure applies only to Turks. Every day 30–40 people, along with their animals, are compelled to work in building a road outside the town … This is human rights abuse. And worse of all this goes on amidst a generalised atmosphere of terror. People are so fearful that they can not even approach their MPs and talk to them. The times are such that nobody would refuse to help, either for military or civilian purposes. But nobody could accept such treatment that is both illegal and inhumane … We don't refer to what is happening in the villages. This is happening in Komotini and the only ones forced into compulsory work are Turks.[72]

After another, less conspicuous but revealing, incident in February 1947 *Trakya* criticised the attitude of an Army officer named Dimitris Ioannidis offering, perhaps, an early sign of the character of the man who would later rise to the top of the Greek Junta in the 1970s (see Box 7.7).

---

[72] *Trakya*, 30 August 1948.

Trakya's frequent reports of state violence against the Muslim community in Western Thrace offer a fascinating insight into the complicated relationship between its publisher, Osman Nuri, and the Greek authorities. This relationship is explored in more detail at the end of this chapter.

Court-Martial cases involving members of the Muslim community

Members of the Muslim community suspected for collaboration with the DSE forces were court-martialled. This was, indeed, a widespread practice across Greece which saw thousands of suspected DSE sympathisers sentenced to lengthy imprisonment and, often, death. Unfortunately, state archives (GAK, *Γενικά Αρχεία το Κράτους, ΓΑΚ*) for the Prefectures of Xanthi, Rhodope and Evros have been so depleted that it has not been possible to retrieve full court hearings involving members of the Muslim Community as alleged collaborators of the DSE. Hence, the accounts here are based primarily on local publications of the time, which provide an indicative, but possibly incomplete, picture of the way in which these cases were pursued in court.

A first observation in this respect is that the number of Muslims accused of collaboration with the Communist forces is very small and certainly (even in proportional terms) much smaller than that of the Greek-Orthodox majority in the area. In the cases examined here it is apparent that court-martials often showed leniency towards the Muslims accused who, in the vast majority of cases, were able to convince the military judges that their association with the DSE was the product of compulsion and threats. At the same time, however, it is worth noting that the authorities often offered amnesty to DSE fighters who surrendered themselves to the EES (as was the case with many Muslims recruits).[73]

One of the most important court-martial cases involving Muslims took place in Xanthi in October 1947. A few months earlier, in mid-July, the military authorities of Komotini arrested a large number of Muslims on suspicion of collaboration with the DSE. In total, 63 Muslim citizens were arrested alongside 20 members of the Greek-Orthodox community. Following the preliminary judicial investigations a total of 36 Muslims were

---

[73] For example, *Trakya* on 7 April 1947 reported: 'On Friday and Saturday the court-martial of Xanthi heard the case of 14 people, 12 of which are guerrillas who were captured in various battles against governmental forces. The other 2 are Turks who were arrested as suspects [of collaboration with the DSE]. The trials lasted for two days. 8 guerrillas were sentenced to death, 3 in life imprisonment and 3 were found innocent, of which 2 were the Turks suspects and the other was a guerrilla. The innocent verdict for the guerrilla is due to the fact that he surrendered himself during a time where the government had announced an amnesty, a fact that was confirmed by the soldiers that arrested him'.

charged.[74] Those charged were placed alongside 29 more Muslims who had been charged on similar grounds previously. During the trial the judge acknowledged mitigating circumstances for the accused; namely that they were subjected to blackmail by the DSE forces. At the end, of the 65 men accused, only four were convicted to a year-long imprisonment (Hüseyin Karahasan, Kazim Nazifoğlou, Abukat Hasan Mustafaoğlou and Hüseyin Hasanoğlou).[75] The leniency shown by the court-martial to the members of the Muslim community was appreciated by *Trakya* which reported that 'this trial involving Turks seems to be ending in the best possible manner'.[76]

A report by the Turkish newspaper, *Son Telegraf,* in March 1948, also made reference to the arrest of 43 Muslim DSE guerrillas following a battle with government forces in the region of Xanthi. The ruling of the Xanthi court-martial, however, found all the accused innocent, on the grounds that they were forcefully recruited by the DSE, and it ordered their release.[77] Equally lenient was the outcome of the court-martial case against Muslim villagers from Alkyoni all of whom were found innocent with the exception of Ibrahim Arifoğlu and Rasim Müminoğlou who received six months in prison.[78]

There were, however, cases where court-martials imposed heavy sentences on Muslim suspects. In August 1949 the Xanthi court-martial heard the case of seven Muslim villagers from Miki and two (one Muslim and one Greek Orthodox) from Megali Mersini on charges of collaboration with the DSE. At the end, two (Imam Mümin Hasan Kabze Feizullah and Hafiz Hasan Topaloğlu) of the accused were found guilty and received prison sentences of 17 years each.[79] A similarly long sentence was reported in March 1947 by *Agonistis*, the official newspaper of the KKE's Committee of Macedonia and Thrace. It involved two Muslim soldiers accused of disobeying orders for a transfer to Katerini (in Macedonia) on the grounds that they would fight their 'Greek brothers'. Although the court-martial recognised mitigating circumstances for one of the two accused, the other was sentenced to 20 years imprisonment.[80] There are also reports that some Muslim suspects

---

[74] AYE 1947.28.4, Higher Gendarmerie Command, Thessaloniki, General Security Desk, to the Administration-General of Thrace, Komotini, 7 August 1947. Despite the fact that the total number of those charged was 36, the police report associated with this investigation makes (presumably by mistake) mention of '35 Ottoman' arrests.

[75] *Trakya,* 20 October 1947.

[76] *Trakya,* 20 October 1947.

[77] AYE/1948/105.3, Greek Embassy in Turkey, Skeferis, to the Foreign Ministry, Department of Turkey, 1 April 1948.

[78] *Trakya,* 10 October 1949.

[79] *Trakya,* 21 August 1949. For a similar conviction see also *Trakya,* 17 October 1949.

[80] *Agonistis*, 29 March 1947 (available at ASKI/3122).

were exiled to the open prison of Makronissos, but soon returned.[81] More controversially, a number of Muslim suspects were obliged to undertake forced labour, while their trials were pending. Fifty such cases were picked up by the Turkish Embassy in Athens who protested against this practice (which was routinely used against suspected Communist sympathisers throughout Greece).[82] An internal communication by the Administration-General of Eastern Macedonia and Thrace to the Aliens' Department in Athens suggests that such practices were soon terminated.[83]

The court-martials involving Muslims attracted strong interest by the local Turkish-language press and prompted prominent minority members to unite around the accused. In some cases, however, it appears that members of the Muslim community took advantage of the anti-Communist frenzy of the period to settle personal scores. One such example must have been the court case of Ferezler Mehmet Bey, a prominent land owner of the Muslim community. As *Trakya* reported in November 1949:

> The trial of the land owner, Ferezler Mehmet Bey, started on 25 October (and lasted for one week) which the whole community of Xanthi and Komotini has been eagerly awaiting. Many witnesses were heard from which some were supportive, others not. People who were known to be his enemies before the war were prosecution witnesses and they tried by all means to get him convicted. The court-martial heard all details. It did not accept the accusations that he was an old EAM member, that he sheltered guerrillas in his farm and that he was working for the secession of Thrace and Macedonia. One of his workers was found innocent; another one who was elderly received a 9-month suspended sentence and the owner himself [Ferezler Mehmet Bey] was sentenced to 20 months imprisonment because he gave a bottle of *Raki* [local alcoholic drink] and other minor provisions to the guerrillas. The reasons that led to the bringing of this case to court, spread a climate of discontent and anxiety within the minority.[84]

Both the limited number of court-martial cases brought against Muslims and the relative leniency of the sentences imposed on those found guilty provide an interesting insight into the way in which the local Greek authorities perceived the involvement of the Muslim community with the

---

[81] *Trakya*, 1 August 1949.

[82] AYE/1948/105.7, Foreign Ministry, Department of Turkey, to the Ankara Embassy, 3 December 1948.

[83] AYE/1948/105.7, 8. Aliens' Centre-General for Eastern Macedonia and Thrace, Director, A. Grevenitis, Thessaloniki, to Aliens' Department, Athens, 8 January 1948.

[84] *Trakya*, 7 November 1949.

Communist insurgents. Although suspicion over the minority's 'national loyalty' remained widespread amongst the local military and civilian elite, there is no evidence to suggest that anti-Communist legislation (and the draconian penalties it entailed) was systematically used as a pretext in order to 'cleanse' the area from its Muslim inhabitants. Faced with more pressing security problems elsewhere, the authorities appeared to give the Muslim community the benefit of the (Communist) doubt. Plenty more doubts remained. These would come to the surface later (in the mid-1950s), framing, in the eyes of the Greek establishment, Western Thracian Muslims as the 'enemy within'.

7.4   The battle for Muslim hearts and minds

Compulsion and violence were central to the hunt for new recruits and the conduct of military operations on both sides of the civil war divide. Yet the military campaign of the Communist insurgents and the state-sponsored violence employed for their defeat, reveal only a part of the overall picture of the conflict. For both warring parties, the support of the local, non-combatant, population was a vital ingredient of their overall strategy for military dominance. For the DSE, the geographically limited area of its dominance underlined its heavy reliance on local communities for both recruits and logistical support. For the government forces, the undermining of the insurgents' revolutionary agenda in the eyes of the local Muslims was equally important. Its pool of recruits was certainly bigger than that of the DSE and the cooperation of the villagers of the Rhodope Mountains was vital for gathering intelligence on the enemy as well as navigating a difficult terrain in the context of its military operations. The propaganda war discussed in the next sections reveals much more than the ideological conflict between the two warring parties. As already noted in Chapter 2, issues of memory, religion, ethnicity, and social norms that had shaped the outlook of the Muslim community of Western Thrace for centuries presented a fascinating interface with the political and military imperatives of the civil war conflict.

Communist propaganda in the Rhodope Mountains

The main propaganda instrument for the DSE in the Rhodope Mountains was the Turkish-language newspaper *Savaş* (War-Struggle), published monthly between November 1947 and June 1948. The newspaper was printed in Kardzhali (Bulgaria) and edited by Captain Kemal and Lufti Hoca, a Muslim member of the BCP.[85] In addition to *Savaş* the news bulletin *Radio Haberleri*

---

[85] AYE/1948/105.7, Royal Gendarmerie, Aliens' Centre, Komotini, to Ministry of Public Order, Aliens' Directorate, 1 January 1948.

(Radio News) was published twice in June 1948. The DSE's propaganda material also included a series of proclamations, all of which, according to Greek government intelligence, was printed in Bulgaria.[86]

The DSE's propaganda targeted the members of the Muslim community with short and rather simple messages. All material, however, was written in the new Turkish alphabet (promoted in parallel by the Kemalists) which was not widely used in the area at the time. In contrast to the DSE's propaganda material in other parts of Greece, such as the *Demokratikos Stratos* bulletin, *Savaş* made no use of long and detailed analyses of political and ideological content. A typical example of its editorial style can be found in the simple dialogues between the 'Lowland villager' (living under the control of the *Monarchofascists*) and the 'Highland villager' (living under DSE control) often used by *Savaş* in order to convey its message (see Box 7.8).

Savaş published regular reports on the military achievements of the DSE in Western Thrace and around Greece, news from abroad, the activity of the People's Committee's and orders issued by DSE's HQ EMT. It also included obituaries of DSE fighters who died in battle (see Box 7.9).[87]

Security services' reports in the archives of the Greek Ministry of Foreign Affairs also contain information on the musical tastes of the DSE Muslim fighters in the Rhodope mountains, including the official ELAS anthem translated into Turkish, the 'The Mountains of Rhodope', 'Go Ahead Farmers', 'Antartis and Villager' and 'I Left in Sadness, I Returned in Joy' (see Box 7.10).

A central point in the DSE's propaganda efforts was the defeat of the government's strategy of evacuating mountainous villages in order to starve the guerrillas from provisions and new recruits. The DSE responded by launching a series of raids against the main towns of Western Thrace (particularly Komotini) where many of the displaced villagers were temporarily housed. The purpose of such an offensive was, amongst others, to disprove the government's claims that a move to the lowlands was the only guarantee for the villagers' safety. The DSE raids were accompanied by a large-scale propaganda campaign. In March 1948, *Savaş* warned:

Attention! Attention! Brothers! Get away from the cities and the places where the *Bourandades* have camped. These places are heading for destruction by the fire weapons of the Democratic Army. Brothers please spare your lives. Go back to your villages, your ox and your vineyard. You have nothing to fear from the democrats. We do not want anything from

---

Box 7.8 Extract from *Savaş*, Two Villagers Discussing Life under the DSE, February 1948

Highland Villager: Good morning lowland villager, how are you?
Lowland Villager: So and so, not so bad, God save us from worse, how are you?
Highland Villager: Thank God I am very well. Under the Democratic administration for the first time I am free. We are very satisfied with the administration and they are very satisfied with us. We have a nice life, but we also have a problem. From the time that the fascists do not allow us to travel to the valley, its very difficult to find soap, salt, petrol, corn flour. God will punish them. They will pay very quickly for the fight they have picked with the people.
Lowland Villager: You look very confident. What do you think, will this war end soon? Will the nation find peace?
Highland Villager: It will end very soon, but only if we all do our duty for the fatherland [Greece].
Lowland Villager: What duty?
Highland Villager: What duty! For us, the Turkish minority, there is only one route to salvation and this is the victory of the democrats. Every Turk who is loyal to his religion, nation and honour has his own share in this struggle by the democrats for the salvation of the people. If our youth take the gun in their hand and go up the mountain and if those who are left behind do any necessary sacrifice to help the Democratic Government and the Democratic Army, then this war will be over. A few days ago my son joined the army. I am not sad because I know that it is necessary for the whole nation to unite and fight. That's the only way. Otherwise if I step aside, if you step aside there will not be an end.
Lowland Villager: Yeah. Many young men from our village also joined the Democratic Army. I wonder how they are doing. I've got a brother in law in the Democratic Army and I am worried.
Highland Villager: Don't you worry about them, they are strong like lions. The Democratic Army is looking after them like father and mother. I saw them during training the other day. They are made of steel. We Turks are very good with guns. I saw them after the training was over. They were playing the clarinet and the tabor. They were playing, laughing and singing. Their joy is unbelievable. Don't worry about them, worry about yourself. Since I saw those young Turks I truly believed in the victory of the democrats. In fact the people are going to win this war and they are going to win it very soon.
Lowland Villager: God bless you. Your words brought serenity in my soul. Goodbye.
Highland Villager: Goodbye.

Source: *Savaş*, Issue 4, 16 February 1948.

Box 7.9   Savaş Obituary for Ali Memetoğlu, February 1948

Brave Ali Fell like a Hero

Ali Memetoğlu from Milia, fell gloriously in the battle of Metaxades. His death meant the loss of the bravest and most beloved comrade. It was long ago since Ali joined ELAS and fought the Germans in Macedonia. Ali was with ELAS on the Acropolis of Athens when the British imperialists landed in our country as new oppressors. After Varkiza, Ali returned to his village and he was called to duty [by the EES] but he escaped on the first chance, bringing many of his friends into the Democratic Army. He joined the Evros Headquarters without having a weapon. When the Bourandades [police forces hostile to Communist sympathisers]* attacked the Headquarters, the battle started and Ali stormed into it. Without saying anything to anyone, he took a broken machine-gun, fixed it and fought heroically. He took prisoners and gave us victory. He took part in all battles in Evros on the first line, starring death in the eye.

In the battle of Metaxades, however, he showed the utmost bravery. The enemy had encircled our forces and this Turk broke the enemy's lines and saved hundreds of democratic soldiers. Our position was very exposed. The place where Ali had set his machine-gun was under heavy fire by the enemy. A bullet hit Ali on his right arm and a friend told him 'Ali you are wounded, go back'. Ali laughed and said 'I'm not going anywhere, this is nothing' and continued shooting the fascists. Another bullet wounded him badly on his chest. Ali knew that he was going to die and he said to the comrade next to him 'Take the machine-gun and kill the fascists. Take revenge for me'. Then a mortar shell exploded and shred his body into pieces.

Ali had become a hero. The man who had saved a whole battalion was now dead. Ali was the most beloved within the battalion. A friend of his who was also wounded, when he heard the news said 'Ali is dead and I am still alive. Why?' and he was beating his chest. Once, the battalion's commander was asked to send Ali to train Turkish guerrillas in the use of the machine-gun. The commander refused and told his colleague "I am not giving you Ali. Let's fight for him". The Turkish minority can be very proud for Ali's bravery. All of us who knew the brave machine-gunner will never forget him. The participation of fighters like Ali in the Democratic Army proves why victory is certain. The blood of the brave will not be spilled in vain.

Note: *The name probably originates from police chief Nikos Bourandas who led an active campaign against Communist sympathisers during the War. In August 1944 he was also involved in the 'Kokkinia roadblock' where German and Greek security forces rounded-up and executed hundreds of suspected resistance fighters and members of the KKE.

Source: *Savaş*, Issue 4, 16 February 1948.

---

you and we will not do anything against the people's interests. Everyone must stay close to his own nest and job.[88]

---

[88] *Savaş*, Issue 5, 10 March 1948. For similar warnings see *Savaş*, Issue 5, 20 December 1947 and Issue 7, 13 May 1948.

Box 7.10   The Lyrics of the DSE Song *I Left in Sadness, I Returned in Joy*

I left in sadness, I returned in joy
Open your arms, I'm back
Give me some water to drink
I came a long way back

Rhodope Mountains, Oh Rhodope Mountains
Forest on my right, forest on my left
Spring of Democracy the antartes [guerrillas] hideout

We took the gun in our hands
We all threw ourselves in the fight
And we all joined Democracy

We are brave antartes [guerrillas]
We don't know what fear means
We will smash the fascist's head

Let us breathe the air of freedom
Let us live like humans
The days of freedom are close
This we must all understand

Source: AYE 1948/105/7.

Similar warnings were also issued to those seeking refuge in Turkey:

> Many Turks emmigrate to Turkey. After they have sold everything they got, they return here in poverty. Have no doubt about that, Turkey has deviated from the path shown by the great Atatürk. Their government, as indeed ours, is a government of foreign enemies of the Turkish Nation. Whoever tries to persuade you to go to Turkey is an enemy of yours.[89]

Another conversation between 'villagers', published in *Savaş* revealed its contempt for the leadership of the Muslim Community and the Turkish Consul in Komotini (see Box 7.11).

DSE propaganda in the Rhodope Mountains thus made a concerted effort to deconstruct the position of the Turkish government as the 'natural' protector of its kin in Western Thrace. Indeed Ankara's support for the government of Athens during the civil war and its well-known anti-Communist predisposition attracted much criticism from the DSE. For example, various *Savaş* articles at the time made clear its opposition to the prospect of Turkish troops being despatched, on American orders, to Western Thrace in order to assume the role of a local Gendarmerie. The impact of these rumours, propagated by the DSE radio station in Belgrade and various

---

[89] *Savaş*, Issue 2, 20 December 1947.

Box 7.11   Extract from *Savaş*, Two Villagers Contemplating Emigration to Turkey, March 1948

Highland Villager: Hello comrade from the lowlands, how are you. What do I see? Your face looks sad. What is wrong? Did your boats sink?

Lowland Villager: I wish my ships had sunk. Don't even ask. One says this, the other says that, I am all confused; I don't know what to do.

Highland Villager: What is your trouble? Tell me.

Lowland Villager: Because of the civil war, life is no longer sweet. Now some Beys in Komotini are advising us to leave for Turkey. The Consul says the same. Some wealthy people believed this advice and have already left for Turkey by sea. They say that the tickets are very expensive.

Highland Villager: I see, they started again with the same old story. Leave your house, your property, your farm, your ox and your vineyard and move out of this beautiful country where your ancestors lived for hundreds of years and where your grandfathers are buried. Go and live as a refugee in a valley in Anatolia without trees, without water. Save yourself from the fascists of Greece to become a victim, a beggar of the fascist government of Ankara. No my friend! I am full of such stories. I am not moving a step away from my home and my farm. Anyway the civil war is coming to an end. The fascists are over. One last push to get rid of them and then we will live free in Greece under Democracy. Leave your home? Now, that's stupid!

Lowland Villager: Ok, but what about the Beys in the city?

Highland Villager: Ignore them. A few days ago they tried to recruit volunteers against the antartes [guerrillas], don't you remember? That is why our youth are against Hafız Galip [i.e. local Muslim MP, Kemalist sympathiser] in Komotini. All those who say these are trying to lead us to misery.

Lowland Villager: Ok, but the Consul also says the same.

Highland Villager: My friend you need to understand this for good. The Turkish Consul in Komotini does not represent the Turkish people. We love the Turkish people and we want what is best for them. However, you have to make a distinction between the Turkish people and the fascist government in Ankara which is a servant of the Americans. The Consul is an instrument of the Turkish government which oppresses the Turkish people and guides them to many hardships. Don't listen to the words of your nation's enemies and don't destroy your life and property. Anyway the worst is over, just a little more patience.

Lowland Villager: You are right, we can't live anywhere else. Many have left for Turkey, but many have returned having spent everything they had. If it was nice for us there, they would not return. We are smarter now. I am going to tell my friends not to do anything stupid. It is not worth it. Farewell.

Highland Villager: Farewell.

Source: *Savaş*, Issue 5, 10 March 1948.

newspapers in Bulgaria,[90] on the Western Thracian Muslims is difficult to assess. Local DSE leaders, like Lambros, however, appeared unimpressed:

> Is the fascist government of Ankara a friend of the Turkish minority in Western Thrace? No! Just as the Greek Fascist Government of Athens is an instrument of the Americans, the Turkish Government is also under their orders and oppresses the Turkish nation. It is a great delusion for one to expect salvation from such a government. Is there anyone who does not know that the royalist fascists are the vicious tyrants of the Turkish nation? We know this, you know this, the government in Ankara knows this. Why didn't the Turkish Government raise its voice, even once, to protect you? Why do the Turkish fascists embrace the Greek royalists, who kill you, jail you, exile you and degrade you in every possible way?[91]

With a strongly secular and reformist message and having attacked all pre-existing sources of leadership within the Muslim community (including the government of 'Mother Turkey'), the DSE propaganda in the area adopted a high risk strategy placing too much confidence in the moral superiority of the Communist cause and its appeal to the local population. However, the promised rewards of Socialist victory and the idealised portrayal of the DSE conduct sat uncomfortably with the much harder realities of life in the Rhodope Mountains. For its part, the government in Athens was preparing to do everything at its disposal to 'enlighten' the Muslim community about the evils of the Communist insurgency.

State-organised anti-communist propaganda

The government's propaganda activity towards the Muslim community was subjected to similar operational constraints to those already discussed in the case of the DSE. As significant parts of the Rhodope Mountains remained, by and large, outside the control of EES, the government's propaganda activities focused predominantly on the lowland areas and the big towns of Western Thrace. The content of such propaganda was informed by both strategic considerations (namely, to minimise the recruitment pool of the DSE and to boost the morale of the local population) and deeply entrenched perceptions about the 'national trustworthiness' of the Muslim community. The latter were also important in shaping government preconceptions about the extent of the problem (i.e. Muslim sympathy for the DSE) that its propaganda activities would seek to remedy.

---

[90] AYE/1947/73.1, 'Briefing of Bulgarian Press', 11 November 1947.
[91] AYE/1948/105.7, DSE Command of Eastern Macedonia-Thrace, to the Turkish minority of Western Thrace (undated Proclamation signed by Lambros).

> *Box 7.12*   Extract from a Report of the Komotini Gendarmerie on Muslim Sentiments towards the Government, August 1947
>
> [....] It is an undisputed fact that all Muslims, regardless of their ethnic identity, do not have a national Greek conscience and their only aim is to save money and have a nice living without empathy to the state's struggle against the [Communist] bandits. They maintain a passive attitude both towards the state and the bandits and many of them say 'what do we care about what Greeks do to one another. We live under foreign occupation anyway, why should we get involved? If things get worse, we can always leave [for Turkey]'. This is also the reason why they collude with the bandits and they do not give any support or information about them [the 'bandits'] to the army and the police. On the contrary they hide information and twist the truth. On the one hand this attitude is due to their indifference and their lack of national Greek conscience. On the other hand, it is also due to the terror and threats that the bandits direct against them. Especially those who live in villages have been terrorised by the murders, looting and arson committed by the bandits and they are trying to safeguard their property and life by colluding with the bandits. They say that you can't save yourself from the bandits, but you are not in danger by the military authorities [.....]
>
> *Source*: AYE/1947/28.4, Aliens' Centre, Komotini, to Government-General of Thrace, Directorate of Political Affairs, 12 August 1947.

A first observation in this regard is that the local security forces massively overestimated the DSE inroads into the Muslim communities. In August 1947, the Komotini Gendarmerie estimated that approximately 20 per cent of the Pomak villagers on the Rhodope Mountains were supportive of the DSE, attracted by its promise that it would redistribute the lands of wealthy farmers to the poor.[92] The view of a local Gendarmerie Captain on Muslim sentiments towards the government cause is given in Box 7.12.

In a separate report to the Ministry of Public Order in January 1948, the Komotini Gendarmerie depicted a much bleaker picture:

> Unfortunately, the propaganda of the [Communist] bandits in the remote villages under their control has succeeded in attracting almost 60% of the residents to the Communist ideas. The remaining 40% does not react due to a reign of terror. All of them provide their services to the bandits in every possible way. On the other hand, they do not provide the government forces with any information or favours and they often try to hide facts from us.[93]

---

[92] AYE/1947/28.4, Aliens' Centre, Komotini, to Administration-General of Thrace, Directorate of Political Affairs, 12 August 1947.
[93] AYE/1948/105.7, Aliens' Centre Komotini, to the Ministry of Public Order, Aliens' Directorate, 1 January 1948.

Acknowledging the government's inability to restore its authority in the mountainous areas of Western Thrace, the Minister of the Administration-General of Northern Greece, Aristeidis Basiakos, outlined the main axis of state propaganda towards the local Muslim community.

> For the time being the liberation of the villages controlled by the [Communist] bandits by military means is impossible. Therefore we believe that it is necessary to enlighten the law-abiding and peaceful Muslim population of Western Thrace through the Turkish newspapers of Xanthi and Komotini. We must make clear to this population that they must abstain from every kind of contact and cooperation with the bandits, who are the enemies of Greece and Turkey. We need to stress the fact that the bandits aim to enslave [the minority] to communist Bulgaria, in taking their property (as it happens in all Communist countries) and in abolishing their religion.[94]

The propagation of the government's line in the Muslim areas was pursued through three main channels: the establishment of special Committees for the Enlightenment of the Rural Population (*Επιτροπές Διαφωτίσεως του Λαού της Υπαίθρου*), official visits and state events in the area and (most importantly) the penetration of the local Turkish-language press.

The idea for the creation of Committees for the Enlightenment of the Rural Population was floated by the Administration-General of Thrace in summer 1947. The main objective of these committees was the dissemination of the government's promise to grant an amnesty to all those (both Greek Orthodox and Muslims) that deserted DSE units and provided information on Communist activities. The Committee made regular visits to the local villages (such as Xylagani, Sappes, Aratos, Iasmos, Arriana, Kavakli and others) during Sundays and public holidays.[95] The Administration-General issued specific instructions on the line that the Committee should follow (see Box 7.13).

---

[94] AYE/1948/105. 7, Administration-General of Northern Greece, to the Foreign Ministry, Directorate of Political Affairs, 4 February 1948.

[95] Members of the Rhodope Committee were the Metropolitan of Maroneia and Thasos; one local MP from each party (or their representative); the (two) Muslim MPs; the Mayor of Komotini; an army officer of the regional army headquarters-general; a higher officer of the Gendarmerie and a State Prosecutor. For more details see GAK (Athens), K108/B, Administration-General of Thrace, The Governor, G. Kosmas, Komotini, to: Members of the Committee; Battalion; Gendarmerie Higher Command; the Administrations's Secretary-General, 24 July 1947; GAK (Athens), K108/B, Administration-General of Thrace, The Governor, G. Kosmas, Komotini, to the Committee for the Enlightenment of the Rural Population of the District of Rhodope, 6 August 1947.

Box 7.13   Instructions of the Administration-General of Thrace to the Members of the Committees for the Enlightenment of the Rural Population, August 1947

1. The conflict is not a 'civil war', as the anarchist guerrillas claim, but an uprising organised from abroad by the Slavs and their followers.
2. Every Greek has an obligation to work for the defeat of the 'thieves', providing all available support to the Government, the Army and the Gendarmerie.
3. The Committee must provide advice to the relatives of young rebels who were lured into joining the DSE and convince them to abandon the guerrillas and surrender to the authorities, safe in the knowledge that mother Greece will embrace them with tears in her eyes once more and will protect them in every possible many way.
4. Everybody should assist the families whose men have been conscripted to the Army and do not have spare hands to work in the fields.
5. Everyone should be willing to make sacrifices for the struggle of the motherland with the belief that the rebel uprising will be shattered.
6. People should be convinced that this struggle is a matter of life and death for the nation.
7. Slavism cannot succeed against the superior power of the Anglo-Saxons.

Source: GAK (Athens), K108/B, Administration-General of Thrace, The Governor, G. Kosmas, Komotini, to the Committee for the Enlightenment of the Rural Population of the District of Rhodope, 6 August 1947.

In order to ensure greater penetration into the Muslim populations of the lowlands a number of 'trusted' members of the minority were employed to supplement the activities of the Committees for the Enlightenment of the Rural Population. One such was Hasan Hatipoğlu, son of the pro-Kemalist former MP and senator Hatip Yusuf from Komotini, who at that time served as an officer in the Greek Army and was later elected as a Member of Parliament (1952–1967). According to Aarbakke (2000: 117) one of the 'few stable features in Hatipoğlu's career is his disdain for the Left'.

Official visits and national celebrations also provided a major channel for the dissemination of the government's anti-Communist line. Royal tours, in particular, offered a first class opportunity for such propaganda. At least three visits by members of the royal family (January 1947, October 1947, June 1949) are recorded in the local press of the time, which pro-vided extensive coverage of the royal whereabouts and published morale-boosting articles targeting the local population.[96] Prominent members of the Muslim community featured regularly in these visits. *Eleftheri Thraki* reported on the visit of King Paul to Alexandroupolis in October 1947 (see Box 7.14).

---

[96] See, indicatively, *Proia*, 22 June 1949; *Eleftheri Thraki*, 22 January 1947, 8 October 1947 and 2 July 1949; *Ergatikos Agon tis Thrakis*, 24 June 1949 and 2 July 1949.

> *Box 7.14* Report by *Eleftheri Thraki* on King Paul's Visit to Alexandroupolis, October 1947
>
> On 6 October, at 13:15 His Majesty King Paul arrived from Komotini by car, which he drove himself. The King, who wore an Army General's uniform...was accompanied by General Alexandros Papagos, the British General Rawlings, the Commander-in-Chief of the 3rd Army Corps, Mr. D. Papageorgiou, the Governor-General of Thrace D. Kosmas, the Commander-in-Chief of the 7th Brigade, Mr. Al. Asimakopoulos and the rest of his entourage.
>
> Outside the Brigade's building he greeted the gathered crowd who applauded and cheered with great enthusiasm. The Queen was waiting for him there and they subsequently went together to the Metropolitan Church to attend service.
>
> Such was the crowd gathered outside the church to see the royal couple that the police barely managed to open a narrow passageway for the officials to cross into the church.
>
> Although in the middle of the church there were carpets and armchairs for the Royal couple, they both attended the whole mass standing. [...]
>
> Source: *Eleftheri Thraki*, 8 October 1947.

Equally laborious, albeit less glamorous, were the efforts of the authorities to strengthen the 'national', law abiding credentials of the local population. These included frequent parades celebrating Greek national holidays, attended by both Greek Orthodox and Muslim dignitaries, where students from minority schools were invited to carry the Greek flag. Such festivities were frequently supplemented by performances from schoolchildren and scouts,[97] while, on a more serious note, history-inspired theatrical plays, such as *Belomorie* (premiered in March 1947) reminded the locals of the suffering brought by the Bulgarian occupation during WWII.[98] The local press also reported in detail the funerals of fallen soldiers and gendarmes which were routinely attended by senior military and civilian officials, re-iterating their unfaltering commitment to defeat the Communist evils.[99]

The mobilisation of local Greek and Turkish-language newspapers in Xanthi and Komotini became a key instrument of anti-Communist propaganda in the area. The importance of the local press for the government's interests was recognised by the Deputy Governor-General of Thrace, Zahos Xirotyris, who suggested that state subsidies should be directed to all pro-government local newspapers in order to counter financial problems caused by decreasing circulation. The loss of such valuable local allies: 'would cause great damage to our national interests, since these newspapers

---

[97] See, indicatively, *Proia*, 31 October 1946; 30 October 1947, 31 March 1948, 30 March 1949, 2 November 1949, and *Eleftheri Thraki*, 29 March 1947 and 29 March 1948.
[98] *Eleftheri Thraki*, 4 March 1947.
[99] See, for example, *Proia*, 6 December 1946.

are our only means of reacting to raging hostile propaganda and preserving morale in this area that has suffered so much'.[100]

For the Muslim community, in particular, Xirotyris floated the idea of an anti-*Savaş* newspaper, published exclusively in Turkish, but this suggestion never got off the ground. For his part, the Minister for the Administration-General of Northern Greece, Aristeidis Basiakos, advised Athens to issue strict guidelines to all public authorities and, especially, local journalists:

> To abstain from passing any kind of judgment or criticism against the Muslim population in Western Thrace. To maintain the existing policy which is never to imply that they are under suspicion, but at the same time keep them under surveillance in the same way that every Greek needs to be under surveillance.[101]

Xirotyris also believed that the government should engage the local Muslim elite in its anti-Communist propaganda. This should involve:

> Appropriate suggestions and orders to the Muslim religious and community leaders to take advantage of any public or private encounter to enlighten and educate their co-religionists against the disastrous communist ideas and to draw their attention to the hazards which the misleading and subversive preaching of the [Communist] bandits may cause to them personally or to the minority in general.[102]

Minister Basiakos also argued for the mobilisation of Muslim MPs, suggesting that they tour their constituencies in order to boost the morale of the local Muslim communities.[103] Indeed, the vast majority of the local Muslim elite responded positively to the government's call. A typical example was Osman Nuri, the editor of *Trakya* newspaper and a local MP for the centrist *National Political Union*, who adopted a strong anti-Communist stance and

[100] AYE/1948/105.7, Administration-General of Thrace, Press Office, to the Ministry of Press and Information, 26 October 1948. The Minister for Northern Greece, Basiakos, also stressed that 'wherever it is not possible for some villagers to escape from the control of the guerrillas through the operations of the army, it is imperative that the task of enlightening the law-abiding and pious Muslim population of Thrace should be undertaken by the Turkish newspapers printed in Komotini and Xanthi'. AYE/1948/105.7, Administration-General of Northern Greece, A. Basiakos, to Foreign Ministry, Directorate of Political Affairs, 4 February 1948.
[101] AYE/1948/105.7, Administration-General of Northern Greece, to the Foreign Ministry, Directorate of Political Affairs, 12 February 1948.
[102] AYE/1948/105.7, Administration-General of Thrace, Press Office, to the Ministry of Press and Information, 26 October 1948.
[103] AYE/1948/105.7, Administration-General of Northern Greece, to the Foreign Ministry, Directorate of Political Affairs, 4 February 1948.

later claimed that, without him, a much larger number of Muslims would have joined the Communist forces (Aarbakke 2000: 91).

Nuri's anti-communism provided the Greek government with a temporarily valuable, if a highly volatile, ally. The Greek security services were highly suspicious of Nuri's frequent criticisms against the government's minority policy and his close links with the Turkish Consulate in Komotini.[104] An intelligence report in 1947 also referred to Nuri's regular contacts with the Military Attaché of the Turkish Embassy in Athens.[105] Yet, there is no evidence to suggest that the Greek authorities suspected Turkish officials of defaulting on their commitment to support the Greek government during the civil war. Indeed, communication between Minister Basiakos and the Foreign Ministry in Athens, reveals that Greek officials appeared to have discussed the effect of Communist propaganda on the Muslim population with Turkish consular officials and that both sides agreed that the Muslim population in Western Thrace was not a 'natural' ally for the DSE forces.[106]

The entanglement between the Greek authorities, local Muslim notables and the Turkish Consulate in Komotini, might have been sustained by the imperatives of the Greek civil war and the onset of the Cold War, but it offered no stable basis for longer-term collaboration. Indeed, a secret report by the Greek security services in 1952 (shortly after the end of the civil war) revealed the extent to which mutual suspicion had returned to Western Thrace:

> The Muslim MPs and other notables are frequent visitors to the Consulate and, having monitored certain movements, we can safely conclude that they constitute a sort of advisory council to the Consul. Quite often, when the Consul wants to get in touch with the Muslim element in the province, he does so escorted by certain Muslims under the pretext

---

[104] The Greek security services attributed Nuri's outbursts on his party political ambitions in the area and the cultivation of his image as a self-proclaimed 'protector' of the local Muslim community. For more see AYE/1948/105.6, Greek Royal Gendarmerie, Aliens' Centre, Komotini, to the Aliens' Centre-General of Macedonia-Thrace, 9 August 1948; AYE/1948/105.6, Greek Royal Gendarmerie, Aliens' Centre, Komotini, to the Aliens' Centre-General of Macedonia-Thrace, 14 September 1948; AYE/1948/105.6, Greek Royal Gendarmerie, Aliens' Centre, Komotini, to the Aliens' Centre-General of Macedonia-Thrace, 20 October 1948; AYE/1948/105.6, Government-General of Northern Greece, The Minister Korozos, to the Foreign Ministry, Directorate of Political Affairs, Department of Turkey, 12 August 1948. For more on Osman Nuri see also Aarbakke 2000: 9, 83 and 110–112.

[105] AYE/1947/28.4, Ministry of Public Order, Aliens' Directorate-General, II Office, 'Intelligence Report', 6 November 1947.

[106] AYE/1948/105.7, Minister of Northern Greece, A. Basiakos, to Foreign Ministry, Directorate of Political Affairs, 12 February 1948.

of going for an excursion or hunting. Needless to say, the Consulate is informed on most – if not all – our affairs, through its many informants among the minority. It is said that the Muslim newspaper from Xanthi, *Trakya*, receives supplementary [secret] funds from the Consulate. The Consulate supports the Muslim Youth associations and their bonds are really close.[107]

The issue of *Trakya*'s funding, it seems, had gone full circle: from Basiakos' 'subsidies' to the Turkish Consulate's 'supplementary funds'. The desperate battle for the hearts and minds of the Muslim community during the civil war necessitated opportunistic friendships on the ground. With many of the underlying sources of (mutual) frustration still simmering in the background, however, the spark to ignite fresh inter-communal tensions was only a short way off. The events in Cyprus and Istanbul during the 1950s would provide such ignition.

7.5   Conclusion

The recruitment and propaganda strategy of the two warring parties of the Greek civil war towards the Muslim community of Western Thrace was shaped by a mixture of military imperatives and deeply entrenched stereotypes as to whether the minority could ever become a 'reliable ally'. In terms of Muslim recruitment, the Communist insurgents lacked a coherent strategy for the implementation of the Party's earlier commitments on Thracian independence or autonomy from the Greek state. Throughout the 1930s and, certainly during the first half of the 1940s, such rhetorical flourishes were never seriously pursued on the ground. As a result, the Muslim community only entered the 'radar' of the DSE at a late stage. The DSE strategy in this respect was driven by the imperative of finding new recruits against the background of an increasingly hopeless campaign against the government. This strategy received, in the face of Mihri Belli, a major and unlikely boost. Yet even 'Captain Kemal's charisma was not enough to galvanise sufficient (or consistent) support on the ground. The minority, locked in its own isolation and suspicious as to the promised rewards of Communist revolution, never became a loyal ally of the DSE and collaborated, by and large, only when it had no other option. As the territorial spread of DSE forces was confined to small mountainous pockets, the pressure for new recruits turned ugly, aggravated by the fact that the enlistment of female Muslims was unrealistic. The widespread incidents of Communist reprisals

---

[107] GAK Kavalla, Archive of Foreign and Minority Schools, F.95B, Ministry of Interior, Aliens' Directorate-General, II Office, D. Vlastaris, 'Report of the Muslims living in Greece', July 1952.

against those who failed to collaborate as well as the massive waves of Muslim desertion from the ranks of the DSE testify to this troubled relationship.

The government in Athens found, in the Muslim community of Western Thrace, a useful ally in its anti-Communist campaign. But here too there was no love at first sight. The Muslims never really regarded the conflict between the government and the DSE forces as 'their war'. Fear and respect for state authority might have brought Muslim conscripts into the ranks of the EES (until mid-1948), but there are few stories of anti-Communist heroism to report. The Muslim community was far more eager to join government-sponsored militias in order to protect their own localities and kin. Yet as the government's civil war strategy began to build the foundations of a restrictive police state, the members of the Muslim community were amongst the first to feel the consequences. True, court-martials were lenient to those Muslims suspected of Communist sympathies. Yet attitudes of suspicion and animosity towards the Muslim/Turkish 'other' regularly bubbled up and escalated into violence. Such incidents strained relations between Greek state officials and local Muslim leaders, but did not threaten to fundamentally destabilise their front against their common enemy; the Communist insurgents. This front, however, was built largely on mutual convenience rather than a commitment, on either side, to the virtues of multi-cultural co-existence. In subsequent years, it would be shattered by the increasing bilateral tensions between Greece and Turkey.

The propaganda of both sides was constrained by the fortunes of war. The main objective of the DSE propaganda was to stop the depopulation of the Rhodope Mountains which had become a key strategic aim for the government forces. The image of a victorious Communist army enjoying the full support of the locals, however, became increasingly difficult to sustain as the DSE's faltering military campaign reduced the geographical spread of its control and mounted unbearable pressure on poor mountainous villages to provide support for the guerrillas. For the government forces, the portrayal of their Communist opponents as instruments of a Slavic conspiracy aiming at the abolition of religion and property was designed to stir widespread anti-Bulgarian sentiments among Western Thracian Muslims and remind their pious communities of their incompatibility with the insurgents. However, both the DSE and the government forces faced significant geographical limitations in reaching some of their key Muslim audiences. The DSE's presence in the lowlands was sporadic and in the big towns almost non-existent. This fatally undermined its ability to engage with a potentially much bigger pool of recruits or indeed convince some of the evacuees to return to their villages. By contrast, the government's dominance in the urban centres allowed it to control the local flow of information. Yet, its weakness in the mountainous villages left it in a difficult position to counter the DSE's propaganda there. The very small number of government-appointed teachers who took up their posts in minority schools during the course of the civil war is another testament of this limitation (for more on this see Chapter 8).

In ideological terms, the DSE's message towards the local Muslim community also suffered from (inevitable) contradictions. The rhetoric of the DSE propaganda was kept simple (presumably to appeal to uneducated villagers), but contained a strong secular and modernist message. Kemalist ideals were praised (and the new Turkish alphabet used) and much attention was directed towards an ethnic (Turkish), rather than religious, identification of the local community. Yet, much of this modernity had not yet penetrated the rural communities in the Rhodope Mountains which remained, by and large, unreceptive audiences. All relics of the Ottoman power structures within the Muslim community (its Islamic leadership, the local Beys or the land-owning elites) were 'natural' enemies of the DSE's agenda. The Turkish government in Ankara and the Consulate in Komotini were also dismissed as American stooges or allies of the *Monarchofascists* in Athens. The DSE had chosen to ignore all pre-existing power-bases within the local community, propagating instead a message of 'social liberation' which, it hoped, would sweep away all of its local enemies. As it turned out, this was a strategic mistake; a step too far for a local community which valued its traditional way of life more than the promised rewards of the Socialist revolution.

The conservative predisposition of Western Thracian Muslims made them a more receptive audience for the government's propaganda. The resources at the disposal of government authorities were far greater than those of the DSE as, indeed, was the number of local Muslims under its influence. The need to keep the minority on its side forced the government to build alliances with local minority leaders who were influential opinion leaders for the Muslim middle classes in the big towns. The sincerity of such an alliance, however, was questionable from the start. For local Muslims it meant siding with the least threatening of the two warring parties of the civil war. For the Greek government it meant the implicit recognition of an increasingly 'mediated' access to the minority, through a local elite that was progressively looking to the Turkish Consulate of Komotini for protection and guidance. For Athens, such a compromise might have been easier to swallow during the desperate times of the civil war. Later on, however, the compromise of this period would lead to a profoundly dysfunctional *modus vivendi* in Western Thrace.

8
Parallel Universes

8.1 Introduction

The changing fortunes of the military conflict between the government forces and the DSE exposed the Muslim community of Western Thrace to two very different kinds of authority. In the big towns and (most of) the lowland villages, the pre-war state apparatus began to return gradually from March 1945 onwards, ending the *de facto* dominance that EAM had in the area since the withdrawal of the Bulgarian forces the previous autumn. In the Rhodope Mountains, however, the Greek state maintained only a nominal presence and this did not last very long as the outbreak of the civil war brought many of these areas under the control of the Communist forces. Indeed, by mid-1947, the two warring parties had largely consolidated their power in their respective areas of control. Yet, the delineation of the battle lines was far from tidy. Mopping-up operations by government forces in the mountains and DSE incursions into the lowlands produced a volatile security situation where military authority varied over time and geographically. Such volatility, along with the mounting ideological polarisation of the conflict, had profound implications for the way in which both the Communists and the Greek state sought to organise their educational and welfare policies towards the Muslim communities. In this context of having to negotiate an increasingly precarious militarisation at home, many Western Thracian Muslims sought a better fortune by escaping to Turkey. For those who remained, the experience of the civil war (and more generally of the 1940s) would transform the way in which they perceived their own self-interest and their relation with the Greek state.

8.2 The Muslim community between two authorities

The return of the Greek state to Western Thrace

The gradual return of state authority to Western Thrace (as indeed in most other parts of the country) took place in the context of extreme political instability and heavy foreign interference. The discussion of the basic state apparatus in the area forms an important part of the narrative that follows, both in terms of locating the main interlocutors between the Muslim community and the Greek state, but also in contextualising the extensive primary material that informs much of the story that is being told here. Indeed, the climate of political instability is evident from the fact that, during the five years between the arrival of Georgios Papandreou in Athens as Prime Minister in October 1944 and the end of the civil war in late 1949, a total of 17 different governments were formed under ten different prime ministers.[1] As the security situation in the country began to deteriorate rapidly after the *Dekemvriana* – the outbreak of military clashes in Athens in December 1944 – the outlook and structure of successive Greek governments became increasingly militarised. The pressing emergencies confronting the first post-war Greek governments is reflected in the names of some of their key ministerial and vice-ministerial portfolios such as Welfare (Πρόνοιας), Food (Επισιτισμού),[2] Repatriation of Refugees (Παλιννοστήσεως Προσφύγων), Reconstruction (Ανοικοδομήσεως), Press and Enlightenment (Τύπου και Διαφωτίσεως). It is also indicative that many of the prime ministers of the period retained under their personal authority the (then separate) ministries of the Military (Στρατιωτικών), the Air-Force (Αεροπορίας) and the Navy (Ναυτικών), as well as the Ministry of Foreign Affairs.

The increasing militarisation of the Greek state was further reinforced in the aftermath of the March 1946 elections (the first post-war elections that had been marred by much violence; see also Chapter 6) and the subsequent descent of the country into a fully-fledged civil war. As a result, the government in Athens implemented a series of measures on public order and security which brought draconian punishments for anybody suspected of Communist sympathies, frequently leading to summary executions. As the north of the country became the centre stage of the civil war, subversive activities 'against the integrity of the State' (law 2803/1941) in Epirus, Thessaly, Macedonia and Western Thrace commanded even harsher punishments than those committed elsewhere. Amongst the measures employed

---

[1] The sequence was: Georgios Papandreou (18 October 1944 to 3 January 1945), Nikolaos Plastiras (3 January to 8 April 1945), Petros Voulgaris (8 April to 11 August 1945 and 11 August to 17 October 1945), Regent, Archbishop Damaskinos (17 October to 1 November 1945), Panagiotis Kanellopoulos (1 November to 22 November 1945), Themistocles Sofoulis (22 November 1945 to 4 April 1946), Panagiotis Poulitsas (4 April to 18 April 1946), Konstantinos Tsaldaris (18 Apil to 2 October 1946 and 2 October 1946 to 24 January 1947), Demetrios Maximos (24 January to 29 August 1947), Konstantinos Tsaldaris (29 August to 7 September 1947), Themistocles Sofoulis (7 September 1947 to 18 November 1948; 18 November 1948 to 20 January 1949; 20 January to 14 April 1949 and 14 April to 30 November 1949), Alexandros Diomedes (30 June 1949 to 6 January 1950).

[2] This was renamed, in 1945, Ministry of Supply (Εφοδιασμού).

by the Greek government was the creation of right-wing 'security' militias (or the re-armament of existing ones) and the opening of special 'rehabilitation camps' in remote islands in which suspected Communist supporters were exiled. (Alivizatos 1981)

After liberation – and throughout the duration of the civil war – the civilian administration of all northern regions of Greece came under the Administration-General of Northern Greece (*Γενική Διοίκηση Βορείου Ελλάδας*), headed by a senior government minister as Governor-General.[3] The post had been a feature of the Greek administration since the aftermath of the Balkan Wars as a means of consolidating the authority of the state in the 'new lands' (i.e. the territories captured by Greece from the Ottoman Empire). The post was strengthened further during the last prime-ministerial tenure of Eleftherios Venizelos (1928–1932) when all governor-generals became members of the government (either as Ministers or Vice-Ministers). The powers ascribed to these posts were indeed extensive, covering the exercise of all ministerial powers in the area of their competence (with the exception of Justice, Military and Foreign Affairs). After 1950, many of these responsibilities were gradually transferred to prefects,[4] before the post of Governor-General was abolished altogether in 1955.

Throughout the course of the civil war, the Governor-General of Northern Greece was assisted by a number of deputy governor-generals each of whom headed a separate Administration-General for a specific geographical sub-division of Northern Greece, such as Western Thrace.[5] The Administration-General of Thrace was re-established in March 1945 by the Plastiras government.[6] The basic structure of the Administration-General of Thrace

---

[3] During the period 1945–1950, this post was held successively by Athanasios Theodorou, Alexandros Merentitis, Nikolaos Kottas, Konstantinos Rodopoulos, Aristeidis Basiakos, Konstantinos Korozos.

[4] The administrative division of Greece into Prefectures pre-dated WWII. In mid-1945 five such Prefectures came under the competence of the Administration-General of Thrace: Kavalla, Drama, Xanthi, Rhodope and Alexandroupolis. The Prefecture of Xanthi was created for the first time on 21 December 1944 after the carving-up of the (larger) Rhodope and Drama Prefectures. However, due to the instability in the region, the first Prefect, Nikolaos Grammatikakis, did not assume his duties until March 1945. Generally on the administrative history of Greece see Andronopoulos and Mathioudakis 1988: 119–127.

[5] Deputy Governor-Generals existed for the regions of Western Macedonia, Central Macedonia, Eastern Macedonia, as well as Western Thrace. Each Deputy Governor-General also had the rank of Vice Minister (*Υφυπουργός*) in the government. In some early post-war governments, the areas of Crete, Epirus, the Aegean and the Ionian islands also came under the competence of a Governor-General.

[6] The first Deputy Governor-General for Thrace was Alexandros Papathanasis who was replaced in succession by Charalambos Rouchotas, Michael Mavrogordatos, Christos Goulopoulos and Nikolaos Panagiotopoulos who resigned in June 1949 shortly before the end of the civil war in the area. Immediately after liberation, a

Box 8.1   The Basic Structure of the Administration-General of Thrace, 1946–1949

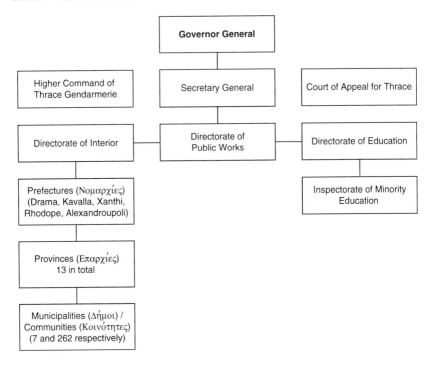

(listing the most relevant services to the Muslim community) is presented in Box 8.1.

Much of the early post-war security apparatus dated back to the Metaxas period. The Aliens' Department within the Ministry of Public Order in Athens was the central point for intelligence-gathering, with a powerful regional branch located in Thessaloniki (Aliens' Centre-General). In Western Thrace, branches of the Aliens' Department existed both in the Higher Gendarmerie Command (located in Komotini) and the local Commands

---

number of Special Committees were established in preparation for the restitution of the Greek pre-war administration. In this context, PM Papandreou appointed as Commissioner to the General-Administration of Macedonia and Thrace his old aide and ex-MP for Drama, Lambrinidis. For more see WO/201/1606A, Leeper to British Embassy, Greece, Telegram No. 58, 22 September 1944. Generally for the structure of the Administration-General of Thrace see WO/252/800, Greece, Zone Book No. 8, Macedonia and Thrace, Part 1, People and Administration, 29 February 1944, and Greece, Zone Book No.8, Macedonia and Thrace, Part 2, Local Information, 31 March 1944. *Leykoma Thrakis-Makedonias* 1932: 244–246. Also see Aarbakke 2000: 683; Divani 1999: 75–81; Soilentakis 2004: 461–464, Vol. II.

and Stations across the region. The activities of the Aliens' Department were also supplemented by the Army's military intelligence (known as the 2nd Office). Later, in February 1949, a root and branch reform of the Greek intelligence services led to the creation of the Central Information and Research Service (*Κεντρική Υπηρεσία Πληροφοριών και Ερευνών*).

With respect to the policies of the Greek government towards the Muslim community in Western Thrace after the war, the continuing importance attached to the Lausanne Treaty (1923) and its reciprocity principle, led to the reinstatement of the Ministry of Foreign Affairs as a key player in the decision-making on minority affairs.[7] The Ministry of Foreign Affairs' powerful A' Directorate of Political Affairs and, particularly, the Department for Turkey featured prominently in much of the internal correspondence on the elaboration of minority policy on a wide range of issues such as religious affairs, education and the administration of Muslim communal properties. At the same time, the return of the Greek state in Western Thrace also removed all remnants of Bulgarian rule and saw the reinstatement of all 'self-governing' institutions of the Muslim minority to their pre-war status.

Yet, the return of such institutions met a much changed landscape. Throughout the course of the Bulgarian occupation the Kemalist/modernist tendency within the minority had been significantly strengthened, aided, in part, by the skilful manoeuvring of the Turkish Consulate in Komotini to position itself as the protector of the minority in difficult times. For the Greek government, its own earlier alliances with the Kemalists were now overtaken by an increasing suspicion of their nationalist agenda. As a result, Athens turned to the conservative/old-Muslim guard in the area in search of more conducive allies.[8] The emerging tension between the Greek authorities and the minority's Kemalist elite manifested itself most clearly in the row over the membership and role of the Commissions for the Management of Muslim Properties (*Διαχειριστικές Επιτροπές Μουσουλμανικών Περιουσιών or Vakıf*).

These commissions were set up in accordance with the terms of the Lausanne Treaty which provided for the self-government of mosques, schools and other community-owned property by local Muslims. Before the war, the independence and competences of these commissions were compromised by the constant interference of the Greek authorities, which retained control over the appointment of their members (despite Law 2345/1920 providing for their election). The Greek government also

---

[7] However, communication and coordination between the Ministry of Foreign Affairs and other relevant agencies (the sectoral Ministries, the Administration-General of Thrace, security services) was marked by much uncertainty during this period.

[8] GAK (Kavalla), 'Archive of Foreign and Minority Schools', F. 95B, Ministry of Interior, Aliens' Directorate, 'Report on the Muslims of Greece', July 1952.

refused to recognise their self-assumed role as representative institutions of the local community; arguing, instead, that their role, as provided for in the 1920 legislation, was merely managerial.[9] The practice of appointing the members of the Commissions for the Management of Muslim Properties was reversed in 1944, when, local EAM forces, which controlled the area at the time, allowed the Muslim community to hold direct elections for this purpose, leading to a widespread victory for the Kemalists (for more on this see Chapter 6). Following the return of the 'official' Greek administration in early 1945, however, the results of the 1944 election were annulled. In October 1946 the Governor-General of Thrace, Christos Goulopoulos, appointed new members of the Xanthi Committee, prompting a string of complaints by the local Kemalist elite and, particularly, Osman Nuri, who was himself ejected from the Commission.[10] On 23 December 1946, *Trakya*'s editorial thundered:

> The wounds that the administrative authorities are trying to inflict upon our ethnic and religious sentiments and, now, upon our economic existence are beginning to overstep the mark. This change of administrative practice is not just the policy of one party. Just one drop of water is enough for the glass to overflow. From our next issue we will reveal the [Greek] state policy for the annihilation of our ethnic, religious and economic existence.[11]

The return of Greek state authority in the towns of Western Thrace might have averted the immediate danger of a Communist takeover, but it certainly had not brought harmony to the Muslim community. As the priorities of both the local Muslim elite and the Greek authorities shifted towards an increasingly antagonistic relationship, their cooperation, even in the face of a common Communist enemy, became difficult to sustain.

The Soviet Muslim Republic of Western Thrace

At the same time as the government of Athens was re-asserting the apparatus of the Greek state in Western Thrace, the DSE was busy building its own structures. The Communist leadership of DSE had recognised that 'if a revolution is to prevail, it must not just antagonise the old regime, but it will have to create its own state and replace the old one that is crushing under the

---

[9] GAK (Kavalla), 'Archive of Foreign and Minority Schools', F. 95B, Ministry of Interior, Aliens' Directorate, 'Report on the Muslims of Greece', July 1952.

[10] For more on the Commissions for the Management of Muslim Properties see Aarbakke 2000:85–88; Andreades 1980: 12–14; Nikolakopoulos 1990–1991: 185–189; Soltarides 1997: 81–86; Tsioumis 2006: 53–55.

[11] *Trakya*, 23 December 1946.

blows of the rebelled people'.[12] DSE thus had a dual strategy: armed struggle along with state-building. The point to prove was clear: the Communist
movement was capable of much more than fighting a war; it was able to
deliver its ideas and care for the citizens of 'new Greece' by introducing a
new style of government based on a different rule of law.

The building of a parallel administration by the DSE served more practical
imperatives too. The DSE was not simply a collection of guerrilla groups that
could survive on the occasional 'requisition' of resources from local communities. Zachariadis had transformed the DSE into a regular army with a
centralised command structure and with increased needs for recruitment,
provisioning, transportation, fortification, communications, etc. Such an
outlook required a centralised system of effective logistical support. In this
sense, the development of a state administration was inextricably linked
with the pursuit of the DSE's military objectives. One could not survive
without the other. To this end, in August 1947, the Headquarters-General of
the DSE issued a decree of five acts on the administration of the areas under
its control. These referred to the organisation of the people's administration,
the delivery of justice, the redistribution of land, the administration of forests and education.[13] A few months later, in December 1947, the 'Provisional
Democratic Government of Greece' was established with Markos Vafiadis as
Prime Minister and Minister of Military Affairs.

In Western Thrace, the geographical spread of the DSE's administration
extended over two 'zones' along the region's most remote and mountainous
areas, populated almost exclusively by Pomaks. The first zone was north-
east of Komotini, along the Greco-Bulgarian border, covering the villages
Sarakini, Kardamos, Drania, Kimi, Drosini, Vyrsini, Organi, Ragada, Smigada,
Esochi, Mirtiski, Vourla, Chloe, Kechros and extending eastwards to the village of Mikro Dereio (in Evros) which was also a key DSE stronghold. The second zone included a cluster of villages north of the Xanthi such as Dimario,
Kotyli, Pachni, Melivia, Thermes, Medousa and Kotani, all near the Greco-
Bulgarian border. It is rather difficult to be precise about the exact limits
of both zones as these were formed gradually after mid-1947 and control
over them shifted frequently between DSE and the government forces. The
administration set up by the DSE in these areas was, therefore, challenged by
a series of incursions and mopping-up operations by the EES.

The imposition of DSE rule in the Rhodope Mountains met with little
enthusiasm on the part of local Muslims whose scarce resources (being by
far the poorest communities in Western Thrace) now had to sustain a large
number of Communist fighters. Moreover, participation in the new administrative structures involved a significant element of compulsion and fear.
The main instrument for the setting-up of the new administration was the

---

[12] *Dimocratikos Stratos*, Issue 6, June 1949.
[13] *Kommounistiki Epitheorisi*, No. 9, 1947, 421–423.

> *Box 8.2*   DSE Propaganda Material on Taxation in Western Thrace, March 1948
>
> *The people's contribution to the Democratic Army*
>
> The people in the free area are on alert. Everyone is rushing to help the Democratic Army. Every Turkish village is doing its utmost to help the Democratic Army and the thousands of its Turkish soldiers. In the Mosaikon village, a villager offered the whole of his provisions in food, 2 *okas* [1oka=1, .280grams] of cornflour and some fruit. The Democratic Commissar knew of his poverty and told him "take back your food and let your kids eat it". But the villager from Mosaikon insisted 'I cannot exclude myself from the collection for the Democratic Army, I want to contribute my share'. The women of Organi opened their 'marriage dot chests' and offered their clothes saying that 'this is how we can prove our bond with the Democratic Army'. On 2 January the women of Organi offered 114 pairs of socks, 104 towels, 16 blankets, 16 *okas* of wheat, 120 chicken, 22 eggs, 15 *okas* of grape juice syrup, 20 *okas* of walnuts and 5 *okas* of butter. The women of Kechros offered 69 pairs of socks, 6 *okas* of wheat, 63 towels, 5 pairs of gloves, 170 *okas* of pasta, 45 *okas* of butter, 87 *okas* of fruit, 7 chicken and 112 eggs. The women of Kechros said that they will keep contributing.
>
> *Source*: Savaş, Issue 5, 10 March 1948.

People's Committee, led by a local Commissar. According to the 1st Act On the Organisation of the People's Rule issued by DSE's Headquarters-General, every village or city was to have its own People's Committee which comprised seven regular and five reserve members elected directly by the People's Assembly.[14] The authority of the People's Committee covered every aspect of the economic and social life of the village, including education, welfare, the management of public property and resources and taxation.

DSE's tax decrees were translated into Turkish and distributed to the people's committees in Muslim villages. According to their provisions, the poor were not taxed, while the maximum tax was 15 per cent of an individual's income or production (the latter regardless of profitability).[15] The presidents of the people's committees were responsible for tax collection and for the delivery of taxes. The People's Committees were also responsible for organising fundraising campaigns and collections in food and provisions for DSE fighters. Such activities were idealised in DSE propaganda material (see Box 8.2).

In reality, however, such contributions had a compulsory character and were often underpinned by threats of reprisals. Taxation never developed

---

[14] For towns with more than 2500 inhabitants, nine regular and seven acting members were elected.

[15] *Savaş*, 19 June 1948.

Box 8.3   Extract from *Savaş* on the Work of People's Committees, November 1947

Although some time has passed since the elections, the People's Committees in the free areas do not seem to be active enough. This is mainly due to the fact that the villagers are still backward as they have been oppressed by fascism for so many years that they are unable to administer all the issues that democracy brings forth.

One of the most important tasks that the People's Committees have to deal with is education. Have the schools been prepared? Is there a teacher appointed in every school? How many pupils are there? Is there a list of names? What is the condition of the desks?

Another serious task is provisioning for the villagers. Not a single stretch of land will be left uncultivated. Is that the case in every village? Do the locals get help? Did the People's Committees find shelter for all those whose houses have been burnt by the fascists? The village has a lot of running costs; did the People's Committee prepare a revenue list of how much each villager will be taxed? How will the taxes be collected?

Since the People's Committee was elected, how many meetings have they had in order to find solutions for all these crucial issues that their fellow villagers have entrusted them with? It is not just us who ask all these questions, but the people who voted for you. The people are watching and they are expecting you to deliver.

Go on People's Committees, move!

[...]

Source: Savaş, 25 November 1947.

---

into a structured or organised exercise as it was driven by the immediate needs of DSE fighters. As the area under DSE control was poor and shrinking, the local communities came under increasing pressure to contribute most of their food production to the cause of the DSE. The realities of exercising this 'duty' were much harsher than the DSE propaganda suggested.

Another contribution 'in kind' demanded from the villagers was compulsory labour in building bunkers, repairing infrastructure and transporting weapons and provisions. The people's committees were also put under huge pressure to maintain essential services at the village level, a task that demanded large numbers of 'volunteers' who were not always willing. The *Savaş* newspaper often vented its frustration about the slow progress made by the people's committees in this respect (see Box 8.3).

The DSE also introduced an extensive People's justice system (2nd Act on the Organisation of the People's Rule). Accordingly, every village or town established its own People's Court composed by a Commissar in the role of Prosecutor and three elected members of the People's Assembly, whereas two Courts of Appeal were set up in the DSE's zone of control in Xanthi

---

Box 8.4   Extract from *Savaş* on the People's Courts, January 1948

The People's Courts are working non-stop. Here are some cases they have heard recently. The People's Court in Drania heard three cases on 5 and 6 December. The first one was a land ownership dispute between Kiâşif Hüseyin and Sadık Hüseyin from Kardamos. The court heard both sides as well as witnesses and annulled the Mufti's verdict issued ten years ago, since it was against the will of the deceased owner of the land. The Court ruled that the land should be taken way from Sadık Hüseyin and be returned to Kâşif Hüseyin. The other case was about the maltreatment of a woman by Ahmet Oğlu Hasan from Kato Drosini. The Court sentenced the accused to one month imprisonment and a 200,000 drachma fine. The Court also fined Kozdereli Bekir Kâzim with 50,000 drachma because he beat up his wife. Since Bekir Kâzim was the People's Court President he could not take part in the trial. The man who told us the news said "Well done Bekir Kâzim, you are brave. You have shown how brave you are to your wife. Do it again if you dare".

The People's Court in Kato Vyrsini on 30 October 1947 heard a case of civil dispute and sentenced Kasabalı Hasan to 20 days imprisonment and a 100,000 drachma fine. Köse Mustafa Resif was sentenced to 15 days imprisonment and a 75,000 drachma fine. Köşe Mustafa Ahmet, Köşe Mustafa Hasan, Cemile daughter of Bayram and Şaban son of Bayram were also fined.

The People's Court in Mytikas heard a case of abduction. Mehmet Oğlu Ahmet abducted a young girl who, nevertheless, was not hurt. The Court awarded a 300,000 drachma in compensation. His associates, Ali and Hüseyin Oğlu İsmail, were fined 250,000 drachma each while Mustafa Mehmet was fined 150,000 drachma. They were all given a deadline to pay the fines.

Source: *Savaş*, 10 January 1948.

---

and in Organi. The DSE translated the people's justice legislation into Turkish and distributed it to the local people's courts.[16] The latter were able to adjudicate not only on civil cases such as land-ownership disputes and commercial and economic crimes, but also on more serious cases of theft and bodily harm. Crimes against the rule of DSE were heard by special court-martials. This is how *Savaş* reported on the progress of the People's Court (see Box 8.4).

Despite the relatively trivial penalties referred to in the *Savaş* reports, the operation of the people's courts along strongly secular lines no doubt aggravated the conservative Muslim communities where the implementation of *Sharia* Law on civil matters (particularly family law) had been a fact of life for centuries and one recognised by the Lausanne Treaty. In his memoirs, Captain Kemal himself acknowledged this conflict when he recalled an incident (in the village Kechros) in which DSE soldiers intervened to stop the administration of *falanga* (foot whipping) as punishment

---

[16] *Savaş*, 20 December 1947.

for a rather minor civil offence (Belli 2009: 115). The DSE court-martials, on the other hand, showed no such leniency to those who dared to challenge Communist authority. The accounts of local interviewees and those given at the time to the Greek state's army and police interrogators by Muslim villagers who had escaped from DSE zones of control spoke of 'show-trials' and summary executions for those suspected of collaboration with the EES. No such incidents were reported in *Savaş*.

DSE's system of administration had become much stronger by early 1948 in the areas it controlled. During that time, plans were drawn-up for the formation of an organisation that would offer political representation to the Muslim community. According to DSE's propaganda:

In areas that have been liberated by the Democratic Army, Turkish villagers made a wonderful suggestion. Some citizens have already made preparations to implement this idea. They go around the villages explaining the necessity of creating an inclusive Turkish organisation in which the whole of the Turkish minority will participate and which will be administrated by Turks, focusing on their issues.[17]

Eventually the organisation was set up on 29 March 1948 in Organi where the '1st National Conference of the Turkish Minority' took place. The conference was attended by the Provisional Democratic Government's Minister of Health and Welfare, Petros Kokkalis, KKE officials from Eastern Macedonia and Western Thrace and 150 representatives from the Muslim villages under DSE's control. Captain Kemal, who chaired the conference, argued:

Compared to Greeks, we the Turkish minority have suffered more under the fascist yoke and the rule of all reactionary governments. We had never been granted equality or our basic human rights. Today things are even worse......What is there for us to do? There is only one way for us, to fight with the Democratic Army, to help it win so that we can live like humans in freedom, in our common country, Greece.[18]

At the conference, representatives from the villages also argued that there was a great need for a new organisation to replace the Mufti and the Commissions for the Management of Muslim Properties and take over all of their administrative authority.[19]

The conference ended with the formation of the Greece's National Democratic Union of Turks (*Εθνική Δημοκρατική Ένωσις Τούρκων Ελλάδας*). The Union's first objective was 'the mobilization of the whole

---

[17] AYE/1948/105.
[18] *Drasis*, 18 April 1948.
[19] *Savaş*, 16 April 1948.

of the minority to the struggle against *Monarchofascism* and the American rule'.[20] The Union would also exercise authority over religious, economic, political and agricultural issues and would become the supreme institution of political representation of the minority 'with the objective to reclaim all [of its] rights'.[21] The conference issued the Union's declaration (see Box 8.5) and addressed calls to the minority itself (see Box 8.6), the Democratic (DSE) Government, General Markos Vafiadis, the Greek and Turkish people and to all Muslims around the world.[22]

The formation of the Greek National Democratic Union of Turks featured prominently in the propaganda broadcast by DSE's state radio in Belgrade.[23] Yet, despite its high propaganda value, the activities of the Union remained rather limited in subsequent months. On 18 February 1949 a second conference of the Union was held for which little is known other than it issued an address to the Muslim world.[24] The following month, a delegate of the Greek National Democratic Union of Turks took part in the second NOF conference in Prespes (chaired by KKE's leader Nikos Zahariadis) along with 700 representatives of the Slav-Macedonian minority.[25]

The appeals of the DSE authorities to the Muslim community had been carefully crafted to combine revolutionary fervour with local sensitivities. This was an uncomfortable marriage between tradition and (Communist) modernity. Captain Kemal was keen to remind all 'ethnic Turks' of their oppression by the Greek authorities, but at the same time pledged their 'desire to live in a free Greece'; a significant reminder that the agenda of the DSE was not sympathetic to secessionist aspirations (by contrast to the case of Macedonia). A great deal of emphasis was placed on the social liberation of the Muslim community, even from its own self-governing institutions. The attacks against the Mufti and the commissions for the management of Muslim properties, however, were justified on the basis of their corrupt practices (and their collusion with the Greek authorities), not on a principled stance against its religious and traditionalist power structure. Yet, as Captain Kemal himself acknowledges in his memoirs, village elders remained the backbone of the People's Committees on the ground (Belli 2009: 115). This was, in other words, a very Muslim Communist revolution.

---

[20] *Drasis*, 18 April 1948.

[21] *Savaş*, 16 April 1948.

[22] *Savaş*, 19 June 1948.

[23] AYE 1948.105.7, Ministry of Public Order, Aliens Department, to Foreign Ministry, Department of Political Affairs, 20 May 1948.

[24] AYE 1949/21.2, Greek Ministry of Foreign Affairs, 'Radio Broadcasts from Bucharest', March 1949.

[25] AYE 1949.25.3, Report of Contact of the 6th Group of Observers of the UN, 10 May 1949.

Box 8.5 The Declaration of the Greece's National Democratic Union of Turks, March 1948

In order to take the fate of the ethnic Turkish minority into our hands, the delegates of Komotini's free areas gathered on 29 March 1948 in the village of Organi and decided the following:

1. The ethnic Turkish minority, as every other minority and the people of Greece, believe that the fascist administration, both now and in the past, is very bad. Due to exploitation by the capitalists and the fascists, production and standards of living are very low compared to neighbouring countries. Our political rights, our language, our customs and traditions, our religion are in the hands of people who are instruments of the fascist government. On many occasions the ethnic Turkish minority was deprived of its rights by reactionary governors. It gave many struggles against the landowners.
2. The situation for the Turkish minority got worse after the American and British imperialists started helping the Greek Monarchofascists. The ethnic Turkish minority could no longer suffer this oppression. It revolted and joined the struggle for freedom, independence and democracy.
3. For two years now, the ethnic Turkish minority joined the Democratic Army's struggle and has done its duty. Even today the ethnic Turkish minority continues to carry out that duty with the gun in its hand.
4. The ethnic Turkish minority participates with all its strength in the struggles and efforts of the Democratic Army because it is convinced that the Democratic Army will achieve its goal and bring freedom. The People's Committees, the People's Courts, the schools in all villages, the distribution of forests and land estates, the respect for our religion and tradition, these are the political objectives of the Democratic Government. These objectives are totally identical with the objectives of the Turkish minority. This makes the bond between us a brotherly bond and it condemns anyone who tries to break it.

For the benefit and progress of the ethnic Turkish minority we decide:

1. We institute the "Greece's National Democratic Union of Turks" which will embrace the whole of the Turkish minority of Greece.
2. The purpose of the Union is to be the administrator of all political, social, religious, educational issues concerning Turks and the defence of their rights. The Union will mobilize the whole of the Turkish minority for the success of the Democratic Army and its final victory.
3. The Union is administrated by a Central Committee of 21 members and another 9-member Commission which has the high command. The Commission will undertake its duties immediately.
4. The Union will establish branches in all Turkish villages and towns.
5. The Union's objective is to become operational within the shortest period of time. Until the second National Conference, the Union will be run by a provisional administrator. Only after the second National Conference will the administration take its final form. The second conference will take place in a year at the latest.
6. Membership of the Union is free of charge and applications are judged by the Commission.

7. The Union's seal is round. It reads the Union's title and year of establishment and in the centre it has a "Δ" and two hands shaking.

The Conference Committee,
Hüseyin Kemal (i.e. Captain Kemal),   İmam Faik Kâşif,
Mustafa Mehmet,   Ahmet Hasan,   Imam Ahmet

Source: *Savaş*, Issue 7, 13 May 1948.

Box 8.6   Address of Greece's National Democratic Union of Turks to the Muslim Minority, March 1948

Brothers of religion and blood,

On the 29th March 1948 the Turkish people of free Greece exercised their rights as free people, came to a national assembly, and founded the 'Greek National Democratic Union of Turks.

The Union's purpose is to unite and represent all ethnic Turks in Greece. The Union of Turks was founded because there is a need to administer and settle all issues affecting the minority, defend its rights and abide to its responsibilities to the fatherland. The Union declares that until now Turks have been oppressed and that the fascist regimes of the past are responsible for making Turks backward. Only through the Union can we preserve and improve our culture and education.

The Union of Turks – not just the Turks of free Greece, but also the Turks under the fascist yoke – is formed according to the terms of this Conference.

In the areas under fascist rule, the Muslim Community [i.e. the Commission for the Management of Muslim Properties] is responsible for the administration, whereas the Mufti is responsible for religious issues. These institutions however do not benefit the minority since the Americans and the fascists have made them their puppets. They put in charge individuals who have abused the people. These individuals do not defend the rights of the minority. They betray the Turks. Our Union of Turks was formed in this conference in order to defend freedom.

In the free areas, freedom and progress are opening their gates. All the necessary help is given for education and progress. The Democratic Union of Turks represents the will and the desire of the Turkish minority.

Brothers of religion and blood,

Our desire is to live in a free Greece, to liberate our brothers who live under the fascist yoke, to fulfil our duty to Democracy and to make our Union strong. We must form branches of our Union in every city and village and solve all issues affecting the Turks.

By uniting our forces the National Union of Turks will become a stronghold against the imperialist Americans and the native fascists.

Long live the National Democratic Union of Turks!
Long live the brotherhood with the fighting Democratic Greek people!
Long live the liberator of the Turkish ethnic minority and the leader of the Democratic Army, Markos!
[...]

Source: AYE/1948/105.7.

Table 8.1 Estimate by Öksüz of Western Thracian Immigration to Turkey, 1946–1949

Year	Legal Immigration	Illegal Immigration
1946	2318	4630
1947	1824	2100
1948	2934	2360
1949	677	950
Total	7753	10,040

Source: Öksüz 2000/01: 62.

8.3 Muslim immigration to Turkey during the civil war

The tremendous pressure exerted upon the Muslim community during the course of the civil war resulted in a renewed exodus. Those fleeing the area were divided into two main groups. The first involved the rural inhabitants of the Rhodope Mountains who, either through their own initiative or on orders of the EES, evacuated their villages, seeking refuge in the lowland areas and the larger towns of Western Thrace. The plight of this group of people, labelled by the Greek government as 'guerrilla-stricken' (*ανταρτόπληκτοι*), will be discussed in more detail in the next section. A second, numerically significant, group tried to escape the dangers of the Greek civil war through immigration to Turkey.

The overall number of Western Thracian Muslims who emigrated to Turkey during the course of the Greek civil war is difficult to estimate, particularly as a significant number of refugees crossed the borders without possessing the necessary travel documents. The available primary evidence on this matter is scattered and rather contradictory. A report by the British Consul in Thessaloniki in September 1946 estimated the number of Muslim refugees at 2000.[26] In February 1948, the Turkish newspaper *Vatan* offered a similar estimate.[27] A more realistic figure is offered by Öksüz, (see Table 8.1), although here too the methodology behind the compilation of these statistics is far from clear.

Also unknown is the number of Muslims, particularly Pomaks, who escaped from Western Thrace through the Rhodope Mountains into Bulgaria (or, indeed, of Bulgarian Muslims who moved south of the border). Neither archival material nor oral testimonies shed significant light on this issue.

---

[26] FO/371/58868, British Consulate-General, Salonica, Peck, to the British Embassy, Athens, 18 September 1946.
[27] AYE/1948/105.3, Greek Embassy, Ankara, to Foreign Ministry, A' Directorate of Political Affairs, 27 February 1948.

Hence the extent and nature of population movement between Greece and Bulgaria during that period remains largely unexplored.

Immigration tales

Chapter 7 discussed the hardship experienced by the Muslim communities that had become caught in the middle of the government's fight against the Communist insurgents. Insights into why local Muslims decided to emigrate to Turkey are available through a variety of sources, including personal testimonies, newspaper reports of the time and documents of the Greek administration. A report in the Turkish newspaper *Memleket* in November 1947, for example, quoted one such account by a newly-arrived immigrant from Western Thrace:

> We had a quiet life in Greece and, apart from nostalgia for our motherland [Turkey], we really had no complaints. Yet, the activities of Communist guerrillas changed everything and our lives, properties and honour came under threat. When the night came, all sense of security was lost in our villages. When the government forces withdrew from a village, guerrilla bands came from the mountains and, when daylight returned, the army was back. In this game of hide and seek between bandits and the army, the poor villages suffered all evils. Fortunately we are now in Turkey.[28]

The Turkish press at the time published a number of stories (based on refugee evidence) about armed bands, pretending to be Communist fighters, which exerted pressure upon the Muslim population in order to leave, with a view to taking over their property.[29] *Trakya* too referred to an armed band of Roma fighters, dressed in DSE uniform, who pillaged Muslim villages across the area.[30] Similar incidents were also confirmed by an interviewee from Mega Dereio: 'I know that there were two Gypsies in the DSE, E.M. and T.B., who committed crimes and looting'.[31]

It is quite possible that such testimonies were coloured by what the immigrants thought they should say or what the journalists believed would fit the prevailing political climate. It is impossible to determine the extent of such influences. Nevertheless, the basic sentiments expressed here are confirmed by other sources and they may therefore be taken as illustrating some basic truths. Oral testimonies from those who decided to immigrate highlight

---

[28] *Memleket*, 8 November 1947. A similar story of a group of 57 villagers who arrived in Turkey was published in *Yeni Sabah*, 9 November 1947.

[29] *Yeni Gazete*, 9 May 1948.

[30] The band was eventually arrested by the Greek security forces and many of its members were executed. *Trakya*, 29 March 1948.

[31] Interview 5.

some of the security dilemmas facing the local population. A former villager from Mega Pisto (near Komotini) recalled:

> In late 1946 a Communist band came to our village and took two sons from a rich family. They returned one, but asked for a ransom for the second. My father decided then that we should definitely leave for Turkey.[32]

Another former resident of the village of Mesohori (near Komotini) recalled:

> The guerrillas often passed by our farm and, following threats, they took the supplies they needed. One day, the head of the [Communist] band was waiting for my father early in the morning. My father did not recognise him in his uniform and beard, but the guerrilla asked him, "don't you recognise me? I used to work in your fields before the war. Please take me to the authorities, I want to surrender myself". My father did, indeed, hand him in, but, as a result, the guerrillas became his enemies.[33]

A different perspective is offered by the then Governor-General of Thrace, Zahos Xirotyris, who, in his communication to the Ministry of Foreign Affairs, suggested that a number of those emigrating sought to escape conscription to the Army. Xirotyris wrote:

> It has been observed that a large proportion of those emigrating illegally, either on their own or with their families, are young people that should have already enlisted in the Army or were soon about to do so. For example, on the 20th of this month [April 1948], amongst a large group of around 200 people that was arrested by the police in a quiet beach ready to depart, 11 were deserters and 15 had been invited to present themselves on 21 of the current month at the Army barracks in Drama.[34]

Whatever the reasons, the escape from Western Thrace and the passage into to Turkey was recalled as a major traumatic experience by all interviewees. The main escape routes involved either the crossing of the River Evros or the boarding of small boats from the costal areas south of Komotini and Alexandroupolis with direction to Samothrace and from there, through

---

[32] Interview 46.
[33] Interview 38.
[34] AYE/1948/105.6, Government-General of Thrace, Directorate of Political Affairs, Xirotyris, to the Foreign Ministry, Department of Turkey, 28 April 1948.

Gökçeada, to the coast of Turkey.[35] In both cases those seeking to escape paid hefty fees to local human traffickers. The alternative – the crossing of the River Evros (near its delta) without aid – carried with it mortal dangers. This is how one refugee recalled his experience:

> We moved everything we could – including our animals – to a safe place in the city [Komotini]. It was a difficult situation, but we had no choice. We did not feel safe and we decided to cross the border in secret. In Evros, we saw many dead bodies of Turks who died there as a result of the bad conditions.[36]

Others recalled their encounters with Greeks offering to ease their passage, sometimes involving extortion:

> My parents went to Alexandroupolis and found some Greeks offering to help them cross the river to Turkey. I believe that these people also got a fee from the [Greek] state when refugees left. A trafficker took us to a village barn where we stayed for two nights with closed windows. With our carts and property we crossed the River Arda [in Greece]. From the other side of the river another Greek brought two cows to pull the carts out of the water. He then took us to his house to dry our clothes and give us something to eat. He told us he would not betray us to the authorities. After a day there we went to the River Evros. A small boat came after a while to pick us up.[37]
>
> We took a boat from the coast near Xylagani. It cost 4 gold Ottoman sovereigns per head. The boat was Greek. On the first night we reached Samothrace and stopped there because of bad weather. The traffickers hid us somewhere. We were a group of 25–30 people. However, in order to continue the trip we had to pay more money. Eventually, we were dropped near the coast of Imvros [Gökçeada].[38]

This is how a returning refugee reported his escape to the authorities upon his return to Greece:

> I went to the coast near Porto-Lago where, together with 48 of my minority kin, we boarded a boat on the night of 15–16 April 1948. We went to

---

[35] According to a report published in the Greek newspaper *Elliniko Aima* (22 April 1948), the Turkish authorities considered settling all Western Thracian refugees to the Turkish island of Gökçeada.

[36] Interview 38.

[37] Interview 49.

[38] Interview 50.

the islet of Kömür Burnu next to Imvros [Gökçeada]. This is where the boat left us. I paid 335,000 drachmas for this trip.[39]

The journey to Turkey carried with it high expectations of safety and well-being. Rumours in Western Thrace had suggested that all refugees arriving in Turkey would receive a daily allowance and be guaranteed a job. The reality, however, was harsher. A camp in Uzunköprü (near Edirne) received a number of refugees, but most emigrants were initially cared for in make-shift facilities in Turkish towns and villages near the border. The Turkish authorities did, indeed, offer to settle the refugees in designated locations, but for those who refused to accept what they were offered, there was little further help.[40]

This is how some refugees recalled their experiences in Turkey:

We reached Evros with a horse and cart and went to Uzunköprü where there was a refugee camp. We stayed there 3–5 days in order to complete our paperwork. The authorities wanted to settle us in Tekirdağ, but my father preferred to be free to go wherever we liked and so we moved to Izmir.[41]

They [the traffickers] took us to Enez [on the Turkish side of the Evros/Maritsa delta]. When we settled there the local Turks took us to the mosque and brought us food. We then went to Edirne and from there to Akhisar [near Izmir] inside a cargo train. Because it was the religious celebration of Kurban Bayram wherever we stopped people offered food. We stayed in Akhisar for four years before moving to Izmir.[42]

Turkish soldiers took us to a school building to spend the night. After a week we were transferred to Istanbul where we stayed for another week in a refugee hostel. They asked us where we wanted to go and we said Izmir. When you agreed to settle in the place proposed by the authorities, the state provided accommodation, money and food (for, at least, a year). If you chose to stay in a different place you did not receive anything except for travel expenses and some small amount of money until being

---

[39] AYE/1948/105.7, Ministry of Public Order, Aliens' Directorate, to the Foreign Ministry, Directorate of Political Affairs, 1 June 1948.

[40] The assistance provided by the Turkish government was only made available to those who travelled illegally to Turkey and could, thus, substantiate the claim that they were refugees. Those travelling with the necessary documents did not receive any help. This, according to the Greek authorities, encouraged many Western Thracian Muslims to cross the border without any travel documentation. AYE/1948/105.6, Greek Royal Gendarmerie, Aliens' Centre, Komotini, to the Aliens' General Centre of Macedonia-Thrace', 11 April 1948.

[41] Interview 46.

[42] Interview 49.

properly settled. We had some family already in Izmir, so we chose to go there.[43]

For some refugees the conditions they encountered in Turkey were a source of considerable disappointment. Writing to the Turkish newspaper *Kör Kadı* (24 June 1948), a refugee for Western Thrace, Riza Ahmet, complained:

> When we arrived in Turkey we expected to get a house, some land and any other assistance we could. This is why so many of us abandoned our properties there [in Western Thrace] and came destitute to live in the motherland. After our arrival the government put as in a refugee camp in Istanbul and shortly afterwards sent us to Izmir. There our families found themselves left alone without money or provisions in a place that was foreign to us…those who believed in state help and came here became very miserable.

In his account to the Greek authorities, a former resident of Komotini also regretted the journey to Turkey:

> I stayed in Istanbul for a week. During this time the Turkish state provided food and bread…The rest of my fellow travellers had relatives in Istanbul and settled with them, but I had none. I regretted getting into all that trouble…I took the train back to Uzunköprü and from there I went by car to Edirne. Someone to whom I said I was interested in crossing into Greece advised me to go to the borders by Nea Vyssa (south of Kastanies). From there I entered in secret Greek territory and presented myself to the police station of Nea Vyssa.[44]

The response of the Greek authorities to the Muslim emigration

The response of the Greek authorities to the Muslim exodus from Western Thrace displayed confusion and striking contrasts between hard-line nationalists and more liberal elements.

A more accommodating stance was taken during the course of 1947–1948 when the Greek government reassured its Turkish counterpart that the properties of those who had decided to emigrate to Turkey would not be subjected to the relevant Greek legislation providing for all properties left vacant for over ten years to revert to the ownership of the Greek state.

---

[43] Interview 50.
[44] AYE/1948/105.7, Ministry of Public Order, Aliens' Directorate, to the Foreign Ministry, Directorate of Political Affairs, 1 June 1948. This file contains a number of similar stories.

According to *Vatan* (24 February 1948), the Turkish authorities agreed, in exchange, to issue visas for a number of Western Thracian Muslims seeking refuge in Turkey. A few months earlier, in October 1947, *Trakya* had also warned those intending to leave that, upon arrival in Turkey, they should contact Greek consular authorities in order for their properties in Greece to be made safe.[45] Indeed reports in *Yeni Sabah* (1 May 1948) suggested that the Turkish government was satisfied with the initiatives taken by the Greek authorities in order to facilitate those wishing to go to Turkey, by providing them with all the necessary travel documents.

Some in the Greek administration recognised the emigration of local Muslims to Turkey as a problem, not least because of the adverse consequences for the lucrative local tobacco production and the mounting numbers of defaulting debts to the Agricultural Bank.[46] There were also a number of reported cases of the police successfully prosecuting local (both Greek-Orthodox and Muslim) human traffickers who made fortunes exploiting those seeking to emigrate.[47] Reports by local authorities in Evros suggested that efforts were made to reverse the wave of immigration towards Turkey. The Provincial Administrator (*Έπαρχος*) of Orestiada, for example, reported to the Administration General of Thrace in September 1947 that:

> I summoned the heads of the families and advised them to remain in their village [Komara], since measures had been taken to safeguard their lives and properties and no one is in danger. Yet, they insisted on leaving, arguing that they face all sorts of danger from the [Communist] guerrillas. I managed to convince them to stay and file applications for travel permits. After a few days, however, they left in secret and only one family of 14 persons [out of 45 families who had expressed a wish to leave] and 4 Pomaks [out of 5] remained in the village.[48]

Similarly, the Prefect of Evros wired the Ministry of Foreign Affairs reporting that the deteriorating security situation in the Arda area (near Orestiada) had so alarmed the local Muslim population that '...it is very difficult for us to prevent them from leaving'.[49] Indeed, as government forces struggled to contain the activity of DSE guerrillas during the course of 1947, many police

---

[45] *Trakya*, 13 October 1947. On this see also the report in *Son Posta,* 1 March 1948.

[46] AYE/1950/52.4, Administration-General of Thrace, Directorate of Political Affairs, Kaligatsis, to the Government-General of Northern Greece, Directorate of Political Affairs, Komotini, 27 September 1950.

[47] AYE/1947/28.4, Ministry of Public Order to the Aliens' Centre-General of Macedonia-Thrace, 15 September 1947. See also *Proia* 23 June 1948.

[48] AYE/1948/28.4, Sub-Prefecture of Orestiada, The Sub-Prefect, to the Government-General of Thrace, Orestiada, 29 September 1947.

[49] AYE/1947/31.2, Prefect of Evros, Nikolaidis, to Foreign Ministry, 7 June 1947.

stations in the villages near the Greco-Turkish border were abandoned so
that the larger towns in the area could be better defended.[50] This move frustrated the Turkish side which was suspicious that the Greek government was
turning a blind eye to border security in order to 'encourage' more Western
Thracian Muslims to leave the area.[51]

Turkish fears on this matter were certainly not unfounded. Although the
Minister of the Administration-General for Northern Greece, Konstantinos
Korozos, described the Muslim exodus from Western Thrace as 'damaging',[52]
other senior members of the Greek government took a more hard-line
approach. In March 1949, for example, the Minister of Public Order,
Konstantinos Rendis, urged the Aliens' Centre-General of Macedonia-
Thrace that:

> Through a series of orders, we have communicated that the national
> interest dictates the partial evacuation of the population of foreign eth-
> nic origin [αλλογενών] from the border areas, as the presence of such a
> compact [ethnic] group presents a constant and serious danger for our
> national borders.
>
> [...]
>
> We therefore urge you to issue the relevant orders to all competent
> authorities so that the largest possible number of those of foreign eth-
> nic origin is evacuated from our northern provinces. For this reason you
> should refrain from any action that could reduce the [legal] emigration
> flow of those of foreign ethnic origin. When illegal, their departure
> should be silently assisted.[53]

Similarly, in July 1949, the Minister for the Navy, Gerasimos Vassiliadis,
communicated to the Ministry of Foreign Affairs:

> [Naval patrols]…capture power boats that transfer illegal immigrants
> from the coastal areas of Thrace to the Turkish coast. The Director of the
> Aliens' Centre-General in Macedonia informed the Navy Commander
> that they have oral instructions from their superiors to tolerate silently

[50] AYE/1928/28.4, Aliens' Centre-General of Macedonia-Thrace, 2nd Office, to
GES/A2, 30 August 1947.

[51] AYE/1950/52.1, Foreign Ministry, Department of Turkey, to the War Office, Army
Headquarters-General, 23 March 1948.

[52] AYE/1950/52.1, Administration-General of Northern Greece to Ministry of
Foreign Affairs, 10 May 1948.

[53] AYE/1950/52.1, Ministry of Public Order, Aliens' Department, The Minister
Rendis, to the Aliens' Centre-General of Macedonia-Thrace, 6 March 1949. See
AYE/1950/52.1, Ministry of Public Order, Aliens' Department, The Minister Rendis,
to the Foreign Ministry, Department of Turkey, 5 April 1948.

the illegal immigration of Pomaks because, due to their weak character, they are easy prey for the KKE recruiters and the subversive instruments of [Communist] bands.[54]

The military successes of the EES against the DSE and the improving security situation in Western Thrace during the second half of 1948 encouraged a number of refugees to return. This was further facilitated by the suspension, since mid-1948, of conscription to the army for all Muslim men. The exact number of those who returned to Greece is impossible to estimate. The Greek Embassy in Turkey concluded that, between July 1945 and October 1948, some 3020 Muslims returned through the Kastanies border crossing (near Edirne), while the number of those who crossed (either legally or illegally) through other parts of Evros is unknown.[55]

Despite the significant number of repatriated refugees, the emigration flow of Western Thracian Muslims into Turkey continued in the immediate aftermath of the civil war. The response of the Greek authorities to this trend is vividly reflected in a report of the Aliens' Centre-General in Thessaloniki in 1950:

> Many Muslim owners of large estates wish to leave and permanently settle in Turkey, but they cannot find buyers for their property. From a national point of view it would be desirable to facilitate them so that their estates could eventually come under the ownership of the state, the Agricultural Bank or Greeks of known patriotic beliefs. This way, alien financial centres, around which the Turkish minority actively rallies, will be gone.[56]

In subsequent decades the issue of property transactions would become one of the major points of friction between the Muslim community and the Greek authorities in the area.

The response of 'official' Greece to the exodus of Muslims from Western Thrace into Turkey thus reflected embedded ambiguities of state policy. The minority remained the unreliable 'other': being not of 'us', whether they should stay or go was a question to be judged by reference to Greece's overarching diplomatic – and perhaps, economic – strategic interest. For the Muslim community itself, emigration was seen by some as the best escape from a civil war that threatened their very existence. Emigration was by no

---

[54] AYE/1950/52.1, Ministry of the Navy, The Minister, Vassileiadis, to the Foreign Ministry, 22 July 1949.
[55] AYE/1948/105.6, Greek Embassy in Turkey, Skeferis, to the Foreign Ministry, Department of Turkey, 27 November 1948.
[56] AYE/1950/52.1, Aliens' Centre-General of Macedonia-Thrace, 2nd Office, to Ministry of Public Order, Aliens' Directorate-General, 24 August 1950.

means an easy option: it involved tremendous danger and hardship and was often met by profiteering, duplicity and neglect on the part of their 'host' country, Greece. The urge to leave clearly reflected the plight suffered beforehand.

8.4   Welfare provision for the 'guerrilla-stricken'

Aside from the phenomenon of emigration, one of the greatest humanitarian dramas of the civil war was the plight of the internally displaced: namely those, who under various circumstances, abandoned their villages and sought refuge elsewhere in Greece. The overall number of the so-called 'guerrilla-stricken' is very difficult to estimate with national and local sources often providing widely divergent numbers. In periods of escalating violence, the number of the internally displaced rose significantly, but often the nature of this movement was temporary as many were able to return to their homes soon afterwards, creating further problems of estimation. Moreover, depending on the changing definition of the term 'guerrilla-stricken' by the Greek government, a number of those affected shifted from one category to another. Overall, the term 'guerrilla-stricken' referred to three main categories of people:

1. Those who remained in their villages, but were listed as refugees because their homes had been looted or destroyed;
2. Those who left their villages voluntarily because of guerrilla activity;
3. Those who were evacuated on a compulsory basis by the EES for security purposes.[57]

Official estimates of the number of the internally displaced throughout Greece ranged between 700,000 and 850,000.[58] Laiou (2002: 88) estimates that the number of the internally displaced in Western Thrace reached its peak in May 1949 at 62,215. According to statistics provided by the Administration-General of Thrace, in July 1949 there were 21,689 'guerrilla-stricken' in Evros, 7036 in Rhodope and 5553 in Xanthi.[59] The number of

---

[57] FO/371/78373, British Consul-General, Salonika, to British Embassy, Athens, 27 October 1949.

[58] A Greek report by the Ministry of Press referred to 684,607 'guerrilla-stricken' receiving welfare and being resettled by the state by May 1949. Another 18,000 children were housed in the 52 Children's Centres under the patronage of Queen Frederica. AYE/1950/32.1, Ministry of Press and Information, Research Department, 17 October 1949. On this see also Laiou 2002: 87 and Margaritis 2001: 595–600, Vol. II.

[59] At the time the Administration-General of Thrace also included the Prefectures of Drama and Kavalla. The former had 11,760 'guerrilla-stricken' and the latter 5106,

Muslims included in these figures was a matter of much contestation at the time. The minority newspaper *Trakya*, maintained that, in May 1948, less than 25 per cent of recognised 'guerrilla-stricken' in the Komotini area were Muslim.[60] The Greek authorities, on the other hand, put that figure at 40 per cent for Rhodope and 70 per cent for Xanthi (see below). Either way, the phenomenon of such displacement was a point of major strategic interest for both the DSE and the EES.

The distribution of government aid in Western Thrace

Greece – Western Thrace included – came to rely heavily on state relief from the deprivations of the civil war. The relief-aid to the 'guerrilla-stricken' provided by the Greek state included a daily allowance in cash, bread rations, as well as other forms of assistance such as temporary help with lodging, lighting, heating, transport, repatriation, reconstruction of properties and provision of building material.[61] An essential element of this operation was the distribution of aid provided by the United Nations Relief and Rehabilitation Administration (UNRRA), between April 1945 and September 1947. Greece was one of the major beneficiaries of this programme receiving $351 million worth of aid, more than 12 per cent of all aid distributed by UNRRA worldwide. The aid included basic food supplies (such as powder milk, wheat and sugar), building materials, fertilizers, fuel, agricultural machinery and cattle. From 1948 onwards, in the context of the Truman Doctrine and the Marshall Plan, the reconstruction of Greece was taken over by the American Mission for Aid to Greece (AMAG) and the Economic Cooperation Administration (ECA), which channelled US military, financial and humanitarian aid, in an effort to reconstruct the Greek economy and strengthen its armed forces (Stathakis 2004; Vetsopoulos 2007; Tsilaga 2008).

Foreign aid thus became an essential lifeline for Greece and it featured heavily in the government's anti-Communist propaganda. In Western Thrace, the main point of entry for foreign aid was the port of Alexandroupolis where the local authorities often organised official ceremonies to celebrate its arrival.[62] The distribution of foreign aid, however, was also a source of great resentment for those not able to access it. In this and other matters,

---

giving a total 51,144 for the whole of the Administration's territory. AYE/1949/25.2, Ministry of Press and Information, Statistical Table of Guerrilla-Stricken Refugees until 31 July 1949, 12 September 1949.

[60] *Trakya*, 17 May 1948.

[61] FO/371/78370, British Embassy, Athens, to Foreign Office, 6 April 1949.

[62] See, for example, *Eleftheri Thraki*, 19 February 1948. A number of reports were also published with regards to the plundering of aid by the local authorities and/or those responsible for keeping it safe. On this see *Eleftheri Thraki*, 4 March 1947 and 7 March 1947.

the Muslim community claimed much discrimination in comparison to the majority population. *Trakya*, for example, frequently published editorials criticising the authorities for mishandling aid destined for those most in need.[63] In May 1948 it wrote:

> Among Turks there are many who, for 80 days now, make ends meet with just 5,000 drachma provided to them in aid. These people walk around the streets of Komotini without a job; the locals gather some bread from their own houses and distribute it to them. We haven't seen such suffering among Greeks…These people [a family that escaped from the mountainous village of Paterma in the Rhodopes] sleep on borrowed mattresses. There is no such tragic case to be found amongst the Greeks. Yet, this family, from the beginning of March to the beginning of May, has not received any help from the authorities. It only received a "guerrilla-stricken" certificate, i.e. that it is now eligible for help…These are not isolated incidents.[64]

The government's programme of re-housing those displaced from the Rhodope Mountains in Komotini was also attacked by *Trakya*, which reported that internal refugees were re-housed exclusively in Muslim households without the prior agreement of their owners.[65] According to government guidelines, the issuing of a 'guerrilla-stricken' certificate – an entitlement to aid for relocation to 'safe areas' – was conditional on:

- Total damage to property;
- Abduction or death of a family member by the guerrillas;
- Threats against the families of those enlisted in the Army or damage to their properties by the guerrillas;
- Guerrilla threats against the families of those who had deserted the DSE under the terms of the government's amnesty;
- Abandonment of property for 'strategic reasons' and relocation under the auspices of the Army.

Trakya maintained that these conditions discriminated against the Muslim population in the mountainous areas who, despite suffering frequent looting by the DSE forces, were often disqualified from government assistance and were consequently forced to move to the lowlands on their own accord.[66] The same newspaper also criticised the decision of the authorities to ban the distribution of aid to the villages in the Rhodope Mountains for

---

[63] See indicatively *Trakya*, 20 January 1947 and 14 April 1947.
[64] *Trakya*, 31 May 1948.
[65] *Trakya*, 6 October 1947.
[66] *Trakya*, 13 September 1948.

fear of vital supplies getting into the hands of the guerrillas.[67] Many of these frustrations were vented in a letter by the minority MPs of Rhodope, Osman Üstüner and Faik Engin, to the Minister of Social Welfare on 15 April 1948 (see Box 8.7). It explained the discrimination by reference to the clientelism of the local Greek authorities.

Inevitably, the complaints of the two minority MPs became a source of fierce mutual recrimination. In its response to the Ministry of Welfare, the Rhodope Prefecture claimed that:

> The vague accusations against every state authority and the systematic defamation of the Community and Police authorities and the services of Social Welfare and the Prefecture illustrate clearly the motivation and purpose of those who advised the two MPs, who no doubt in good faith, relied [for drafting their letter] on malicious rumours by irresponsible local elements.[68]

The memorandum then went on to argue that, in May 1948, 875 Muslims were recognised as 'guerrilla-stricken' (out of 948 applications), compared with 2035 members of the Greek-Orthodox community (out of 2365 applications). The authorities were keen to emphasise that the rejection rate of applications made by Greek-Orthodox citizens (14 per cent) was higher than the equivalent for Muslims (7.6 per cent), but offered no explanation as to why the absolute number of Muslim 'recognitions' was less than half of that granted to Greek-Orthodox citizens (even though the worst affected areas in the Rhodope Mountains were populated overwhelmingly by Muslims).[69] The response from the Prefecture of Xanthi made similar references to their commitment to equal treatment of all citizens, reporting that, in May, 1948 out of a total of 1130 'guerrilla-stricken', 750 were Muslims.[70] A precise picture here is not possible – given the political usage of the statistics – but it may well have been the case that local Muslims received significantly worse treatment in the distribution of the foreign aid.

On the issue of re-settlement, the authorities in Xanthi acknowledged that members of the Greek-Orthodox community were the first to be accommodated as their villages were the first to be attacked by the guerrillas. When security in these areas was re-instated, their inhabitants were ordered to

---

[67] *Trakya*, 10 May 1948.

[68] AYE/1948/105.7, Prefecture of Rhodope, Social Welfare Service, to the Ministry of Social Welfare, The Minister's Office, 11 May 1948.

[69] AYE/1948/105.7, Prefecture of Rhodope, Social Welfare Service, to the Ministry of Social Welfare, The Minister's Office, 11 May 1948.

[70] In June 1948 the numbers of the 'guerrilla-stricken' had risen to 6522 Muslims and 4342 Greek Orthodox. For more see AYE/1948/105.6, Social Welfare Service, Xanthi, to Xanthi Prefecture, 9 September 1948.

> *Box 8.7* Letter by the Minority MPs of Rhodope to the Minister of Social Welfare, April 1948
>
> Dear Minister,
>
> It has come to our attention that you recently began touring Northern Greece and we are looking forward to welcoming you in Komotini, in order to present to you the just complaints of the Muslim population in the region.
>
> As you know, half of the population of the district of Rhodope is Christian and the other half Muslim, whilst the mountainous region of Rhodope is inhabited exclusively by the Muslim element. This region is completely controlled by the guerrillas and the locals who managed to take their women and children and come to Komotini, have abandoned everything at the disposal of the guerrillas. The Muslims of Komotini have welcomed them, offering to share their rooms with them so that the refugees do not remain homeless. They have not approached the state authorities to settle them. However, they are all in need of food supplies for their families. Moreover, because of the situation, they are unable to find a job and support their families.
>
> There exists in our Prefecture – as well as in all Prefectures – a Welfare Department and a Committee that determine who gets given the status of 'guerrilla-stricken', thus enjoying the benefits provided by the relevant decrees of your Ministry.
>
> We hold the opinion that, as a consequence of the prevailing conditions, the population in question should be the first in line of those recognised as 'guerrilla-stricken'. Yet, no one so far has been granted this status. On the contrary, according to the certificates supplied by Community Presidents and Police Stations, there are people recognised as 'guerrilla-stricken' who are not in need of state aid and are, indeed, rather prosperous. The reason for this situation is the fact that the local authorities, the Police staff, as well as the Committee wish to favour their own clientele. Hence, the issue of the 'guerrilla-stricken' has become subjected to favouritism.
>
> We have repeatedly presented this situation to our Prefecture authorities without any result. On the other hand, the Muslim element, faced with this situation and under the threat of starvation, is looking to depart for Turkey.
>
> We do not wish to add anything more, although we are aware that similar complaints have been expressed by the Christian element too, due to the prevailing favouritism.
>
> We appeal to you and look forward to your orders for a re-assessment of those recognised as 'guerrilla-stricken', as well as of those who have not yet received this status by competent staff dispatched here from the central services.
>
> Otherwise, we must think of another course of action in order to protect our discriminated fellow citizens.
>
> *Source*: AYE/1948/105.7, Social Welfare Service, District of Rhodope, Komotini 15 April 1948.

return and Muslim refugees were housed in their place.[71] The authorities in Komotini argued that, due to the persistent reaction of the Muslim population of the city, the Prefecture did not requisition any Muslim houses

---

[71] AYE/1948/105.6, Social Welfare Service, Xanthi, to Xanthi Prefecture, 9 September 1948.

and 'only after having requisitioned every available space in Greek houses, did the authorities requisition a few rooms in Muslim houses'.[72]

The controversy over the welfare to the 'guerrilla-stricken' was vividly reflected in the local press with both *Proia* (the main Greek-language newspaper of Komotini) and *Trakya* publishing a series of articles containing a number of claims and counter-claims about the discrimination.[73] For the local security forces, the role of the minority MP, Osman Nuri (also the editor of *Trakya*) was, once again, the focus of much frustration. A report by the Komotini Aliens' Centre accused Nuri of 'hiding behind his parliamentary immunity' and being 'one of the most fanatic anti-Greek Muslims, a blind instrument of the Turkish Consulate and more nationalist than the Turks of Turkey who ... loses no opportunity to criticize and defame the Greek administration'.[74] The Deputy Governor-General of Thrace, Zahos Xirotyris, also urged the Greek Ministry of Foreign Affairs to adopt a more aggressive campaign against *Trakya's* claims in order,

> To avert their negative effects which are two-fold. On the one hand, internally, the poisoning of the Muslim element and the nurturing of its negative attitude towards the Greek state and its authorities. On the other hand, externally, as this newspaper is sent to Turkey and the newspapers there, based on its articles, published misleading reports on the Muslim minority here and make negative remarks against our country, as you probably know from the news summaries received from our Embassy in Ankara.[75]

If the welfare of the 'guerrilla-stricken' became a flashpoint in the increasingly nationalist-driven encounters between the Greek authorities and the leadership of the Muslim minority, the fate of children in the war-ravaged areas of the Rhodope mountains took an altogether more sinister turn.

The welfare of children as an instrument of war

From a relatively early stage of the civil war, the welfare of children became both a humanitarian concern and a strategic imperative for both the government forces and the Communist insurgents. During the summer of 1947 Queen Frederica took the initiative to establish a network of camps

---

[72] AYE/1948/105.7, Prefecture of Rhodope, Social Welfare Service, to the Ministry of Social Welfare, The Minister's Office, 11 May 1948.

[73] See, indicatively, *Proia*, 19 May 1948.

[74] AYE/1948/105.6, Komotini Aliens' Centre, to Aliens' Centre-General of Macedonia-Thrace, Office II, 14 September 1948.

[75] AYE/1948/105.6, General Administration of Thrace, Department of Political Affairs to Ministry of Foreign Affairs, Turkey Department, 20 July 1948.

and shelters for affected children throughout the country. These institutions, named παιδουπόλεις (children centres), were established in order to provide care for both orphans and displaced children who lived in areas that had become theatres of operations. The total number of children who lived in these centres has been estimated to be around 20,000 (Margaritis 2001: 613, Vol. II; Baerentzen, 2002).[76] According to data provided by the Greek authorities to the United Nations Special Committee in the Balkans (UNSCOB),[77] by April 1948, 5000 children had been taken from the area administered by the General-Administration of Thrace. With their parents' consent 2300 of them were transferred from the port of Alexandroupolis to other parts of Greece. Care for these children, aged between three and 14 years, was provided by the Ministry of Social Welfare, the Greek Red Cross, the Committee for the Relief of the Northern Provinces of Greece (of which the Queen was patron),[78] and the Greek-American Relief.[79]

The archives of the Prefecture of Xanthi contain a wealth of information regarding the preparations, in 1947, for the transfer of the first cohort of children to the newly-created shelter in Kavalla. The names of several Muslim children are contained in the relevant lists. For example, out of a total of 40 children transferred from Xanthi, seven were Muslim. In order to qualify for the scheme, applicant children had to have fulfilled the following conditions:

- To have lost at least one parent (either during the civil war or the occupation);
- To suffer from the lack of an existing family to protect or support them;
- Be resident in a village with no security;
- Be aged between six and 12 years;[80]
- Not be suffering from contagious diseases.[81]

---

[76] According to the digitised Historical Archive of the Greek Royal Family, approximately 30,000 'war-children' were hospitalised in the Queen's 53 παιδουπόλεις. See: http://www.greekroyalfamily.org/el/index.cfm?get=archive&show=documents&ItemID=179 (accessed 10 September 2009).

[77] The UNSCOB was established by the UN General Assembly on 21 October 1947 in order to examine the allegations of the Greek government that Albania, Bulgaria and Yugoslavia were providing assistance to the DSE. In this context, the Committee also examined the issue of the 'abduction' of children from the northern regions of Greece and their transfer to countries of the Soviet Block (Coufoudakis 1981; Jones 1985; Nachmani 1990).

[78] The Fund for the Northern Provinces of Greece continued to provide financial support for 'war-stricken' children until 1955. See Andreades 1980: 40–44.

[79] FO/371/72229, UNSCOB, Annex A, Reply to Questions submitted by UNSCOB, 21 April 1948.

[80] This contrasts the respective information stated in the FO document above, which refers to ages 3–14.

[81] GAK (Thessaloniki), 'Xanthi Prefecture', F.623.

Later, in April 1948, children from Western Thrace were transferred to shelters in Athens, an event that received much attention in the press. The Athens newspaper *Elliniko Aima* published an extensive report of the first group of 1186 children that arrived from Western Thrace, containing several photographs and an emotional article by the writer Stratis Myrivilis.[82] *Eleftheri Thraki* also reported on the arrival from Alexandroupolis to Athens of another group of 875 children, which were welcomed by a number of dignitaries and a large local crowd.[83]

On the other side of the ideological divide, the DSE also implemented its own programme for the evacuation of children from northern Greece, the region most ravaged by the civil war. The evacuated children were sent to Communist countries to be raised in similar 'children centres'. This operation, labelled by the Greek government as 'children-snatching' (παιδομάζωμα, a term also used to describe the Ottoman recruitment of *Janissaries*) – and portrayed as such in the novel *Eleni* by Nicholas Gage (1983) – resulted in the transfer of some 25,000–28,000 children to Eastern Europe. By contrast, the DSE maintained that the evacuation of children was dictated by humanitarian concerns and that the operation was only carried out following the full consent of parents, many of whom were themselves DSE fighters. Both sides argued that the evacuation of children averted the risk of their abduction by the enemy. For the DSE, 'children centres' sponsored by Queen Frederica, were anti-Communist propaganda schools. For the government, the DSE policy was regarded as a cynical attempt to indoctrinate future Communist fighters, a modern equivalent of the Ottoman recruitment of *Janissaries*.[84]

In his memoirs, Captain Kemal strongly maintains that no Muslim children were displaced by DSE forces in Western Thrace (Belli 2009: 98–103). He argues that the separation of a child from its parents was alien to the customs and ethos of the Muslim community and refers to a particular incident to back up his claim. On one occasion, Kemal argues, his men found out that the DSE was planning to displace Muslim children from Organi and that DSE officials on the ground had already started counting those ready to depart. This move caused a furious reaction on the part of the Muslim guerrillas. Kemal tried to re-assure his men and travelled to Organi to find out for himself. There, he found two officials of the DSE enlisting the names of children in the village. Kemal asked the DSE officials what they were doing and they replied that they were carrying out the orders of the Political Commissar.[85] Kemal was enraged and

---

[82] *Elliniko Aima*, 3 April 1948.
[83] *Eleftheri Thraki*, 27 June 1948.
[84] For more details see Baerentzen (2002: 137–164).
[85] Kemal does not mention the Political Commissar's name in his book, but it is certain that it was Dimitris Vatousianos. Vatousianos' relation with Kemal was strained. According to Captain Kemal when the member of KKE's Central Committee,

tore-up the list in public, before ordering the two officials to be arrested. He shouted:

> They are lying; the Political Commissar could not have possibly given such an order. These people are spies of the enemy and they will be punished. No one is going to separate a child from its mother by force as long as this land is occupied by the Democratic Army. (Belli 2009: 101)

Following this incident Kemal claims to have contacted the Political Commissar and the two men had an intense row. The Commissar did not change his views, but Kemal was reassured that Muslim children would never be displaced (Belli 2009: 102).

Despite Captain Kemal's assertions, however, there is evidence that the DSE policy on the evacuation of children was indeed implemented in Western Thrace. After the end of the civil war, parents of displaced children across Greece submitted over 12,000 applications to the International Red Cross for the repatriation of their children.[86] In the archives of the Ministry of Foreign Affairs in Athens, among a plethora of similar cases, a number of applications by Muslim parents exist, demanding the return of their children.[87] Although these petitions do not give an accurate picture of the number of children affected, they do, nevertheless, confirm beyond doubt that a number of children were indeed evacuated from the area without the consent of their parents. This evidence is supplemented by local interviews suggesting that at least 30 Muslim children were involuntarily displaced by DSE forces from the village of Chloe.[88] Responding to reports in the British press that Muslim children were evacuated to Eastern Europe at the demand of their parents, the Governor-General of Northern Greece, Sotiris Stergopoulos, expressed the view that 'the Muslims of Western Thrace definitely did not give their consent to the abduction of their children or to the forced recruitment [to the DSE] of their adult offspring'.[89] This squares with

---

Yannis Ioannides, visited Thrace, he (Kemal) briefed him on the issue of the evacuation of children and expressed the view that the whole project was wrong. Ioannides agreed with Kemal's view and the way that he handled the case. According to Captain Kemal, during the discussion between himself and Ioannides, Vatousianos was nodding, approving what Kemal was saying and he kept whispering to him 'well done'. Belli (2009: 102).

[86] By the end of 1952 just 538 children had returned home, all of them from Yugoslavia which was the only Socialist country that collaborated with the International Red Cross. For more see Baerentzen (2002: 160–1).

[87] AYE/1950/124. See, indicatively, the petitions of I.S, M.S, A.H.K, M.A, M.N, M.S, M.M and MN concerning the return of 15 children.

[88] Interview 7.

[89] AYE/1950/124.2, Administration-General of Northern Greece, The Governor S. Stergopoulos, to the Foreign Ministry, Greek attaché to the UN Balkan Committee, 31 January 1950.

the interview evidence, though interviewees were reluctant to talk further of the circumstances under which Muslim children were displaced by the DSE during the civil war.[90]

8.5 Minority education during the civil war

Ever since the end of the Greco-Turkish war in 1923, minority education in Western Thrace had been shaped by the provisions of the Lausanne Treaty which, with Article 40, afforded their respective minorities the right:

> To establish, manage and control at their own expense, any charitable, religious and social institutions, any schools and other establishments for instruction and education, with the right to use their own language and to exercise their own religion freely therein. (Ministry of Foreign Affairs of Greece 1999: 140)

Administratively the supervision of minority schools in Western Thrace came under the Ministry of Education working closely with the Ministry of Foreign Affairs in its capacity as the overall 'guardian' for the implementation of the terms of the Lausanne Treaty. On the ground, the responsibility of regulating and supervising minority schools in the area fell on the Inspectorate of Minority Schools (part of the Administration-General of Thrace) in Komotini which reported to the Inspectorate-General of Foreign and Minority Schools (part of the Administration-General of Northern Greece) in Thessaloniki. The legal framework for the operation of these schools was put together by a series of legislative initiatives during the 1920s. These provided, amongst other things, for a joint appointment system for minority schools. Minority (i.e. Turkish-language) teachers were selected by the local Muslim communities who were also responsible for paying their salaries. However, these appointments were subjected to close scrutiny by the Inspector of Minority Schools which ensured that the appointees were 'adequately qualified' and operated within the 'principles' of the Greek educational system.[91] On the other hand, Greek-language teachers in minority schools were appointed by and paid for the Ministry of Education. The legislation also provided for state subsidies for minority (Muslim, Armenian and Jewish) schools which were not able to meet their own costs.[92]

Throughout the inter-war period literacy levels across all minority areas were extremely low, with only a tiny minority of local Muslims attending school. Investment in educational infrastructure, either by the Greek authorities or the local Muslim communities, was also minimal. The main

---

[90] Interview 7.
[91] Law 3179/1924, 7 August 1924. See also Law 3578/1928, 30 June 1928.
[92] Law 2781/1922, 4 June 1922.

providers of minority education were either 'secular' primary schools or religiously-run *Medrese*. The former only catered for pupils aged 6–12 who received their education[93] in either modern Turkish or old Ottoman (depending on the wishes of the local teacher), with the exception of Greek-language training (and, subsequently, history and geography). Until 1952, there was no secondary minority education in Western Thrace (Askouni 2006: 69). The handful of pupils who wished to progress with their studies had to either register in a Greek-language *Gymnasium* or emigrate to Turkey for secondary schooling. Instruction in the religious *Medrese* included learning the Holy Koran, Muslim law and the Prophet's teachings in Turkish and Arabic.

By the late-1920s, the majority of the minority teachers were graduates of the local religious schools. Indicatively in 1929, out of 277 minority teachers, 253 were graduates of the religious schools, 20 had a basic teaching education and only four had graduated from Turkish teaching academies. To a large extent, this also determined that the Ottoman/Arabic alphabet would be used for instruction in most minority schools. Later on, however, the emergence of the modernist/Kemalist fraction within the minority brought about demands for educational reforms (e.g. the introduction of the new Turkish alphabet and a more secular curriculum), similar to those implemented in Turkey by Kemal Atatürk in 1928. Within this context, the demand for 'modern' teachers, who had graduated from teaching academies in Turkey, increased substantially in the early 1930s. Also indicative of this trend was the opening, by Osman Nuri in 1928, of the first minority school in Xanthi which used exclusively the new Turkish alphabet (Aarbakke 2000: 129–130).

During the Metaxas dictatorship (1936–40) the Greek authorities became increasingly restrictive both with regards to the content and the administration of minority education. As a result, the practice of importing textbooks from Turkey was ended and replaced by much tighter controls over the content of the Turkish-language curriculum. By contrast, the teaching of the Greek language in minority schools was strictly enforced. In 1930, there was Greek-language instruction in only 44 out of 305 minority schools.[94] By the end of the decade, knowledge of Greek had become a precondition for the appointment of minority teachers and larger numbers of Greek-Orthodox teachers had been appointed in minority schools. The authorities also banned all foreign inscriptions within public buildings (including schools) and the requirements for establishing new private schools were significantly

---

[93] Turkish language, religious instruction, practical arithmetic, basic geometry, basic elements of physics, chemistry, hygiene, calligraphy, painting, music, arts and crafts and physical education.

[94] Archive of Eleftherios Venizelos, F.251/1931, Stylianopoulos, Report on my tour in Western Thrace on 15–30/6/1931, 15 January 1930.

tightened to ensure that 'national ideals' were not compromised (Aarbakke 2000: 130–131; Tsioumis 1998: 153–156).

Educating 'nationally-minded' Greeks

The outbreak of the civil war and the presence of the DSE in a number of Muslim villages in the Rhodope Mountains created major problems for the operation of minority schools. By February 1948 a total of 58 minority schools in the Prefecture of Rhodope, 50 in that of Xanthi and a handful in that of Evros were under the control of the DSE forces.[95] For the local authorities, the exact nature of the DSE's educational agenda in the mountainous areas was something of an unknown, as information about the condition of some remote villages was fragmented and sketchy. Their biggest fear centred on the DSE's commitment to enforce the teaching of the new Turkish alphabet (using Latin characters), in all minority schools under its control.[96] The shift from the teaching of old Ottoman to modern Turkish by the DSE mirrored the educational policy of the Bulgarian (Communist) government towards its own Turkish minority at the time. In the eyes of many Greek nationalists, however, such a policy only served the purpose of accelerating the minority's 'Turkification'. Local government officials expressed frustration that *Savaş* made no reference to the accommodation of the educational needs of the Pomaks, calling, instead, all local minority schools 'Turkish'. This prompted the government authorities to speculate that the DSE was ready to 'sacrifice' Pomak sensitivities in order to appease the, politically more active, Turkish element of the minority.[97]

Significant disruption was also felt by a number of minority schools in less remote areas that were caught up in the middle of the conflict between the EES and the Communist forces. With the majority of Muslim notables having fled to the lowlands, local school boards – responsible for the hiring of teaching staff – became slow to react, causing significant delays to the start of the 1947–1948 academic year.[98] Under these circumstances, education provision for the Muslim community contracted significantly during the

---

[95] AYE/1948/105.6, Inspector of Muslim Schools of Western Thrace, Minaidis, to the Ministry of Education, Directorate of Primary Education, 'The Situation of the Muslim Schools of Western Thrace', 7 February 1948.

[96] AYE/1948/105.6, Inspector of Muslim Schools of Western Thrace, Minaidis, to the Ministry of Education, Directorate of Primary Education, 'The Situation of the Muslim Schools of Western Thrace', 7 February 1948.

[97] AYE/ 1948/105.6, Inspectorate-General of Foreign and Minority Schools, Papaevgeniou, to Ministry of Education, Department of Private Primary Education, 13 February 1948.

[98] AYE/1948/105.6, Inspector of Muslim Schools of Western Thrace, Minaidis, to the Ministry of Education, Directorate of Primary Education, 'The Situation of the Muslim Schools of Western Thrace', 7 February 1948.

course of the civil war. According to data compiled in 1948 by the Inspector-General for Foreign and Minority Schools, in 1939–1940 there had been 270 operational minority schools. In 1946–1947, their number had increased to 287, but in 1947–1948 it was reported to have decreased to 252.[99] By the end of the civil war (the academic year 1949–1950), the Greek authorities estimated that from a total of 309 minority schools in Western Thrace, only 184 were operational.[100] The Greek authorities put forward a number of reasons for the decline: damage to educational infrastructure, inability of the locals to pay for teaching staff as well as active interference by the Turkish Consulate and leading local Kemalists who withdrew their support from schools that insisted on the instruction of Ottoman/Arabic alphabet.[101]

The minority schools that remained operational during the conflict faced major problems in recruiting teachers. For the 1939–1940 academic year, there had been a total of 264 Turkish-speaking and 174 Greek-speaking teachers in minority schools. By 1946–1947 the number of Turkish-speaking teachers had increased to 320, but Greek-speaking recruits collapsed to just 12. The situation changed little in the 1947–1948 academic year when the numbers of teachers were 304 and 21 respectively[102]. The collapse in the number of Greek-speaking teachers in minority schools became the subject of frequent reporting by Komotini's local newspaper, *Proia*. The newspaper claimed that only 60 per cent of all teaching vacancies were filled, blaming the poor security conditions in the area as well as problems with the remuneration of teachers (e.g. the non-payment of overtime work) and the inefficiencies of the system of transferring teaching staff to local schools.[103] Particular attention was paid to the activation of clientelist networks that allowed teachers (and civil servants more widely) to avoid despatch to Western Thrace, a region that was perceived as an 'unappealing' destination due to its geographical distance from the big urban centres of Athens and Thessaloniki.[104]

[99] AYE/1948/105.6, Inspector-General for Foreign and Minority Schools, Papaevgeniou, Thessaloniki, to the Education Ministry, 'Report on the Muslim Schools of Thrace', 29 October 1948.

[100] In Rhodope there were 164 schools in total (109 were operating), in Xanthi 129 (66 operated) and in Evros 16 (9 operated).

[101] See AYE/1950/52.1, Inspector-General for the Muslim Schools of Western Thrace, M. Minaidis, 'Report on the operation of the Muslim schools of Western Thrace during 1949–1950', 7/8/1950. See also *Proia*, 24 August 1949.

[102] AYE/1948/105.6, Inspector-General for Foreign and Minority Schools, Papaevgeniou, Thessaloniki, to the Education Ministry, 'Report on the Muslim Schools of Thrace', 29 October 1948.

[103] *Proia*, 24 August 1949. The newspaper also reported shortages of staff across the local civil service. *Proia*, 22 June 1949.

[104] On this se also *Proia*, 22 December 1948 and 5 October 1949.

In addition to the chronic lack of staff, many minority schools faced severe shortages in teaching materials and educational infrastructure. *Trakya*, for example, complained that the disruption in the supply of school textbooks from Turkey during the War, had allowed the Greek government to print its own teaching material for minority schools which, nevertheless, used 'forms of the Turkish language that were outdated for more than a decade, due to the radical language reform that occurred in Turkey during the interwar period'.[105] In January 1947, Turkey agreed to send 25,000 new textbooks, but according to *Trakya*, these were blocked by the relevant Greek authorities for a lengthy period, as they checked the contents for any material that could have been regarded as inappropriate.[106]

Student numbers also fell. In 1939–1940, the total number of minority students was 11,368. In 1946–1947 this number had increased to 17,392, but the following year it dropped to 11,546 students.[107] Although there is no available data for the academic years 1948–1949 and 1949–1950 (during which the civil war in the area reached its peak), it is safe to assume that minority student numbers would have faced a substantial further decrease.

The education of the minority in the context of the civil war also provoked rising tensions between the Greek authorities and the leadership of the minority. The case of the Central (Muslim) School in Komotini elicited major disputes. The Greek authorities had requisitioned the school in the autumn of 1947 to house the 'guerilla-stricken', together with six Greek schools and all Armenian and Jewish schools.[108] This elicited sharply differing responses: the local Greek officials noted that the Muslims had been treated lightly; local Muslims themselves issued a barrage of complaints, as did the Turkish Consulate; and the issue was taken up in the Turkish press, leading Ankara to launch a wide-ranging criticism against Greece's educational policies in the area.[109] Eventually, in January 1948, Athens instructed that the school be re-opened, though this was only done in phases.[110] The

---

[105] *Trakya*, 9 December 1946.

[106] *Trakya*, 13 January 1947.

[107] AYE/1948/105.6, Inspector-General for Foreign and Minority Schools, Papaevgeniou, Thessaloniki, to the Education Ministry, 'Report on the Muslim Schools of Thrace', 29 October 1948.

[108] AYE 1948 105/6, Inspector of Muslim Schools of Western Thrace, Minaidis to the Ministry of Education, Directorate of Primary Education, 'The Situation of the Muslim Schools of Western Thrace', 7 February 1948.

[109] See, indicatively, AYE/1948/105.6, Administration-General of Thrace to Foreign Ministry, Directorate for Turkey, 28 April 1948. and AYE/1948/105.6, Ministry of Education to Administration-General of Thrace, 3 January 1948.

[110] See AYE/1948/105.6, Minister of Education to the Administration-General of Thrace, 3 January 1948 and AYE/1948/105.6, Greek Embassy, Ankara to the Ministry of Foreign Affairs, Department of Turkey, 16 June 1948.

case signalled that Athens and Ankara were now in an increasingly fraught struggle over the plight and the cultural identity of the Muslims of Western Thrace.

A similar tension arose over scholarships granted by the Turkish government to Muslim children in the region.[111] These scholarships had first been made available during the interwar period of Greco-Turkish rapprochement. Their purpose was to encourage minority students (10–12 per year) to receive 'modern' secular education in Turkey before returning to Western Thrace in order to replace 'traditionalist' teachers in minority schools.[112] Although, these scholarships were meant to be allocated on merit, the Greek administration grew increasingly suspicious of what it regarded as excessive interference in this matter by the Turkish Consulate in Komotini. This, according to the Inspector of Muslim Schools in Komotini 'create[d] among local Muslim circles the impression, or the belief rather, that all matters affecting the Muslim minority of Western Thrace are being arranged by the Turkish Consul and that the Greek administration, out of fear of Turkey, does not have the will to resolve essential issues of the Muslim minority'.[113] The Greek authorities certainly took this issue seriously: intelligence officials of the 3rd Army Corps were also informed of the names of the recipients of these scholarships.[114] The Administration-General of Northern Greece expressed similar fears when urging Athens to:

> Take action for the training of teaching staff for Thrace, otherwise we give the pretext to Turkey to assume this role, which can accuse us of neglecting on purpose this matter in order to keep the Muslim population

---

[111] In 1947, 35 scholarships were granted (there were 38 candidates) instead of the usual number of 10–12. The reason for this increase in numbers was the interruption of this process during the Bulgarian occupation. The selection committee for these scholarships included the Turkish Consul, the Deputy Consul and the Consulate's Secretary and four Muslim teachers. The candidates were examined in Mathematics, Physics and Writing Composition (Topic: 'What should a student and the youth in general, know and do for the prosperity and greatness of the Turkish nation?'). AYE/1948/105.6, Administration-General of Thrace, to Foreign Ministry, Department of Turkey, 10 January 1948. AYE/1948/105.6, Greek Gendarmerie, Aliens' Centre, Komotini, to Aliens' Centre-General of Macedonia-Thrace, 20 September 1948.

[112] AYE/1948/105.6, Administration-General of Thrace, to Foreign Ministry, Department of Turkey, 22 September 1947.

[113] AYE/1948/105.6, Inspector for the Muslim Schools of Western Thrace, Minaidis, Komotini, to Ministry of Education, Directorate of Primary Education, 3 September 1948. See also AYE/1948/105.6, Administration-General of Thrace, Department of Political Affairs, to the Foreign Minister, Department of Turkey, 2 September 1948 and AYE/1948/105.6, Foreign Ministry, Department of Turkey, to Administration-General of Thrace, 8 October 1947.

[114] AYE/1948/105.6, DES. A2 III, 'Education of Muslim Students in Turkish Schools', 24 January 1948.

ignorant. The claim [of the Inspector of Minority Education in Komotini] that out of the hundreds of students sent to Turkey only three returned to Thrace to assume their teaching duties should not be taken for granted. We cannot dismiss the possibility of these teachers – fully trained with the ideals of Turkish nationalism – returning en masse someday to Thrace, becoming the spearhead of Muslim education and [getting involved] in other minority activities.[115]

In this context, a special meeting was held in the Administration-General of Thrace, in late 1948, in order to prioritise the dispatch of fully trained Greek-language teachers to Western Thrace to improve the knowledge of Greek by Muslim school children. The report that followed warned that:

> Turkish propaganda is acting upon a specific plan and towards a particular direction. This [plan] is the national awakening of the Muslim mass. An indication of this plan is the clear decision of Muslim villages not to hire any teachers wearing the fez and having a religious background, for being agents of backward and conservative ideals. They rather opt for young – aged 17 – secular teachers, inspired by the ideology of the well-organised Turkish Youth.[116]

As the Greek civil war neared its end, the local educational authorities shifted much of their attention away from the 'Communist danger' in the Rhodope Mountains and onto the 'Turkish danger' nearer to home. With an increasing number of Muslims congregating (either willingly or not) in the main towns of Western Thrace, the fate of those subjected to the Communist-inspired education in the areas controlled by the DSE disappeared almost entirely from the 'radar' of local policy makers. The mountainous areas were now a matter for military planners. Instead, in the lowlands the local Greek authorities were forced to square their own nationalist fervour with that of an increasingly confident Kemalist elite which now commanded significant influence over large parts of the minority. Education stood at the very centre of this tension. The turmoil of the civil war had produced fertile ground for the settling of old scores between rival fractions within the minority, with the old-Muslim traditionalists very much on the defensive. The increasingly nationalist profile of the minority's leadership also raised awkward questions about the content of Greek educational policies in the area. The later period of the civil war offered just a glimpse of the problems to come. The

---

[115] AYE/1948/105.6, Inspectorate-General for Foreign and Minority Schools, to Ministry of Religions and National Education, 20 September 1948.

[116] AYE/1948/105.6, Inspector-General for Foreign and Minority Schools, Papaevgeniou, Thessaloniki, 'Report on the Muslim Schools of Thrace', 29 October 1948.

legacies of the Lausanne Treaty were still to unfold their full shadow over the international and local politics of Western Thrace.

Educating Muslim Communists

The DSE administration in the Rhodope Mountains gave high priority to the education of Muslim children. Indeed, the control of minority education brought significant benefits to the Communist cause. It was one of the best means of radicalising the 'reactionary' Muslim communities and combating their attachment to tradition. In addition to shaping the character of good Communists, education also served a very useful propaganda purpose against the *Monarchofascist* government of Athens and its local allies.

The 5th Act of DSE's Headquarters-General on the Organization of the People's Rule in August 1947 highlighted the basic principles of DSE's education policy:

Article 1: Primary schooling is compulsory for six years and free for all children.

Article 2: Every People's Committee has the responsibility to organise a school in every village [.....]

Article 3: In case that there is no availability qualified teachers, the People's Committee will appoint as teachers those who are educated enough. Teachers' salaries are determined by the People's Committee and are covered by its budget.

Article 4: Modern Greek (*Δημοτική*)[117] is the official language and is taught in all grades.

Article 5: For the children who belong to ethnic minority groups, special schools are established by the People's Committees. The minority's own language is used in such schools.

Article 6: The People's Committees provide the books and stationary, especially for poor children. In case where it is impossible to find books, teaching is conducted orally.[118]

These principles were put into practise in minority schools under the control of the DSE in Western Thrace. School boards were formed by the respective People's Committee in every village and they enjoyed significant freedom on administrative issues such as the building of new schools or maintenance of existing ones (such as in the village of Kardamos).[119] However, the DSE maintained a close watch over the appointment of teachers.[120] The DSE also

---

[117] Until 1976 the curriculum in all state schools was taught in Old Greek (*Καθαρεύουσα*).

[118] *Kommounistiki Epitheorisi*, 10/1947, 466.

[119] *Savaş*, 10 March 1948.

[120] *Savaş*, 20 December 1947.

> **Box 8.8**   Extract from *Savaş* Regarding DSE Propaganda in Minority Schools
>
> In Ragada, two schools opened and they work like beehives. The first school's teacher is comrade Hasan Oğlu Mehmet, while that of the other, is comrade Abdullah Molla Hüseyin. Both are teaching children the new Turkish language [i.e. alphabet] with great zeal and the little children are eager to learn. Although the spelling books are not yet in print, everyone knows how to read the new letters. The children also learn to sing DSE's songs. The other day after a battle with the *monarchofascists* the children heard that the enemy was defeated and they sang the 'Spring of Democracy' song and cheered 'Long live the Democratic Army', 'Long Live General Markos'. The children are waiting for books, pens, writing books and they know that the Democratic Government will gladly cover these needs. Well done comrades Mehmet and Hüseyin. Well done little children of Ragada. Don't worry, the spelling books are ready.
>
> *Source: Savaş*, 10 January 1948.

assisted school boards by providing construction materials for the building or repair of schools, pencils and chalk for the students and, in some cases, school meals.[121]

Teachers in local schools were both Christian and Muslim, provided they held sympathetic views to the Communist cause. The DSE HQ EMT organised two conferences for the teachers of Muslim schools, the first being held in December 1947.[122] The second one took place in February 1948 where:

> All teachers from the free areas were gathered in Ballica [Melitena] for a 10-day conference. The conference was chaired by the Director of Education in Eastern Macedonia and Thrace, Stratis. The conference focused on several issues such as school administration, student education etc. All Hocas [teachers in religious schools] were satisfied with the conference and they promised to apply in their schools what was discussed in the conference. At the end of the conference a telegram of love and solidarity was sent on behalf of all teachers to General Markos, the leader of the Democratic government and the Democratic Army.[123]

As far as the school curriculum was concerned, the DSE suspended teaching in the Arabic alphabet and adopted the use of the new Turkish. Teaching was heavily driven by propaganda (see Box 8.8).

The drafting of the spelling book was probably the most important educational project for the DSE with respect to the minority schools. In autumn 1947, Captain Kemal was ordered by Lambros to write a spelling

---

[121] *Savaş*, 25 November 1947.
[122] *Savaş*, 25 November 1947.
[123] *Savaş*, 10 March 1948.

book for primary school children. Kemal used the 1940 official spelling book distributed to Muslim students by the Greek Ministry of Education as a guide. He kept the same format, but he made considerable changes to the book's content, deleting all references to the old regime and enriching it with socialist ideals. There were also considerable changes in the book's illustrations. The picture of King George II, for example, was replaced with a picture of a guerrilla. Pictures of gendarmes, school parades, the Greek flag and the drachma coin, were replaced by pictures of a clarinet, or of *Faik, the village boy*. Also entries with traditionalist or nationalist connotations, such as *Our flag, We are Muslims, My mummy, Our house, A good child, Respect to the teacher* were deleted altogether.

Other entries in the spelling book were amended:

- *25 March* [the Greek national holiday celebrating independence from the Ottoman Empire]: the phrase 'with the flag in the hand the children are joyful' was replaced with the phrase 'with the flag in the hand the children are joyful in Free Greece'.
- *Hasan and the little bird*: the phrase 'birds are like us, they want to be free' was added.
- *Greece*: the phrase 'we want our county's freedom. The Democratic Army is fighting for the fatherland. We are democrats and we want democracy in Greece' was added.
- *Our homeland Greece*: the phrase 'we live in free Greece and we are happy for this. We want to see the whole of Greece free and we will see it' was added.
- *Our village*: the phrase 'yesterday we had elections in our village. Everyone voted for the village's People's Committee. My father was elected. The People's Committee governs our village' was added.

New entries included:

- *The antartes* [guerrillas]: where a little boy tells its grandfather:
  'Granddad, today I saw the *antartes* again. They came in our village and drank water from the spring. They gave us chocolate. They are so nice! Where do they live granddad? Don't they have children, homes and villages?
  Of course they do my child. They have all of these things.
  Why are they here then?
  Like your father, they fight for the homeland'.
- *The spring*: 'Our [village's] spring was dry. On a Friday the People's Committee decided to call the people and fix the spring. The democratic youth carried the stones. The pipe work was provided by the Democratic state'.

- *Cleanliness in our village*: 'The Little Eagles [*Τα Αετόπουλα*, the youth organisation of EAM] came το our school. The democratic youth started building roads. The elderly are watching with joy. My grandfather says:
  We were not as lucky as you are when we were young. We were not free. You must always appreciate the value of democracy'.
- *Go ahead Farmers!*: followed by the poem,

> We are the cornerstone of the world
> Rise up farmers
> Wake up to save ourselves from the darkness
> Let's break the chains
> Let's succeed in our objective
> Let's unite farmers
> To save ourselves from ignorance
> To slaughter the Fascists in Thrace
> The mountains are flourishing
> The *bourandades* are disappearing like the wind
> Let's go, there is no going back for the *antartes* [guerrillas].[124]

The publication of the DSE spelling book, which was probably printed in Bulgaria,[125] was delayed by Captain Kemal's injury in July 1947. It was eventually distributed to primary schools in the early months of 1948 where it was used for only a year. The government authorities were soon informed about its publication and ordered its confiscation.[126]

DSE propaganda advertised aggressively the educational achievements of 'Free Greece' and reminded local Muslims of their complaints against the Greek authorities with regards to minority education. According to a report by *Savaş* in November 1947:

While the DSE has made education compulsory for every child in its zone and has done the utmost for teachers and schools to be ready on time, the *Monarchofascists* are constantly putting obstacles to the opening of Turkish schools. Schools should have opened by early October. The Turkish schools in Komotini, however, have not opened yet and haven't even started the registration of students. The dictatorial, royalist government has requisitioned a central school and filled it with people and animals. Classes in Greek schools have already started, while Turkish

---

[124] The DSE spelling book for Muslim children is available at, AYE/1948/105.7.

[125] In the cover of the book, the Greek letter 'H' is typed using the letter 'И' of the Cyrillic language.

[126] AYE/1948/105.7, Ministry of Public Order, Aliens' Directorate, to Foreign Ministry, Directorate of Political Affairs, 22 March 1948.

schools do not even have teachers. Twenty one [minority] teachers live in poverty and cannot support their families. The DSE administration invites these teachers to the free zone and promises to give them work and the means to sustain themselves.[127]

Despite investing precious political capital (and resources) in its educational policy in minority villages, the success of the DSE's endeavour in this respect was very limited. The difficulty of Communist forces to maintain uninterrupted military control of their strongholds made the implementation of a consistent educational policy impossible. The following incident illustrates this imperative. During a raid in the village of Arisvi in February 1948, DSE forces left five copies of the new spelling book with the members of the local school board and ordered them to use it in the school. The local school teacher, Molla Şerifoğlu Mehmet, however, had different ideas. Instead of distributing the spelling book to his pupils, he informed the government's authorities and delivered the books to the Inspector of Muslim Schools of Western Thrace.[128]

Although this might have been an isolated incident, it highlighted some wider limitations in the application of the DSE policy on the ground. For many of the remote mountainous villages under the control of the Communist forces, levels of illiteracy were extremely high. In the few villages where educational facilities existed, teaching duties were often performed by the local religious leaders (İmams/Hocas) with the preoccupation of maintaining the Islamic tradition though the reading of the Koran in Arabic. For those local parents who chose to send their children to school, this was often a means of freeing up hands to work in the fields. As soon as children were old enough to join their parents, they too would spend their day engaged in agricultural work. The compulsory education system envisaged by the DSE disrupted these practises. The content of the prescribed curriculum (with its socialist/secular undertone) and the compulsory use of the new Turkish alphabet must have also alienated many of the locals with traditionalist views. Despite the DSE's protestations to the opposite, in the eyes of the local villagers suspicious about the Communist promise, the DSE's educational agenda would have looked remarkably similar to that pursued previously by the official Greek authorities: an attempt to engineer loyalty to principles that were alien to the minority's own tradition and Islamic values.

---

[127] *Savaş*, 25 November 1947.
[128] AYE/1948/105.7, Inspectorate of Muslim Schools of Western Thrace, to Administration-General of Thrace, Department of Political Affairs, 'The new Turkish language textbooks distributed in the guerilla-occupied region', 20 February 1948.

8.6   Conclusion

During the course of the Greek civil war various sections of the Muslim community came under two strikingly different systems of authority, one organised by the Communist insurgents in the areas under their control and one answerable to the government of Athens. Given the ideological and logistical imperatives that shaped them, the two systems appeared to have created two parallel universes; each producing a very different set of experiences. Yet, given the nature of the conflict and the changing military fortunes of the two warring parties (the DSE and the EES), the two universes often intersected and overlapped with each other (particularly in areas of 'contested' military control), producing glimpses of each other's aspirations and sense of vulnerability.

In the Rhodope Mountains, the DSE forces were keen to envelope their authority within the context of a functioning People's Republic which possessed all the key attributes of a state apparatus. A number of institutions for civilian administration were established, including a system of justice and tax collection. In this context, educational provision in the guerrilla-controlled areas became a significant endeavour with multiple benefits. It not only educated good Communists, but proved to the local population that the DSE was more than just a fighting machine. The DSE cared. And the DSE was here to stay.

Yet, the implementation of the DSE's agenda on the ground met with serious challenges. Its revolutionary fervour rejected the authority of all pre-exiting power structures within the minority such as its community notables, its religious leadership and the Turkish Consulate in Komotini. The DSE's educational policy too, with its compulsory nature and uncompromisingly modern undertone represented a radical break. Its target audience, however, remained attached to its conservative traditions and was sceptical. The DSE promised to build a 'new Greece', but the material available to it in Western Thrace was very much moulded by the old order. With few locals eager to embrace its agenda of 'liberating' Greece, the DSE's authority in the Rhodope Mountains turned increasingly tyrannical. Its faltering military campaign and the shrinking area under its control also placed a heavy burden on local Muslim communities whose scarce resources now had to sustain larger numbers of DSE fighters. The realities of life under the DSE administration must have been very different to that suggested by its propaganda material. The large numbers of those desperate to escape the socialist experiment in the Rhodope Mountains was an uncomfortable testament to this failure.

On the other hand, the gradual consolidation of the authority of the Greek government in Western Thrace brought with it new challenges. The Muslim community overwhelmingly shared the anti-Communist agenda of the local authorities, but there were other tensions simmering in the background. By the time the civil war was underway both the government in Athens and the minority itself were undergoing a process of significant transformation. Both were shifting towards more nationalist paradigms and both sought to redefine their relationship with each other. For the minority, in particular, the growing influence of the Kemalist faction – as highlighted both in the outcome of the 1946 election and in the shifting balance of power within minority institutions – brought a more assertive challenge to the dictates of the Greek authorities in the area and a much greater attachment to the Turkish Consulate in Komotini. Evidence of the emerging tension became apparent in many key aspects of state authority in Western Thrace such as education, welfare and border control. Weakened by the civil war conflict and compounded by early Cold War diplomatic imperatives, the Greek government watched in frustration its access to the local Muslim population becoming increasingly 'mediated' through a network of minority 'leaders' whose loyalty could not be taken for granted and, possibly, did not deserve to be. By the end of the 1940s, the Muslim minority of Western Thrace was both less diverse and more purposefully led. This was no longer the Ottoman relic that resisted the lure of modernity and nationalism.

9
Conclusion

The primary aim of the case study that has been presented in the previous chapters was to address the historical puzzle of why the Muslim minority in Western Thrace remained passive and disengaged from collaboration or resistance under the Axis occupation and insurgency during the civil war. The puzzle was founded on a number of factors that might have led the minority to a different course of action.

The case study has elaborated how many of these factors turned out differently. The key factors were: the counter-veiling strategic interests of Turkey; the fragmentation of the 'minority', both in terms of the plurality of its identities and in its leadership capacity; the neglect of the minority by the main resistance organisations during the Bulgarian occupation; the exercise of the 'exit' option, with so many fleeing to Turkey; the absence of ethnic polarisation within Western Thrace as a spur to insurgency; and, the limited engagement with either the Communists or the Government forces in the civil war. The 'story' of the Muslims in the 1940s raises a number of issues, therefore, and it is not one that can be easily confined.

A number of issues might be taken up at this point: notably, the contradictions between rhetoric and actions on the part of the Greek Communists; the enduring realities of Balkan irredentism, following the aspirations of both Bulgaria (whose troops lingered in Western Thrace after 'liberation') and Greece (over the Pomak areas of Bulgaria); the inter-play between the Great Powers of WWII and their Balkan satellites; and the longer-term socio-economic consequences of the conflicts.

But, following Chapters 1 and 2, the discussion here will focus on three priority themes. These can be placed in an order for reasons of clarity, rather than of significance. A first theme is of the strategic relevance of minorities within international relations: what explains the variation in how Turkey has defined and pursued the issue of the position of its 'kindred' minority? The second theme is the original core puzzle: what local conditions led the minority of Western Thrace to passivity

291

and disengagement in the 1940s? The third theme concerns what the case study indicates as to the sense of shared identity on the part of the minority and how this might have changed over time. The core history of the case study has investigated a largely barren territory and this has been its primary task. At this point, it is appropriate to consider the wider themes – albeit briefly – in order to help locate the study in parts of the broader social science literature.

9.1 The strategic relevance of kindred minorities

Since 1923, Turkish foreign policy has displayed some variation in how it has defined and prioritised the 'problem' of the Muslim minority in Western Thrace. It is evident that this variation has been prompted by a number of factors drawn from domestic politics: notably leadership; the current climate of Greco-Turkish relations; the public reaction to conflicts; and assessments of regional security threats. Such factors have continued to be relevant from the 1920s to the present day, though latterly an additional dimension of European and international criticism of Greek policy as support for Turkey's engagement in Western Thrace has been added.

The prioritisation given to the plight of the Muslim minority seems readily suited to a 'realist' frame of analysis. Initially, the new Republic's 'National Pact' signalled the retention of an irredentist claim over Western Thrace. Thereafter, strategic calculations have trumped other considerations during critical threat periods. The 1930 Treaty of Friendship and the Greco-Turkish rapprochement that followed met Ankara's concern for its security, allowing attention to its domestic reform programme and then providing reassurance as instability grew in Europe. The effect was to downgrade Ankara's public concern for its kindred community: the immediate issues lingering from the population exchange had been resolved, thereafter the issue of their condition all but disappeared from Turkey's agenda. In effect, a path was now set. When German troops marched into Western Thrace in 1941, followed by the establishment of Bulgarian rule, Turkey quickly dropped its actual or implied commitments to rally to Greece's defence. Official policy switched from mutual support to one of 'active neutrality', seen by its critics as a misnomer for opportunistic manoeuvring. A new unpredictability arose in Turkish policy. Revised security calculations led to the same outcome, however: public pronouncements on the treatment of Muslims in Western Thrace were not to occur. After the occupation, and with a less threatening situation, Turkey took up the plight of the minority with Athens. With the descent into the Greek civil war, however, Ankara now feared Bulgarian irredentism and Soviet expansionism (Kuniholm 1980: 256–259; Athanasopoulou 1999; Hale 2000: 111–112). Moscow's access to the Aegean would not serve Turkey's security interests and certainly not those of the embryonic Atlantic Alliance.

In this context, many in Turkey appeared supportive of Greek post-war territorial claims on the Dodecanese.[1] On the issue of Greek claims on Bulgarian Pomak lands, no official Turkish reaction has been recovered, although government correspondence in Ankara highlighted Turkish frustrations over the assimilation strategy of the Fatherland Front in Bulgaria against both 'Turks' and 'Pomaks'.[2] In the case of Western Thrace, Ankara's fears (particularly during the opening stages of the civil war) revolved around the potential threat of a Communist victory, rather than the increasing authoritarianism of the Greek government. Subsequently, although the flow of Muslim refugees from Western Thrace into Turkey did become a source of contention between the two governments, the overall stability of bilateral relations were never seriously threatened. As with the case of the Bulgarian occupation of Western Thrace, larger geo-political considerations had forced Ankara to put the protection of its local kin on the diplomatic backburner.

In parallel to Turkey's diplomatic caution, however, were the actions of the Turkish Consulate in Komotini during both the occupation and the civil war. There is no reason to suggest that these actions were undertaken without Ankara's approval and resources. It must be assumed, therefore, that they were part of a coordinated strategy, based on careful calculation. At the heart of this strategy was a consistent conditionality: local support depended on an allegiance to Kemalism. Thus, when the Bulgarian authorities sacked 'Kemalist' school teachers, the Consulate stepped in to sustain those who had lost their jobs. More generally, the Consul's representations to the Bulgarian and German authorities moderated the impact of the Axis occupation (particularly in the lowlands) and reinforced Turkey's image as the guardian of the local Muslims. The Consulate's increasing influence, however, is to be seen within the severe constraints posed by the disruption and vulnerabilities of war. But the Consulate emerged as the only show in town for the Muslims.

---

[1] According to *Vakit* (25 July 1946), 'the presence of Mussolini's fascists in the Dodecanese had tuned the islands into a military base that threatened international security in the Eastern Mediterranean. The withdrawal of the Italians from them will bring a new period of cooperation between Turkey and Greece'. Similarly, *Haber* (1 July 1946) noted, that 'if the cession of the Dodecanese to Greece was discussed 25 years ago, it would cause an outrage in Turkey. Yet, today it causes only satisfaction. We now feel that a part of our coastline is much safer. This cession brings big benefits to international politics, as it creates the prospects for the creation of a very strong Turco-Greek cooperation in the Middle East and a peaceful block committed wholeheartedly to the UN'.

[2] See, for example, BCA/426847/3010/2436467, Filibe [Plovdiv] Consulate, to Foreign Ministry, 'On the efforts of the Bulgarian Government to Bulgarize the Pomaks and cause their immigration', 29 May 1946; and BCA/426846/3010/243/646/6, Foreign Ministry, to Prime Ministry, 'Report of the Filibe Consulate on the attitude of the Communist government regarding the Turkish population', 1 August 1946.

Beyond realist-inspired calculation at the diplomatic level, the actions of the Consulate are also to be understood as part of how Turkey defined – or 'constructed' – the issue of the minority. A continuing feature is the stress on kinship: the Muslims of Western Thrace were 'Turks': they are identified as 'kin' and as 'brothers', belonging to the 'motherland'. The minority's civil and religious rights, its education and the 'modernisation' of its social life, are all considered within the terms of it being part of the national family, needing to keep pace with the rest. The recognition of the Pomaks as part of the 'Turkish' family, however, was more problematic. The Pomaks might have been Muslims too, but their linguistic and cultural distinctiveness remained a poignant reminder of their 'otherness' to the Turks of the lowlands. This 'otherness' was also reinforced by the constraints of geography and their limited contact during times of war.

Whether Ankara's strategy is seen as deft diplomatic strategy or as unprincipled, the 1940s proved a formative period in its relationship with Western Thrace. Diplomatically, the minority would not become a significant issue until after the civil war had ended, but the actions of the Consulate served to encourage wider and stronger feelings of attachment to the Republic on the part of the minority. As will be discussed later, they contributed to the process of 'Turkification', however partial that was in the 1940s.

9.2   Resistance and insurgency

The case study was prompted by an historic puzzle: why did a minority – having lost so much by the collapse of the Ottoman Empire, suffering much adversity thereafter, living in an unstable, powder-keg region, remain overwhelmingly passive and disengaged when confronted with an exceptionally gruesome Bulgarian occupation? At this point it is appropriate to leave the various exogenous factors aside – the non-intrusion of Turkey and the neglect of the 'Greek' resistance movements. What were the local conditions militating against resistance and insurgency during the occupation and the civil war? This requires a two-part answer. The next section will consider the minority's 'groupness' and leadership capacity, as well as its geographic fragmentation, as conditions affecting its reaction. Here, the focus is on the motivational factors on behalf of the minority prompting a response.

The levels of hardship and of violence were not correlated with the strength of local response. As outlined in Chapter 4, the severity of the Bulgarian occupation – re-awakening bitter memories of past Bulgarian rule – *a priori* seemed sufficient to provoke a response. Moreover, the Bulgarian authorities could not win significant support – local collaboration was minimal – thus they had to rule by fear and repression. The regime was over-stretched in logistical terms, lacking resources and marked by some lawlessness. When resistance occurred, near Drama in September 1941 – organised by the Greek Communists – the response of the occupation regime was swift and brutal (see Chapter 5). The severity of the response dampened all subsequent resistance activity in the area until the defeat of the Axis Powers looked certain in 1944. What had been proclaimed as the first uprising in occupied Europe led, paradoxically, to some of the lowest levels of resistance activity. The Bulgarians were universally despised. Interviewees recalled their families feeling helpless in the face of the demands of the occupation authorities. 'What could we do?' was a common refrain, though one that contrasted with responses in some other parts of Europe.

The numbers involved in resistance activities were very much lower proportionately than those estimated for France or the Netherlands, both of which were societies criticised for their levels of collaboration. Estimating the proportion of the populations actually involved in 'active' resistance is enormously difficult, but Moore (2000) points out that Paxton put the figure for France at no more than 2 per cent (Paxton 1972) and De Jong puts the number for the Netherlands at less than 0.6 per cent (De Jong 1990). The vast majority of the population were neither involved in active resistance or collaboration (Moore 2000: 254, 260). But, even applying these figures to the Muslim minority of Western Thrace would produce a crude hypothesis of some 500–1700 persons directly involved in resistance against the Axis (Bulgarian) occupation. The evidence presented in this case study suggested that nothing like this number of Muslims engaged in resistance against the Bulgarians.

A defence was given that the Muslims did not have much to join: the activity of the Greek Communists in the area was limited and, in any case, their agenda was unappealing to the conservative Muslims. Closer ideological and linguistic proximity to the nationalist resistance groups (of EAO) might have produced greater incentive for engagement, but right-wing resistance in the area was only scattered in nature and appeared late in the day. That said, however, the puzzle of Muslim passivity is not simply a 'supply-side' problem. Local conditions relating to the ideological outlook, internal fragmentation, and culture of the Muslim community also played a crucial part in shaping the response, or lack of it, to the violence that surrounded them during the Axis occupation.

A similar passivity was evident during the civil war. Here, the minority suffered greatly as it was squeezed between the demands of both the Communist insurgents and the Government troops. The Communist side enforced Muslim recruitment to the DSE and extracted precious food supplies, leaving local Muslim families in a parlous state. For its part, the government conscripted Muslim soldiers, though it made a notable exemption of them in 1948. Even so, the progresssively nationalist outlook of the local Greek authorities produced an uncomfortable climate for the Muslims, whose loyalty to Greece was consistently questioned. In exchange, the minority felt strongly that the civil war was not 'their' conflict: it had little sympathy for the Communists and, whilst it craved the return of peace and stability, it could not fully align itself with Athens' agenda. Many took the exit option and fled to Turkey, but there was no independent response to the civil war, no assertion of a distinct interest. The absence of a separate response was due to several factors – the strategy of Turkey included – but it rested on the local fragmentation of the minority and its lack of 'groupness'.

The argument that local conditions proved so important is consistent with Kalyvas' study of the Greek civil war (2006). He examined the levels of violent activity across the Argolida (north-east Peloponnese in southern Greece) to ascertain what he termed its 'microdynamics' (Kalyvas 2006).[3] Master historical narratives or grand theories crudely infer 'on-the-ground dynamics from the macrolevel', neglecting the interaction between rival elites, elites and the population, and among individuals (2006: 391). Yet there was much variation in violent activity between villages of the same social type. He found that political violence became privatised to individuals, as locals manipulated opportunities and harmed their rivals. Yet, in the case of the minority in Western Thrace, no similar process of internalisation occurred: there is little evidence of individual Muslims, let alone groups, exploiting the conflict of the civil war to exact revenge over their non-Muslim neighbours or to denounce them. Behaviour was defensive, protecting households and neighbourhoods from intrusion and attack by one or other 'Greek' side. When Kalyvas compared his cases with that of Almopia (in Pella, Macedonia) he found that ethnic polarisation could not account for different levels of violence (2006: 314). As this study has indicated, in Western Thrace, ethnic polarisation did not prove to be a spur for Muslims to assert themselves, either.

This contrasts with the situation elsewhere in Macedonia. There, the secessionist aspirations of the local Slav minority clearly underscored the conflict during the Greek civil war. An opportunity was seized. Koliopoulos (1999) describes how the minority had preserved its pro-Bulgarian sentiments throughout the inter-war period, leading to increasing mistrust against the Greek authorities. As Danforth (1995: 41) describes it: '...when Bulgaria, an ally of Nazi Germany, occupied a large portion of Greek Macedonia, many of the Slav speakers in the area identified themselves as Bulgarians and collaborated with the Bulgarian forces in their *persecution* of the Greeks of Macedonia' (emphasis added). No equivalent movement of the Muslims in Western Thrace against their Greek Orthodox neighbours was evident. Thereafter, Yugoslav partisans organised 'Slav-Macedonian' resistance units with the aim of winning Greek Slav-speakers over to the 'Macedonian' nation (Kofos 1964; Danforth 1995). Again, the Slav-Macedonian National Liberation Front (SNOF) and its civil war successor National Liberation Front (NOF), which allied with the Greek Communists against the Axis and the EES respectively, were different in form and far larger than 'Captain Kemal's'

---

[3] Kalyvas (2006) makes no reference to Western Thrace.

Battalion in Western Thrace and they had a stronger, shared political purpose.

In Epirus, many Chams – an Albanian ethnic minority – had sided with Mussolini and then the Axis occupation. Ethnicity made a difference here. Manta (2004) and Margaritis (2005) in their respective studies on the Chams describe a discontented minority, which was challenged by the influx of the refugees from Asia Minor and suffered property loss in the context of the Greek government's refugee-settlement programme. A number of appeals against Greece were launched to the League of Nations, but no properties were returned (Divani 1999: 218–258). Although relations between the Chams and the Greek authorities improved following Venizelos' return to power in 1928, the Albanian government continued to support Cham irredentism in Epirus. When the area was eventually occupied by Italy (Albania's patron since the 1930s), the Chams collaborated enthusiastically with their new masters. Once again, the contrast with Western Thrace is stark. There, very few isolated incidents of collaboration with the Bulgarian forces were reported.

In his study on Turkish-speaking Pontians in Macedonia, Marantzidis (2001) discusses how shared historical experiences and common linguistic and cultural characteristics led to their overwhelming participation in nationalist resistance groups (EAO). Other studies on the Greek-Orthodox majority have pointed out how local socio-economic cleavages have shaped collaboration and resistance during the occupation period and the Greek civil war (Aschenbrenner 2002; Sakkas 2000; Mamarelis 2004). In Western Thrace, there was little in the form of collective ideologies, cultures or an independent nationalism to mobilise the local Muslim minority. These limitations point to the issue of identity and 'groupness'.

9.3 Identity, 'groupness' and war

An important theme of the case study has been of the need to disaggregate the 'minority' in Western Thrace to better distinguish its experiences of the occupation and of the civil war, but also to gain a clearer understanding of the extent to which it possessed a capacity for collective leadership and action. The use of 'minority' has been bequeathed by the Treaty of Lausanne and sustained by both Athens and Ankara, each contesting singular notions of the 'Muslim minority' or the 'Turkish minority'. This is not helpful in analysing the 1940s, however.

Chapter 4 differentiated the impact of occupation on the various socio-ethnic groups, contrasting the suffering by geographical location (mountain/lowland; towns/villages) and by sub-group. The Pomaks suffered the most by comparison to all other sub-groups of the Muslim community. The forced assimilation policies of the Bulgarians largely failed – unlike those the regime pursued with the Slav-Macedonians next door – as the Pomaks rejected them and sustained their sense of independence. In the lowlands, the economic impact of the occupation was to shake the pre-war social structure. Significant differentiation occurred both between and within the various ethnic groups each of which was confronted with contrasting opportunities for escape from Western Thrace. Large numbers of both Greek Orthodox and Muslims did, indeed, opt for better fortunes elsewhere. Chapter 8 also noted the relevance of geography to the impact of the civil war on the various minority communities. To Government forces struggling to assert control in the mountains, the early assumption was of Pomak support for the Communists. Later, this was shown to be much exaggerated. The various parts of the minority experienced the ebb and flow of control between the Communists and Government forces differently, depending on their location. This left the most exposed vulnerable to conflicting demands and raids, placing them in a dilemma as to how to respond. Overall, it was very evident that the minority's experience of the occupation and of the civil war was far from uniform: suffering depended largely on location: a theme that is again consistent with Kalyvas (2006).

The variation of experience by geography paralleled the fragmentation of the minority in other ways. Geography meant that the minority lacked easy communication: its various parts were often isolated from each other and had little interaction. This dispersal structured community life and the existence of leadership. Following Brubaker et al. (2006), the conditions militated against 'groupness' across the minority *per se*: shared interests, agency and will were heavily constrained. There was no meaningful sense in which the 'minority' acted as a common group during either the occupation or the civil war; rather activity was limited to distinct and confined geographic communities. The minority lacked unity and 'actorness'. War exposed the fragmentation and limitations of the minority's leadership structures that had existed in peacetime. Now, these features greatly affected the scope for resistance or insurgency.

Yet, geographic fragmentation also underscored distinctions of self-identity. Smith (1981) asserts a plausible proposition: group cohesion intensifies when reacting to a common threat. Communities bind together, sharing the misery, to overcome the external shock. However, across Western Thrace the threat could not be experienced in common. Physical isolation, reinforced by a differentiation of treatment by the prevailing forces, created separate shocks and experiences. Occupation and civil war did not, of themselves, lead to a shared, coordinated response by 'the' minority.

Against this backdrop, there are important questions concerning the spread and intensity of feelings of a common identity on the part of the minority. The now classic question posed by Walker Connor (1988) – 'when is a nation?' – focuses on the relevant issue of determining when or if a shared (national) consciousness has emerged amongst a people. As Chapter 2 noted, the minority of Western Thrace could not claim a shared ancestry – the defining condition of a 'nation', according to Connor. The minority was conscious of its internal ethnic distinctions. The 'ethno-symbolic' dimension to the minority's identity was limited (Smith 2000: 796). In these respects, the minority shared primarily only those features associated with its religious faith.

Crucially, these features did not extend to identification with a primordial 'nation'; pre-war Thracian nationalism had left no legacy of a distinct somnolent movement waiting to rise-up. As Chapter 2 indicated, the three attempts to establish a separate Thracian rule – in 1878, 1913 and 1920 – had come to nought. Each was essentially a defensive response to the threat posed by 'neighbouring' nationalisms, they were not expressions of a separate nationalism. The 'Turkish Republic of Western Thrace' (1920) had been prompted by an alliance of Bulgarians and Turks opposing Greek supremacy over both Eastern and Western Thrace, but when Greece was pushed back the alliance collapsed. Instead, in the absence of a distinct Thracian nationalism, the area was carved up between Bulgaria, Greece and Turkey (treaties of Neuilly and Lausanne) and transformed by large population movements. The internal diversity of the local population – and the linguistic division of Pomaks and Turks – stood against the sweep of a single nationalism.

Indeed, the extent of shared values, symbols, memories, myths and traditions with the new Republic of Turkey was constrained by both geography and ideology. West Thracian Muslims were disconnected from the 'motherland' both by means of a foreign border and by an evident gap with Kemal's modernism. In this new world, the default Ottomanist outlook of Western Thracian Muslims meant little specific in terms of an alternative national or civic identity. Moreover, lacking a common ethnic identity, this was a minority comprising several *ethnies* but each of which, in their various ways, had failed to develop a strong sense of national feeling (on ethnic groups not developing nationhood, see Fearon and Laitin 2003). Thus, the mobilising force of nationalism was not readily available.

This is not to say that ethnicity was unimportant. Rather, it is a matter of *how* ethnicity worked (Brubaker et al. 2006). In Western Thrace, social life at the local level was, to a significant extent, structured along ethnic lines, with interaction anchored in particular communities. The voting behaviour of the minority illustrates this point: although both before and after the 1940s the Muslim vote was overwhelmingly given to 'minority' candidates, their political expression never led to the creation of a separate 'minority' party (as was to be the case later in post-Communist Bulgaria). Arguably, the integration of minority candidates within mainstream 'Greek' political parties has served as a counter-weight to a political expression built on the premise of a separate nationhood or a distinct nationalist discourse shared across the 'Muslim minority'. At best, such a discourse was felt only weakly or partially within the minority's sub-groups and it was propagated mainly by a committed (but, at that point, not dominant) group of local Kemalist activists.

The interesting turn, in this respect, came with the response to occupation and war. The numbers of Muslims exiting the conflicts to flee – under much hardship – to Turkey indicates a strong identification of that nation as a source of rescue. A by-product was that it disturbed the demographic character of the region: more refugees fled from the lowlands, though the numbers in the lowlands were partially compensated by the shift of Pomaks down from the mountains. The shift of the Pomaks into the more overtly 'Turkish' milieu of the lowlands enabled them to become more receptive to Kemalism and Turkish nationalism. The involvement of the Turkish Consulate in Komotini in the social and educational life of the minority in the 1940s also appears to have strengthened the local feelings of attachment in the lowland communities to the Kemalist Republic. Given the constraints of war, the Pomaks in the mountains were beyond its reach, but Turkey as a means of rescue and support entered the consciousness of the larger part of the minority very strongly in the 1940s. The minority lacked the structural capacity to express a shared agenda or interests, but the orientation towards Turkey was the closest it came in that regard.

Paradoxically, the major Greek forces in Western Thrace – during both the occupation and the civil war – tended to view the 'minority' through the established singular lens of the Lausanne Treaty. The *idée fixe* was of the minority as a largely undifferentiated 'other', placed in an antagonistic and suspicious opposition to the majority. Communists and nationalists alike were wary of engagement: the prism of Lausanne essentially remained in tact.

With such wariness and relative detachment, Turkey was left as the prime option for escape and succour. Despite Ankara's restraint in taking up their cause, and despite seeking to stem the flow of refugees, the effect of the wariness of the Greek Communists and later the suspicion of the Government was to strengthen the 'pull' of Turkey. The process of the 'Turkification' of the minority has been historically punctuated, but the experience of the occupation and the civil war formed one of the strongest episodes in overcoming the Ottomanist/Kemalist cleavage of identity in favour of the latter. This was evident in the growing strength of Kemalist candidates in the 1946 elections, by contrast to those of 1936. That said, the process of growing closer to Turkey – 'process' being central to Brubaker's notion of group identity – remained partial within the minority. It was a process that was far weaker in the case of the mountainous Pomaks: having rejected identification with Bulgaria, most retained a sense of distinction from Turkey. The minority thus finished the 1940s still with major points of internal differentiation: it would remain more meaningful to refer to the 'minorities'.

Turkification would be significantly strengthened and shaped by later events. Moreover, with Turkification came the prime means of the minority's 'modernisation'. For much of the minority, both before and immediately after the 1940s, the impact of the economic and technological changes felt long before in the 'West' had only loosely and limitedly affected their local circumstances. With a Greek state suspicious of them and largely preferring that they remain in their traditional stupor, it was the ideology of 'Kemalism' – and with it the nationalist orientation towards Ankara – that became the dominant purveyor of 'modernisation'. The minority's position in an economy rooted in the tobacco industry and traditional agriculture displayed much 'backwardness' in the mid-twentieth century. Echoing Janos' study of Hungary, this was a local society facing exogenous more than indigenous pressures for 'modernisation' (Janos 1982). Kemalist ideology, policies and mores were the main stimulus to their social change and adaptation and one that gradually pressed a singular identity of their kinship as 'Turks'. In so doing, this nationalist ideology encouraged a 'groupness'.

9.4   Future research

The present study was prompted by an historical puzzle of passivity and disengagement when other reactions and outcomes might have been expected. Explaining passivity – why something did *not* happen – is no easy task. As an investigation into why 'the dog didn't bark', it rested on the assertion that conditions existed that could have led to a very different historical path. Such an assertion is always going to be hazardous: the informed reader already knows the route that history followed; some will challenge the likelihood that events might have been different. The reasons why the dog might have barked will always be well short of overwhelming: after all, history did not work out that way. The task for the researcher is to provide credible reasons why this could have been a dog that barked, citing factors that had the potential to prompt the reaction. In the present study, there was an array of factors to consider: Turkey's geo-strategy and the proximity of the border; the relevance of the minority's kinship with Turkey; the severity of life under the occupation and the civil war; the rejection of Bulgarian rule; the minority's sense of identity, separateness and political agenda; the geographic conditions facilitating insurgency, etc. The reader will judge whether any or some of these factors had the potential to set a different course and whether the explanation of why they did not is convincing. In this case, the relevant Greek actors not only behaved as if the minority were acting or might have acted differently, Greek opinion sustained assumptions of it as a threat in itself or as a Trojan-horse for Turkey. Explaining why something did not happen can be as revealing as accounting for something that did: for it can challenge misjudgements.

The case study here was prompted by the dearth of historical accounts of the Muslim minority. It is hoped that the study fills a significant gap by covering the occupation and the civil war. There are, of course, other lacunae to be addressed. Most notably there is an absence of comparative work on response to the Axis occupation and the Greek civil war of the different ethnic communities of Greece. Within the more specific context of Western Thrace, the attitudes and experiences of those Muslims migrating to Turkey after the civil war and beyond would be an important dimension of the minority's story: both in terms of what was left behind and also what they confronted on arrival in Turkey. Such migration often took place within a climate of increasing Greco-Turkish tension. Sometimes it involved personal histories of being denied passports and citizenship by the Greek authorities; and it frequently involved a block on a return to Western Thrace. Such migrant stories are the history between conflicting nationalisms and prejudices. Another interesting dimension that could not be explored here are the experiences of the Bulgarian settlers to Western Thrace in the 1940s. Here, a narrative of a 'lost country' – with apparent 'Greek' and 'Turkish' parallels, may connect the experiences of those Bulgarians uprooted from the region in the aftermath of WWI with those who returned in the 1940s. More particularly, further exploration of the Pomak response to occupation in the 1940s is warranted in order to ascertain what degree of interaction taking place between the Pomaks of Greece and those of Bulgaria. The impression is that such interaction was limited. Each of these dimensions would enrich this small, but complex case.

9.5   The nexus between past and present

A further perspective on the case study here is that its findings contradict established assumptions within both Greece and Turkey. Since the Lausanne Treaty, official Greece has seen the Muslim minority of Western Thrace as an inconvenient remnant of the Ottoman Empire. It has been the unreliable 'other', a likely conduit for Turkey's irredentism. Prior to 1941, Greek strategy had assumed the minority's potential disloyalty. Again, despite official reports confirming that the minority had not collaborated with the Bulgarian occupation, the Athens government continued to misjudge the minority in the civil war. Its suspicions matched those of the Communists. Contrary to such interpretations, however, the Muslim minority of Western Thrace did not pose any threat to Greece or the Greeks in a period when existing structures were collapsing and contested, despite ample opportunity to do so. Official Greece has continued to misunderstand the minority thereafter.

The Lausanne Treaty had placed the West Thracian Muslims in the same strategic frame as that of the Greek Orthodox minority in Istanbul. New Greco-Turkish tensions in the 1950s over Cyprus underscored this equivalence. The demands of the Greek Cypriots for *'enosis'* (union) with Greece raised fears amongst Turkish Cypriots as to their own fate and the violent campaign of the former inflamed Turkish nationalism. Popular tensions ran high. The bombing of the Turkish Consulate in Thessaloniki – the house in which Kemal Atatürk had been born – led to large scale riots in Istanbul directed at the Greek minority there. Later reports indicated that the Thessaloniki bombing had been planted by Turkish nationalists as an apparent pretext for action in Istanbul (Vryonis 2005; Güven 2006; Özkırımlı and Sofos 2008: 171). The Istanbul riots weighed on the Greek psyche as the *Septemvriana* (Events of September). An expulsion of Greeks from Istanbul in 1964 – again prompted by the actions of Greek Cypriots vis-à-vis their Turkish counterparts – further decimated a once large community. Since the Lausanne Treaty, the Greeks of Istanbul have declined from 111,000 to 2–3000, a reduction clearly brought about by the repression and intimidation of their host government and society (Niarchos 2005: 9). The position of the Ecumenical Patriarch in the city – recognised internationally as the spiritual leader of the world's second largest Christian Church, but seen by official Turkey as merely a local bishop – has been kept bound and vulnerable. At the same time, successive Turkish governments in the post-war period have looked to the 'outside Turks' (*Diş Türkler*) of Western Thrace, stressing their common 'Turkish' identity and criticising their mistreatment by the Greek authorities since the 1950s.

For its part, official Greek policy towards the Muslims of Western Thrace was repeatedly justified by perceptions of a Turkish threat. After the restoration of democracy in 1974, the fear wrought by Turkey's invasion of Cyprus and its claims over the Aegean continued to sustain policies that involved a significant curtailment of the basic economic and social rights of the minority. Moreover, located in a poor periphery of Greece, the minority suffered much economic inequality: a periphery of a periphery (Anagnostou and Triandafyllidou 2006). With a rising tension between local Muslims – mobilised by Turkish nationalism – and the Greek Orthodox community, the Mitsotakis Government in 1991 announced a new approach, abolishing discriminatory measures, and applying the principles of 'equality before the law' and 'equal citizenship' (*isonomia kai isopolitia*). Though not mandated by any external body, the opprobrium that Greece received from the European Court of Human Rights, the Council of Europe, and the EU – quite apart from Turkey – underscored such moves. The policy of designating the mountainous (Pomak) areas as 'restricted zones', requiring the outside traveler to obtain special clearance and permits, for example, lasted until 1996 (Anagnostou, 2007: 160).

Today, the minority in Western Thrace continues to suffer from disadvantages of public provision and of economic circumstance. Though the path of Muslims into Greek universities has been greatly eased by measures of positive discrimination, the places available in local secondary schools offering tuition in Turkish remains inadequate and the number of local Muslims exiting education at an early age (sometimes as young as 12 years) continues to cause major concern. Deeper than the provision of services, however, are the social attitudes that affect the life of the minority community. Changed circumstances can hide enduring myths. Dragona (2008), for example, in her study of the present-day problems evident in the education of the minority notes that whilst there are superficial acceptances that similarities exist between the majority and minority communities, these are likely to be soon qualified by an assertion of the latent distinctiveness of the 'other'. Schoolteachers and other members of the Greek majority are apt to project onto the minority the 'other' features that are threatening and unwanted. Such stereotypes both simplify and exacerbate the sense of difference, reinforcing what Bourdieu (1977) termed 'symbolic capital' underlying social interaction.

The irony is that if today the minority is, in part, alienated and resentful of its host country, then official Greek policy has – repeatedly since the Lausanne Treaty – treated it with suspicion and discrimination, reinforcing whatever sense of 'otherness' the minority has historically possessed. The evidence of the present case study, however, is an apt reminder that at a crucial stage in modern Greek history – when so much seemed uncertain – the Muslims of Western Thrace chose not to rebel and were definitely not the 'enemy within'.

Sources

A. List of Archival Material

1. AYE – Diplomatic and Historical Archive of the Greek Foreign Ministry (Υπηρεσία Διπλωματικού και Ιστορικού Αρχείου του Ελληνικού Υπουργείου Εξωτερικών), Athens, Greece

AYE/1926/5.1
AYE/1926/61.2
AYE/1927/91.1
AYE/1927/92.2
AYE/1927/93.3
AYE/1929/B/61
AYE/1929/37
AYE/1930/B/28/I
AYE/1930/25
AYE/1940/8.A/3/2
AYE 1941/14/A/3/3
AYE/1941/14.3
AYE/1941/26.B/4/T
AYE/1944/1.1
AYE/1944/1.3
AYE/1944/4.1
AYE/1944/4.4
AYE/1944/6.1
AYE/1944/8.5
AYE/1944/10.1
AYE/1944/10.3
AYE/1944/11.3
AYE/1944/21.6
AYE/1944/22.2
AYE/1945/21.3
AYE/1945/41.3
AYE/1945/75.11
AYE/1946/42.3
AYE/1946/61.1
AYE/1947/28.4
AYE/1947/28.5
AYE/1947/31.2
AYE/1947/73.1
AYE/1947/111.1
AYE/1948/27.1
AYE/1948/56.4
AYE/1948/105.3
AYE/1948/105.6
AYE/1948/105.7

AYE/1949/21.2
AYE/1949/22.3
AYE/1949/25.1
AYE/1949/25.2
AYE/1950/32/1
AYE/1950/52.1
AYE/1950/52.4
AYE/1950/70.1
AYE/1950/81.5
AYE/1950/124.2

2. BCA – Turkish Republic, Prime Ministry Republican Archives (*Başbakanlık Cumhuriyet Arşivleri*), Ankara, Turkey

BCA/77D80/301000/7348113
BCA/6176/301000/63214
BCA/10253/301000/12387412
BCA/14530/301000/1432811
BCA/14532/301000/144292
BCA/426846/3010/243/646/6
BCA/426847/3010/2436467
BCA/43323/301000/25370623
BCA/433591/301000/25672512
BCA/433592/301000/25672513

3. BOA – Prime Ministry Ottoman Archives (*Başbakanlık Osmanlı Arşivleri*), Istanbul, Turkey

BOA/HR.SYS/2426/37
BOA/HR.SYS/2424/54
BOA/HR.SYS/2454/37
BOA/HR.SYS/2457/19
BOA/HR.SYS/2461/77

4. CSA – Bulgarian Central State Archives (ЦЕНТРАЛЕН ДЪРЖАВЕН АРХИВ), Sofia, Bulgaria

177/3/2665
177/5/83
177/7/170
177/7/189
177/8/13
264/1/185
264/1/497
264/7/848
284/3/62
471/1/1082
471/1/1311n
662/1/9
662k/1/14
662/1/26

662/1/51
798/2/48

5. NARA – National Archives and Records Administration, Maryland, USA

NARA/M1221/1174
NARA/M1221/4209
NARA/RG 59/R&A 2165

6. PRO – Public Record Office, London, United Kingdom

CAB – Records of the Cabinet Office

CAB/66/48/36
CAB/120/710
CAB/120/715

FO – Records created and inherited by the Foreign Office

FO/12/292
FO/195/2478
FO/195/2483
FO/195/2486
FO/371/33211
FO/371/37158
FO/371/37179
FO/371/37465
FO/371/43775
FO/371/48764
FO/371/48784
FO/371/58535
FO/371/58537
FO/371/58868
FO/371/72229
FO/371/78370
FO/371/78373

HW – Records created and inherited by Government Communications Headquarters

HW/12/261
HW/12/262
HW/12/263
HW/12/264
HW/12/265
HW/12/287
HW/12/305
HW/12/314
HW/12/315
HW/12/320

HS – Records of Special Operations Executive (SOE)
HS/5/152
HS/5/185
HS/5/317

MFQ – Maps and plans extracted to flat storage from records of various departments held at the Public Record Office
MFQ/1/458

WO – Records created or inherited by the War Office, Armed Forces, Judge Advocate General, and related bodies
WO/178/48
WO/178/50
WO/201/1606A
WO/201/1606B
WO/204/360
WO/252/800

7. ASKI – Contemporary Social History Archives (Αρχεία Σύγχρονης Κοινωνικής Ιστορίας)

ASKI/3122: *Agonistis* (*Αγωνιστής*) – Official newspaper of the KKE's Committee of Macedonia and Thrace
ASKI/20/16/62: *Savaş* (certain issues) – Turkish-language organ of the Headquarters of Eastern Macedonia and Thrace of the DSE
Kommounistiki Epitheorisi (*Κομμουνιστική Επιθεώρηση*) – Monthly theoretical organ of KKE

8. Benaki Museum (Μουσείο Μπενάκη), Athens, Greece

Archive of Eleftherios Venizelos, File 251/1931

9. ELIA – The Hellenic Literary and Historical Archive (Ελληνικό, Λογοτεχνικό και Ιστορικό Αρχείο), Greece

Athens
ELIA/24/02, 'Archive of Epameinondas Vrettos'.

Thessaloniki
ELIA/37/02, 'Archive of Harisios Vamvakas'.
ELIA/47, 'Archive of Bulgarian Occupation in Macedonia and Thrace'.

10. GAK – General State Archives (Γενικά Αρχεία του Κράτους), Greece

Athens
K65/92, Metaxas Archive
K65/93, Metaxas Archive
K108/B

Kavalla
F.95B, Archive of Foreign and Minority Schools

Thessaloniki (Historical Archive of Macedonia)
F.623, Archive of Xanthi Prefecture
F.150 (B10), Archive of Xanthi Prefecture

11. HoC – House of Commons, Parliamentary Papers on line, United Kingdom

HoC, 1878 [C.2089] Turkey. No. 42 (1878). 'Further correspondence respecting the affairs of Turkey'.
HoC, 1878 [C.2135] Turkey. No. 45 (1878). 'Further correspondence respecting the affairs of Turkey'.
HoC, 1878 [C.2141] Turkey. No. 49 (1878). 'Correspondence respecting the proceedings of the International Commission sent to the Mount Rhodope District'.
HoC, 1878 [C.2009] Turkey. No. 31 (1878). 'Correspondence respecting the objections raised by populations inhabiting Turkish provinces against the territorial changes proposed in the preliminary treaty signed at San Stefano, 19th February, 3rd March, 1878'.
HoC, 1878–79 [C.2204] [C.2205] Turkey. No. 53 (1878). 'Further correspondence respecting the affairs of Turkey'.
HoC, 1880 [C.2552] Turkey. No. 5 (1880). 'Correspondence respecting the condition of the Mussulman, Greek, and Jewish populations in Eastern Roumelia'.
HoC, 1880 [C.2610] Turkey. No. 10 (1880). 'Report of the commission appointed to inquire into the occurrences in the Kirdjali district'.

12. Vovolinis Archive (Αρχείο Βοβολίνη), Athens, Greece

Elliniko Aima (*Ελληνικό Αίμα*).
Leykoma Trakis-Makedonias 1932. (*Θρακική Στοά, Λεύκωμα Θράκης-Μακεδονίας*). Komotini: Drakopoulos.

13. Personal Archive of Dr. John Iatrides

Personal letter of Alexandros Gregoriadis to Dr John Iatrides, 7 February 1973.

B. Press

Bulgaria
Zora (newspaper)

Greece
Azınlıkça – Turkish-language magazine published in Western Thrace
Demokratikos Stratos (*Δημοκρατικός Στρατός*) – Monthly bulletin of the Headquarters-General of the DSE
Drasis (*Δράσις*) – Newspaper of the Headquarters of Eastern Macedonia and Thrace of the DSE
Ergatikos Agon tis Thrakis (*Εργατικός Αγών της Θράκης* – Newspaper, Alexandroupolis)
Eleftheri Thraki (*Ελεύθερη Θράκη* – Newspaper, Alexandroupolis)
Governmental Gazette (*Εφημερίδα της Κυβερνήσεως* – ΦΕΚ)
Proia (Πρωϊα – Newspaper, Komotini)
Proodeutiki (Προοδευτική – Newspaper, Xanthi)

Radio Haberleri – Turkish-language Radio News of the Headquarters of Eastern Macedonia and Thrace of the DSE
Rizospastis – (*Ριζοσπάστης* – Newspaper, Athens)
Savaş – Turkish-language newspaper of the Headquarters of Eastern Macedonia and Thrace of the DSE
Trakya (Turkish-language newspaper, Xanthi)

Turkey

Haber (newspaper)
Memleket (newspaper)
Kör Kadı (newspaper)
Republique (French-language edition of *Cumhuriyet* newspaper)
Son Posta (newspaper)
Vakit (newspaper)
Yeni Gazete (newspaper)
Yeni Sabah (newspaper)

United Kingdom

The Times (newspaper)

Bibliography

A Report of the Professors of the Universities of Athens and Salonica. 1945. *Bulgarian Atrocities in Greek Macedonia and Thrace, 1941–1944*. Athens.

Aarbakke V. 2000. *The Muslim Minority of Greek Thrace*. PhD Thesis. University of Bergen.

Aarbakke V. 2004. 'Πρόσφυγες και προσφυγικές οργανώσεις στη Βουλγαρία, 1940–1990'. ['Refugees and Refugee Organizations in Bulgaria, 1940–1990'], in Gounaris V.K. and Michailidis I.D. (eds). *Πρόσφυγες στα Βαλκάνια. Μνήμη και Ενσωμάτωση*. [*Refugees in the Balkans. Memory and Incorporation*]. Athens: Patakis. 382–447.

Ahmad F. 1969. *The Young Turks: The Committee of Union and Progress in Turkish Politics, 1908–1914*. Oxford: Clarendon.

Ahmad F. 2003. *Turkey, The Quest for Identity*. Oxford: Oneworld.

Akar R. 1992. *Varlık Vergisi, Tek Parti Rejiminde Azınlık Karşıtı Politika Örneği*. Istanbul: Bilim Dizisi.

Akçura Y. 1991. *Üç Tarz-ı Siyaset*. Ankara: Türk Tarih Kurumu.

Akgönül S. 1999. *Une communauté, Deux Etats: La Minorité Turco-Musulmane de Thrace Occidentale*. Istanbul: ISIS.

Akgönül S. (ed.). 2008. *Reciprocity. Greek and Turkish Minorities. Law. Religion and Politics*. Istanbul: Bilgi University Press.

Akşin S. 2007. *Turkey, From Empire to Revolutionary Republic. The Emergence of the Turkish Nation from 1789 to the Present*. London: Hurst.

Aktar A. 2006. 'Το πρώτο έτος της ελληνοτουρκικής ανταλλαγής πληθυσμών: Σεπτέμβριος 1922-Σεπτέμβριος 1923'. [The First Year of the Greco-Turkish Population Exchange: September 1922-September 1923'], in Tsitselikis K. (ed.). *Η ελληνοτουρκική ανταλλαγή πληθυσμών. Πτυχές μιας εθνικής σύγκρουσης. [The Greek-Turkish Population Exchange. Aspects of a National Conflict]*. Athens: Kemo/Kritiki. 111–156.

Alexandris A. 1982. 'Turkish Policy Towards Greece During the Second World War and its Impact on Greek-Turkish Détente'. *Balkan Studies*. Vol.23. Part 1. 157–197.

Alexandris A., Veremis T., Kazakos P., Coufoudakis V., Rozakis H.L. and Tsitsopoulos G. 1991. *Οι Ελληνοτουρκικές Σχέσεις 1923–1987*. [*Greco-Turkish Relations 1923–1987*]. Athens: Gnosi.

Alexandris A. 1992. *The Greek Minority of Istanbul and Greek-Turkish Relations 1918–1974*. Athens: Centre for Asia Minor Studies.

Alexandris A. 2003. 'Religion or Ethnicity, The Identity Issue of the Minorities in Greece and Turkey', in Hirschon R. (ed.). *Crossing the Aegean, An Appraisal of the 1923 Compulsory Population Exchange Between Greece and Turkey*. Oxford: Bergham Books. 117–132.

Ali R. and Hüseyinoğlu T. 2009. *1946–1949. Yunan İç Savaş'nda Batı Trakya Türk Azınlığı*, Komotini: PEKEM/BAKEŞ.

Alivizatos N.C. 1981. 'The "Emergency Regime" and Civil Liberties, 1946–1949', in Iatrides J.O. (ed.). *Greece in the 1940s. A Nation in Crisis*. Hanover and London: University Press of New England. 220–228.

Altinoff I. 1921. *La Thrace Interalliée*. Sofia: Imprimerie de la Cour.

American Geographical Society. 1923. 'Geographical Elements in the Turkish Situation: A Note on the Political Map'. *Geographical Review*. 13(1) (January). 122–129.

Anagnostou D. and Triandafyllidou A. 2006. *Regions, Minorities and European Integration: A Case Study on Muslims in Western Thrace, Greece*. Athens: ELIAMEP, http://www.eliamep.gr/en (last accessed 7 February 2010).

Anagnostou D. 2007. 'Development, discrimination and reverse discrimination: effects of EU integration and regional change on the Muslims of Southeast Europe', in Al-Azmeh A. and Fokas E. (eds). *Euro-Islam at the Turn of the Millennium: Present Conditions and Future Perspectives*. Cambridge: Cambridge University Press. 149–182.

Anastasiadou I. 1982. *Ο Βενιζέλος και το Ελληνοτουρκικό Σύμφωνο Φιλίας του 1930*. [*Venizelos and the 1930 Greco-Turkish Friendship Pact*]. Athens: Filippotis.

Anderson P. 2008. 'Kemalism'. *London Review of Books*. 11 September.

Andreades K.G. 1980. *The Moslem Minority in Western Thrace*. Amsterdam: Adolf Hakkert.

Andronopoulos V.K. and Mathioudakis M. 1988. *Νεοελληνική διοικητική ιστορία: περιφερειακή διοίκηση, τοπική αυτοδιοίκηση*. [*Administrative History of Modern Greece: Regional Administration, Local Government*]. Athens.

Antonovski Hristo. 1961. *Η εξέγερσις της Δράμας του 1941 κα τα βουλγαρικά φασιστικά εγκλήματα*. [*The Drama Uprising and the Bulgarian Fascist Crimes*] Skopje (translated by I.T. Lampsidis 1963 for the Institute for Balkan Studies).

Armstrong H.G. 1932. *The Grey Wolf, Mustafa Kemal, An Intimate Study of a Dictator*. London: Arthur Barker.

Aschenbrenner S. 2002. 'Ο Εμφύλιος από την οπτική ενός μεσσηνιακού χωριού' ['The Civil War from the Local Perspective of a Messinian Village'], in Baerentzen L., Iatrides J.O. and Smith O.L. (eds). *Μελέτες για τον Εμφύλιο Πόλεμο 1945–1949*. [*Studies in the History of the Greek Civil War 1945–1949*]. Athens: Olkos. 115–136.

Askouni N. 2006. *Η εκπαίδευση της μειονότητας στη Θράκη. Από το περιθώριο στην προοπτική της κοινωνικής ένταξης*. [*The Education of the Minority of Thrace. From Marginalisation to the Prospect of Social Incorporation*]. Athens: Alexandreia.

Atatürk (Mustafa Kemal). 2009. *Nutuk*. Vol. I–II. Athens: Papazisis.

Athanasopoulou E. 1999. *Τουρκία. Αναζήτηση ασφαλείας. Αμερικανο-Βρετανικά συμφέροντα.* [*Turkey. In Search of Security. Americano-British Interests*]. Athens: Papazisis/ELIAMEP.

Averoff-Tositsas E. 1974. *Φωτιά και Τσεκούρι, Ελλάς 1946–1949 και τα προηγηθέντα, Συνοπτική Ιστορική Μελέτη* [*Fire and Axe, Greece 1946–1949 and the Precedent, Concise Historical Study*]. Athens: Estia.

Baerentzen L. and Close D.H. 1998. 'Η ήττα του ΕΑΜ από τους Βρετανούς 1944–45', ['The Defeat of EAM by the British 1944–45'] in Close D.H. (ed.) *Ο ελληνικός Εμφύλιος Πόλεμος 1943–1950. Μελέτες για την Πόλωση.* [*The Greek Civil War 1943–1950. Studies of Polarization*]. Athens: Filistor. 100–128.

Baerentzen L. 2002. 'Το Παιδομάζωμα και οι παιδουπόλεις της βασίλισσας' ['The "Paidomazoma" and the Queen's Camps'], in Baerentzen L., Iatrides J.O. and Smith O.L. (eds). *Μελέτες για τον Εμφύλιο Πόλεμο 1945–1949.* [*Studies in the History of the Greek Civil War 1945–1949*]. Athens: Olkos. 137–164.

Baev J. 1997. The Greek Civil War. A View from Outside. [Ο εμφύλιος πόλεμος στην Ελλάδα – Διεθνείς διαστάσεις]. Athens:Filistor.

Bahcheli T. 1990. *Greek-Turkish Relations Since 1955.* London: Westview Press.

Bamberger-Stemmann S. 2000. Der europäische Nationalitätenkongress 1925 bis 1938. Nationale Minderheiten zwischen Lobbyisten und Grossmachtinteressen. Marburg: Herder Institut.

Barker E. 1996. *Η Μακεδονία στις Διαβαλκανικές Σχέσεις και Συγκρούσεις* [*Macedonia in the Balkan Power Politics*] Thessaloniki: Paratiritis.

Barker E. 2002. 'Η Γιουγκοσλαβική πολιτική προς την Ελλάδα στα 1947–1949' ['Yugoslav Policy towards Greece 1947–1949'], in Baerentzen L., Iatrides J.O and Smith O.L. (eds). *Μελέτες για τον Εμφύλιο Πόλεμο 1945–1949.* [*Studies in the History of the Greek Civil War 1945–1949.*] Athens: Olkos. 285–318.

Barlas D. and Güvenç S. 2009. 'Turkey and the Idea of a European Union during the Inter-war Years, 1923–39'. *Middle Eastern Studies.* 45(3). 425–446.

Bartziotas V. 1986. *60 χρόνια κομμουνιστής. Κριτική αυτοβιογραφία, Αναμνήσεις.* [*Being Communist for 60 Years. Critical Autobiography, Memoirs.*] Athens: Syghroni Epochi.

Batıbey K. Ş. 1970. *Batı Trakya Türk Devleti (1919–1920).* [*The Turkish State of Western Thrace.*] Istanbul: Boğaziçi Yayınları.

Batıbey K. Ş. 1976. *Ve Bulgarlar geldi. Batı Trakya'da teneke ile alarm.* [*There Came the Bulgarians. The Cutlery Alarm of Western Thrace*]. Istanbul, Bogazici Yayinlari.

Bayülken Ü.H. 1963. 'Turkish Minorities in Greece'. *The Turkish Yearbook of International Relations.* Vol. IV. 145–164.

Belli M. 2009. *Καπετάν Κεμάλ. Αναμνήσεις από τον Ελληνικό Εμφύλιο.* [*Captain Kemal. Memoirs from the Greek Civil War*]. Istanbul: Telos International.

Bourdieu P. 1977. *Outline of a Theory of Practice.* Cambridge and New York: Cambridge University Press.

Bravos T. 2001/2003, 'Κατοχή και Εμφύλιος στον Γερμανοκρατούμενο Έβρο, Η περίπτωση των τεσσάρων χωριών του', ['Occupation and Civil War in German-occupied Evros']. *Θρακικά* [*Thrakika*]. 13(2). 145–172.

Brewer D. 2001. *The Flame of Freedom. The Greek War of Independence 1821–1833.* London: John Murray.

Broun J. 2007. 'Rehabilitation and Recovery: Bulgaria's Muslim Communities', in *Religion, State & Society.* 35(2). 105–138.

Brubaker R., Feischmidt M, Fox J. and Grancea L. 2006. *Nationalist Politics and Everyday Ethnicity in a Transylvanian Town.* Princeton and Oxford: Princeton University Press.

Brunnbauer U. 1998. 'Histories and Identities: Nation-State and Minority Discourses. The Case of the Bulgarian Pomaks', in Bulgarian Center for Regional Cultural Studies (Sofia). *In and Out of the Collective: Papers on Former Soviet Bloc Rural Communities.* Vol. I. February. 1–10.

Bulgarian Political Mission to Washington. *The Truth About Bulgaria.* May 1946.

Carabott P. and Sfikas T.D. (eds). 2004. *The Greek Civil War, Essays on a Conflict of Exceptionalism and Silences.* London: Ashgate.

Carnegie Endowment for International Peace. 1914. *Report of the International Commission to Inquire into the Causes and Conduct of the Balkan Wars.* Washington DC.

Carnegie Endowment for International Peace. 1924. *The Treaties of Peace 1919–1923.* Vol. II. New York.

Carpenter T. 2003. *The Miss Stone Affair. America's First Modern Hostage Crisis.* New York: Simon and Schuster.

Chatzianastasiou T. 2003. *Αντάρτες και Καπεταναίοι, Η εθνική αντίσταση κατά της Βουλγαρικής κατοχής της Ανατολικής Μακεδονίας και της Θράκης, 1942–1944.* [*Guerrillas and Kapetanios. The National Resistance against the Bulgarian Occupation of Eastern Macedonia and Thrace, 1942–44*]. Thessaloniki: Kyriakidis Bros.

Chatzianastasiou T. 2006. 'Οι εθνικιστές οπλαρχηγοί στη βουλγαροκρατούμενη Μακεδονία και Θράκη' ['The nationalist war-lords leaders in Bulgarian-occupied Macedonia and Thrace'], in Marantzidis N. (ed.). *Οι άλλοι Καπετάνιοι. Αντικομουνιστές ένοπλοι στα χρόνια της Κατοχής και του Εμφυλίου* [*The Other Kapetanios. Anti-Communist Fighters during the Occupation and the Civil War*]. Athens: Estia. 297–374.

Chatzinikolaou N.V. (Kapetan Mavros). 2008. *Ταραγμένα χρόνια στο Νέστο. Κατοχή-Αντίσταση-Εμφύλιος.* [*Troubled Years in Nestos. Occupation-Resistance-Civil War*]. Thasos: Niragos Publications.

Chatzitheodoridis V.G. 2002. *Η Κατοχή στην Ανατολική Μακεδονία-Θράκη (1941–45), Μια ιστορικο-ερμηνευτική και κοινωνική προσέγγιση της Αντίστασης του λαού μας.* [*The Occupation in Eastern Macedonia-Thrace (1941–45). A Historical and Social Approach of the Resistance of our People*]. Drama: NEPOTA.

Chatzis T. 1983. *Η νικηφόρα επανάσταση που χάθηκε.* [*The Victorious Revolution that was Lost*]. Vol. I-IV. Athens: Dorikos.

Christopoulos D. and Tsitselikis K. 2003. 'Legal Aspects of Religious and Linguistic Otherness in Greece. Treatmenet of Minorities and Homogeneis in Greece: Relics and Challenges'. *Jahrbuecher fuer Geschichte und Kultur Suedosteuropas.* [*History and Culture of South Eastern Europe – An Annual Journal*]. 5: 'Minorities in Greece. Historical Issues and New Perspectives' edited by Trubeta S. and Voss C. 81–93.

Chrysochoou A. 1949. *Η Κατοχή εν Μακεδονία. Τόμος Ι. Η δράσις του ΚΚΕ.* [*The Occupation in Macedonia. Vol. I. The Activities of the KKE*]. Thessaloniki, Etaireia Makedonikon spoudon.

Clark B. 2006. *Twice a Stranger. The Mass Expulsions that Forged Modern Greece and Turkey.* Cambridge: Harvard University Press.

Claude I. L. 1955. *National Minorities: An International Problem.* Cambridge: Harvard University Press.

Clogg R. 1975. 'Pearls from Swine: the Foreign Office Papers, SOE and the Greek Resistance', in Clogg R. and Auty P. (eds). *British Policy towards Wartime Resistance in Yugoslavia and Greece.* London: Macmillan. 167–205.

Clogg R. 1981. 'The Special Operations Executive in Greece', in Iatrides J.O. (ed). 1981. *Greece in the 1940s. A Nation in Crisis.* Hanover and London: University Press of New England. 102–118.

Clogg R. 1992. *A Concise History of Greece*. Cambridge: Cambridge University Press.

Clogg R. 2000. *Anglo-Greek Attitudes: Studies in History*. Basingstoke: Palgrave Macmillan.

Close D.H. (ed.). 1998. *Ο ελληνικός Εμφύλιος Πόλεμος 1943–1950. Μελέτες για την Πόλωση*. [*The Greek Civil War 1943–1950. Studies of Polarization*]. Athens: Filistor.

Coakley J. 1990. 'National minorities and the government of divided societies: A comparative analysis of some European evidence'. *European Journal of Political Research*. 18(4). 437–456.

Connor W. 1994. *Ethnonationalism: The Quest for Understanding*. Princeton: Princeton University Press.

Coufoudakis V. 1981. 'The United States, the United Nations and the Greek Question 1946–1952', in Iatrides J.O. (ed.). *Greece in the 1940s. A Nation in Crisis*. Hanover and London: University Press of New England. 275–297.

Cowan J.K. 2001. 'Ambiguities of an Emancipatory Discourse: The Making of a Macedonian Minority in Greece', in Cowan J.K., Dembour M.B. and Wilson R.A. (eds). *Culture and Rights: Anthropological Perspectives*. Cambridge: Cambridge University Press. 152–176.

Cowan J.K. 2003. 'Who's Afraid of Violent Language? Honour, Sovereignty and Claims-making in the League of Nations'. Special Issue on 'Violence and Language'. *Anthropological Theory* 3(3). 271–291.

Cowan J.K. 2007. 'The Success of Failure? Minority Supervision at the League of Nations', in Dembour M-B. and Kelly T. (eds). *Paths to International Justice: Social and Legal Perspectives*. Cambridge: Cambridge University Press. 29–56.

Crampton R.J. 1997. *A Concise History of Bulgaria*. Cambridge: Cambridge University Press.

Dagkas A. and Leontiadis G. 1997. *Κομιντέρν και Μακεδονικό ζήτημα, Το ελληνικό παρασκήνιο, 1924* [*Comintern and the Macedonian Issue. The Greek Backstage, 1924*]. Athens: Trochalia.

Dalègre J. 1995. *Populations et Territoire en Thrace depuis 1878*. Thèse de Doctorat. Univerisité de Paris X. Nanterre.

Dalègre J. 1997. *La Thrace Grecque. Populations et Territoire*. Paris: L'Harmattan.

Danforth L. 1989. *Firewalking and Religious Healing: The Anastenaria of Greece and the American Firewalking Movement*. Princeton: Princeton University Press.

Danforth L.M. 1995. *The Macedonian Conflict. Ethnic Nationalism in a Transnational World*. Princeton: Princeton University Press.

Daskalov G. 1992a. 'Демографските процеси в Източна Македония и Западна Тракия (1 Януари 1942 – 25 Октомври 1944)'. ['Demographic Developments in Eastern Macedonia and Western Thrace (1 January 1942–25 October 1944)']. – *Военноисторически сборник* [*Voennopoliticheski Sbornik – Military-Political Journal*]. Issue 1. 17–48.

Daskalov G. 1992b. 'Установяване на Българската Администрация и Политическата Система в Новоосвободените Земи на Западна Тракия и Източна Македония (1941–1944)'. ['The Establishment of the Bulgarian Administrative and Political System in the Newly Liberated Lands of Western Thrace and Eastern Macedonia. (1941–1944)']. *Военнополитически Сборник* [*Voennopoliticheski Sbornik – Military-Political Journal*]. Issue 6. 103–127.

De Jong F. 1980. *Names, Religious Denominations and Ethnicity of Settlement in Western Thrace*. Leiden: E.J. Brill.

De Jong L. 1990. *The Netherlands and Nazi Germany*. Cambridge: Harvard University Press.

Dede A. 1980. 'Andartlık Hikâyeleri'. *Türk Dünyası Araştımaları Dergisi*. 1(4). 90–97.

Demetriou O. 2002. *Divisive Visions: A Study of Minority Identities among Turkish-Speakers in Komotini, Northern Greece*. PhD Thesis. The London School of Economics and Political Science.

Demetriou O. 2004. 'Prioritizing "ethnicities": The uncertainty of Pomak-ness in the urban Greek Rhodope'. *Ethnic and Racial Studies*. 27(1). 95–119.

Denniston R. 1997. *Churchill's Secret War, Diplomatic Decrypts, The Foreign Office and Turkey 1942–44*. New York: St.Martin's Press.

Deringil S. 1982. 'The preservation of Turkey's neutrality during the Second World War: 1940'. *Middle Eastern Studies*. 18. 30–52.

Deringil S. 1992. 'Active Neutrality: 1942'. *Turkish Review, Quarterly Digest*. 6(28). 45–72.

Deringil S. 2004. *Turkish Foreign Policy during the Second World War. An 'Active' Neutrality*. Cambridge: Cambridge University Press.

Dimokratikos Stratos. 1996. *Φωτογραφική αναπαραγωγή από τα πρωτότυπα τεύχη του περιοδικού Δημοκρατικός Στρατός'*. [*Photographic Reproduction of the Original Issues of the Magazine 'Demokratikos Stratos'*]. Vol. I. January-December 1948. Athens: Rizospastis.

Dimokratikos Stratos. 1996. *Φωτογραφική αναπαραγωγή από τα πρωτότυπα τεύχη του περιοδικού Δημοκρατικός Στρατός'*. [*Photographic Reproduction of the Original Issues of the Magazine 'Demokratikos Stratos'*]. Vol. I. January-September 1949. Athens: Rizospastis.

Divani L. 1999. *Ελλάδα και Μειονότητες. Το σύστημα διεθνούς προστασίας της Κοινωνίας των Εθνών*. [*Greece and Minorities, The System of International Protection of the League of the Nations*]. Athens: Kastaniotis.

Dragona T. and Frangoudaki A. 2006. 'Educating the Muslim Minority in Western Thrace'. *Islam and Christian-Muslim Relations*. 17(1). 21–41.

Dragona T. 2008. 'Εκπαιδεύοντας τον "ανοίκειο" άλλο: ταυτότητες, ψυχικοί μηχανισμοί και ιδεολογία' ['Educating the Unfamiliar "Other": Identities, Psychological Mechanisms and Ideology'], in Dragona T. and Frangoudaki A. (eds.). *Πρόσθεση Όχι Αφαίρεση, Πολλαπλασιασμός Όχι Διαίρεση: Η Μεταρρυθμιστική Παρέμβαση στην Εκπαίδευση της Μειονότητας της Θράκης*. [*Addition not Subtraction, Multiplication not Division: The Reformative Intervention in the Education of the Minority of Thrace*]. Athens: Metaichmio. 423–435.

Economides K.P. 1989. *Το Νομικό Καθεστώς των Νησιών του Αιγαίου, Απάντηση σε Τουρκική Μελέτη*. [*The Legal Status of the Aegean Islands, Response to a Turkish Study*]. Athens: Gnosi.

Eddy C.B. 1931. *Greece and the Greek Refugees*. London: George Allen and Unwin.

Eminov A. 2007. 'Social Construction of Identities: Pomaks in Bulgaria'. *Journal of Ethnopolitics and Minority Issues in Europe* (JEMIE) 2. 1–24.

Enepekides P. 1969. *Οι διωγμοί των Εβραίων εν Ελλάδι, 1941–1944, Επί τη βάσει των μυστικών αρχείων των ΕΣ-ΕΣ* [*The Persecution of the Jews in Greece, 1941–44. Based on the Secret Archives of the SS*]. Athens. Papazisis.

European Roma Rights Centre. 2003. *Country Reports Series. A Short History of the Roma in Greece*, Issue 12. 28–41 (www.ceeol.com).

Exarchou T. 1999. *Δεκαπέντε μήνες μιας πόλης, Ξάνθη, Ιανουάριος 1940–Απρίλιος 1941* [*Fifteen Months of a City, Xanthi, January 1940–April 1941*]. Xanthi: Politistiko Anaptyksiako Kentro Thrakis.

Exarchou T. 2000. *Εφτά Χρόνια μιας Πόλης, Ξάνθη 1933–1939* [*Seven Years of a City, Xanthi 1933–1939*]. Xanthi: Politistiko Anaptyksiako Kentro Thrakis.

316   *Sources*

Exarchou T. 2001. *Οι Εβραίοι στην Ξάνθη, (Ο κόσμος που χάθηκε αλλά δεν ξεχάστηκε.* [*The Jews in Xanthi (A World that was Gone but not Forgotten)*] Xanthi: Politistiko Anaptyksiako Kentro Thrakis.

Exarchou T. 2002. *Ξάνθη 1941–44, Όμηροι Βουλγαρίας (Μια πρώτη συστηματική προσέγγιση)* [*Xanthi 1941–44. Hostages of Bulgaria (A First Systematic Approach)*] Xanthi: Politistiko Anaptyksiako Kentro Thrakis.

Farakos G. 2004. *Β Παγκόσμιος Πόλεμος, Σχέσεις ΚΚΕ, και Διεθνούς Κομμουνιστικού Κέντρου* [*World War II, Relations Between KKE and the International Communist Centre*]. Athens: Ellinika Grammata.

Fearon J.D. and Laitin D.D. 2003. 'Ethnicity, Insurgency and Civil War'. *American Political Science Review*. 97(1). 75–90.

Fleischer H. 1988. *Στέμμα και Σβάστικα, Η Ελλάδα της Κατοχής και της Αντίστασης,* [*Crowns and Swastika, Greece during the Occupation and Resistance*]. Vol. I-II. Athens: Papazisis.

Foot M.R.D. 1999. *SOE: An Outline History of the Special Operations Executive 1940– 1946*. London: Pimlico.

Fostiridis A. 1959. *Ηεθνική αντίστασις κατά της Βουλγαρικής κατοχής, 1941–45* [*National Resistance Against the Bulgarian Occupation, 1941–45*]. Thessaloniki.

Foteas P. 1978. *Οι Πομάκοι της Δυτικής Θράκης. Μια μικρή συμβολή σε ένα μεγάλο θέμα.* [*The Pomaks of Western Thrace. A Small Contribution to a Big Issue*]. Komotini. Morfotikos Syllogos Komotinis. 3–33.

Friedman V.A. and Dankoff R. 1991. 'The Earliest Text in Balkan (Rumelian) Romani: A Passage from Evliya Çelebi's Seyahat nameh'. *Journal of the Gypsy Lore Society*. Fifth Series. 1(1). 1–20.

Gage N. 1983. *Eleni*. New York: Ballantine Books.

Gagoulias G.D. 2004. *Η αθέατη πλευρά του Εμφυλίου. Τα τραγικά γεγονότα της 7ης Μεραρχίας του ΔΣΕ.* [*The Invisible Side of the Civil War. The Tragic Events of the 7th Division of the DSE*]. Athens: Iolkos.

Georgantzis P.A. 1993. *Θρακικός Αγώνας 1912–1920. Ύστατοι απελευθερωτικοί αγώνες Δ. Θράκης.* [*The Struggle for Thrace 1912–1920*]. Xanthi: Stegi Grammaton kai Kalon Tehnon.

Geragas K. 2005. *Αναμνήσεις εκ Θράκης 1920–1922.* [*Memoirs from Thrace 1920–1922*]. Katerini: Mati.

Gerolymatos A. 2005. *Κόκκινη Ακρόπολη, Μαύρος Τρόμος. Από την Αντίσταση στον Εμφύλιο 1943–1949* [*Red Acropolis, Black Terror. From Resistance to Civil War 1943–1949*]. Athens: Kochlias.

GES. 1951. *Οι μάχες του Βίτσι και του Γράμμου 1949, Επιχείρησις 'Πυρσός'.* [*The Battles of Vitsi and Grammos 1949. Operation 'Pyrsos'*]. Athens: DIS.

GES/DIS. 1971. *Ο Ελληνικός Στρατός κατά τον Αντισυμμοριακόν Αγώνα: το πρώτον έτος του αγώνος, 1946.* [*The Greek Army in the Anti-Bandit Struggle: the First Year of the Struggle, 1946*]. Athens: DIS.

GES/DIS. 1976. *Ο Ελληνικός Στρατός κατά τον Αντισυμμοριακόν Αγώνα (1946–49): επιχειρήσεις Γ' Σώματος Στρατού* [*The Greek Army during the Anti-Bandit Struggle (1946–1949): Operations of the 3rd Army Corps*]. Athens: DIS.

GES/DIS. 1990. *Αγώνες και Νεκροί του Ελληνικού Στρατού κατά το Δεύτερο Παγκόσμιο Πόλεμο, 1940–45* [*Struggles and Casualties of the Greek Army during World War II, 1940–45*]. Athens: DIS.

GES/DIS. 1998. *Αρχεία Εμφυλίου Πολέμου, (1944–49). Τόμος 3* [*Civil War Archives (1944–1949). Vol. 3*]. Athens: DIS.

GES/DIS. 1998. *Αρχεία Εθνικής Αντίστασης (1941–1944). Τόμος 8. (Κατοχικές Αρχές-Τάγματα Ασφαλείας, Εγκληματικές Ενέργειες των Βουλγάρων).* [*Archives of National*

Resistance (1941–1944). Vol.8 (Occupation Authorities, Security Battalions, Bulgarian Criminal Activities)]. Athens: DIS.

Ghazarosyan H. 1998. Ἡ συμμετοχή τῶν Ἑλληνο-Ἀρμενίων στον εθνικο-απελευθερωτικό αγώνα του ελληνικού λαού (1941–1944)' ['The Participation of Greek-Armenians in the National-Liberating Struggle of the Greek People (1941–1944)'], in Μακεδονία και Θράκη, 1941–44. Κατοχή-Αντίσταση-Απελευθέρωση. [Macedonia and Thrace, 1941–44. Occupation-Resistance-Liberation]. International Conference. Thessaloniki 9–11 December 1994. Thessaloniki: Institute for Balkan Studies. 279–295.

Gladstone W.E. 1876. Bulgarian Horrors and the Question of the East. London: John Murray.

Gökalp Z. 2005. Αρχές Τουρκισμού. [The Principles of Turkism]. Athens: Kurier.

Güven D. 2006. Εθνικισμός, κοινωνικές μεταβολές και μειονότητες. Τα επεισόδια εναντίον των μη μουσουλμάνων της Τουρκίας (6/7 Σεπτεμβρίου 1955). [Nationalism, Social Changes and the Minorities. The Riots against the Non-Muslimsof Turkey (6/7 September 1955)]. Athens: Estia.

Hale W. 2000. Turkish Foreign Policy 1774–2000. London and Portland: Frank Cass.

Hall R.C. 2000. The Balkan Wars 1912–1913. Prelude to the First World War. London and New York: Routledge.

Haslinger P. 2003. 'Minorities and Territories – Ways to Conceptualise Identification and Group Cohesion in Greece and in the Balkans'. Jahrbuecher fuer Geschichte und Kultur Suedosteuropas. [History and Culture of South Eastern Europe – An Annual Journal]. 5: 'Minorities in Greece. Historical Issues and New Perspectives' edited by Trubeta S. and Voss C. 15–26.

Hassiotis I.K. 2002. 'Armenians', in Clogg R. (ed.). Minorities in Greece. Aspects of a Plural Society. London: Hurst. 94–111.

Helsinki Watch. 1990. Report, Destroying Ethnic Identity, The Turks of Greece. New York: Human Rights Watch.

Helsinki Watch. 1999. Report, Greece: The Turks of Western Thrace. Vol. 11. No. 1 (D). New York: Human Rights Watch.

Herakleides A. 2001. Η Ελλάδα και ο 'εξ ανατολών κίνδυνος'. [Greece and the 'Eastern Threat']. Athens: Polis.

Herzfeld M. 1980. 'Honour and Shame: Problems in the Analysis of Moral Systems'. Man (New Series). 15(2). 339–351.

Hiden J. 2004. Defender of Minorities: Paul Schiemann 1876–1944. London: Hurst.

Hiden J. and Smith D.J. 2006. 'Looking beyond the Nation State: A Baltic Vision for National Minorities between the Wars'. Journal of Contemporary History. 41. 387–399.

Hirschon R. 1998. Heirs of the Greek Catastrophe. The Social Life of Asia Minor Refugees in Piraeus. New York and Oxford: Berghahn Books.

Hirschon R. (ed.). 2003. Crossing the Aegean, An Appraisal of the 1923 Compulsory Population Exchange Between Greece and Turkey. New York and Oxford: Bergham Books.

Hirschon R. 2006. 'Knowledge of Diversity : Towards a more Differentiated Set of "Greek" perceptions of "Turks"'. South European Society and Politics. 11(1). 61–78.

Hirschon R. 2009. 'Religion and Nationality: The Tangled Greek Case', in Rik Pinxten and Lisa Dikomitis (eds), When God Comes to Town. New York and Oxford: Berghahn Books. 3–16.

Hupchick D. 2002. The Balkans: From Constantinople to Communism. New York: Palgrave.

Hondros J.L. 1993. Occupation and Resistance: The Greek Agony 1941–44. New York: Pella.

Iatrides J.O. (ed.). 1981. *Greece in the 1940s. A Nation in Crisis*. Hanover and London: University Press of New England.

Iğsiz A. 2008. 'Documenting the Past and Publicizing Personal Stories: Sensescapes and the 1923 Greco-Turkish Population Exchange in Contemporary Turkey'. *Journal of Modern Greek Studies*. 26. 451–487.

Iliou Ph. 2005. *Ο Ελληνικός Εμφύλιος Πόλεμος, Η εμπλοκή του ΚΚΕ* [*The Greek Civil War, The Entanglement of the KKE*]. Athens: Themelio/ASKI.

Ioannidis G. 1979. *Αναμνήσεις, προβλήματα της πολιτικής του ΚΚΕ στην εθνική αντίσταση* [*Memoirs, Problems of the KKE Policy on National Resistance*]. Athens: Themelio.

Janos A.C. 1982. *The Politics of Backwardness in Hungary*. Princeton: Princeton University Press.

Jelavich B. 1997. *History of the Balkans. Vol. I. Eighteenth and Nineteenth Centuries*. Cambridge: Cambridge University Press.

Jenkins R. 1961. *The Dilessi Murders*. London: Longman.

Jonchev D. 1993. *България и Беломорието (октомври 1940–9 септември1944г.) Военнополитически аспекти*. [*Bulgaria and the Aegean Region (October 1940 – September 1944) from a Military and Historical Perspective*]. Sofia: Dirum.

Jones H. 1985. 'The Diplomacy of Restraint: The United States' Efforts to Repatriate Greek Children Evacuated During the Civil War of 1946–49'. *Journal of Modern Greek Studies*. 3(1). 65–85.

Justice for Bulgaria Committee (The). 1946. *Bulgaria Claims Western Thrace*. Sofia.

Kalantzis E. 1969. *Σαράντα Χρόνια Αναμνήσεις, 1920–1961: Μια ζωή αφιερωμένη στην Πατρίδα* [*Forty Years of Memories, 1920–1961: A Lifetime Dedicated to the Fatherland*] Athens.

Kalionski A. and Kolev V. 2004. Οι πρόσφυγες στη Βουλγαρία την εποχή του Μεσοπολέμου: Προβλήματα ένταξης'. ['Refugees in Bulgaria during the Interwar Period. Problems of Integration'], in Gounaris V.K. and Michailidis I.D. (eds). *Πρόσφυγες στα Βαλκάνια. Μνήμη και Ενσωμάτωση. [Refugees in the Balkans. Memory and Incorporation*]. Athens: Patakis. 287–328.

Kalyvas S. 2003. 'Μορφές, Διαστάσεις και πρακτικές της βίας στον Εμφύλιο (1943–1949): Μια πρώτη προσέγγιση' ['Forms, Dimensions and Practices of Violence in the Civil War (1943–1949): A First Approach'], in Nikolakopoulos E., Rigos A. and Psallidas G. (eds). *Ο Εμφύλιος Πόλεμος, Από τη Βάρκιζα στο Γράμμο, Φεβρουάριος 1945 – Αύγουστος 1949*. [*The Civil War, From Varkiza to Grammos, February 1945– August 1949*]. Athens:Themelio. 188–207.

Kalyvas S. 2003a. Εμφύλιος Πόλεμος (1943–1949): Το τέλος των μύθων και η στροφή προς το μαζικό επίπεδο. [The Civil War (1943–1949): The End of Myths and the Turn toward the Mass Level]. *Επιστήμη και Κοινωνίας. [Epistimi kai Koinonia]*. 11. 37–70.

Kalyvas S. 2006. *The Logic of Violence in Civil War*. Cambridge: Cambridge University Press.

Kandylakis M. 2006. *Ο μυστικός τύπος της εθνικής αντιστάσεως στη βόρεια Ελλάδα, Καταγραφή των εφημερίδων που κυκλοφόρησαν στη Θεσσαλονίκη και στη Μακεδονία και Θράκη* [*The Secret Press of National Resistance in Northern Greece, A List of the Newspapers Circulating in Thessaloniki and Macedonia and Thrace*]. Thessaloniki: University Studio Press/Ekfrasi.

Karal E.Z. 1997. 'The Principles of Kemalism', in Kazancigil A. and Özbudun E. (eds). *Ataturk, Founder of a Modern State*. London: Hurst. 11–35.

Karamandjukov H.I. 1934. *Западнотракийските Българи в своето културно-историческо минало, с особен поглед към тяхното политико-революционно дҗизхение, Книга I, Историята им до 1903г.* [*Western Thracian Bulgarians in their Cultural-Political Past, with particular Attention to their Political-Revolutionary Movement, Volume I. Their History up until 1903*]. Sofia. 1934.

Karpat K.H. 1982. 'Millets and Nationality: The Roots of the Incongruity of Nation and State in the post-Ottoman Era', in Braude B. and Lewis B. (eds). *Christians and Jews in the Ottoman Empire. Vol. I. The Central Lands.* London: Holmes and Meier. 141–169.

Karpat K. 1985. *Ottoman Population, 1830–1914: Demographic and Social Characteristics.* Madison: University of Wisconsin Press.

Kasaba R. (ed.). 2008. *The Cambridge History of Turkey. Volume 4: Turkey in the Modern World.* Cambridge: Cambridge University Press.

Kasapis V. (Kriton). 1977. *Στον Κόρφο της Γκύμπρενας, Χρονικό της Εθνικής Αντίστασης στον Έβρο* [*On the Slopes of Gkybrena, A Chronicle of National Resistance in Evros*]. Vol I–II. Alexandroupolis.

Kasapis V. (Kriton). 1999. *Ο Εμφύλιος στον Έβρο (1946–1949)* [*The Civil War in Evros (1946–49)*]. Alexandroupolis.

Kayali H. 2008. 'The Struggle for Independence', in Kasaba R. (ed.). 2008. *The Cambridge History of Turkey. Volume 4: Turkey in the Modern World.* Cambridge: Cambridge University Press. 112–146.

Kazamias G. 2002. 'Το τέλος της Κατοχής. Το διεθνές και διπλωματικό παρασκήνιο και η αποχώρηση των Βουλγάρων από την Ανατολική Μακεδονία και τη Θράκη', in Kotzageorgi-Zymari X. (ed.) *Η Βουλγαρική Κατοχή στην Ανατολική Μακεδονία και τη Θράκη 1941–1944* [*The Bulgarian Occupation in Eastern Macedonia and Thrace 1941–1944*]. Thessaloniki: Paratiritis. 235–272.

Kazamias G. 2008. 'The Politics of Famine Relief for Occupied Greece', in Clogg R. (ed.). *Bearing Gifts to Greeks. Humanitarian Aid to Greece in the 1940s.* London: Palgrave Macmillan. 39–57.

Kazancigil A. and Özbudun E. (eds). 1997. *Ataturk, Founder of a Modern State.* London: Hurst.

Ker-Lindsay J. 2007. *Crisis and Conciliation, A Year of Rapprochement between Greece and Turkey.* London: I.B. Tauris.

Kerner R.J. and Howard H.N. 1936. *The Balkan Conferences and the Balkan Entente 1930–1935, A Study in the Recent History of the Balkan and Near Eastern Peoples.* Berkeley: University of California Press.

Keyder Ç. 2003. 'The Consequences of the Exchange of Populations for Turkey', in Hirschon R. (ed.). *Crossing the Aegean, An Appraisal of the 1923 Compulsory Population Exchange Between Greece and Turkey.* Oxford: Bergham Books. 39–52.

Keyder Ç. 2005. 'A History and Geography of Turkish Nationalism', in Birtek F. and Dragonas Th. (eds). *Citizenship and the Nation-State in Greece and Turkey.* London: Routledge. 3–17.

Kinross P. 1995. *Ataturk, The Rebirth of a Nation.* London: Phoenix.

Kitromilides P.M. 1990. '"Imagined Communities" and the Origins of the National Question in the Balkans' in Blinkhorn M. and Veremis Th. (eds). *Nationalism and Nationality.* Athens: ELIAMEP. 23–66.

Kitsikis D. 1990. *Η Ελλάς της 4ης Αυγούστου και οι Μεγάλες Δυνάμεις, Τα Αρχεία του Ελληνικού Υπουργείου Εξωτερικών 1936–1940.* [*Greece of the 4th August and the Great Powers, The Archives of the Greek Foreign Ministry 1936–1940*]. Athens: Eleftheri Skepsis.

KKE. 1974. *Επίσημα Κείμενα. Τόμος 2. 1925–1928.* [*Official Documents. Vol. 2. 1925–1928*]. Athens: Synchroni Epochi.

KKE. 1975. *Επίσημα Κείμενα. Τόμος 4. 1934–1940. [Official Documents. Vol. 4. 1934–1940]*. Athens: Synchroni Epochi.

KKE. 1981a. *Επίσημα Κείμενα. Τόμος 5. 1940–1945. [Official Documents. Vol. 5. 1940–1945]*. Athens: Synchroni Epochi.

KKE. 1981b. *Ιστορικό Τμήμα της ΚΕ του ΚΚΕ, Κείμενα της Εθνικής Αντίστασης. Τόμος I (ΕΑΜ,ΕΕΑΜ,ΕΛΑΣ,ΕΑ,ΕΠΟΝ,Κίνημα Μέσης Ανατολής). [History Department of the Central Committee of the KKE. Documents of the National Resistance. Vol. I. (EAM, EEAM, ELAS, EA, EPON, Movement in the Middle East)]*. Athens: Synchroni Epochi.

KKE. 1981b. *Ιστορικό Τμήμα της ΚΕ του ΚΚΕ, Κείμενα της Εθνικής Αντίστασης, Τόμος 2 (ΠΕΕΑ, Εθνικό Συμβούλιο). [History Department of the Central Committee of the KKE. Documents of the National Resistance. Vol. II. (PEEA, National Council)]*. Athens: Synchroni Epochi.

KKE. 2001. *Δοκίμιο Ιστορίας του ΚΚΕ, 1918–1949, Τόμος I. [Historical Documents on the History of the KKE, 1918–1949, Vol. I]*. Athens: Synchroni Epochi.

Knatchbull-Hugessen H. (2000). *Β' Παγκόσμιος Πόλεμος, Απομνημονεύματα (1939–1945). [World War II, Memoirs (1939–1945)]*. Athens: Thetili.

Kofos E. 1964. *Nationalism and Communism in Macedonia*. Thessaloniki: Institute for Balkan Studies.

Koliopoulos J. 1987. *Brigands with a Cause. Brigandage and Irredentism in Modern Greece, 1821–1912*. Oxford: Clarendon Press.

Koliopoulos J. 1999. *Plundered Loyalties. Axis Occupation and Civil Strife in Greek West Macedonia, 1941–49*. London: Hurst.

Koliopoulos J.S. and Veremis T.M. 2002. *Greece, The Modern Sequel, From 1831 to the Present*. London: Hurst.

Kondis. V. 1986. *Η Αγγλοαμερικανική πολιτική και το ελληνικό πρόβλημα: 1945–1949. [The Anglo-American Policy and the Greek Problem: 1945–1949]*. Thessaloniki: Paratiritis.

Konstantaras K. 1964. *Αγώνες και Διωγμοί. [Struggles and Persecutions]*. Athens.

Konstantinov Y. 1997. 'Strategies for Sustaining a Vulnerable Identity: The Case of the Bulgarian Pomaks', in Poulton H. and Taji-Farouki S. (eds). *Muslim Identity and the Balkan State*. London: Hurst & Co. 33–53.

Kontogiorgi E. 2006. *Population Exchange in reek Macedonia. The Rural Settlement of Refugees 1922–1930*. Oxford: Oxford University Press.

Kotzageorgi-Zymari X. (ed.). 2002. *Η Βουλγαρική Κατοχή στην Ανατολική Μακεδονία και τη Θράκη 1941–1944 [The Bulgarian Occupation in Eastern Macedonia and Thrace 1941–1944]*. Thessaloniki: Paratiritis.

Kotzageorgi X. and Kazamias G. 1994. 'The Bulgarian Occupation of the Prefecture of Drama (1941–44) and its Consequences on the Greek Population'. *Balkan Studies*. 35(1). 81–112.

Kotzageorgi X. and Kazamias G. 2002. 'Οι επιπτώσεις της Βουλγαρικής Κατοχής στον οικονομικό βίο της Ανατ. Μακεδονίας και της Θράκης'. ['The Consequences of the Bulgarian Occupation on the Economic Life of Eastern Macedonia and Thrace'], in Kotzageorgi-Zymari X. (ed.). *Η Βουλγαρική Κατοχή στην Ανατολική Μακεδονία και τη Θράκη 1941–1944. [The Bulgarian Occupation in Eastern Macedonia and Thrace 1941–1944]*. Thessaloniki: Paratiritis. 107–135.

Kourtovik G. 1997. 'Justice and the Minorities', [Δικαιοσύνη και Μειονότητες] in Tsitselikis K., and Christopoulos D. (eds). *The Minority Phenomenon in Greece. A Social Sciences Contribution. [Το μειονοτικό φαινόμενο στην Ελλάδα. Μια συμβολή των κοινωνικών επιστημών]*. Athens: Kritiki/Kemo. 245–280.

Kousoulas E. 1965. *Revolution and Defeat, The Story of the Greek Communist Party*. London: Oxford University Press.

Küçükcan T. 1999. 'Re-claiming Identity: Ethnicity, Religion and Politics among Turkish-Muslims in Bulgaria and Greece'. *Journal of Minority Affairs*. 19(1). 59–78.

Kuniholm B.R. 1980. *The Origins of the Cold War in the Near East, Great Power Conflict and Diplomacy in Iran, Turkey and Greece*. Princeton: Princeton University Press.

Kyriakidis S.P. 1919. *Η Δυτική Θράκη και οι Βούλγαροι*. [*Western Thrace and the Bulgarians*]. Athens: Sideris.

Kyrou A.K. 2008. 'The Greek-American Community and the Famine in Axis-occupied Greece', in Clogg R. (ed.). *Bearing Gifts to Greeks. Humanitarian Aid to Greece in the 1940s*. London: Palgrave Macmillan. 58–84.

Ladas S.P. 1932. *The Exchange of Minorities, Bulgaria, Greece and Turkey*. New York: Macmillan.

Laiou A. 2002. 'Μετακινήσεις πληθυσμού στην ελληνική ύπαιθρο κατά τη διάρκεια του εμφυλίου πολέμου'. ['Population Movements in the Greek Countryside during the Civil War'], in Baerentzen L., Iatrides J.O. and Smith O.L. (eds). *Μελέτες για τον Εμφύλιο Πόλεμο 1945–1949*. [*Studies in the History of the Greek Civil War 1945–1949*]. Athens: Olkos. 67–114.

Landau J.M. 2004. *Exploring Ottoman and Turkish History*. London: Hurst.

League of Nations. 1934a. *Treaty Series*. Vol. 3514.

League of Nations. 1934b. *Treaty Series*. No. 4493.

Leitz C. 2000. *Nazi Germany and Neutral Europe during the Second World War*. Manchester: Manchester University Press.

Lewis B. 1965. *The Emergence of Modern Turkey*. London: Oxford University Press.

Lewis G. 1965. *Turkey*. London: Ernest Benn.

Lipordezis G. 2002. *Τρεις Αιώνες Έξη Γενεές Μια Ιστορία*. [*Three Centuries Six Generations, One Story*], Sapes.

Lithoxoou D. 2006. *Μειονοτικά ζητήματα και εθνική συνείδηση στην Ελλάδα*. [*Minority Issues and National Consciousness in Greece*]. Thessaloniki: Batavia.

Llewellyn Smith M. 1998. *Ionian Vision, Greece in Asia Minor 1919–1922*. London: Hurst.

Lory B. 1989. 'Ahmed Aga Tamrashliyata: The Last Derebey of the Rhodopes'. *International Journal of Turkish Studies*. 4(2). 179–201.

Lymberatos M. 2006. *Στα πρόθυρα του Εμφυλίου Πολέμου, Από τα Δεκεμβριανά στις εκλογές του 1946. Κοινωνική πόλωση, αριστερά και αστικός κόσμος στη μεταπολεμική Ελλάδα*. [*On the Verge of Civil War. From Dekemvriana to the Elections of 1946. Social Polarization, the Left and the Bourgeois World in Post-War Greece*]. Athens: BiBliorama.

Lymberiou T. 2005. *Το κομμουνιστικό κίνημα στην Ελλάδα. Τόμος I*. [*The Communist Movement in Greece. Vol. I*). Athens: Papazisis.

Macar E. 2008. 'The Turkish Contribution to Famine Relief in Greece during the Second World War' , in Clogg R. (ed.). *Bearing Gifts to Greeks. Humanitarian Aid to Greece in the 1940s*. London: Palgrave Macmillan. 85–96.

Macartney C.A. 1931. *Refugees. The Work of the League*. London: League of Nations Union.

Macartney C.A. 1934. *National States and National Minorities*. London: Humphrey Milford and Oxford University Press.

Mair L. P. 1928. *The Protection of Minorities: The Working and Scope of Minorities treaties under the League of Nations*. London: Christophers.

Malkidis Th. 2004. 'Η διαμάχη "παλαιομουσουλμάνων" – κεμαλικών στην ελλαδική Θράκη την περίοδο του Μεσοπολέμου'. ['The Dispute between "Old-Muslims" – Kemalists in Greek Thrace during the Interwar Period]. *Νέα Κοινωνιολογία*. [*Nea Koinoniologia*]. 39. 73–87.

Malkidis Th. and Kokkas N. 2006. *Μετασχηματισμοί της συλλογικής ταυτότητας των Πομάκων* [*Transformations of the Collective Identity of the Pomaks*]. Xanthi: Spanidis.

Mamarelis A. 2004. *The Rise and Fall of the 5/42 Regiment of Evzones: A Study on National Resistance and Civil war in Greece 1941–1944*. PhD thesis. The London School of Economics and Political Science.

Mango A. 2008. 'Atatürk', in Kasaba R. (ed.). *The Cambridge History of Turkey. Volume 4: Turkey in the Modern World*. Cambridge: Cambridge University Press. 147–173.

Mango A. 1999. *Atatürk*. London: John Murray.

Manta E. 2004. *Οι μουσουλμάνοι Τσάμηδες της Ηπείρου (1923–2000)*. [*The Muslim Chams of Epirus (1923–2000)*]. Thessaloniki: Institute for Balkan Studies (IMXA).

Marantzidis N. 2001. *Γιασασίν Μιλλέτ, Ζήτω το Έθνος, Προσφυγιά, Κατοχή και Εμφύλιος: Εθνοτική Ταυτότητα και Πολιτική συμπεριφορά στους τουρκόφωνους ελληνορθόδοξους του δυτικού Πόντου*. [*Yaşasin Millet, Long Live the Nation. Refugees, Occupation and the Civil War, Ethnic Identity and Political Behaviour amongst the Greek-Orthodox of Western Pontus*]. Heracleion: University Press of Crete.

Marantzidis N. (ed.). 2006a. *Οι Άλλοι Καπετάνιοι, Αντικομμουνιστές ένοπλοι στα χρόνια της Κατοχής και του Εμφυλίου*. [*The Other Kapetanios. Anti-Communist Fighters during the Occupation and the Civil War*]. Athens: Estia.

Marantzidis N. 2006b. 'Οι ένοπλοι εθνικιστές αρχηγοί της Κατοχής στην Βόρεια Ελλάδα'. ['The armed nationalist war-lords of northern Greece during the Occupation], in Marantzidis N. (ed.). *Οι Άλλοι Καπετάνιοι, Αντι-κομμουνιστές ένοπλοι στα χρόνια της Κατοχής και του Εμφυλίου*. [*The Other Kapetanios. Anti-Communist Fighters during the Occupation and the Civil War*]. Athens: Estia. 27–61.

Margaritis G. 2001. *Ιστορία του Ελληνικού Εμφυλίου Πολέμου, 1946–1949* [*History of the Greek Civil War (1946–49)*]. Vol. I–II. Athens: Bibliorama.

Margaritis G. 2005. *Τσάμηδες – Εβραίοι. Ανεπιθύμητοι συμπατριώτες. Στοιχεία για την καταστροφή των μειονοτήτων της Ελλάδας*. [*Chams – Jews. Unwanted Compatriots. Evidence about the Elimination of Minorities in Greece*]. Athens: Vivliorama.

Marushiakova E. and Popov V. 2002. 'The Muslim Minorities in Bulgaria'. (http://www.islamawareness.net/Europe/Bulgaria/bulgaria_article0003.pdf, accessed on 10 August 2009).

Mavrogordatos G. 1981. 'The 1946 Election and Plebiscite: Prelude to Civil War', in Iatrides J.O. (ed). *Greece in the 1940s. A Nation in Crisis*. Hanover and London: University Press of New England. 181–194.

Mavrogordatos G. 1983. *Stillborn Republic. Social Coalitions and Party Strategies in Greece, 1922–1936*. Berkeley: University of California Press.

Mavrommatis G. 2004. *Τα παιδιά της Καλκάντζας. Εκπαίδευση, φτώχεια και κοινωνικός αποκλεισμός σε μια κοινότητα μουσουλμάνων της Θράκης*. [*The Kids of Kalkantza. Education, Poverty and Social Exclusion in a Muslim Community of Thrace*]. Athens: Metaichmio.

Mazower M. 1998. *Dark Continent. Europe's Twentieth Century*. London: The Penguin Press.

Mazower M. (ed.) 2000. *After the War was Over. Reconstructing the Family, Nation and State in Greece, 1943–60*. Princeton and Oxford: Princeton University Press.

Mazower M. 2001. *Inside Hitler's Greece. The Experience of the Occupation, 1941–44*. New Haven and London: Yale University Press.

Mehmet H. 2007. *Помаците и торбешите в Мизия, Тракия и Македония*. [*The Pomaks and the Torbeshes in Moesia, Thrace and Macedonia*]. Sofia.

Meinardus R. 2002. 'Muslims: Turks, Pomaks and Gypsies', in Clogg R. (ed.). *Minorities in Greece, Aspects of a Plural Society*. London: Hurst. 81–93.

Mekos Z.K. 2002. *Ριζώσαμε στην Κομοτηνή. Πόλεμοι, Καταστροφές, προσφυγιές, εμφύλιες διαμάχες, κατοχές, Ιστορική και Λαογραφική προσέγγιση της Ιστορίας της νεότερης και σύγχρονης Θράκης και Κομοτηνής.* [*We Settled in Komotini. Wars, Destructions, Refugees, Civil Wars, Occupations. A Historical and Laographic Approach to the Modern History of Thrace and Komotini*]. Thessaloniki: Herodotus.

Melas S. 1958. *Οι πόλεμοι 1912–1913.* [*The Wars of 1912–1913*]. Athens: Biris.

Metaxas I. 1964. *Το Προσωπικό μου Ημερολόγιο,* [*Diary*], Vol. I–VI, Athens.

Michail D. 2003. 'From "Locality" to "European Identity": Shifting Identities among the Pomak Minority in Greece'. Paper presented at the *2nd Conference of the International Association for Southeasterm Anthropology* (in ASEA). Graz. February 20–23.

Michailidis I.D. 2003. *Μετακινήσεις σλαβόφωνων πληθυσμών (1912–1930). Ο πόλεμος των στατιστικών.* [*Population Movements of the Slavophone Population (1912–1930). The War of Statistics*]. Athens: KEMO/Kritiki.

Miller W. 1913. *The Ottoman Empire 1801–1913.* Oxford: Oxford University Press.

Miller W. 1931. 'The Greco-Turkish Friendship'. *Contemporary Review.* 140. 718–726.

Miller M.L. 1975. *Bulgaria during the Second World War.* California: Stanford University Press.

Minaidis M. 1984. 'Συμβολή στην Ιστορία της Θράκης'. ['A Contribution to the History of Thrace']. *Θρακική Επετηρίδα* [*Thrakiki Epetirida*]. 5. 111–126.

Ministry of National Economy. General Statistical Service of Greece. 1928a. *Στατιστική των βουλευτικών εκλογών της 7ης Νοεμβρίου 1926.* [*Statistics of the National Elections, 7 November 1926*]. Athens: Ethniko Typografeio.

Ministry of National Economy. General Statistical Service of Greece. 1928. *Απογραφή του πληθυσμού της Ελλάδος κατά την 19 Δεκεμβρίου 1920* [*Statistic Results of the Greek Population Census of 19 December 1920*]. Athens: Ethniko Typografeio.

Ministry of National Economy. General Statistical Service of Greece. 1931a. *Στατιστική των βουλευτικών εκλογών της 19ης Αυγούστου 1928.* [*Statistics of the National Elections, 19 August 1928*]. Athens: Ethniko Typografeio.

Ministry of National Economy. General Statistical Service of Greece. 1931. *Στατιστική των γερουσιαστικών εκλογών της 21ης Απριλίου 1929.* [*Statistics of the Elections for the Senate, 21 April 1929*]. Athens: Ethniko Typografeio.

Ministry of National Economy. General Statistical Service of Greece. 1933. *Στατιστική των βουλευτικών εκλογών της 25ης Σεπτεμβρίου 1932.* [*Statistics of the National Elections, 25 September 1932*]. Athens: Ethniko Typografeio.

Ministry of National Economy. General Statistical Service of Greece. 1934. *Στατιστική των γερουσιαστικών εκλογών της 25ης Σεπτεμβρίου 1932 και των μέχρι τέλους του 1933 αναπληρωματικών τοιούτων.* [*Statistics of the Elections for the Senate, 25 September 1932 and of the Supplementary ones in 1933*]. Athens: Ethniko Typografeio.

Ministry of National Economy. General Statistical Service of Greece. 1935a. *Στατιστική των εκλογών της Εθνικής Συνελεύσεως της 9ης Ιουνίου 1935.* [*Statistics of the Elections for the National Assembly, 9 June 1935*]. Athens: Ethniko Typografeio.

Ministry of National Economy. General Statistical Service of Greece. 1935. *Στατιστικά αποτελέσματα της απογραφής του πληθυσμού της Ελλάδος της 15–16 Μαΐου 1928* [*Statistic Results of the Greek Population Census of 15–16 May 1928*]. Vol. 1 and 4. Athens: Ethniko Typografeio.

Ministry of National Economy. General Statistical Service of Greece. 1938. *Στατιστική των βουλευτικών εκλογών της 26ης Ιανουαρίου 1936.* [*Statistics of the National Elections, 26 January 1936*]. Athens: Ethniko Typografeio.

Ministry of National Economy. General Statistical Service of Greece. 1947a. *Στατιστική των βουλευτικών εκλογών της 31ης Μαρτίου 1946.* [*Statistics of the National Elections, 31 March 1946*]. Athens: Ethniko Typografeio.

Ministry of National Economy. General Statistical Service of Greece. 1947b. *Στατιστική του δημοψηφίσματος της 1ης Σεπτεμβρίου 1946.* [*Statistics of the Plebiscite of 1 September 1946*]. Athens: Ethniko Typografeio.

Ministry of National Economy. General Statistical Service of Greece. 1950. *Πληθυσμός της Ελλάδος κατά την απογραφήν της 16 Οκτωβρίου 1940* [*Statistic Results of the Greek Population Census of 16 October 1940*]. Athens: Ethniko Typografeio.

Ministry of National Economy. General Statistical Service of Greece. 1958. *Αποτελέσματα της απογραφής του πληθυσμού της 7 Απριλίου 1951* [*Statistic Results of the Greek Population Census of 7 April 1951*]. Vol. 1 and 2. Athens: Ethniko Typografeio.

Ministry of Foreign Affairs of Greece. Service of Historical Archives. *The Foundation of the Modern Greek State. Major Treaties and Conventions (1830–1947).* Athens: Kastaniotis.

Moore B. (ed.) 2000. *Resistance in Western Europe.* Oxford and New York: Berg.

Morgenthau H. (in collaboration with Strother F.). 1930. *An International Drama.* London: Jarrolds.

Myers E.C.W. (1975). *Η Ελληνική Περιπλοκή, Οι Βρετανοί στην Κατεχόμενη Ελλάδα.* [*The Greek Entanglement*]. Athens: Exandas.

Nachmani A. 1990. 'Civil War and Foreign Intervention in Greece: 1946–49'. *Journal of Contemporary History.* 25(4). 489–522.

Naltsas C.A. 1946. *Τα ελληνοσλαυϊκά σύνορα. Αι προς βορράν εθνικαί μας διεκδικήσεις.* [*The Greco-Slav Borders. Our National Claims towards the North*]. Thessaloniki: Etaireia Makidonikon Spoudon.

Nefeloudis P. 1974. *Στις Πηγές της κακοδαιμονίας. Τα βαθύτερα αίτια της διάσπασης του ΚΚΕ 1918–1968. Επίσημα κείμενα και προσωπικές εμπειρίες.* [*The Sources of Misfortune. The Deeper Reasons for the Split of the KKE 1918–1968. Official Documents and Personal Experiences*]. Athens: Gutenberg.

Neuburger M. 2000. 'Pomak Borderlands: Muslims on the Edge of Nations'. *Nationalities Papers.* 28(1). 181–198.

Niarchos G. 2005. *Between Ethnicity, Religion and Politics: Foreign Policy and the Treatment of Minorities in Greece and Turkey, 1923–1974.* PhD Thesis. The London School of Economics and Political Science.

Nikolakopoulos E. 1990–1991. 'Πολιτικές Δυνάμεις και Εκλογική Συμπεριφορά της Μουσουλμανικής Μειονότητας στη Δυτική Θράκη: 1923–1955'. ['Political Forces and Electoral Bahaviour of the Muslim Minority of Western Thrace: 1923–1955']. *Δελτίο Κέντρου Μικρασιατικών Σπουδών* [*Deltio Kentrou Mikrasiatikon Spoudon*]. Vol. 8. Athens. 171–199.

Nikolakopoulos E. 2009. *Η Καχεκτική Δημοκρατία. Κόμματα και Εκλογές, 1946–1967.* [*The Struggling Democracy. Parties and Elections, 1946–1967*]. Athens: Patakis.

Ökte F. 1987. *The Tragedy of the Turkish Capital Tax.* London: Croom Helm.

Öksüz H. 2000/2001. 'Western Thracian Turks in Greek Civil War (1946–1949)'. *Turkish Review of Balkan Studies.* 5. 53–65.

Öksüz H. 2002. 'Representation of the Western Thracian Turkish Minority in the Greek Parliament'. *Turkish Review of Balkan Studies.* 135–152.

Öksüz H. 2003. 'The Reason for Immigration from Western Thrace to Turkey (1923–1950)'. *Turkish Review of Balkan Studies.* 249–278.

Oran B. 1984. 'The Inhanli Land Dispute and the Status of the Turks in Western Thrace'. *Journal of Muslim Minority Affairs*. 5(2). 360–370.

Oran B. 1986. *Türk-Yunan İlişkilerinde Batı Trakya Sorunu*. Ankara: Mülkiyeliler Birliği Vakfı.

Oran B. 1988. 'La minorité Turco-Musulmane de la Thrace Occidentale (Gréce)', in Vaner S. (ed.). *Le Différent Gréco-Turc*. Paris: Editions L' Harmattan. 145–161.

Oran B. 1994. 'Religious and national identity among the Balkan Muslims: A Comparative Study on Greece, Bulgaria, Macedonia, and Kossovo'. *CEMOTI* (Cahiers d'études sur la Méditerranée Orientale et le Monde Turco-Iranien). No. 18. 308–323.

Oran B. 2003. 'The Story of Those Who Stayed, Lessons from Articles 1 and 2 of the 1923 Convention', in Hirschon R. (ed.). *Crossing the Aegean, An Appraisal of the 1923 Compulsory Population Exchange Between Greece and Turkey*. Oxford: Bergham Books. 97–115.

Örs I.R. 2006. 'Beyond the Greek and Turkish dichotomy: the Rum-Polites of Istanbul and Athens'. *South European Society and Politics*. 11(1). 79–94.

Özkırımlı U. and Sofos A.S. 2008. *Tormented by History: Nationalism in Greece and Turkey*. London: Hurst.

Pallis A.A. 1925. *Στατιστική μελέτη περί των φυλετικών μεταναστεύσεων Μακεδονίας και Θράκης κατά την περίοδο 1912–1924*. [*Statistical Study of the Racial Migrations in Macedonia and Thrace during 1912–1924*]. Athens.

Pallis A.A. 1930. 'The End of the Greco-Turkish Feud'. *Contemporary Review*. 138. 614–620.

Papadimitriou P.G. 2003. *Οι Πομάκοι της Ροδόπης, Από της εθνοτικές σχέσεις στους Βαλκανικούς Εθνικισμούς 1870–1990*. [*The Pomaks of Rhodope, From Ethnic Relations to Balkan Nationalisms 1870–1990*]. Thessaloniki: Kyriakidis Bros.

Papaevgeniou A. 1946. *Βόρειος Ελλάς. Μειονότητες από στατιστικής απόψεως εν σχέσει με τον πληθυσμόν και την εκπαίδευσιν*. [*Northern Greece. Minorities from a Statistical Perspective with Respect to the Population and Education*]. Thessaloniki.

Papagos A. 1995. *Ο πόλεμος της Ελλάδος 1940–41*. [*The War of Greece 1940–41*]. Athens: Goulandri-Horn Foundation.

Papagos A. 1997. *Ο Ελληνικός Στρατός και η προς πόλεμον προπαρασκευή του. Από Αυγούστου 1923 μέχρι Οκτωβρίου 1940*. [*The Greek Army and its War Preparation. From August 1923 until October 1940*]. Athens: Goulandri-Horn Foundation.

Papanikolaou A. 2007. *'Hak Verimler, Alınır' (Rights are not Granted, They are Taken): The 'Politicization of Rights in the Case of the Muslim-Turkish Minority in Greece*. Phd Thesis. University of Sussex.

Papastratis Th.O. 2001. *Οι Εβραίοι του Διδυμοτείχου*. [*The Jews of Didimoteichon*]. Athens: Tsoukatos Publications.

Papathanasi-Mousiopoulou K. (ed.). 1975. *Η απελευθέρωση της Δυτικής Θράκης από το αρχείο του Χαρισίου Βαμβακά*. [*The Liberation of Western Thrace. From the Archive of Harisios Vamvakas*]. Athens.

Papathanasi-Mousiopoulou K. 1982. 'Συμβολή στη διπλωματική ιστορία της Θράκης κατά το 1913 (ανέκδοτα έγγραφα Χ. Βαμβακά, Ι. Δραγούμη, Ε. Κανελλόπουλου, Α. Χαλκιοπούλου)'. ['A Contribution to the Diplomatic History of Thrace during 1913 (Unpublished Documents of H. Vamvakas, I. Dragoumis, E.Kanellopoulos, A. Chalkiopoulou]. *Θρακική Επετηρίδα*. [*Thrakiki Epetirida*]. Vol. 3. Komotini: MOK. 45–83.

Papathanasi-Mousiopoulou K. 1984. *Σελίδες Ιστορίας. Θράκη 1870–1886.* [*History Pages. Thrace 1870–1886*]. Athens: Pitsilos.

Papathanasi-Mousiopoulou K. 1991. *Θράκη. Μορφές και γεγονότα 1902–1922.* [*Thrace. Protagonists and Events 1902–1922*]. Athens: Pitsilos.

Papathanasiou I. 2004. 'The Cominform and the Greek Civil War, 1947–49', in Carabott P. and Sfikas T.D. (eds). *The Greek Civil War, Essays on a Conflict of Exceptionalism and Silences.* London: Ashgate. 57–71.

Paschalidis D. And Chatzianastasiou T. 2003. *Τα γεγονότα της Δράμας (Σεπτέμβριος-Οκτώβριος 1941). Εξέγερση ή προβοκάτσια;* [*The Events of Drama (September–October 1941). Uprising or Provocation?*]. Drama: Dimotiki Epiheirisi Koinonikis Politismikis kai Touristikis Anaptyxis Dimou Dramas.

Paxton R.O. 1972. *Vichy France.* New York: A.A. Knopf.

Pazarci H. 1989. *Το Καθεστώς Αποστρατικοποίησης των Νησιών του Ανατολικού Αιγαίου.* [*The Status of Demilitarization of the Islands of Eastern Aegean*], Athens: Gnosi.

Pentzopoulos D. 1962. *The Balkan Exchange of Minorities and its Impact upon Greece.* Paris: Mouton.

Pesmazoglou S. 1993. *Ευρώπη-Τουρκία. Αντανακλάσεις και διαθλάσεις. Η στρατηγική των κειμένων.* [*Europe-Turkey, Reflections and Refractions, The Strategics of Texts*]. Volume I. Athens: Themelio.

Petsalis-Diomidis N. 1978. *Greece at the Paris Peace Conference 1919.* Thessaloniki: Institute for Balkan Studies (IMXA).

Pikros I.P. 1996. *Τουρκικός Επεκτατισμός, Από το Μύθο της Ελληνοτουρκικής Φιλίας στην Πολιτική για την Αστυνόμευση των Βαλκανίων 1930–1943.* [*Turkish Expansionism, From the Myth of the Greek-Turkish Friendship to the Policy for the Policing of the Balkans 1930–1943*]. Athens: Estia.

Pirjevec J. 2002. 'Η ρήξη Τίτο-Στάλιν και το τέλος του Εμφυλίου στην Ελλαδά'. ['The Tito-Stalin Split and the End of the Civil War in Greece'], in Baerentzen L., Iatrides J.O. and Smith O.L. (eds). *Μελέτες για τον Εμφύλιο Πόλεμο 1945–1949.* [*Studies in the History of the Greek Civil War 1945–1949*]. Athens: Olkos. 331–338.

Popovic A. 1986. *L'Islam Balkanique, Les Musulmans du Sud-Est Europeen dans la periode post-Ottoman.* Berlin: Otto Harrassovitz.

Poulton H. 1997. 'Changing Notions of National Identity among Muslims in Thrace and Macedonia: Turks, Pomaks and Roma', in Poulton H. and Taji-Farouki S. (eds). *Muslim Identity and the Balkan State.* London: Hurst. 82–102.

Poulton H. 1999. *Ημίψηλο, Γκρίζος Λύκος και Ημισέληνος.* [*Top Hat, Grey Wolf and Crescent. Turkish Nationalism and the Turkish Republic*]. Athens: Odysseas.

Richter H. 1981. 'The Varkiza Agreement and the Origins of the Civil War', in Iatrides J.O. (ed.). *Greece in the 1940s. A Nation in Crisis.* Hanover and London: University Press of New England. 167–180.

Richter H. 1985. *British Intervention in Greece: from Varkiza to Civil War, February 1945 to August 1946.* London: Merlin Press.

Rousos P. 1982. *Η μεγάλη πενταετία, 1940–45.* [*Great Five Years, 1940–1945*]. Vol. I–III. Athens.

Sakkas J. 2000. 'The Civil War in Evrytania', in Mazower M. (ed.) 2000. *After the War was Over. Reconstructing the Family, Nation and State in Greece, 1943–60.* Princeton and Oxford: Princeton University Press. 184–209.

Sarris N. 1992. *Εξωτερική πολιτική και πολιτικές εξελίξεις στην πρώτη Τουρκική Δημοκρατία, Η άνοδος της στρατογραφειοκρατίας (1923–1950).* [*Foreign Policy and Political Developments in the First Turkish Republic, The Rise of Military Bureaucracy (1923–1950)*]. Athens: Gordios.

Schechtman J.B. 1946. *European Population Transfers, 1939–1945*. New York: Oxford University Press.

Shaw S.J. and Shaw E.K. 1977. *History of the Ottoman Empire and Modern Turkey. Volume II. Reform, Revolution and Republic. The Rise of Modern Turkey 1808–1975*. Cambridge: Cambridge University Press.

Schurman J.G. 1914. *The Balkan Wars: 1912–1913*. Princeton: Princeton University Press.

Seferiades S. 1928. 'L' Echange des Populations'. *Academie de Droit International Recueil des Cours*. 4. 311–433.

Simon A. 2000. *Balkan Reader: First Hand Reports by Western Correspondents and Diplomats for Over a Century*. Florida: Simon Publications.

Sfikas T.D. 1994. *The British Labor Government and the Greek Civil War, The Imperialism of Non-Intervention*. Keele: Keele University Press.

Skopetea E. 1988. *Το 'πρότυπο βασίλειο' και η Μεγάλη Ιδέα. Όψεις του εθνικού προβλήματος στην Ελλάδα (1830–1880)*. [*The 'Model Kingdom' and the Great Idea. Aspects of the National Pronlem in Greece (1830–1880)*]. Athens: Polytypo.

Skordylis K. 1994. Μειονότητες και Προπαγάνδα στη Βόρειο Ελλάδα κατά το Μεσοπόλεμο. Μια Έκθεση του Γ.Θ. Φεσσόπουλου. [Minorities and Propaganda in Northern Greece during the Inter-War Period. A Report of G.Th. Fessopoulos]. *Ίστωρ*. [*Istor*]. Issue 7. 43–91.

Smith E.D. 1959. *Turkey: Origins of the Kemalist Movement and the Government of the Grand National Assembly 1919–1923*. Washington: Judd and Detweiler Inc.

Smith A. 1981. *The Ethnic Revival*. Cambridge: Cambridge University Press.

Smith A.D. 1999. *The Ethnic Origins of Nations*. Oxford: Blackwell Publishers.

Smith A.D. 2000. 'The Sacred Dimension of Nationalism'. *Millennium: Journal of International Studies*. 29(3). 791–814.

Smith D.J. and Cordell K. (eds). 2008. *Cultural Autonomy in Contemporary Europe*. London: Routledge.

Soilentakis N. 2004. *Ιστορία του Θρακικού Ελληνισμού*. [*History of Thracian Hellenism*]. Vol. I–II. Athens: Papazisis.

Soltarides S.A. 1997. *Ιστορία των Μουφτειών της Δυτικής Θράκης*. [*The History of the Mufti Institutes of Western Thrace*]. Athens: Livanis.

Sonnichen A. 2004. *Αναμνήσεις ενός Μακεδόνα Αντάρτη*. [*Confessions of a Macedonian Bandit*]. Athens: Petsiva Publications.

Sonyel S.R. 1975. *Turkish Diplomacy 1918–1923, Mustafa Kemal and the Turkish National Movement*. London: Sage Publications Ltd.

St. Clair S.G.B. and Brophy C.A. 1869. *Residence in Bulgaria, or Notes on the Resources and Administration of Turkey*. London: John Murray.

St Clair. S.G.B. 1876. *Bulgarian Horrors and Mr. Gladstone's Eastern Policy*. London: Blanchard and Sons.

Stathakis G. 2004. *Το Δόγμα Τρούμαν και το Σχέδιο Μάρσαλ. Η ιστορία της αμερικανικής βοήθειας στην Ελλάδα*. [*The Truman Doctrine and the Marshall Plan. The History of American Aid in Greece*]. Athens: Bibliorama.

Stolingas K. 2006. *Με αίμα και δάκρυ, Από τη δοκιμασία της Αν. Μακεδονίας-Θράκης*. [*Blood and Tears. The Hardships of Eastern Macedonia-Thrace*]. Thessaloniki: Kyriakidis Bros.

Svolopoulos C.D. 1973. 'Le Probléme de la Sécurité dans le Sud-Est Européen de l'Entre-Deux-Guerres: A la Recherche des Origines du Pacte Balkanique de 1934'. *Balkan Studies*. 14. 247–292.

Svolopoulos K. 1997. *Η Ελληνική Εξωτερική Πολιτική 1900–1945*. [*The Greek Foreign Policy 1900–1945*]. Athens: Estia.

Terzoudis L. 1985. *Η εθνική αντίσταση στον Έβρο, Οι αγωνιστές μιλούν και γράφουν*. [*The National Resistance in Evros. The Fighters Speak and Write*]. Athens: Democritus.

Thrax P. 1944. *The Bulgars. Self-Styled Prussians of the Balkans*. New York: Greek Government Office of Information.

Todorova M. 1998. 'Identity (Trans)Formation among Bulgarian Muslims', in Crawford B. and Lipschutz R.D. (eds). *The Myth of 'Ethnic Conflict': Politics, Economics, and 'Cultural' Violence*. Berkeley: University of California International and Area Studies Digital Collection. 471–510.

Toynbee A.J. 1922. *The Western Question in Greece and Turkey. A Study in the Contact of Civilizations*. London: Constable and Company Ltd.

Toynbee A.J. and Kirkwood K.P. 1926. *Turkey*. London: Ernest Benn.

Toynbee A.J. (ed.). 1953. *Survey of International Affairs, 1938*. Vol. III. London: Oxford University Press.

Trifonov S. 1988. *Българското национално-освободително движение в Тракия 1919–1934*. [*Bulgarian National Liberation Movement in Thrace 1919–1934*]. Sofia. 1988.

Trubeta S. 2001. *Κατασκευάζοντας Ταυτότητες για τους Μουσουλμάνους της Θράκης, Το Παράδειγμα των Πομάκων και των Τσιγγάνων* [*Constructing Identities for the Muslims of Thrace, The Case of Pomaks and Roma*]. Athens: Kritiki/KEMO.

Trubeta S. 2003. '"Minorisation" and "Ethnicisation" in Greek Society: Comparative Perspectives on Muslim Immigrants and the Thracian Muslim Minority'. *Jahrbuecher fuer Geschichte und Kultur Suedosteuropas* [*History and Culture of South Eastern Europe – An Annual Journal*]. 5: 'Minorities in Greece. Historical Issues and New Perspectives' edited by Trubeta S. and Voss C. 95–112.

Tsekou. K. 2007. *'Οι Έλληνες πολιτικοί πρόσφυγες στη Λαϊκή Δημοκρατία της Βουλγαρίας'*. ['Greek Political Refugees in the People's Republic of Bulgaria']. *Συνέδριο: Ελληνικός Εμφύλιος πόλεμος – 60 χρόνια μετά*. [*Conference: The Greek Civil War – 60 Years After*]. Prague 5–7 October 2007.

Tsibiridou F. 2000. *Les Pomak dans la Thrace Grecque: Discours Ethnique et Pratiques Socioculturelles*. Paris: L' Harmattan.

Tsilaga F. 2008. 'UNRRA's Relief Efforts in late 1944 Greece: Political Impartiality versus Military Exigencies', in Clogg R. (ed.). *Bearing Gifts to Greeks. Humanitarian Aid to Greece in the 1940s*. London: Palgrave Macmillan. 189–211.

Tsioumis K. 1995. *'Ηγεσία και προσωπικότητα στη μουσουλμανική μειονότητα της Δυτικής Θράκης κατά την περίοδο του Μεσοπολέμου (1923–1940)'*. ['Leading Personalities of the Muslim Minority of Western Thrace during the Interwar Period (1923–1940)']. *Ενδοχώρα. [Endohora]*. 2. Alexandroupolis. 120–126.

Tsioumis K. 1997. *Οι Πομάκοι στο ελληνικό κράτος (1920–1950). Ιστορική προσέγγιση*. [*The Pomaks in the Greek State (1920–1950). A Historical Approach*]. Thessaloniki: Promytheus.

Tsioumis K. 1998. *'Η νομοθετική πολιτική για την εκπαίδευση της μουσουλμανικής μειονότητας της Δυτικής Θράκης 1923–1940'*. ['The Legislative Policy for the Education of the Muslim Minority of Western Thrace 1923–1940']. *Παιδαγωγική Επιθεώρηση. [Paidagogiki Epitheorisi]*. 27(98). 141–158.

Tsioumis K. 2006. *Η μουσουλμανική μειονότητα της Θράκης (1950–1960. Πολιτικοδιπλωματικές διεργασίες και εκπαιδευτική πολιτική*. [*The Muslim Minority of Thrace (1950–1960). Political and Diplomatic Developments and Educational Policy)*]. Thessaloniki: Ant. Stamoulis Publications.

Tsitselikes K. and Christopoulos D. (eds). 1997. *Το Μειονοτικό Φαινόμενο στην Ελλάδα, Μια Συμβολή των Κοινωνικών Επιστημών*. [*The Minority Phenomenon in Greece, A Contribution of the Social Sciences*]. Athens: Kritiki.

Tsitselikis K. (ed.). 2006. *Η ελληνοτουρκική ανταλλαγή πληθυσμών. Πτυχές μιας εθνικής σύγκρουσης. [The Greek-Turkish Population Exchange. Aspects of a National Conflict]*. Athens: Kemo/Kritiki.

Tsitselikis K. 2008. 'Reciprocity as a Regulatory Pattern for the Treatment of Greece's Turkish/Muslim Minority', in Akgönül S. (ed.). *Reciprocity. Greek and Turkish Minorities. Law. Religion and Politics*. Istanbul: Bilgi University Press. 69–102.

Tsolakoglou G. 1959. *Απομνημονεύματα. [Memoirs]*. Athens: Akropolis.

Tsonidis T.Ch. 1980. *Η Ορεστιάδα μας [Our Orestiada]*. Orestiada: Ekpolitistikos Syllogos Neon.

Tsouderos E.I. 1950. *Διπλωματικά Παρασκήνια 1941–1945. [Diplomatic Backstages 1941–1944]*. Athens: Aetos.

Turan O. 2005. 'Turkish Migrations from Bulgaria'. *Forced Ethnic Migrations on the Balkans: Consequences and Rebuilding of Societies*. Conference Proceedings. Sofia. 22–23 February. 77–93.

Türkeş M. 1994. 'The Balkan Pact and its Immediate Implications for the Balkan States, 1930–34'. *Middle Eastern Studies*. Vol. 30. Part 1. 123–144.

Vakalopoulos K.A. 2000. *Ιστορία του Βόρειου Ελληνισμού. Θράκη. [History of Northern Hellenism, Thrace]*. Thessaloniki: Kyriakidis.

Van Creveld M. 1973. *Hitler's Strategy 1940–1941. The Balkan Clue*. London: Cambridge University Press.

Vaner S. (ed.). 1988. *Le Different Greco-Turc*. Paris: Editions L' Harmattan.

Volkan V.D. and Itzkowitz N. 1994. *Turks and Greeks, Neighbors in Conflict*. Huntington: The Eothen Press.

Vervenioti T. 2002. 'Οι μαχήτριες του Δημοκρατικού Στρατού Ελλάδας'. ['The women fighters of the Democratic Army of Greece'], in Nikolakopoulos E., Rigos E. and Psallidas G. (eds). *Ο Εμφύλιος Πόλεμος. Από τη Βάρκιζα στο Γράμμο, Φεβρουάριος 1945-Αύγουστος 1949*. ['Civil war from Varkiza to Grammos, February 1945-August 1949']. Athens: Themelio. 125–142.

Vetsopoulos A.B. 2007. *Η Ελλάδα και το σχέδιο Μάρσαλ. Η μεταπολεμική ανασυγκρότηση της ελληνικής οικονομίας. [Greece and the Marshal Plan. The Post-War Reconstruction of the Greek Economy]*. Athens: Gutenberg.

Vlavianos H. 1992. *Greece 1941–49. From Resistance to Civil War. The Strategy of the Greek Communist Party*. London: Macmillan.

Von Papen F. 2000. *Β' Παγκόσμιος Πόλεμος, Απομνημονεύματα (1939–1945). [World War II, Memoirs (1939–1945)]*. Athens: Thetili.

Vryonis S. 2005. *The Mechanism of Catastrophe. The Turkish Pogrom of September 6–7, 1955, and the Destruction of the Greek Community of Istanbul*. New York: Greekworks.com.

Vukmanovic S. 1985. *How and Why the People's Liberation Struggle of Greece met with Defeat*. London: Merlin Press.

Weber F.G. 1983. *Ο Επιτήδειος Ουδέτερος, Η Τουρκική Πολιτική κατά τον Β' Παγκόσμιο Πόλεμο, Στόχοι: Δωδεκάνησα-Κύπρος-Ανατολικό Αιγαίο-Ιράκ-Συρία-Κριμαία-Καύκασος. [The Evasive Neutral]*. Athens: Thetili.

Wittner L.S. 1982. *American Intervention in Greece, 1943–1949: A Study in Counterrevolution*. New York: Columbia University Press.

Wolff S. 2003. *The German Question Since 1919: An Introduction with Key Documents*. Westport: Praeger.

Woodhouse C.M. 1976. *Το Μήλον της Έριδος, Η Ελληνική Αντίσταση και η Πολιτική των Μεγάλων Δυνάμεων. [The Apple of Discord]*. Athens: Exandas.

Woodhouse C.M. 2002. *The Struggle for Greece, 1941–1949*. London: Hurst.

Woods C. 1916. 'Communications in the Balkans'. *The Geographical Journal.* 47(4) (Apr). 265–290.
Woolsey T. S. 1920. 'The Rights of Minorities Under the Treaty with Poland'. *The American Journal of International Law.* 14(3). July. 392–396.
Xydis S.G. 1963. *Greece and the Great Powers 1944–47. Prelude to the 'Truman Doctrine'.* Thessaloniki: Institute for Balkan Studies.
Yağcıoğlu D. 2004. *From Deterioration to Imprtovement in Western Thrace, Greece. A Political Systems Analysıs of a Triadic Ethnic Conflict.* PhD Thesis. George Mason University.
Yıldırım O. 2006. *Diplomacy and Displacement. Reconsidering the Turco-Greek Exchange of Populations, 1922–1934.* New York and London: Routledge.
Zachariadis N. 1978. *10 χρόνια πάλης [10 Years of Struggle].* Athens: Poreia.
Zafeiropolous D. 1956. Ο Αντισυμμοριακός Αγών 1946–1949. [The Anti-Bandit Struggle 1946–1949]. Athens.
Zenginis E.C. 1994. *Οι μουσουλμάνοι αθίγγανοι της Θράκης. [The Muslim Roma of Thrace].* Thessaloniki: Institute for Balkan Studies (IMXA).

Internet Sources

http://www.emz-berlin.de/projekte/pj41_1.htm (accessed 15 October 2009).
www.armenians.gr/index1024.html (accessed on 30/10/2008).
Central Board of Jewish Communities in Greece. www.kis.gr
Greek Royal Family, Historical Archive (digitized) http://www.greekroyalfamily.org/el/index.cfm?get=archive&show=documents&ItemID=179 (accessed 10 September 2009).

CODIFIED INTERVIEWS

No	Status	Place of Birth	Place of Interview	Date
1	High-ranked DSE officer	Turkey	Alexandroupolis	18/6/2007
2	Senior official in the Turkish Ministry of Foreign Affairs	Turkey	Komotini	24/6/2007
3	Group interview (8+)		Organi-Rhodope	25/6/2007
4	Group interview (10+)		Echinos-Xanthi	26/6/2007
5	Muslim villager	Mega Dereio-Evros	Mega Dereio	27/6/2007
6	Muslim Cleric	Charadra-Evros	Charadra	27/6/2007
7	Muslim villager	Chloe-Rhodope	Chloe	30/6/2007
8	Muslim Cleric	Echinos-Xanthi	Komotini	31/6/2007
9	Greek-Orthodx soldier in the Middle East		Komotini	18/7/2007
10	Group interview (5–6)		Iasmos-Rhodope	20/7/2007
11	Local politician		Komotini	21/7/2007

Continued

Continued

No	Status	Place of Birth	Place of Interview	Date
12	Group interview (5–6)		Echinos-Xanthi	22/7/2007
13	Muslim villager	Dimarion-Xanthi	Komotini	27/7/2007
14	Greek-Othodox resistance fighter	Gratini-Rhodope	Gratini	29/7/2007
15	Senior official in the Greek Ministry of Foreign Affairs		Xanthi	1/8/2007
16	Muslim MAY fighter	Chloe-Komotini	Komotini	2/8/2007
17	Muslim villager	Oraion-Xanthi	Oraion	2/8/2007
18	Muslim villager	Sminthi-Xanthi	Sminthi	2/8/2007
19	Roma villager		Komotini	3/8/2007
20	Roma villager	Evlalo-Xanthi	Drosero	3/8/2007
21	Roma villager	Nea Karya-Xanthi	Drosero	3/8/2007
22	Roma villager	Evlalo or Kyrnos-Xanthi	Drosero	3/8/2007
23	Roma villager	Kyrnos-Xanthi	Drosero	3/8/2007
24	High-ranked DSE official	Soufli	Alexandroupolis	4/8/2007
25	Muslim town-dweller	Komotini	Komotini	7/8/2007
26	Muslim town-dweller		Komotini	7/8/2007
27	Muslim city-dweller		Thessaloniki	6/9/2007
28	Muslim Journalist	Rizoma-Rhodope	Komotini	9/9/2007 and 10/9
29	Greek-Orthodox resistance fighter	Proskynites-Rhodope	Komotini	9/9/2007
30	Muslim Cleric	Kechros-Rhodope	Komotini	10/9/2007
31	Greek Orthodox town-dweller	Komotini	Komotini	10/9/2007
32	Muslim city-dweller	Thrace	Istanbul	7/11/2008
33	Muslim town-dweller	Xanthi	Istanbul	7/11/2008
34	Muslim villager	Medousa-Xanthi	Istanbul	7/11/2008
35	Muslim town-dewller	Xanthi	Istanbul	7/11/2008
36	Muslim town-dewller	Komotini	Istanbul	7/11/2008
37	Mulim town-dweller	Komotini	Istanbul	7/11/2008
38	Muslim villager	Mesochori-Rhodope	Istanbul	7/11/2008

Continued

Continued

No	Status	Place of Birth	Place of Interview	Date
39	Muslim town-dweller	Orestiada	Uzunköprü	7/11/2008
40	Muslim villager	Salmoni-Rhodope	Uzunköprü	7/11/2008
41	Muslim villager	Neo Cheimonio-Evros	Uzunköprü	7/11/2008
42	Muslim villager		Uzunköprü	7/11/2008
43	Muslim town-dweller	Komotini	Uzunköprü	7/11/2008
44	Muslim town-dweller	Komotini	Uzunköprü	7/11/2008
45	Muslim town dweller	Komotini	Izmir	8/11/2008
46	Muslim villager	Mega Piston-Rhodope	Izmir	8/11/2008
47	Muslim villager	Mega Piston-Rhodope	Izmir	8/11/2008
48	Muslim villager	Mischos-Rhodope	Izmir	8/11/2008
49	Muslim villager	Mischos-Rhodope	Izmir	8/11/2008
50	Muslim villager	Sostis-Rhodope	Izmir	8/11/2008
51	Muslim villager	Mega Piston-Rhodope	Izmir	8/11/2008
52	Muslim town-dweller	Xanthi	Izmir	8/11/2008
53	Muslim villager	Tsalapeteinos-Xanthi	Izmir	8/11/2008
54	Muslim villager		Izmir	8/11/2008
55	Muslim town-dweller	Demarion-Xanthi	Komotini	Various dates
56	Greek-Othodox local politician	Komotini	Komotini	Various dates
57	Local Muslim politician		Komotini	Various dates
58	Muslim villager	Sidiro-Evros	Email contact	Various dates

Index

WWII (World War II) 1, 4, 5, 7, 9, 21,
24, 35, 41, 50, 51, 55, 71, 123, 126,
158, 166, 173, 189, 191, 198, 215, 239,
245, 291

Xanthi 7, 12–13, 18–23, 27–8, 30–1,
43–4, 48–51, 56, 65–7, 69–71,
77–8, 80, 83, 92–3, 97, 101, 107,
110–16, 119, 122, 126, 136,
140–5, 148–51, 155–6, 163,
171–3, 175, 177–81, 183, 186–9,
193–5, 199–200, 203, 205, 207,
213–14, 217–18, 222–8, 237, 239–40,
242, 247–8, 250–1, 253, 268–9, 271–2,
274, 278–80
Xanthi Youth Association 43
Xirotyris, Zahos 239–40, 261, 273
Xylagani 144, 237, 262

Yarin 43
Yeni Adım 43–4
Yeni Yol 43
Yeni Ziya 43
Young Turks *17*, 28, 31–2, 43, 150, 178,
202, 231
Yugoslavia 1, 2, 25; Balkan
Entente 56–7, 59; and Bulgaria 100,
167; Bulkes 184, 194, 221; expelled
from Comintern 210; German
invasion 83; Greek civil war 193, 210,
274; return of evacuated children 276

Zachariadis, Nikos 185–6, 189, 208,
210–12, 251
Zervas, Napoleon 133, 186
Zeybek, Hüseyin 173, 187
Zora 114